Black Morocco

Black Morocco: A History of Slavery, Race, and Islam chronicles the experiences, identity, and agency of enslaved black people in Morocco from the sixteenth century to the beginning of the twentieth century. Chouki El Hamel argues that we cannot rely solely on Islamic ideology as the key to explain social relations, particularly the history of black slavery in the Muslim world, for this viewpoint yields an inaccurate historical record of the people, institutions, and social practices of slavery in northwest Africa. El Hamel focuses on black Moroccans' collective experience beginning with their enslavement as members of the loyal army of Sultan Isma'il. By the time the sultan died in 1727, the army had become a political force, making and unmaking rulers well into the nineteenth century. The emphasis on the political history of the black army is augmented by a close examination of gender and concubinage as well as the continuity of black Moroccan identity through the musical and cultural practices of the Gnawa.

Chouki El Hamel is an Associate Professor of history at Arizona State University.

African Studies

The African Studies Series, founded in 1968, is a prestigious series of monographs, general surveys, and textbooks on Africa covering history, political science, anthropology, economics, and ecological and environmental issues. The series seeks to publish work by senior scholars as well as the best new research.

A list of books in this series will be found at the end of this volume.

Black Morocco

A History of Slavery, Race, and Islam

CHOUKI EL HAMEL

Arizona State University

CAMBRIDGE
UNIVERSITY PRESS

32 Avenue of the Americas, New York NY 10013-2473, USA

Cambridge University Press is part of the University of Cambridge.

It furthers the University's mission by disseminating knowledge in the pursuit of education, learning and research at the highest international levels of excellence.

www.cambridge.org
Information on this title: www.cambridge.org/9781107651777

First published 2013
First paperback edition 2013

A catalogue record for this publication is available from the British Library

Library of Congress Cataloguing in Publication data
El Hamel, Chouki.
Black Morocco : a history of slavery, race, and Islam / Chouki El Hamel.
p. cm. – (African studies; 123)
Includes bibliographical references and index.
ISBN 978-1-107-02577-6 (hardback)
1. Blacks – Morocco – History.   2. Slavery – Morocco – History.
3. Concubinage – Morocco – History.   4. Slavery and Islam – Morocco.
5. Soldiers, Black – Morocco – History.   6. Isma'il, Sultan of Morocco,
d. 1727. 7. Gnawa (Brotherhood)   I. Title.
DT313.6.B5E5   2013
326.089'96064–dc23
2012023658

ISBN 978-1-107-02577-6 Hardback
ISBN 978-1-107-65177-7 Paperback

To my mother and all the mothers of Morocco, for paradise lies under their feet!

To Malaika and Kanza

In memory of the silenced members of the Soudani and the Gania families

The executioner kills twice, the second time [by silence].
Elie Wiesel[1]

We cannot sustain an open and free society if we do not remain mindful of the lessons of the past. Because with ignorance comes indifference. With indifference comes incomprehension. And with incomprehension comes the foundation upon which systems of injustice, exploitation and racism can flourish freely.
Michaëlle Jean[2]

[1] Elie Wiesel, *The Oath* (New York: Random House, 1973), 237.
[2] Michaëlle Jean's speech on the occasion of inaugurating the Harriet Tubman Institute at York University, Toronto, Sunday, March 25, 2007.

Contents

Acknowledgments

I express my vast gratitude to all my friends and colleagues for their support throughout the course of my writing this book. I am, in particular, indebted to Tim Cleaveland, Robert Conrad, and Patrick Manning for their contributions, corrections, and suggestions. Tim Cleaveland, an expert on race, ethnicity, and gender in the western Sahel, has read many drafts of my book and offered invaluable insights toward improving it. I am also grateful to the anonymous readers and the adviser of the African Studies series for their constructive criticism. Paul Lovejoy, Deborah Kapchan, Michael Gomez, Yacine Daddi Addoun, Sarah Shields, Eve Trout Powell, Kim Butler, Gregory Castle, Mohamed Salem Soudani, and Jean Boulègue are friends whose intellectual support and friendship were crucial in enhancing my work. I recall my mentor, Jean Boulègue, with deep sadness, as he passed away in March 2011. Many thanks also go to my colleagues at the Schomburg Center for Research in Black Culture in New York (Class 2001): Colin Palmer, Kim Butler, Rhonda Frederick, Samuel Roberts, Jeffrey Sammons, Barbara Savage, Jeffrey Ogbar, Thomas Reinhardt, Barbara Katz, Geoffrey Porter, and Aisha al-Adawiyya. A special thanks to Doann Houghton-Alico for helping me build the index of my book and Mary Margaret Fonow, director of the School of Social Transformation at ASU.

Many people have contributed directly or indirectly with comments or encouragement to improve the quality of my research: Alice Bullard, Constant Hamès, Myriam Cottias, Barry Gaspar, Karla Holloway, Charles Payne, Louise Meintjes, Paul Berliner, Janet Ewald, Miriam Cooke, Barry Gaspar, Rick Powell, Nichole Green, Martin Klein, John

Hunwick, David Lewis Levering, Joseph Miller, Toyin Falola, Julio Tavares, El Ouafi Nouhi, Mohamed Jouay, Ahmed Toufiq, Mohamed Ennaji, Mokhtar Gania, Suzanne Miers, Ousseina Alidou, Alamin Mazrui, Cynthia Becker, Carolyn Brown, Emmanuel Akyeampong, Renée Soulodre-LaFrance, Mariana Candido, Amal Ghazal, Claudine Bonner, Ismael Montana, Bruce Hall, Brian Gratton, Andrew Barnes, Joe Lockard, Deborah Losse, Stanley James, Victoria Thompson, Lynn Stoner, Rachel Fuchs, James Rush, Anna Holian, Kent Wright, Ann Hobart, Mark Von Hagen, Alex Bontemps, Norma Villa, Sarah Wolfe, Carine Nsoudou, Thierry Etcheverry, Françoise Bordarier, Keith Binkley, Ismael Diadie Haidara, Lahcen Ezzaher, Mohamed El Mansour, Fatima Harrak, Hassan Hakmoun, Alicia Brewer, Philip Thorne, Nikki Taylor, William Merryman, Bouna Ndiaye, Monica Green, Eleanor Green, and the late John Hope Franklin.

I acknowledge my deep gratitude to the wonderful librarians who assisted me in the United States, France, Mali, Mauritania, and Morocco, especially Liliane Daronian, Henry Stevens, Edward Oetting, Ahmed Chouqui Binebine, Khalid Zahri, Mohammed Saïd Hinchi, Nouzha Bensaadoun, Aziz Laghzaoui, Rahma Nagi, Mohamed Abbouti, Chafik Khafajah, Bouâzza El Khalfouni, Meriam Stoni, Mohamed Malchouch, and the late 'Abd al-Wahhab b. Mansur, director of the Royal Archives. I am also grateful to the Soudani and Gania families for allowing me to interview them and to enjoy their warm hospitality.

My initial research was supported by the Scholar-in-Residence fellowship at the Schomburg Center for Research in Black Culture in New York (2001–2002), which helped me broaden my understanding of the similarities and the particularities of the experiences of enslaved black Africans in the global diaspora. The 2005 summer grant from the American Institute for Maghrib Studies (AIMS) allowed me to make another research trip to Morocco to gather more information that was crucial in giving me more insight into the experience of the Gnawa. My institution, Arizona State University, allowed me two sabbatical research leaves. These two semester leaves from full-load teaching, advising, and administrative duties were crucial in allowing me the time to write a great part of my book.

I thank the various universities that invited me as a guest speaker to share my work in progress and to get feedback from my colleagues in different disciplines. Finally, I ask forgiveness from those my memory has failed to remember.

A Summary

This study chronicles the experiences, identities, and achievements of enslaved black people in Morocco. I examine the history of slavery in Morocco from the beginning of the Islamic era through the reign of Mawlay Isma'il, with a special emphasis on the "black army" or 'Abid al-Bukhari. I have written the story of the black army to inform readers beyond those with narrow specialist knowledge. I have explored how the concept of integration in the name of Islam functioned as a source of privilege as well as discrimination by focusing on the agency of black Moroccans. The second part of the book, especially Chapters 4, 5, and 6, oscillates between narrative and analysis in order to give readers a deeper sense of the historical and sociological implications of the story being told across a long period of time, from the seventeenth to the twentieth century. Though the strongest element of these chapters concerns the black army, an important component of my discussion is the role of female slaves. The shortcomings of this analysis rest on a limited "evidentiary base." My goal was to broaden this base and make clear the importance of female slaves in relation to the army and to Moroccan society at large.

Introduction

In the summer of 1994, when I was in Nouakchott, Mauritania, researching my first book on the spread of Islamic scholarship in the western Sahel
(the area of Mauritania and northern Mali),[1] I met a local Arab scholar
at the archives who graciously invited me to his home. He wanted to
share some primary source documents in exchange for some books I had
brought with me. As I enjoyed his hospitality, sipping mint tea, a little girl
of dark complexion appeared at the door. I called for her to come in, but
she did not move or speak. I again called to her and asked, "I have a cam-
era. Do you want to take a picture?" Still she did not react. The scholar's
wife then entered the room and said: "Don't bother with her; she is just
a slave ['abda]." After a while, she added that I should buy one and take
her with me to Morocco in order to assist my mother in her household
chores. I was taken off guard. I had naively believed that Africa was currently free of these cruel practices, yet this little girl was living proof that
slavery still existed. I wanted to do something but felt powerless. I was
enraged and left hastily. While still in Mauritania, I inquired about the
issue of slavery, but as it was a politically sensitive issue in Nouakchott,
people were apprehensive and avoided talking about it. I did learn, however, that when Mauritanians call a black person by the terms 'abd or
'abda (Arabic generic terms that designate male and female slaves respec-
tively), they often refer to the blacks' family origins rather than their
current legal condition. In either case the stigma persisted. I concluded

[1] Chouki El Hamel, *La Vie intellectuelle islamique dans le Sahel ouest africain. Une étude
sociale de l'enseignement islamique en Mauritanie et au Nord du Mali (XVIe-XIXe siècles)* (Paris: L'Harmattan, 2002).

from my conversations with Arab Mauritanians that slavery existed only rarely but its effects were still profound.[2] I realized that field work in Mauritania would be complicated, so I decided to start my research on slavery and its legacies in the country I knew best: Morocco.

Although slavery has practically ceased to exist in Morocco since the 1950s, its legacy persists in a form of prejudice and inherited marginalization. Morocco has traditionally been described in local historiography as a racially and ethnically homogenous nation, defined religiously by Islamic doctrine and linguistically and politically by Arabic nationalism. Written history is generally silent regarding slavery and racial attitudes, discrimination, and marginalization and paints a picture of Morocco as free from such social problems, problems usually associated more with slavery and its historical aftermath in the United States. Slavery and racism are issues that were previously academic taboo in Morocco. In May 1999, at a conference at Duke University entitled "Crossings: Mediterraneanizing the Politics of Location, History, and Knowledge," a Moroccan professor in the French department at the University Mohamed V (Rabat, Morocco) stated that there is no Africanicity (black consciousness) in Morocco. At the same conference, Abdessalam Ben Hamida, a Tunisian professor at the University of Tunis, said that from an ethnic standpoint the Mediterranean is a "melting pot." That same year, at a seminar about slavery in Africa directed by Roger Botte at the Ecole des Hautes Etudes in Paris, a Mauritanian scholar indignantly denied the existence of slavery and Africanicity in Mauritania and stated that "the culture of the Haratin [former black slaves] has been erased."[3] Whatever the real intentions of these Maghreb scholars were in presenting the region as a hybrid and harmonious society, this denial and refusal to admit the injustices of slavery and its legacy produces the unfortunate effect of seemingly eradicating the historical truths surrounding race and slavery and does an injustice to those who were enslaved.

The assumption that one can adequately describe the Maghreb without reference to its past demonstrates the need for more scholarly rigor than current research has so far yielded. Indeed, after a decade of researching, writing, and disseminating the findings of my critical analysis with a diverse audience in African and Islamic studies across four

---

[2] The legal abolition of slavery in Mauritania happened in 1981.
[3] Perhaps she implied a complete integration of the Haratin into the dominant culture. Roger Botte replied that he could provide testimonies that slavery still existed in Mauritania in that year of 1999.

continents, I noticed that progress has been made and that Arabs and Muslims from slaving societies are more receptive to breaking the culture of silence about the history of race and slavery. In July 2011, at a conference in Kuala Lumpur (Malaysia), my paper on "Othering Black Africans in Islamic Traditions" was well received by religious and secular Muslims, Arabs, and non-Arabs. I was excited to hear Sadiq al-Mahdi, the great-grandson of al-Mahdi and former prime minister of Sudan, applauding my work on slavery and its legacy of racism. But there is still a way to go as I was also shocked to hear ʿAbd al-Hamid al-Harrama, a Libyan scholar of ISESCO, downplaying the history of slavery in Libya by reiterating the apologetic discourse. This discourse defends the view that slavery was not harsh in North Africa and contributes to the culture of silence by attacking and dismissing Western scholarship by labeling it as "orientalist," and this discourages Moroccans from benefiting from the rich Western intellectual heritage in the field of race, gender, and slavery.[4] It is important to note that a similar silence about slavery could be found in Europe as well. Jacques Heers, a specialist in European history, in his study of slavery in medieval Europe, has written that this silence reflects an embarrassment felt collectively throughout the centuries.[5] This is better illustrated in a recent study by Sue Peabody entitled *"There Are No Slaves in France"*: *The Political Culture of Race and Slavery in the Ancien Régime*. She writes:

"There are no slaves in France." This maxim is such a potent element of French national ideology that on a recent trip to Paris to do research on "French slaves" I was informed by the indignant owner of a boarding house that I must be mistaken because slavery had never existed in France.[6]

Moroccans do not claim that slavery never existed in their country, but the culture of silence about the history of race and slavery either located black Moroccans outside the community or completely absorbed them in it. Conversely, the most revealing testimony of slavery and its

---

[4] Mohamed Hassan Mohamed, a scholar from Sudan, is a clear example. His scholarship attempts to deny the history of the trans-Saharan slave trade and slavery in North Africa in general and in Morocco in particular and to accuse the West of fabricating the social ills of racism and slavery in Islamic Africa. See Mohamed Hassan Mohamed, "Africanists and Africans of the Maghrib: Casualties of Analogy," *The Journal of North African Studies*, vol. 15, no. 3 (2010): 349–374.

[5] Jacques Heers, *Esclaves et domestiques au Moyen Age dans le monde méditerranéen* (Paris: Fayard, 1981), 10 and 14.

[6] Sue Peabody, *"There Are No Slaves in France"*: *The Political Culture of Race and Slavery in the Ancien Régime* (New York: Oxford University Press, 1996), 3.

legacy in Morocco is the very existence of the Gnawa: a spiritual order of a traditionally black Muslim people who are descendants of enslaved sub-Saharan West Africans.[7] The Gnawa have retained many of the rituals and beliefs of their ancestors, expressed through the unique musical traditions of this distinct social group. Songs dealing with Gnawa origins and assimilation are still performed and are similar to those of black Americans who sang as a way to deal with their plight. In this regard, Gnawa music is analogous to the blues rooted in black American slave songs, which were widespread in the southern United States by the late nineteenth century. During my interviews with many Gnawa musicians in Essaouira and Marrakesh, they pointed out that blacks occupy a marginal position in Moroccan society as a result of their history as slaves. Another crucial testimonial is the historical memory and the living experiences of the descendants of enslaved people living in the rural south of Morocco, for example, in the Tata and Aqqa oases. In the words of as-Sudani, the grandson of an enslaved man who belonged to a rich family in southern Morocco:[8]

This ambivalence [in talking about slavery in Morocco] is further compounded by a deep upwelling of frustration at the beliefs and attitudes shaped by the historical legacy of slavery and injustice to black people. Yet, there is still a fear of stirring up the ashes, lest they would start a fire that might hurt me and my nation, instead of helping it to overcome the scars of the past. Yes, slavery existed, especially in the south of Morocco, for a long time, and into the twentieth century. Of course, it has faded slowly, but in the beginning of the century people were still bought and sold. The majority of African people who were enslaved were Muslims, including my own grandfather and the "guard" slaves in my village. One of my uncles still remembers the names of twenty-five slaves still owned by rich white Berbers.[9]

The history of slavery in Morocco cannot be considered separately from the racial terror of the global slave trade. For racial groups such as blacks in Morocco, the problems of slavery, cultural and racial prejudice, and marginalization are neither new nor foreign. Blacks in Morocco have been marginalized for centuries, with the dominant Moroccan culture defining this marginalized group as 'Abid (plural of 'Abd), "slaves"; Haratin (plural of Hartani, a problematic term that generally meant

---

[7] See the interesting study by Viviana Pâques, *Religion des esclaves: recherches sur la confrérie marocaine des Gnawa* (Bergamo, Italy: Moretti & Vitali, 1991).

[8] The family is that of Shaykh Ma' al-'Aynayn. Ma' al-'Aynayn, a famous religious scholar and anticolonial leader, was born around 1830 in Mauritania. In the early 1890s, he moved with a large number of slaves to the south of Morocco, where he died in 1910.

[9] This is an excerpt of my interview with as-Sudani in June 2001.

free black people and/or formerly enslaved black persons); *Sudan* (plural of *Aswad*), "black Africans"; *Gnawa* (plural of *Gnawi*), "black West
Africans"; *Drawa* (plural *Drawi*), "blacks from the Draa region," used in
a pejorative way; *Sahrawa* (plural of *Sahrawi*), "blacks from the Saharan
region"; and other terms with reference to the fact that they are black
and/or descendants of slaves.[10]

The situation in Morocco was similar to the trans-Atlantic diaspora
with zones of cultural exchange, borrowing, mixing, and creolization as
well as violation, violence, enslavement, and racially segregated zones.
The forced dislocation from a familiar place to an alien territory fits the
trans-Atlantic African diasporic patterns. Colin Palmer, a scholar on the
African diaspora, defines a "diasporic community" as a process and a
condition. Diasporic Africans share an emotional link to their land of
origin. They are conscious of their condition: assimilation, integration,
or alienation and retention of elements of their previous culture in the
host countries. "Members of diasporic communities also tend to possess
a sense of 'racial,' ethnic, or religious identity that transcends geographic
boundaries, to share broad cultural similarities, and sometimes to articu-
late a desire to return to their original homeland."[11] The diaspora of
black West Africans in Morocco, the majority of whom were forcefully
transported across the Sahara and sold in different parts of Morocco,
shares some important traits with Palmer's definition of the trans-Atlantic
diaspora. The legacy of the internal African diaspora with respect to
Morocco has primarily a cultural significance and is constructed around
the right to belong to the culture of Islam and the *umma* (the Islamic
community at large). In this sense, black consciousness in Morocco is
analogous to Berber consciousness and shares the Arab notion of collective identity. Blacks in Morocco absorbed some of the Arabo-centric
values expressed in the dominant interpretation of Islam in order to
navigate within the Arabo-centric discourse. Black Moroccans perceive
themselves first and foremost as Muslim Moroccans and only perceive
themselves secondarily as participants in a different tradition and/or
belonging to a specific ethnic, racial, or linguistic group, real or imagined. For blacks, this Islamic identity is the determining factor in their
social relations with other ethnic groups. In a way, Berbers are to some

---

[10] These various terms for race and their meanings will be explained in greater detail in
Chapter 2.
[11] Colin A. Palmer, "Defining and Studying the Modern African Diaspora," *The Journal of
Negro History* vol. 85, no. 1/2 (Winter 2000): 29.

extent in the same boat as black Moroccans, but neither is in the same boat as the dominant Arabs.

The study of marginalized groups has only recently attracted the interest of Moroccan scholarship, and writing the history of enslaved people is particularly difficult because of the lack of sources. There are no written slave narratives in Morocco, and such narratives are rare in the Islamic world due partly to the lack of a consistent abolitionist movement. One informative exception is found in Sudan, where a few narratives were committed to writing and translation due to the encouragement and sponsorship by European Christian abolitionists. For example, the memoirs of the late-nineteenth-century Sudanese slave soldier Ali Effendi Gifoon[12] and the narrative of Josephine Bakhita (1869–1947) were published at the turn of the twentieth century.[13] Scholars interested in recovering the slaves' views of Moroccan slavery are limited to oral histories and the evidence preserved in the Gnawa slave songs. Hence, all the documents I consulted were written from the Moroccan slaveholders' perspective or written by Westerners. One of the pioneering books on the history of Moroccan slavery, entitled *Serving the Master: Masters and Slaves in Nineteenth-Century Morocco*, was published in 1999 by Mohammed Ennaji.[14] In this book, Ennaji depicts aspects of the slave experience that demonstrate the cruelty of slavery in Morocco. One can also find unpublished dissertations about Moroccan slavery in the universities of Morocco and France, but most tend to describe the lives of slave soldiers in the Moroccan army and/or slavery's legal aspects, often with an emphasis on the benign features of the Islamic institution of slavery.[15] What's more, most North African books on the subject are written

[12] "Memoirs of a Soudanese Soldier (Ali Effendi Gifoon)" dictated in Arabic to and translated by Captain Percy Machell in George Smith et al., *The Cornhill Magazine* (London: Smith, Elder, & Co., 1896).

[13] Trout Powell has analyzed this narrative and other important narratives in Sudan, Egypt, and Turkey at the end of the nineteenth century through the first half of the twentieth century. See her book, *Tell This in My Memory: Stories of Enslavement from Egypt, Sudan and the Ottoman Empire* (Stanford University Press, 2012).

[14] Mohammed Ennaji, *Serving the Master: Slavery and Society in Nineteenth-Century Morocco*, translated by Seth Graebner (New York: St. Martin's Press, 1999). See also the dissertation thesis of another Moroccan scholar, Majda Tangi, *Contribution à l'étude de l'histoire des "Sudan" au Maroc du début de l'islamisation jusqu'au début du XVIIIe siècle* (Paris: Université de Panthéon-Sorbonne Paris I, 1994). The dissertation is very informative; it traces the history of blacks in Morocco from the beginning of Islam to the eighteenth century.

[15] For instance, Muhammad Razzuq, "Qadiyyat ar-Riqq fi Tarikh al-Maghrib," *Revue d'Histoire Maghrébine*, (Tunis: Librairie des Chercheurs Arabes, n. 41–42, June 1986): 114–128. See also 'Imad Ahmad Hilal, *ar-Raqiq fi Misr fi al-Qarn at-Tasi' 'Ashar* (Cairo:

in an apologetic manner: emphasizing the generosity of Islam toward those enslaved and hence undermining the experiences and agency of the enslaved people. As for external study of slavery in Morocco, the bulk of published scholarship on slavery in Islamic lands, with Morocco only as a minor case study, was undertaken by European and American scholars such as William Clarence-Smith[16] and Bernard Lewis.[17] As yet, there is no comprehensive and analytic published book on the history of slavery in Morocco.

As for the primary sources, the records in the libraries and archives of Morocco have so far proved to be abundant and indicative of Morocco's significant historical presence and the participation of blacks in the making of Moroccan society and culture. The Moroccan archives, kept at the Royal Library and the Bibliothèque Générale (now Bibliothèque Nationale), both in Rabat, are largely unedited or unclassified and as of yet not well exploited. Moroccan historiography, mainly unpublished and published historical chronicles, although focused largely on elites and events, provides tremendous assistance on the context of the black Moroccans. Traditional Moroccan historiography is chronically and factually centered on the episodes of dynastic history. It is nonetheless possible to glean from it crucial scattered notations concerning the origins of Morocco's black people, their contributions, and the institution and ideology of enslavement. A great example is *Ithaf A'lam an-Nas Bijamal Akhbar Hadirat Maknas* by historian 'Abd ar-Rahman ibn Zaydan,[18] which is important by reason of the amount of information it contains regarding the critical roles that black individuals played in the politics of the palace and the Makhzan. But caution must be taken because Ibn Zaydan was explicitly biased in favor of the 'Alawi dynasty.

The primary Western sources such as accounts of European voyages and colonial documents present a different and often Eurocentric perspective. To maintain objectivity, I corroborated the European information with other local sources. For instance, Joseph de León, a Spanish officer

al-'Arabi li 'l-Nashr wa-al-Tawzi', 1999) and Ibrahim Hashim al-Fallali, *La Riqq fi 'l-Qur'an* (Cairo: Dar al-Qalam, 1960). See also Abubakar Tafawa Balewa, *Shaihu Umar: A Novel*, translated by Mervyn Hiskett (New York: M. Wiener Pub, 1989). This novel depicts domestic slavery in Islamic societies as on the whole benign.

16 William Clarence-Smith, *Islam and the Abolition of Slavery* (Oxford: Oxford University Press, 2006).

17 Bernard Lewis, *Race and Slavery in the Middle East: An Historical Enquiry* (New York: Oxford University Press, 1990).

18 'Abd ar-Rahman ibn Zaydan, *Ithaf A'lam an-Nas Bijamal Akhbar Hadirat Maknas* (Casablanca, Morocco: Librairie Idéale, 1990).

who spent twenty years in captivity in Morocco (1708–1728), reported that Mawlay Isma'il was possibly strangled by one of his concubines named Zaydana, the mother of the prince Mawlay Ahmad adh-Dhahabi. There are two errors in the author's hypothesis: 1) Zaydana was one of the sultan's legitimate four wives and therefore not a concubine – legally, only a female slave can fulfill the role of a concubine in Morocco,[19] 2) Zaydana died in 1716, about eleven years before Mawlay Isma'il's death, hence the impossibility of this hypothesis. Information on the harem was generally based on rumors and speculations at best, since no man, let alone a foreigner, had access to the sultan's harem, or any harem for that matter, but nevertheless these speculations reflected a glimpse of the agency, intrigues, and rivalries among wives and concubines in the sultan's palace.[20] But, since Arabic sources are short in details on issues related to women, sexuality, race, and slavery, European sources provide crucial details that could fill the gap. For instance, Ibn Marjan (a black eunuch in charge of the treasury as well as the black servants in the palace during the life of Mawlay Isma'il) is mentioned in Arabic sources mostly as an important figure in the palace in charge of the treasury. However, European sources provide important details on his political activities in the palace, especially his critical involvement in the succession process. In fact, late-nineteenth-century and early-twentieth-century European travelers' accounts give testimony to the diverse and important roles that slaves occupied in Moroccan society.

My desire to fill in these historical lacunae has led me to focus on slavery, race, and gender in Morocco from the sixteenth century to the beginning of the twentieth century.[21] Over the course of those four centuries, blacks migrated voluntarily, and many of the Haratin were indigenous to the northern Sahara, but most were victims of the slave trade across the Sahara to Morocco. Although the African diaspora in the Americas is one of the major topics of current historical research on the black diaspora, a less researched but no less important aspect of the global African diaspora is that internal to Africa. The Islamization of northern Africa led to a huge increase in trade, especially in the trans-Saharan

---

[19] De León was probably confused about Zaydana's status as she started out as a concubine but later was promoted to the status of free wife.

[20] Chantal de La Véronne and Joseph de León, *Vie de Moulay Isma'il, roi de Fès et de Maroc: d'après Joseph de León, 1708–1728* (Paris: Paul Geuthner, 1974), Documents d'histoire maghrébine, vol. 2, 14–15.

[21] I am using the racial term *black* in the context in which it was socially constructed. I will address the whole issue of race in much greater detail later in the book.

region. As a case study, Morocco is important for several reasons. First, the library records and archives have proven to be more abundant than other archival sources in the Maghreb. Second, Morocco has a significant historical connection with sub-Saharan West Africa. And third, the black community has played a dynamic role in Moroccan society. Therefore my book is primarily slavery related. But I am by no means suggesting that slavery was the origin of the black African presence in Morocco. I am suggesting, however, that the encounter between the Berbers and Arabs and black Africans has historically been inequitable, generally in favor of the Berbers and the Arabs.

I argue that relying solely on Islamic ideology as a crucial key to explain social relations, particularly the history of black slavery in the Muslim world, yields an inaccurate historical record of the people, institutions, and social practices of slavery in the Arab world. Islam and Islamic law was surely a powerful social dynamic, but other cultural and ethnic factors figure prominently into how Islam was engendered in particular historical social settings. My study poses new questions that examine the extent to which religion orders a society and the extensive influence of secular conditions on the religious discourse and the ideology of enslavement in Morocco. The interpretation and application of Islam did not guarantee the freedom and integration of ex-slaves into society. To understand slavery and its legacy, we must therefore investigate the nature and practice of slavery in Morocco within and beyond Islam. Undeniably, Muslims permitted the enslavement of non-Muslims, of any race or ethnicity, even though the Islamic creed explicitly discourages slavery. Islamic law also prohibits the enslavement of free Muslims. History, however, is witness to many cases of Muslims enslaving other Muslims, the most outstanding Moroccan example being the enslavement of the Muslim Haratin – the so-called free blacks or ex-slaves – during Mawlay Isma'il's reign (1672–1727). The illegal enslavement of the Haratin marked a crucial turning point in Moroccan history, one that shaped the future of racial relations and black identity and that revealed the disjuncture between Islamic ideals and historical realities and between ideology and practice regarding race and gender in Moroccan slavery. During Mawlay Isma'il's reign, physical characteristics and skin color in particular were a crucial factor in identifying at least one group in Morocco – the free black people or so-called ex-slaves (sing. *Hartani*; pl. *Haratin*). The term *Haratin* referred to a group of people who occupied an intermediary position between slaves and free Muslims, and thus their social status was at times unclear. However, in addition to being identified as slaves or freed slaves, the

Haratin were invariably recognized in the historical documents of this period as having been black.[22] The episode of their re-enslavement during the reign of Sultan Mawlay Isma'il raises a series of important historical questions: Who were these Haratin and why were they enslaved? What was their status before their enslavement? How did their status change after they were freed? What conditions precipitated their re-enslavement and what role did skin color play in the decision to categorically re-enslave them? In order to answer these questions, I investigate the construction of "black" as a social category and how this changed diachronically, and explore the contrast between Islamic theories on slavery and the practice of slavery during Mawlay Isma'il's era. My analysis demonstrates that the traditional understanding of the politics and the practice of slavery in Morocco ignores important historical evidence and derives from gross generalizations deduced from Islamic legal treatises regarding the status and practice of slavery. Evidence that I present strongly suggests that in the late seventeenth century Morocco did in fact demonstrate the exploitation of blacks and the ideological foundation for a society divided by skin color. Hence, religious principles were substituted by racial concepts and a racist ideology in order to establish and preserve the social boundaries that demarcate the identities and privileges of the Arabs and the Berbers.

In this study, I focus on slavery and racial attitudes during and after Mawlay Isma'il's time, and I also discuss the beginning of slavery, the legal discourse, and racial stereotypes that existed in Moroccan society before Mawlay Isma'il. I chose this period of the history of blacks in Morocco because it best represents their collective experience and how they were perceived. It was also a special case that ironically allowed the black Moroccans a powerful role in the administration of the country. Mawlay Isma'il's project is crucial in this study because it raises questions about the extent to which the integration of black Muslims was real. Although in Islamic societies and societies influenced by Islam, the institution of slavery was not drawn strictly along racial lines, cases of racial slavery did exist, just as can be seen in the cases when Muslims enslaved other Muslims. It is important to note, however, that the same Islamic teachings provided the enslaved with resources for resistance and an identity that made it possible for them to navigate within society. In the second chapter on race, I analyze how racialist ideas and positions became not only an ideology of enslavement but also a structure based on

---

[22] These historical documents will be discussed in greater detail in the book.

patterns of color and cultural prejudice, providing answers to the following questions: What are the roots of the concept of blackness? What does
it mean to be black in Morocco? What does it symbolize?

I also raise the question of gender. In North Africa, there were more
female slaves than male slaves, and females usually cost more than
males. This gender preference was the foundation of the disproportion-
ate burden that rested on female slaves. Within Morocco's institution
of slavery were two systems based on gender relations: one for women
and the other for men, in part because Islamic law decrees that a female
slave who bears her owner's child will acquire certain legal rights and
her child will be free. This dual system developed partly because slave
owners held differing expectations for male and female slaves. These
expectations, articulated in religious ideology, translated into different responsibilities that often determined the life chances of slaves. The
tragic heroine in North African slavery is *female*. Female slaves had to
endure not only economic exploitation and physical labor, but were also
subjected to sexual violence. Survival and the tragic drama of female
slaves' lives entailed at times emotional and sexual relationships via concubinage, usually initiated by male masters, as enslaved people did not
have the right to engage in sexual relationships.[23] For free Moroccan
men concubinage was legalized and secured their sexual access to female
slaves. Enslaved black women who became concubines of their masters were forced to navigate within the sexual desire of their masters to
secure a better position within a society where gender was hierarchical:
patrilineal and patriarchal. If it was legally and socially established for a
male to be entitled to female slave sexuality, it was, as well, legally and
socially conventional for the progeny of female slaves to inherit their
fathers' legal status. I use the analysis of the concubinage system as a

[23] I have searched to no avail in the archives for any direct evidence describing how enslaved
black women felt or reacted as concubines toward their male owners. There are, however, novelists and sociologists such as 'Abd al-Karim Ghallab (1919–2006), Tahar Ben
Jelloun, Fatima Mernissi, and Leila Abouzeid who have broached such issues in their
works. Ghallab, for instance, gave a vivid description of a young female servant being
raped by the household patriarch in the city of Fez. 'Abd al-Karim Ghallab, *Dafanna
al-Madi* (Beirut: al-Maktab at Tijari li-'t-Tiba'a wa 'n-Nashr wa 't-Tawzi', 1966), 38–46.
See Fatima Bouzenirh, "Race and Ethnicity in African Literature" in *Les Constructions
de l'autre dans les relations interafricaines*. Série: Colloques et Séminaires (N° 11). Sous la
direction de Fatima Harrak and Khalid Chegraoui (Rabat: Publications de l'Institut des
Etudes Africaines, 2008), 87–110 and Evelyne Accad, *Veil of Shame: The Role of Women
in the Contemporary Fiction of North Africa and the Arab World* (Sherbrooke, Canada:
Éditions Naaman, 1978), 60–92.

process to investigate the interplay of agency, emotions, identity, race, and gender in Morocco.

The study of slavery in Morocco provides a rich source for examining how the lens of culture influences religious articulation. Concurrent with the Islamic justification of slavery in the Mediterranean basin, one can find historically analogous circumstances in regions such as Spain. The Spanish *Siete Partidas* advanced religious tenets that declared that "servitude is the vilest and most contemptible thing that can exist among men," and that "slavery is the vilest thing in this world except sin." Nonetheless, the institutions of slavery were justified contrary to the seemingly explicit religious tenets of Catholicism by religious interpreters who found a wealth of "reasons" for enslavement.[24] Additional examination of the *Siete Partidas* demonstrates further similarities between Christian and Islamic positions on slavery. Slavery in Morocco was administered according to rules and regulations of the Islamic law based on the Maliki school. In order to understand slavery in Morocco, it is crucial to examine these rules and regulations according to the Islamic law and its main sources in the Qur'an and the Hadith. I will examine the founding texts of Islam in order to show a contrast and a change in the condition of women in slavery as seen in the Qur'an and the Hadith, and especially the place of women in relation to slavery in Maliki doctrine in the midst of the evolution and expansion of the male political hierarchy by the early Umayyad period.

Moroccan history has generally been written to reflect the past but not to question or to reexamine that history by taking into account the specific cultures of non-Arabs and non-Muslims (or *dhimmi*), such as the participation and contributions of Berbers, blacks, Jews, and women in Moroccan culture. Arabo-centrism combined with the Maliki Islamic doctrine has shaped literary traditions and political discourse throughout the history of Morocco since the tenth century. Certainly Islam as a religion preaches egalitarianism and cuts across all differences in ethnicities, color, and cultures. But when it is related to the issue of slavery, the interpretations of Islamic law seem to admit differences and to enforce or to create identities of the "enslavable" other. These identities are validated through the insistence on differences derived from paganism or unbelief. Historical documents such as the seventeenth-century *Mi'raj as-Su'ud* by

---

[24] For an insightfully researched examination of the intersection of religion and culture in Christian works during this era, see Robert A. Williams, *The American Indian in Western Legal Thought: the Discourse of Conquest* (Oxford: Oxford University Press, 1990).

Ahmad Baba from the city of Timbuktu (a legal document about slavery addressed to Moroccan slave traders), provide examples of legal texts that illustrate how identities were defined, maintained, and violated. Other legal texts, like *Daftar Mamalik as-Sultan Mawlay Isma'il*[25] (the register of the slaves belonging to Mawlay Isma'il) provide a coherent and critical account of the nature of slavery in Morocco under Mawlay Isma'il at the beginning of the eighteenth century. It is clear from this legal register that slavery was associated with blackness.

In recent decades, a number of scholars have revised existing historical constructions of Moroccan society by focusing on the agency of subaltern groups in Morocco. Western and Moroccan scholars like Deborah Kapchan,[26] Cynthia Becker,[27] Bouazza Benachir,[28] and Mohamed Ennaji[29] have presented fresh perspectives that emphasize a different starting point for analysis – that of the emergence of the power relations used under the auspices of Islam as found and practiced within the local and temporal specificities of a society rather than strictly as a religious discourse. These fresh analyses place a special focus on the roles of Muslim individuals acting within the structuring elements of a dynamic Islamic society rather than the traditional manner of treating individuals as mere minor actors against the backdrop of Islam. Their analyses of marginalized groups bring out the complex dynamism of immixture and cultural retention rather than rely on the flawed assumption that assimilation is a kind of unilateral absorption into the social fabric.

In the spirit of these scholars, my research seeks to highlight the forgotten role of blacks in Morocco. Hence, by examining specifics about the institution of slavery in Morocco, my study moves the discussion from the general to the particular. The objective of this book is to challenge the conventional readings of slavery in Islam and in Moroccan society. I explore how the concept of integration in the name of Islam functioned as a source of privilege as well as discrimination. What interests me most is the culture of silence – the refusal to engage in discussions about slavery,

---

[25] *Daftar Mamalik as-Sultan Mawlay Isma'il*. Bibliothèque Générale in Rabat, 394. This is a legal document addressing the acquisition of the slaves from various parties.

[26] See the excellent work of Deborah Kapchan, *Traveling Spirit Masters: Moroccan Trance and Music in the Global Marketplace*, (Middletown, CT: Wesleyan University Press, 2007).

[27] Cynthia Becker, "'We are Real Slaves, Real Ismkhan': Memories of the Trans-Saharan Slave Trade in the Tafilalet of South-Eastern Morocco," *The Journal of North African Studies* 7, no. 4 (2002): 97–121.

[28] Bouazza Benachir, *Négritudes du Maroc et du Maghreb* (Paris: L'Harmattan, 2003).

[29] Ennaji, *Serving the Master*.

racial attitudes, and gender issues – and my goal is to recover the silenced histories of slavery in "Islamic" North Africa. I challenge the conventional readings on the integration of black West Africans in Morocco by deconstructing familiar concepts and focusing on the agency of the enslaved and investigating their subaltern relationships to ruling institutions, power, race, gender, and identity politics.

PART ONE

RACE, GENDER, AND SLAVERY IN THE ISLAMIC DISCOURSE

The Notion of Slavery and the Justification of Concubinage as an Institution of Slavery in Islam

The starting-point of critical elaboration is the consciousness of what one really is, and is "knowing thyself" as a product of the historical process to date which has deposited in you an infinity of traces, without leaving an inventory.[1]

"How dare you enslave people whereas they were born free?"[2]

The truth is that male religious leaders have had – and still have – an option to interpret holy teachings either to exalt or subjugate women. They have, for their own selfish ends, overwhelmingly chosen the latter. Their continuing choice provides the foundation or justification for much of the pervasive persecution and abuse of women throughout the world.[3]

Most Islamic judicial texts, such as *al-Muwatta'* and *ar-Risala*, and the compilations of reports of the Prophet (*kutub al-hadith*), such as *Sahih al-Bukhari* and *Sahih Muslim*, have been employed to condone and to normalize the practice of using slaves as concubines. In this chapter, I argue that, contrary to these Islamic judicial texts, the Qur'an not only does not support this practice but actually places a high priority on manumitting slaves with the ultimate objective of abolishing slavery. The Qur'an, the primary and fundamental source of Islam and Islamic law, does not authorize

---

[1] Antonio Gramsci, *Selections from the Prison Notebooks of Antonio Gramsci*, edited and translated by Quintin Hoare and Geoffrey Nowell Smith (New York: International Publishers, 1971), 324.

[2] 'Umar Ibn al-Khattab, second caliph (d. 644) in 'Abd al-'Aziz ibn Ibrahim al-'Umari, *al-Wilaya 'ala al-Buldan fi 'Asr al-Khulafa' ar-Rashidin* (ar-Riyad: Dar Ishbiliya, 1988), vol. 1, 81.

[3] Jimmy Carter in an editorial published in the July 12, 2009 edition of *The Observer*. http://www.cartercenter.org/news/editorials_speeches/observer_071209.html.

or formalize using slaves as concubines. How, then, do we explain the discrepancy between the interpretations of the Qur'an codified in Islamic law, which condone concubinage, and the Qur'an itself, which promotes a structure of social life aimed at a socially just environment in service to God rather than condoning relations of servitude among people?

To understand how concubinage became legitimized in Islam, it is necessary to trace the development of the notion of slavery in the Qur'an, the Hadith, and Islamic law (*ash-shari'a*). Slavery existed in Arabia centuries before the birth of Islam and continued during and after the revelation of the Qur'an. The Qur'an assumed that the practice of slavery was part and parcel of an existing complex social structure. In the pre-Islamic era, owning slaves was a source of prestige reflecting a household's wealth and social status. Slavery was a social norm deeply rooted in cultural behaviors, beliefs, and institutions. The norms governing slavery in pre-Islamic Arabia were not systematic insofar as such norms were not uniform or homogeneous across the diverse cultural landscapes that existed in the region.[4] In pre-Islamic Arabia, the majority of slaves were of Ethiopian origin. The slave population also included "white" slaves imported from the Byzantine and Persian empires, as well as Arab slaves who were likely war captives and often ransomed, a lucrative practice among nomads.[5] Abu al-Faraj al-Isbahani (d. 967), a literary historian who composed a multivolume work on Arabic poetry and songs, wrote that in the pre-Islamic era, Arabs enslaved their own children born of female slaves who served the sexual desires of their owners along with performing their other domestic duties.[6] According to al-Isbahani, children born of slaves could sometimes be manumitted by their fathers. The famous sixth-century Arab poet 'Antara b. Shaddad is an example, the

---

[4] Pre-Islamic Arabia is known in Islam as *Jahiliyya*. The term *Jahiliyya* is problematic. At the time of the Prophet, it referred mainly to the state of ignorance of the guidance from God. But, according to the Qur'an XXXIII, 33, the term was extended to include all societies in the state of moral ignorance during the intermission of the prophetic teachings. Throughout Islamic history the term became an abstract label used at random, transcending space and time and absorbing multiple meanings: barbarism, paganism, lawlessness, ignorance, heathendom, immorality, and anything or any individual/group outside or even inside Islam.

[5] For more information, see Ibrahim Hashim al-Fallali, *La Riqq fi al-Qur'an* (Cairo: Dar a-Qalam, 1960) and the work of Abduh Badawi, *ash-Shu'ara as-Sud wa-Khasa'isuhum fi ash-Shi'r al-'Arabi* (Cairo: al-Hayat al-Misriyya al-'Amma li-'l-Kitab, 1973) and *as-Sud wa-'l-Hadara al-'Arabiya* (Cairo: al-Hayat al-Misriyya al-'Amma li-'l-Kitab, 1976).

[6] Al-Isbahani did not give details as to the regions or populations, whether nomad or sedentary. See Abu al-Faraj al-Isbahani, *Kitab al-Aghani* (Beirut: Dar ath-Thaqafa, 1955), vol. 8, 237.

son of a free Arab father and a black slave. As a young lad he lived in servitude working as a shepherd, but after proving his bravery by defending his father's tribe in war, his father recognized him as his son and he received his freedom.[7] The practice of manumission in pre-Islamic Arabia was similar to that found in the Code Hammurabi (Babylonian king Hammurabi died in 1750 B.C.) in Mesopotamia, although manumission in pre-Islamic Arabia did not allow for full legal entitlement to fathers' estates as it did under Code Hammurabi.[8] According to the Code Hammurabi, if a man recognized the children of his maidservant as his own, these children, along with any other legitimate, free children, shared any inheritance he left his family.[9] If a man did not recognize the offspring of his concubine while still living, the mother and her children nonetheless gained their freedom after his death, but with no rights of inheritance (paragraphs 170–173). Ancient Roman law also codified the status of slaves and their children sired by free citizens. Under Roman law,[10] if the father was a Roman citizen and the mother was a slave, the children remained slaves: the mother imparted to her child her status of slave or free person.[11] The norms governing slavery in pre-Islamic Arabia varied according to the tribal customs of nomadic and mercantile communities rather than the more uniform Roman law of slavery.

The Prophet Muhammad's (570–632) teachings occurred during a transitional period of Arabian history and created a centralized community. He taught that Muslims should refer to only two sources to decide all their matters: the Qur'an and the Sunna (Muhammad's teachings and practices).[12] Indeed, after the death of the Prophet, Muslim scholars assumed the task of providing legal consultations and decisions using the Qur'an and the Sunna as the primary sources. Schools of legal thought, therefore, formed around leading early scholars such as Abu Hanifa (d. 767), Malik ibn Anas (d. 796), Muhammad ash-Shafi'i (d. 820), and Ahmad ibn Hanbal (d. 855). These schools came to be known as Hanafi,

---

[7] Ibid., 235–243.

[8] See Isaac Mendelsohn, *Slavery in the Ancient Near East; a Comparative Study of Slavery in Babylonia, Assyria, Syria, and Palestine, from the Middle of the Third Millennium to the End of the First Millennium* (Oxford: Oxford University Press, 1949).

[9] See Gerda Lerner, *The Creation of Patriarchy* (Oxford: Oxford University Press, 1987), 91.

[10] See W. W. Buckland, *The Roman Law of Slavery: the Condition of the Slave in Private Law from Augustus to Justinian* (London: Cambridge University Press, 1908).

[11] Ibid., 397–398.

[12] The word *sunna* (pl. *sunan*) literally means "the trodden path." It is the sayings, the actions, and the way of life of the Prophet Muhammad as recorded in the Hadith.

Maliki, Shafi'i, and Hanbali and represented the prominent schools within the Sunni practice. As for the Shi'i practice, the legal system of Imami Shi'a (Twelvers) represents the main Shi'i populations. Ja'far b. Muhammad as-Sadiq (702–765) is considered the founder of the Twelver-Shi'i school of law. These major schools survived and prevailed over the entire Islamic world. All of them condoned and regulated the institution of slavery in Islam. In the view of John Esposito:

The early law schools, which had begun only during the late Umayyad period (ca. 720), flourished under caliphal patronage of the *ulama*. Although Islam has no clergy or priesthood, by the eighth century the *ulama* had become a professional elite of religious leaders, a distinct social class within Muslim society. Their prestige and authority rested on a reputation for learning in Islamic studies, the Quran, traditions of the Prophet, law.[13]

This study refers mainly to the Maliki school, the most prevalent in Africa and the official doctrine in the Maghreb and western Africa. Mansour H. Mansour, scholar of Islam, said of the Maliki school: "[Malikis] rejected human reason and believed that every law must be derived from the Qur'an or the Prophet's Sunna as recorded in the Hadith. Consequently the Madinans [or Malikis] became known as the supporters of Hadith."[14]

What Exactly Does the Qur'an Say about Slavery?

Muslims seeking to apply the Qur'anic teachings to the practice of slavery inspired a uniform legal institution of slavery. The Qur'an is the original and ultimate authority of Islam and represents divine guidance for the Muslim community. The Qur'an has been subjected to many interpretations; it is not all equally comprehensible and the Qur'an itself cautions that it contains two kinds of messages: some clear and self-evident (*ayat muhkamat*) and some allegorical (*ayat mutashabihat*). The Qur'an's hidden meanings are traditionally only accessible to those who have achieved great wisdom through scholarship. The following Qur'anic verse on the complexity of the words of God is meant to demonstrate that the Qur'an should not be understood literally; it is an unambiguous validation that the Qur'an is subject to interpretation for people deeply rooted in scholarship:

[13] John Esposito, *Islam: The Straight Path* (Oxford: Oxford University Press, 1998), 52.
[14] Mansour H. Mansour, *The Maliki School of Law: Spread and Domination in North and West Africa 8th to 14th Centuries C. E.* (London: Austin & Winfield, 1995), 3.

He it is who has bestowed upon thee from on high this divine writ, containing messages that are clear in and by themselves – and these are the essence of the divine writ – as well as others that are allegorical. Now those whose hearts are given to swerving from the truth go after that part of the divine writ which has been expressed in allegory, seeking out [what is bound to create] confusion, and seeking [to arrive at] its final meaning [in an arbitrary manner]; but none save God knows its final meaning. Hence, those who are deeply rooted in knowledge say: "We believe in it; the whole [of the divine writ] is from our Sustainer – albeit none takes this to heart save those who are endowed with insight.[15]

When God says in this passage that none but He knows the final meaning of the Qur'an, this means that anybody who claims to know the absolute truth of the Qur'an and tries to impose it on others is ultimately taking the place of God. Hence the act and the continuous process of interpretation are logical and its outcome is never fixed or closed. Muhammad Asad (d. 1992), a Polish-Austrian Muslim thinker and a translator of the Qur'an, explains that:

[T]here are many statements in the Qur'an which are liable to more than one interpretation but are, nevertheless, not allegorical – just as there are many expressions and passages which, despite their allegorical formulation, reveal to the searching intellect only one possible meaning.[16]

The Qur'anic verses on slavery require particularly careful examination. The Qur'an generally uses the following terms: *fata* (pl. *fatayat*), literally meaning "boy"; *fatat* (pl. *fatayat*), literally meaning "girl"; *raqaba* (pl. *riqab*), meaning "neck"; and the expression *ma malakat aymanukum*, meaning "that which your or their right hands possess." These terms designate slaves as personal property. The Qur'an deliberately avoids calling an enslaved person by the name *'abd* (pl. *'abid*) and for the feminine gender *ama* (pl. *ima'*), literally meaning "slave," because the words *'abd* and *ama* in the Qur'an are reserved for all God's creatures – His servants and worshippers, obeying Him only – hence the use of such indirect language as "what their right hands possess." It is important to note that the word *'abd* (root '.b.d) has different meanings; the difference is clearly rendered in the plurals and the nouns of the adjective *'abd*. The plural *'ibad* means worshipers but the plural *'abid* means slaves, and *'ubudiyya* means slavery but *'ibada* means worship. The classical Arabic dictionaries call attention to these distinctions. Muhammad az-Zabidi (died in Cairo in 1791),

[15] The Qur'an, chapter 3, verse 7 – I have used the translation of Muhammad Asad throughout this book, *The Message of the Qur'an: The Full Account of the Revealed Arabic Text Accompanied by Parallel Transliteration* (Bitton, England: Book Foundation, 2003).
[16] Ibid., 80, footnote 5.

an expert in Arabic lexicography, gave in his voluminous dictionary *Taj al-'Arus* (*Crown of the Bride*) ample details on the word *'abd* and its multiple derivatives.[17] Edward Lane (1801–1876), a British scholar and lexicographer, goes further to say, in his *Arabic-English Lexicon* based on many authoritative Arabic dictionaries such as az-Zabidi's, that "it should be remarked that the common people agree in making a difference between *'abid* and *'ibad*, by the former meaning slaves [and by the latter meaning *servants* of God and also simply with the article al, mankind]."[18]

The Justification of Concubinage

The Arabic expression *ma malakat aymanukum* (literally "those whom your right hands possess") has often been interpreted by experts in Islam as a metonymy for concubines. John Hunwick, a renowned professor of Islam in West Africa, reads this expression to mean concubines.[19] Joseph Schacht, a German orientalist, argues that "[t]he Kur'an permits concubinage with a man's own slaves in several passages."[20] Lamin Sanneh, a professor of Islam in West Africa, writes: "Concubinage (*surriyah*) is recognized in the Qur'an, and one may adopt as many slave-women as concubines as one is able."[21] Sanneh's view on concubinage derives from the work of Neil Baillie (1799–1883), a specialist in Islamic South Asian jurisprudence. In regard to female slaves, Baillie said: "It is lawful for a free man to keep and cohabit with as many female slaves as he pleases."[22] Baillie's report was based on eighth-century theologian Abu Hanifa's interpretation of the Islamic law that was largely observed among the Indian Muslim population. Hanafi codes, as well as the codes of other legal schools that legitimized slavery and concubinage, rely on exegeses of the Qur'an that I argue incorporated existing pre-Islamic social and

---

[17] Muhammad Murtada az-Zabidi, *Taj al-'Arus min Jawahir al-Qamus* (Beirut: Dar al-Kutub al-'Ilmiya, 2007) vol. 8, 189–200.

[18] Edward William Lane, *An Arabic-English Lexicon* (Beirut: Librairie du Liban, 1968), in eight volumes, vol. 5, 1935.

[19] John Hunwick, "African Slaves in the Mediterranean World: A Neglected Aspect of the African Diaspora" in *Global Dimensions of the African Diaspora*, ed. Joseph Harris, 2nd ed. (Washington, DC: Howard University Press, 1993), 290.

[20] See Joseph Schacht, "Umm al-Walad" in *The Encyclopedia of Islam*, CD-ROM Edition v.1.1 (Leiden: E.J. Brill, 2001).

[21] Lamin Sanneh, "Slavery, Islam and the Jakhanke People of West Africa," *Africa: Journal of the International African Institute*, vol. 46, no. 1 (1976): 80–97.

[22] Neil Baillie, *A Digest of Moohummudan Law: Compiled and Translated from Authorities in the Original Arabic, with an Introduction and Explanatory Notes* (Lahore: Premier Book House, 1957), 31.

cultural practices rather than adopting and adhering to what the Qur'an expresses with respect to new ethical tenets for social relations.

The legality of concubinage, widely accepted and repeated in most scholarly works on slavery in Islam, was adopted from popular and respected exegeses of the Qur'an. Almost every generation produces volumes of Qur'anic interpretations. The most widely read exegetes available in most bookstores in the Islamic world are the following: Jalal ad-Din al-Mahalli (d. 1459); Jalal ad-Din as-Suyuti (d. 1505), who wrote a concise volume designed for a large audience that is the most popular *tafsir* (interpretation) in present times; at-Tabari (d. 923);[23] Ibn Kathir (d. 1373);[24] and Sayyid Qutb of the twentieth century.[25]

These sources usually refer to the following verse, arguing that it sanctions the practices of polygyny and concubinage:

And if you have reason to fear that you might not act equitably towards orphans, then marry from among [other] women such as are lawful to you [even] two, or three, or four: but if you have reason to fear that you might not be able to treat them with equal fairness, then [only] one – or [from among] those whom you rightfully possess (*ma malakat aymanukum*). This will make it more likely that you will not deviate from the right course (4:3).

Al-Mahalli and as-Suyuti, authors of *Tafsir al-Jalayn,* interpret this verse as "marriage of the four women or only one, or *at-tasarri* (concubinage)."[26] *At-tasarri* means to take a slave girl as a concubine. These authors adopted the model of an earlier and highly regarded exegesis by Muhammad b. Jarir at-Tabari (born in 839, died in 923 in Baghdad), a famous Muslim historian and exegete of the Qur'an. At-Tabari wrote a massive exegesis of the Qur'an in about thirty volumes entitled *Jami' al-Bayan fi Tafsir al-Qur'an,* representing the most extensive authoritative early works on Islam. He interpreted the part concerning *ma malakat aymanukum* in the previously cited Qur'anic verse as follows: "If you fear that you will not treat so many women (up to four) with equal love and companionship, then [take] one only or take a slave girl as concubine (*tasarrartum*), and this will make it more likely that you will not deviate from the straight

[23] Muhammad at-Tabari, *Jami' al-Bayan fi Tafsir al-Qur'an* (Cairo: al-Matba'a al-Maymaniya, 1904).
[24] 'Imad ad-Din Isma'il bin 'Umar bin Kathir (circa 1300–1373) was a historian and a narrator from Syria. He is famous for two works: *al-Bidaya wa 'n-Nihaya* (on the history of Islam) and *Tafsir al-Qur'an* (a commentary on the Qur'an).
[25] Sayyid Qutb, *Fi Zilal al-Qur'an*, thirty-fifth edition (Beirut: Dar ash-Shuruq, 2005).
[26] Jalal ad-Did al-Mahalli and Jalal ad-Din as-Suyuti, *Tafsir al-Qur'an al-Karim* (Cairo: Dar al-Qalam, 1966), 80.

path."[27] Indeed, at-Tabari uses the circumlocution *ma malakat aymanu-kum* as the equivalent of *as-sarari* (concubines). *As-sarari* (sing. *surriyya*) derives from the verb *sarra* (root s.r.), which means "to conceal or to keep something secret," hence, a concealment of the act of a man taking a female slave for *concubitus* while shielding that act from his wife. *Surriyya* is different from *sirriyya*, as the latter means "a free woman with whom one has sexual intercourse secretly" or "one who prostitutes herself."[28] These interpretations of the Qur'an recognize and give license to the practice of concubinage, as long as the woman is a slave and not a free Muslim woman. These interpretations were endorsed by the majority of scholars from different legal schools, such as at-Tabari; Ibn Abi Zayd al-Qayrawani, a Maghrebian Muslim judge who died in 996; Maghrebian Maliki jurist and mufti al-Wansharasi (1431–1508); the Islamic scholar of Timbuktu, Ahmad Baba (1556–1627); and the leading Egyptian figure in political Islam, Sayyid Qutb (d. 1966), to name a few.

Az-Zamakhshari (1075–1144), a famous Persian exegete, explains in his commentary on the Qur'an that men practice concubinage (*tasarri*) because the *only* goal of marriage is procreation.[29] This is an elitist perspective because not every person in society could afford the acquisition of a female slave for sexual enjoyment. Curiously, this definition of marriage as *only* for procreation contradicts the Qur'an and the Prophet's reports (Hadith), which expressly admit that sexual pleasure is also a crucial part of marriage. On sexual relations, the Qur'an says, "Your wives are your tilth; go, then, unto your tilth as you may desire."[30] The following verse places more emphasis on the companionship within the coupling of marriage: "They are as a garment for you, and you are as a garment for them."[31] One finds additional reports of comments by the Prophet on sexual relations, such as the following Hadith on men and women's mutual right to sexual fulfillment: "Your body has a right over you, your eyes have a right over you and your wife has a right over you."[32]

---

[27] At-Tabari, *Jami' al-Bayan*, vol. 4, 148.
[28] On the etymology of the terms *tasarri*, *sarari*, and *surriyya* (from the verb *tasarrara*) meaning to take a girl as concubine slave, see Lane, *An Arabic-English Lexicon*, vol. 4, 1337, 1339, and 1353.
[29] Mahmud ibn 'Umar az-Zamakhshari, *al-Kashshaf 'an Haqa'iq at-Tanzil wa 'Uyun al-Aqawil fi Wujuh at-Ta'wil* (Misr: al-Babi al-Halabi, 1966), vol. 1, 498.
[30] The Qur'an, 2: 223, Asad's translation.
[31] Ibid., 2: 187.
[32] Al-Bukhari, *Sahih* (Beirut: Dar al-Kutub al-'Ilmiyya, 2004), Book of Marriage, chapter 90, Hadith number 5199, 979.

Sayyid Qutb (d. 1966), a leading Egyptian figure in political Islam, was more flexible in his interpretation regarding the meaning of this periphrasis. In his most famous work, *Fi Zilal al-Qur'an* (*In the Shadow of the Qur'an*), he wrote that when the Qur'an says "from among those whom you rightfully possess (*ma malakat aymanukum*), it means among the female slaves either through wedlock or in concubinage (*tasarri*)."[33] Sayyid Qutb explained that the verse does not explicitly authorize slavery as a means to take concubines. The issue of whether the Qur'an authorizes slavery for the purpose of concubinage appears to have been constructed in Islamic law based on the interpretations of men's interest in preserving the cultural continuity of the practice of concubinage (*tasarri*) from the pre-Islamic era. Bernard Lewis recognized the problem when he pointed out that "a Muslim slaveowner was entitled by law [not the Qur'an] to the sexual enjoyment of his slave women."[34] According to Ahmad Sikainga, a Sudanese scholar in Islamic studies, the Qur'anic references to slavery and, for that matter, female slavery consist of "broad and general propositions of an ethical nature rather than specific legal formulations."[35]

Contrary to most classical exegetes who were of the opinion that *ma malakat aymanuhum* means "concubines," ar-Razi (1149–1209), another famous Persian Islamic theologian and part of the Ash'ari-Shafi'i school, who wrote one of the most authoritative exegeses of the Qur'an, was one of those who questioned the moral implications of such interpretations and practices and suggested that *ma malakat aymanuhum* should mean "those whom they rightfully possess through wedlock (*an-nikah*)."[36] According to Qur'an commentator Muhammad Asad, "Razi, in particular, points out that the reference to 'all married women' (*al-muhsanat min an-nisa'*),[37] coming as it does after the enumeration of prohibited degrees of relationship, is meant to stress the prohibition of sexual relations with any woman other than one's lawful wife."[38] Ar-Razi applied the system of inductive logic in Islamic law and expressed doubts about the Hadith.

[33] Sayyid Qutb, *Fi Zilal al-Qur'an*, vol. 1, 583.
[34] Lewis, *Race and Slavery*, 14.
[35] Ahmad Sikainga, "Shari'a Courts and the Manumission of Female Slaves in the Sudan, 1898–1939." *International Journal of African Historical Studies*, vol. 28, no. 1 (1995): 1–24, 6.
[36] Fakhr ad-Din Muhammad ibn 'Umar ar-Razi, *at-Tafsir al-Kabir* (Beirut: Dar al-Fikr, 1995), vol. 5, part 10, 40–45.
[37] That is in the Qur'an.
[38] Asad, *The Message of the Qur'an*, 124, footnote 26.

Ar-Razi was certainly not the only recorded voice of divergence on this issue. According to Leila Ahmed, al-Qaramita, the ninth-century branch of the Shi'i Isma'ili sect, went as far as to reject concubinage and polygyny.[39] However, these progressive interpretations did not have much echo in societies influenced by the Maliki school, especially in northwest or West Africa.[40] It is important to note that the interpretation of *ma malakat aymanuhum* as an option within the marriage institution has not arisen in modern times. Muhammad Asad explained that the concubinage system was a form of coercing a slave girl to fulfill her master's sexual desires and is surely prohibited because the Qur'an explicitly describes it as prostitution (*bigha'*).[41] Hence, the term *as-sarari* or *at-tasarri* meaning concubinage, which is unknown in the Qur'an and is at odds with what the Qur'an expresses with respect to marriage and to the taking of slaves for concubinage. In his study of early Islamic law, Jonathan Brockopp commented that the Qur'an established new ethics by promoting marriage to slaves; it emphasized "sexual intercourse was to be entirely within marriage bonds."[42] To assert that males are entitled to female slaves' sexuality contradicts the Qur'anic verses 4:3, 24, 25; 23:6; 70:30; and 24:32.[43] I should emphasize here that verse 4:3 means a man who marries a slave must first free her. It is logical then that the concept of *umm al-walad* (literally "mother of the child" and legally a female slave who bears a child for her master) is neither found nor recognized even tangentially in the Qur'an. Therefore, the interpretation of *ma malakat aymanukum* as concubines in most interpretations or exegeses of the Qur'an and as implemented in Islamic law does not reflect the language in the Qur'anic message. A careful examination of all the occurrences of *ma malakat aymanukum* in the Qur'an clearly refers to "male and female slaves."[44]

The interpretation of *ma malakat aymanukum* as a license for taking slaves as concubines was accepted as a norm by the end of the ninth century. Qur'anic scholars of this period, such as at-Tabari and Ibn al-Kathir, codified the deeply entrenched customs of their contemporary societies in their interpretations of the Qur'an, providing religious and legal

[39] Leila Ahmed, *Women and Gender in Islam: Historical Roots of a Modern Debate* (New Haven: Yale University Press, 1992), 66.

[40] See John Cooper, "Al-Razi, Fakhr al-Din" in *Routledge Encyclopedia of Philosophy*, general editor Edward Craig (London: Routledge, 1998), 8: 112–115.

[41] Asad, *The Message of the Qur'an*, 602, note 49. See also the Qur'anic chapter *an-Nur* (*The Light*) 24, verse 33.

[42] Jonathan Brockopp, *Early Maliki Law* (Leiden: Brill, 2000), 133.

[43] See Asad, *The Message of the Qur'an*, 579, note 3.

[44] See Ibid., 602, note 45 and 608, note 78.

foundations to sanction social practices inconsistent with the spirit of and the often explicit letter of Qur'anic verses, thus establishing the main direction for interpreting the Qur'an as legitimizing the practice of taking slaves for concubines for future generations.

Many interpretations in Islam have followed a similar course to the interpretation of *ma malakat aymanukum* that is inconsistent with the Qur'an. Take the example of the Qur'an's epithet of Muhammad as the *ummi* Prophet. The Qur'an says: "Those who follow the messenger, the *ummi* Prophet whom they shall find described in the Torah and the Gospel."[45] Most classical exegetes interpret this epithet as "the illiterate Prophet" but recent research argues that *ummi* refers to the origin of the Prophet as an Arab of a non-Jewish or the Christian faith: "So if they argue with thee (O Muhammad!), say: 'I have submitted myself to God and so have those who follow me. And ask those who received the scriptures and those who have not (*ummiyin*).'"[46] Ar-Razi (d. 1209) is probably the only exegete who explains that *ummiyin* means "other nations who were not revealed the scriptures."[47] Mohamed Talbi, a contemporary Tunisian historian of Islam, explains that the word *ummiyin* (sing. *ummi*) designates goyim or gentiles. Therefore *ummi*, in this context, means "the Prophet of all nations."[48]

Another pertinent example of using the Qur'an to legitimize existing enduring cultural practices is the practice of polygyny. The Qur'an, in chapter 4 on women, verse 3, states:

And if you have reason to fear that you might not act equitably towards orphans, then marry from among [other] women such as are lawful to you – [even] two, or three, or four: but if you have reason to fear that you might not be able to treat them with equal fairness, then [only] one – or [from among] those whom you rightfully possess (*ma malakat aymanukum*). This will make it more likely that you will not deviate from the right course.

This verse is widely interpreted as sanctioning plural marriages, laying the responsibility of fairness upon the moral conscience of the husband. If it is read, however, in conjunction with a later verse in the same chapter, the meaning is directed toward a restriction in plural marriages. This verse, number 129, reads: "And it will not be within your power to treat your wives with equal fairness, however much you may desire it." Hence,

---

[45] 7:157.

[46] 3:20.

[47] Fakhr al-Din Muḥammad ibn 'Umar ar-Razi. *at-Tafsir al-kabir*. (Beirut: Dar al-Fikr, 1995), vol. 15, part 30, 4–5.

[48] Mohamed Talbi, *Universalité du coran* (Arles: Actes Sud, 2002), 11–12.

this verse enlightens the previous verse and unequivocally instructs a man on the impossibility of exercising fairness if he chooses to marry more than one woman; it preaches monogamy. The prevailing interpretation of this verse took a course similar to that of *ma malakat aymanukum*. One of the problems in the interpretations and legislation of the Qur'an is the disregard or the misunderstanding of occasions of revelations (*asbab an-nuzul*). Establishing the reasons and the historical context for any particular verse is a great method for understanding the meanings of the Qur'an. "But [as Fazlur Rahman alerted] the literature on the 'occasions of revelation' is often highly contradictory and chaotic."[49] Since the premise of the Qur'an is to establish a just and egalitarian society, Fazlur Rahman contended that:

> To insist on literal interpretation of the rules of the Qur'an, shutting one's eyes to the social change that has occurred and that is so palpably occurring before our eyes, is tantamount to deliberately defeating its moral-social purposes and objectives. It is just as though, in view of the Qur'anic emphasis on freeing slaves, one were to insist on preserving the institution of slavery so that one could "earn merit in the sight of God" by freeing slaves. Surely the whole tenor of the teaching of the Qur'an is that there should be no slavery at all.[50]

The cultural environment generally determined the purpose of the scholarly inquiry and affected the course of the interpretations regarding a man's right to have sexual relations with female slaves. However, current feminist literature on the subject of gender and women in Islam by Muslim women such as Leila Ahmad,[51] Fatima Mernissi,[52] and Amina Wadud calls attention to a reinterpretation of the Qur'an, arguing that the Qur'an intended monogamous marriage. Amina Wadud writes: "If it [the Qur'an] had been fully implemented in the practical sense, then Islam would have been a global motivating force for women's empowerment."[53] Sisters in Islam, a Malaysia-based nongovernmental organization advocating women's rights, said:

> It is therefore clear that giving a wife such an option for obtaining a divorce through the marriage contract or ta'liq is not against Islamic teachings. It is not a

---

[49] Fazlur Rahman, *Islam & Modernity: Transformation of an Intellectual Tradition* (Chicago: University of Chicago Press, 1984), 17.

[50] Ibid., 19.

[51] See Ahmed. *Women and Gender.*

[52] See Fatima Mernissi, *The Veil and the Male Elite: A Feminist Interpretation of Women's Rights in Islam* (Reading: Addison-Wesley Pub. Co, 1991).

[53] Amina Wadud, *Qur'an and Woman: Rereading the Sacred Text from a Woman's Perspective* (Oxford: Oxford University Press, 1999), xxi.

new interpretation which has only arisen in these modern times. On the contrary, it is supported by traditional practices from the early days of Islam. It is not an innovation introducing anything that is unlawful, since divorce by ta'liq is also lawful in Islam.[54]

At this point in the argument, I will provide the terms used in the Qur'an regarding the issue of slavery. I will begin with *ma malakat aymanukum*, and then turn to *raqaba* (pl. *riqab*), *'abd*, and finally *asir* (pl. *asra*). These terms bear considerable relevance within the context of their use in the Qur'an that I think demonstrates that interpretations of the Qur'an giving license to slave concubinage are inconsistent with what the Qur'an actually says.

Ma Malakat Aymanukum
Ma malakat aymanukum is mentioned fourteen times in the Qur'an: 4:3, 4:24, 4:25, 4:36, 16:71, 23:6, 24:31, 24:33, 24:58, 30:28, 33:50, 33:52, 33:55, and 70:30.

1. And if you have reason to fear that you might not act equitably towards orphans, then marry from among [other] women such as are lawful to you [even] two, or three, or four: but if you have reason to fear that you might not be able to treat them with equal fairness, then [only] one – or [from among] those whom you rightfully possess (*ma malakat aymanukum*). This will make it more likely that you will not deviate from the right course (4:3).
2. And [forbidden to you are] all married women other than those whom you rightfully possess (*ma malakat aymanukum*) [through wedlock] (4:24).
3. And as for those of you who, owing to circumstances, are not in a position to marry free believing women, [let them marry] believing maidens from among those whom you rightfully possess (*ma malakat aymanukum*) (4:25).[55]
4. And worship God [alone], and do not ascribe divinity, in any way, to aught beside Him. And do good unto your parents, and near of kin, and unto orphans, and the needy, and the neighbour from

---

[54] "Campaign for Monogamy," By the Coalition on Women's Rights in Islam, Press Statement – Islamic Family Law, 16 March 2003, from http://www.sistersinislam.org.my/news.php?item.255.8.

[55] The Qur'an recommends freeing enslaved women by marrying them. It is not concubinage that it is recommending because concubinage is a form of prostitution and sexual exploitation that the Qur'an categorically prohibits. See verse 24:33.

among your own people, and the neighbour who is a stranger, and the friend by your side, and the wayfarer, and those whom you rightfully possess (*ma malakat aymanukum*) (4:36).

5. And on some of you God has bestowed more abundant means of sustenance than on others: and yet, they who are more abundantly favoured are [often] unwilling to share their sustenance with those whom their right hands possess (*ma malakat aymanukum*), so that they [all] might be equal in this respect. Will they, then, God's blessings [thus] deny? (16:71).

6. [Not giving way to their desires] with any but their spouses – that is, those whom they rightfully possess [through wedlock] (*ma malakat aymanukum*) (23:6).[56]

7. And tell the believing women to lower their gaze and to be mindful of their chastity, and not to display their charms [in public] beyond what may [decently] be apparent thereof; hence, let them draw their head-coverings over their bosoms. And let them not display [more of] their charms to any but their husbands, or their fathers, or their husbands' fathers, or their sons, or their husbands' sons, or their brothers, or their brothers' sons, or their sisters' sons, or their womenfolk, or those whom they rightfully possess (*ma malakat aymanukum*) (24:31).

8. And as for those who are unable to marry, let them live in continence until God grants them sufficiency out of His bounty. And if any of those whom you rightfully possess[57] (*ma malakat aymanukum*) desire [to obtain] a deed of freedom, write it out for them if you are aware of any good in them: and give them [their share] of the wealth of God which He has given you. And do not, in order to gain some of the fleeting pleasures of this worldly life, coerce your

---

[56] This is the verse that most commentators consider as referring to concubines. If this interpretation is correct, it contradicts verse 3 of chapter 4, where the subject is clearly about marrying female slaves. Asad explains this verse, namely, "those whom they rightfully possess through wedlock (see note on 4:24), with the significant difference that in the present context this expression relates to both husbands and wives, who 'rightfully possess' one another by virtue of marriage. On the basis of this interpretation, the particle *aw* which precedes this clause does not denote an alternative ('or') but is, rather, in the nature of an explanatory amplification, more or less analogous to the phrase 'in other words' or 'that is,' thus giving to the whole sentence the meaning, 'save with their spouses – that is, those whom they rightfully possess [through wedlock]....'" Asad, *The Message of the Qur'an*, 579–580, note 3.

[57] Muhammad Asad explains that the periphrasis "whom your right hands possess" here means male or female slaves. Asad, *The Message of the Qur'an*, 602, note 45.

[slave] maidens (*fatayatikum*) into whoredom[58] if they happen to be desirous of marriage; and if anyone should coerce them, then, verily, after they have been compelled [to submit in their helplessness], God will be much-forgiving, a dispenser of grace! (24:33).

9. O YOU who have attained to faith! At three times [of day], let [even] those whom you rightfully possess (*ma malakat aymanukum*),[59] as well as those from among you who have not yet attained to puberty, ask leave of you [before intruding upon your privacy]: before the prayer of daybreak, and whenever you lay aside your garments in the middle of the day, and after the prayer of nightfall: the three occasions on which your nakedness is likely to be bared. Beyond these [occasions], neither you nor they will incur any sin if they move [freely] about you, attending to [the needs of] one another. In this way God makes clear unto you His messages: for God is all-knowing, wise! (24:58).

10. He propounds unto you a parable drawn from your own life: Would you [agree to] have some of those whom your right hands possess (*ma malakat aymanukum*) as [full-fledged] partners in whatever We may have bestowed upon you as sustenance, so that you [and they] would have equal shares in it, and you would fear [to make use of it without consulting] them, just as you might fear [the more powerful of] your equals? Thus clearly do We spell out these messages unto people who use their reason (30:28).

11. O PROPHET! Behold, We have made lawful to thee thy wives unto whom thou hast paid their dowers, as well as those whom thy right hand has come to possess (*ma malakat yaminuka*) from among the captives of war whom God has bestowed upon thee.[60] And [We have made lawful to thee] the daughters of thy paternal uncles and aunts, and the daughters of thy maternal uncles and aunts, who have migrated with thee [to Yathrib]; and any believing woman who offers herself freely to the Prophet and whom the

---

[58] Asad explains that "the above verse reiterates the prohibition of concubinage by explicitly describing it as 'whoredom' (*bigha*')." Asad, *The Message of the Qur'an*, 602, note 49.

[59] Muhammad Asad explains that *ma malakat aymanukum* may denote, in this context, "those whom you rightfully possess through wedlock, that is, wives and husbands." Asad, *The Message of the Qur'an*, 608, note 78.

[60] For Asad, this verse is proof that "Islam does not countenance any form of concubinage, and categorically prohibits sexual relations between a man and a woman unless they are lawfully *married* to one another." Asad, *The Message of the Qur'an*, 727, note 58. In this verse female slaves are clearly described as captives of war.

Prophet might be willing to wed: [this latter being but] a privilege for thee, and not for other believers – [seeing that] We have already made known what We have enjoined upon them with regard to their wives and those whom their right hands may possess (*ma malakat aymanukum*). [And] in order that thou be not burdened with [undue] anxiety – for God is indeed much-forgiving, a dispenser of grace (33:50).

12. No [other] women shall henceforth be lawful to thee – nor art thou [allowed] to supplant [any of] them by other wives, even though their beauty should please thee greatly – [none shall be lawful to thee] beyond those whom thou [already] hast come to possess (*ma malakat aymanukum*).[61] And God keeps watch over everything (33:52).

13. [However,] it is no sin for them [to appear freely] before their fathers, or their sons, or their brothers, or their brothers' sons, or their sisters' sons, or their womenfolk, or such [male slaves] as their right hands may possess (*ma malakat aymanukum*). But [always, O wives of the Prophet,] remain conscious of God – for, behold, God is witness unto everything (33:55).

14. and who are mindful of their chastity,[62] [not giving way to their desires] with any but their spouses – that is, those whom they rightfully possess (*ma malakat aymanukum*) [through wedlock] – for then, behold, they are free of all blame, whereas such as seek to go beyond that [limit] are truly transgressors (70: 29, 30, 31).

Raqaba

Raqaba (pl. *riqab*) literally means "neck" but in the Qur'an it indicates the whole of a human being. This expression is used metonymically in the Qur'an to mean, as defined by Muhammad Asad, "in the cause of freeing human beings from bondage." This is mentioned six times in the Qur'an: 2:177, 4:92, 5:89, 9:60, 58:3, and 90:13.

15. True piety does not consist in turning your faces towards the east or the west but truly pious is he who believes in God, and the Last Day; and the angels, and revelation, and the prophets; and spends

---

[61] This is similar to verse 4:24.
[62] This is similar to verse 23:6.

his substance – however much he himself may cherish it – upon his near of kin, and the orphans, and the needy, and the wayfarer, and the beggars, and for the freeing of human beings from bondage (*fi ar-riqab*) (2: 177).

16. AND IT IS not conceivable that a believer should slay another believer, unless it be by mistake. And upon him who has slain a believer by mistake there is the duty of freeing a believing soul from bondage (*tahrir raqaba*) and paying an indemnity to the victim's relations, unless they forgo it by way of charity. Now if the slain, while himself a believer, belonged to a people who are at war with you, [the penance shall be confined to] the freeing of a believing soul from bondage (*tahrir raqaba*) (4:92).

17. God will not take you to task for oaths which you may have uttered without thought, but He will take you to task for oaths which you have sworn in earnest. Thus, the breaking of an oath must be atoned for by feeding ten needy persons with more or less the same food as you are wont to give to your own families, or by clothing them, or by freeing a human being from bondage (*tahrir raqaba*); and he who has not the wherewithal shall fast for three days [instead] (5:89).

18. The offerings given for the sake of God are [meant] only for the poor and the needy, and those who are in charge thereof, and those whose hearts are to be won over, and for the freeing of human beings from bondage (*fi ar-riqab*) (9:60).

19. Hence, as for those who would separate themselves from their wives by saying, "Thou art as unlawful to me as my mother," and thereafter would go back on what they have said, [their atonement] shall be the freeing of a human being from bondage (*tahrir raqaba*) before the couple may touch one another again: this you are [hereby] exhorted to do – for God is fully aware of all that you do (58:3).

20. But he would not try to ascend the steep uphill road.... And what could make thee conceive what it is, that steep uphill road? [It is] the freeing of one's neck (*fakk raqaba*) [from the burden of sin] (90:11, 12, 13).

The Word 'Abd

The word 'abd that came to be widely and commonly associated with slaves is in point of fact a practice against the teachings of the Qur'an.

God prefers to use the word *'abd* exclusively for Him to call His creatures. For instance, the Qur'an says about the Prophet Muhammad:

> 21. Limitless in His glory is He who transported His servant (*'abdihi*, e.g., Muhammad) by night from the Inviolable House of Worship [at Mecca] to the Remote House of Worship [at Jerusalem] – the environs of which We had blessed – so that We might show him some of Our symbols: for, verily, He alone is all-hearing, all-seeing (17:1).

This verse is about Jesus:

> 22. [As for Jesus,] he was nothing but [a human being,] a servant (*'abd*) [of Ours] whom We had graced [with prophethood], and whom We made an example for the children of Israel (43–59).

Or, when God speaks about His creatures, He would say, for instance:

> 23. Are they, then, not aware of how little of the sky and the earth lies open before them, and how much is hidden from them? – [or that,] if We so willed, We could cause the earth to swallow them, or cause fragments of the sky to fall down upon them? In all this, behold, there is a message indeed for every servant [of God] (*'abd munib*) who is wont to turn unto Him [in repentance] (34:9).

Consequently the Qur'an uses the word *fata*, which literally means "lad" or "boy" to designate a servant or slave boy. It is used three times in the Qur'an: 12:30, 18:60, and 18:62.

> 24. NOW the women of the city spoke [thus to one another]: "The wife of this nobleman is trying to induce her slave-boy to yield himself unto her! Her love for him has pierced her heart; verily, we see that she is undoubtedly suffering from an aberration!" (12:30).
>
> 25. And lo! [In the course of his wanderings,] Moses said to his servant (*fatah*): "I shall not give up until I reach the junction of the two seas, even if I [have to] spend untold years [in my quest]!" (18:60).
>
> 26. And after the two had walked some distance, [Moses] said to his servant (*fatah*): "Bring us our mid-day meal; we have indeed suffered hardship on this [day of] our journey!" (18:62).

The same can be stated about the word *fatayat* (the singular of *fatat*), which means "maiden" or "slave girl." It is mentioned twice in the Qur'an, 24:33 and 4:25:

27. And as for those who are unable to marry, let them live in continence until God grants them sufficiency out of His bounty. And if any of those whom you rightfully possess (*ma malakat aymanukum*) desire [to obtain] a deed of freedom, write it out for them if you are aware of any good in them: and give them [their share] of the wealth of God which He has given you. And do not, in order to gain some of the fleeting pleasures of this worldly life, coerce your [slave] maidens (*fatayatikum*) into whoredom if they happen to be desirous of marriage; and if anyone should coerce them, then, verily, after they have been compelled [to submit in their helplessness], God will be much-forgiving, a dispenser of grace! (24:33).

28. And as for those of you who, owing to circumstances, are not in a position to marry free believing women, [let them marry] believing maidens (*fatayatikum*) from among those whom you rightfully possess (*ma malakat aymanukum*) (4:25).

There are only two occurrences in the Qur'an when the word *'abd* clearly means slave. The feminine gender of *'abd* is *ama* (pl. *ima'*), meaning "female servant" or "slave girl," and it is mentioned only once with that meaning in the Qur'an:[63]

29. AND [you ought to] marry the single from among you as well as such of your male and female slaves (*ima'ikum*) as are fit [for marriage]. If they [whom you intend to marry] are poor, [let this not deter you;] God will grant them sufficiency out of His bounty – for God is infinite [in His mercy], all-knowing (24:32).[64]

---

[63] There is another verse that contains *ama*: "Do not marry unbelieving women till they believe; for any believing servant of God (*ama*) is better than an unbelieving woman even though she please you (2:221)." It is possible to interpret *ama* as "slave," but Asad translates it to mean "servant of God." Asad, *The Message of the Qur'an*, 59–60. Az-Zamakhshari also explains that the *ama* in this verse means servant of God because all believing human beings, be they free or slaves, are God's servants. Az-Zamakhshari, *al-Kashshaf*, vol. 1, 361.

[64] This is similar to 4:25. The verse implies that the only sexual relations accepted in the Qur'an are through wedlock.

30. God propounds [to you] the parable of [two men –] a man enslaved (*'abdan mamlukan*), unable to do anything of his own accord, and a [free] man upon whom We have bestowed goodly sustenance [as a gift] from Ourselves, so that he can spend thereof [at will, both] secretly and openly. Can these [two] be deemed equal? All praise is due to God [alone]: but most of them do not understand it (16:75).[65]

One last term used in the Qur'an for a slave is *asir* (pl. *asra*), designating captives taken in war who may be kept as slaves.

31. IT DOES NOT behoove a prophet to keep captives unless he has battled strenuously on earth. You may desire the fleeting gains of this world – but God desires [for you the good of] the life to come: and God is almighty, wise (8:67).

These thirty-one Qur'anic verses provided the basis for legal formulations regarding the practice of slavery and the taking of slaves for concubinage in the Islamic world. The Qur'an's recommendations for the emancipation of enslaved people are here, too. These verses recommend gradual steps to end slavery. As Muhammad Asad points out, "the institution of slavery is envisaged in the Quran as a mere historic phenomenon that must in time be abolished."[66] Indeed, the Qur'anic prescriptions of manumission are expressed in the Qur'an as pious deeds, clearly implying that ending slavery was a crucial goal in Islam at times when slavery formed a fundamental part of human culture.

What Does the Hadith Say about Slavery?

The Hadith (pl. *ahadith*) is a collection of reports of what the Prophet Muhammad (570–632) did, said, or answered when asked questions about diverse issues. In the first century of the birth of Islam, the Hadith consisted of oral reports relating to the sayings, actions, and way of life of the Prophet Muhammad.[67] It is important to note that Muhammad did

---

[65] There are only these instances (2:178 and 16:75), when the use of the word *'abd* in reference to an enslaved person was to make a point in a parable about Arabian society.

[66] Asad, *The Message of the Qur'an*, 608, note 78.

[67] I use the term *reports* rather than *traditions* to designate *Hadith*. This is better explained by a great scholar of Islam, Marshall Hodgson, who wrote: "Since there is also, of course tradition among Muslims, in the English sense of the word – and since that tradition is often to be contrasted to *hadith* – such a term as 'narration' or 'report' seems a far more convenient rendering for *hadith* if the term is to be translated at all." Marshall

not recommend that his words should be committed to writing, lest they be perceived as comparable to the words of God. He allowed only the Qur'anic verses to be written and insisted on the shortcoming of human reasoning. Indeed, this distinction was observed during the Prophet's lifetime. The following example illustrates this point well. In Medina, on the eve of the famous battle called Badr against the people of Mecca, Muhammad devised a plan of attack and he shared it with his people. One of his followers named al-Habbab b. al-Mundhir inquired whether the plan was Muhammad's or revealed to him by God. Muhammad replied that it was his own reasoning. Then, al-Habbab b. al-Mundhir, an expert in warfare, advised the Prophet with a different plan. Muhammad followed his recommendation, which led the Muslims to a great victory.[68] Although Muhammad repeatedly insisted his humanity was far from flawless, nevertheless, his words, deeds, and behavior became a written corpus that represents a founding text second only to the Qur'an in Islam.[69] James Robson, a specialist in Islamic traditions, wrote: "At that time there was no idea that Tradition [of the Prophet] was second in authority to the Qur'an because there was no collected body of traditions."[70] Only in the late second century, after the death of the Prophet Muhammad, was the Hadith recognized as the second fundamental source in Islam after the Qur'an. Throughout Islamic history, both sources are constantly referred to in matters of Islamic law, history, and politics.

In view of the fact that Muhammad was the embodiment of Islamic social ideals and therefore the model for every Muslim, Muslim scholars wanted to preserve the knowledge of the Prophet and his Sunna. The apparent inaccuracy of many reports compelled scholars to develop critical tools to assess each report attributed to the Prophet Muhammad. The analysis of the (usually oral) chain of the transmitters of the Hadith is called *isnad* and the transmitted text is called the Hadith. Two of the most respected collections of the Hadith are called *as-Sahihayn* (the authentic collections or collections of sound or correct reports): *as-Sahih*

G. S. Hodgson, *The Venture of Islam: Conscience and History in a World Civilization* (Chicago: University of Chicago Press, 1974), vol. 1, 64. Likewise, I refer to Hadith as reports and traditionists as reporters or transmitters.

[68] At-Tabari, *Tarikh at-Tabari: Tarikh al-Umam wa-'l-Muluk* (Beirut: Dar Sader Publishers, 2003), vol. 1, 70. See the English translation: Al-Tabari. *The History of al-Tabari: Prophets and Patriarchs*, translated and annotated by William M. Brinner (Albany: State University of New York Press, 1986), vol. 2, 21.

[69] See the excellent work on this subject of Mahmoud Hussein, *Al-Sîra: le Prophète de l'Islam raconté par ses compagnons* (Paris: Grasset, 2005).

[70] James Robson, "Hadith" in *The Encyclopedia of Islam*.

of al-Bukhari (d. 870) and *as-Sahih* of Muslim (d. 875). There are other collections with varying degrees of authenticity, such as *Sunan* Ibn Majah (d. 887), *Sunan* Abu Dawud (d. 889), *Sunan* at-Tirmidhi (d. 892), and *Sunan* an-Nasa'i (d. 915). Muslims generally recognize these six collections. The *Muwatta'* of Malik b. Anas (d. 795), the founder of the Maliki school of law, and *Musnad* of Ahmad ibn Hanbal (d. 855), the founder of the Hanbali school of law, were also recognized as important sources in the general corpus of the Prophet's reports.

A highly regarded collection of the Prophet's reports is *Sahih* al-Bukhari. It took al-Bukhari sixteen years to compile his work. He collected about 600,000 reports but accepted only 7,275. This means that more than ninety-eight percent of the Hadith were weak or fabricated.[71] Although a critical analysis was undertaken by the traditionists or, rather, the transmitters, to compile collections of sound Hadith, they were not very successful. The following statement by James Robson sums up good examples of forged traditions attributed to the Prophet Muhammad:

One readily notices phrases from the Old and New Testaments put into the mouth of the Prophet as his sayings. There are references to towns far from Arabia which were to be conquered, even to towns not yet founded in the Prophet's time. Parties which arose in the early Muslim period are named, e.g., Kharidji, Murdji'a, Kadariyya, Djahmiyya. Reference can be found to the rightly-guided Caliphs, and there are unmistakable references to the Umayyads and the 'Abbasids. Many miracles are attributed to the Prophet, although the Kur'an does not represent him as a miracle-worker. There is great detail regarding the tribulations before the end of the world, and regarding the Last Judgment.[72]

Many reports were fabricated for various social reasons and to advance political agendas. Some were invented to preach heretical beliefs or to persuade people to live an ascetic life or the straight path according to Muhammad's model. A famous example of fabricated Hadith is the so-called Israelite traditions (*Isra'iliyyat*), traditions of Jewish origin attributed to the Prophet that found their way into Islamic traditions. Strict Muslim scholars warned against the use of these sources. Ibn Kathir, for instance, considered them dubious and advised caution when using them.[73] Other scholars accept them as legitimate sources as long as they do not contradict the Qur'an or the Hadith. According to al-Bukhari, the Prophet said: "Treat women well, for a woman was created from a rib. The most curved portion of the rib is its upper part, so,

[71] Al-Bukhari. *Sahih*, 9–10.
[72] Robson, "Hadith."
[73] Ibn Kathir, *al-Bidaya wa 'n-Nihaya*, vol. 1, 6.

if you try to straighten it, you will break it, but if you leave it as it is, it will remain crooked, so be kind to women."[74] Ibn Kathir, in a famous book on the stories of the Prophets, popularized in Islamic literature the Jewish creation story of Adam and Eve and their offspring. He wrote that Eve (Hawa') was created from the left short rib of Adam while he slept.[75] However, the Qur'an insists on the creation of men and women from one soul. It says: "O humankind! Be careful of your duty to your Lord Who created you from a single soul and from it created its mate" (4:1). Hence, ad-Dimashqi's Hadith seems to contradict the Qur'an, where there is no mention of women being created from a rib.

The reports of the Prophet are explanatory and complementary to the Qur'an, and the Hadith collections contain many messages on the issue of slavery. The Prophet insisted that the unconditional freeing of a human being from bondage is among the most commendable deeds.[76] Ironically the Hadith did not specifically advocate the abolition of slavery; instead the Hadith was used to create practical advancement in the history of slavery. I want to illustrate this by citing examples from *as-Sahih* of al-Bukhari that are consistent or contradictory with the message of the Qur'an. The Hadith reports that the Prophet warned Muslims not to call any human being by the term "slave." The Prophet said:

One should not say: "Feed your lord (*rabbaka*), help your lord perform his ablution, or give water to your lord," but you should say: "my master (*sayyidi*) or my guardian (*Mawlay*)." And one should not say: "my slave (*'abdi*) or my slave-girl (*amati*)," but should say: "my boy or lad (*fataya*), my lass (*fatati*), and my boy (*ghulami*).[77]

By this Hadith, the Prophet implies that all Muslims are servants of God, the only Master. Yet, ironically, in all Hadith, these very words designate slaves.

As-Sahih of al-Bukhari contains ninety-eight books (divisions); each book (*kitab*, pl. *kutub*) contains many chapters, and every chapter (*bab*, pl. *abwab*) contains one to several reports, for a total of 7,275. If we discount the repetitions, there are only about four thousand reports (Hadith).[78]

---

[74] Al-Bukhari, *Sahih*, Hadith 3331, 608.

[75] Ibn Kathir, *Qisas al-Anbiya'* (Beirut: al-Maktaba al-'Asriyya, 2004), 13.

[76] For a most elaborate discussion of the traditions of the Prophet bearing on this issue, see Muhammad ibn 'Ali Shawkani, *Nayl al-Awtar min Ahadith Sayyid al-Akhyar* (Cairo: Maktabat al-Qahirah, 1978), vol. 7, 226–255.

[77] Al-Bukhari, *Sahih*, Hadith 2552, 462. For English see *The Alim* CD-Rom (ISL Software Corporation, 1986–2000), al-Bukhari, vol. 3, 728.

[78] Ibid., 10.

There are two books on slavery in *as-Sahih* of al-Bukhari listed under numbers 49 and 50. Interesting, the first is entitled "the book of emancipation (*kitab al-'itq*)" and the second "the book on written contracts of emancipation" (*kitab al-mukataba*). The emphasis on the emancipation of the enslaved is in accordance with the teachings of the Qur'an. Examples from "the book of emancipation" (*kitab al-'itq*) include the following:

The Prophet said: "Whoever frees a Muslim slave, God will save all the parts of his body from the Fire [of Hell]."[79]

A Muslim by the name Abu Dharr asked the Prophet: "What is the best deed?" He replied: "To believe in God and to fight for His cause." Abu Dharr asked next: "What is the best kind of manumission?" The Prophet replied: "The manumission of the most expensive slave and the most beloved in the household of the master."[80]

When Abu Huraira [a companion of the Prophet] accompanied by his slave set out intending to embrace Islam they lost each other on the way. The slave then came while Abu Huraira was sitting with the Prophet. The Prophet said: "O Abu Huraira! Your slave (*ghulamuk*) has come back." Abu Huraira said: "Indeed, I would like you to witness that I have manumitted him."[81]

Other reports discuss and provide recommendations for masters to respect, marry and manumit their slaves.[82]

The Prophet said: "He who has a slave-girl and educates and treats her nicely and then manumits and marries her, will get a double reward."[83]

The Prophet said: "Whoever frees his share of a common slave and he has sufficient money to free him completely, should let its price be estimated by a just man and give his partners the price of their shares and manumit the slave; otherwise (i.e., if he has not sufficient money) he manumits the slave partially."[84]

Contractual manumission or the deed of manumission is based on the recommendations of the Qur'an. The Qur'an says in this regard:

And if any of those whom you rightfully possess (*ma malakat aymanukum*) desire [to obtain] a deed of freedom, write it out for them if you are aware of any good in them: and give them [their share] of the wealth of God which He has given you" (24:33).

[79] Ibid., Hadith 2518, 457. For English see *The Alim*, al-Bukhari, vol. 3, 693.

[80] Ibid., Hadith 2517, 457; *The Alim*, al-Bukhari, vol. 3, 694.

[81] Ibid., Hadith 2530, 458; *The Alim*, al-Bukhari, vol. 3, 707.

[82] Ibid., Hadith 2533, 459; *The Alim*, al-Bukhari, vol. 3, 710.

[83] Ibid., Hadith 2544, 461; *The Alim*, al-Bukhari, vol. 3, 720.

[84] Ibid., Hadith 2553, 462; *The Alim*, al-Bukhari, vol. 3, 698.

The Hadith emphasizes the owner's obligation toward the slave who is engaged in buying his or her freedom, but it is curiously amended by the practice of *al-wala'* (client relationship). The Qur'an does not say anything about the *wala'*, which was a pre-Islamic practice. It just stipulates that such a contract may not be refused, using an imperative form of the verb *katibuhum* ("write it out for them").[85]

A report in the *Sahih* says that a slave once asked his master for a *mukataba* (contract of freedom), and although he had money, the owner declined his request. So the slave went to 'Umar ibn al-Khattab (second caliph) and 'Umar said: "Write it out for him." The owner refused, so 'Umar beat him with a whip, reciting the Qur'anic verse, "Write it out for them if you are aware of any good in them." Consequently, the owner gave his slave the contract.[86] This anecdote is an example of how the second elected caliph translated this Qur'anic injunction into a mandatory application in favor of the enslaved person.

The chapter entitled "the book on written contracts of emancipation" (*kitab al-mukataba*) includes other examples. There are six reports (Hadith) in this book, but all are slightly different versions of the same Hadith.

'Aisha told the Prophet that Barira came to seek her help in her writing of emancipation (for a certain sum) and that time she had not paid anything of it. 'Aisha said to her, "Go back to your masters, and if they agree that I will pay the amount of your writing of emancipation and get your *wala'*, I will do so." Barira informed her masters of that but they refused and said: "If she (i.e., 'Aisha) is seeking God's reward, then she can do so, but your *wala'* will be for us." 'Aisha mentioned that to Muhammad who said to her, "Buy and manumit her, as the *wala'* is for the liberator." Muhammad then got up and said: "What about the people who stipulate conditions which are not present in God's laws? Whoever imposes conditions which are not present in God's laws, then those conditions will be invalid, even if he imposed these conditions a hundred times. God's conditions (laws) are the truth and are more solid."[87]

The urging for brotherly conduct is apparent in many Hadith:

Your slaves are your brothers and God has put them under your command. So whoever has a brother under his command should feed him of what he eats and dress him of what he wears. Do not ask them to do things beyond their capacity and if you do so, then help them.[88]

---

[85] See Asad, *The Message of the Qur'an*, 602, note 46.
[86] Al-Bukhari, *Sahih*, 464.
[87] Ibid., Hadith 2560, 464; translation by *The Alim*, al-Bukhari, vol. 3, 735 (my emphasis).
[88] Ibid., Hadith 30, 21; translation by *The Alim*, al-Bukhari, vol. 1, 29 (my emphasis).

Bakr went to the Prophet and said: Apostle of God! To whom should I show kindness? He said: Your mother, your sister, your brother and the slave whom you set free and who is your relative, a due binding (on you), and a tie of relationship which should be joined.[89]

Interesting, among all these reports, only few address the slave in person and speak indirectly about his or her agency. The *Sahih* reports that the Prophet said: "The slave who worships in perfect manner, and is dutiful, sincere and obedient to his master, will get a double reward."[90] In another Hadith concerning the case in which a female slave commits fornication, it is reported in the *Sahih* that the prophet said: "If a female slave commits fornication, scourge her; if she does it again, scourge her again; if she repeats it, scourge her again."[91]

Another category found in the Hadith consists of recommendations for masters to be just and kind to their slaves. The Hadith does not speak of slaves as a class apart but requires Muslims to treat slaves with kindness and respect and to consider a slave as a member of the master's family. It also recommends the marriage of free Muslims with slaves. But the Hadith does not take any extra steps to further the outright abolition of slavery. The Hadith, like the Qur'an, has thus left this decision open and dependent upon the slaveholder's moral conscience and man-made laws articulated in the Shari'a.

A Critical Exam

No single verse in the Qur'an calls for the acceptance of slavery as a normal social practice. The Qur'an contains no word on the treatment of slaves to indicate that it condones slavery's existence and continuity. The Qur'an does not speak in the future tense (prior to enslavement) regarding slavery, that is, "what to do when someone acquires a slave," but it provides recommendations for the past acquisition of slavery, "what to do with slaves already acquired." Hence, the explicit Qur'anic recommendations were to free slaves. Al-Khawarij (sing. al-khariji "seceder or schismatic"), who emerged in the seventh century as an early sect of Islam, was probably the first group to insist on a social justice principle in the name of Islam. The group preached against genealogical privileges and on issues

[89] *The Alim*, abu Dawood, 2439.
[90] Al-Bukhari, *Sahih*, Hadith 2551, 462; *The Alim*, al-Bukhari, vol. 3, 727.
[91] Ibid., Hadith 2555, 462; *The Alim*, al-Bukhari, vol. 3, 731.

related to slavery; it declared social equality with slaves and insisted on the right of any morally qualified Muslim to assume the highest role in the community, even if he was a black slave.[92] Some early scholars understood the message of the Qur'an based on these moral implications and social justice principles and declared that slavery should be abolished. According to Indian Muslim jurist Syed Ameer Ali (1849–1928), Ja'far b. Muhammad Sadiq (702–765), revered as the sixth imam by the Shi'a and highly respected by all Muslims, preached against slavery at the end of the Umayyad dynasty and at the beginning of the Abbasid rule. His views on slavery were not embraced by mainstream Shi'a, but were well received by two small schools of thought, al-Mu'tazila and al-Qaramita, in the ninth century.[93] Syed Ameer Ali wrote that the ninth-century founder of the Qarmati movement in Iraq Hamdan Qarmat's "violent denunciations against domestic slavery constituted the chief reason for his being placed under the ban by a great majority of Mussulmans."[94] Qarmat even decided to join the cause of the revolt of the black slaves in Iraq in the ninth century but his collaboration with its leader failed.[95] Al-Qaramita also rejected concubinage, polygyny, and the veil.[96] In Egypt, the Fatimi ruler al-Hakim (985–1021) implemented the abolition of slavery by freeing all his slaves, male and female.[97] But as far as these issues are concerned, mainstream male interpreters all over the Islamic world prevailed against this ethical voice and did exactly the opposite of what the Qur'an intended. From the beginning, the interpretation and the codification of Islamic law intersected with the great imperial Islamic age. Syed Ameer Ali commented:

Slavery by purchase was unknown during the reigns of the first four Caliphs, the *Khulafai-rashadin*, "the legitimate Caliphs" as they are called by the Sunnis. There is, at least, no authentic record of any slave having been acquired by purchase during their tenure of the office. But with the accession of the usurping House of Ommiah, a change came over the spirit of Islam. Moâwiyah was the first Mussulman sovereign who introduced into the Mahommedan world the practice

[92] Muḥammad ibn 'Abd al-Karim ash-Shahrastani, *Kitab al-Milal wa 'n-Nihal*, edited by William Cureton (London: Printed for the Society for the Publication of Oriental Texts, 1846), vol. 1, 87.
[93] Syed Ameer Ali, *The Personal Law of the Mahommedans, According to All the Schools* (London: W.H. Allen, 1880), 39. Al-Qaramita is a branch of the Islma'ili Shi'i sect.
[94] Ali, *The Personal Law*, 39.
[95] At-Tabari, *Tarikh at-Tabari*, vol. 6, 2145–2146. On the revolt of black slaves in Iraq, see Alexandre Popović, *The Revolt of African Slaves in Iraq in the IIIrd/IXth Century* (Princeton: Markus Wiener Publishers, 1999).
[96] Ahmed, *Women and Gender in Islam*, 1992, 66.
[97] Nejla Abu Izzeddin, *The Druzes: A New Study of Their History, Faith, and Society* (Leiden: E. J. Brill, 1993), 79.

of acquiring slaves by purchase. He was also the first to adopt the Byzantine custom of guarding his women by eunuchs.[98]

Imperial monarchic Islam contradicted the teachings of the Qur'an and Muhammad's model of governing. It was imperative for the rulers to sponsor whoever could reconcile the dynastic pretensions of the new Arab-Umayyad dynastic regime and its conquests with the socially just language of the Qur'an. In the words of two Egyptian experts in early Islamic history, Bahgat Elnadi and Adel Rifaat:

> From 660, the founder of the dynasty of the Umayyads, Mu'awiyya, is considered by some Muslims as a usurper, to have betrayed the fourth Caliph, 'Ali, who is no other than the cousin of the Prophet. Mu'awiya and his descendants, obliged to leave Medina, established their capital in Damascus[...]. Under their influence, certain compilers will go as far as attributing to the Prophet reports which he did not make, to serve the prestige of the lineage of Mu'awiyya. Their opponents will do the same, in favor of the lineage of 'Ali, or that of al-'Abbas, uncle of the Prophet. The descendants of these opponents will finally dethrone the Umayyads, in 750, to found the dynasty of the 'Abbasids.[99]

Hence, through their 'ulama', the leaders, who produced and mediated political knowledge to shape public opinion, forged an interpretation and a form of Islam suited to a dynastic theocracy. The mosque was, and still is, the main instrument to mediate, mobilize, mold, and perpetuate the state of political affairs.

It must be noted that a consistent abolitionist movement is clearly a modernist idea but the moral sensibility against the practice of slavery existed throughout Islamic history. Voices against slavery, albeit isolated or silenced, continued, especially in the nineteenth century during contact with Western ideas and campaigns for abolition. Sayyid Ahmad Khan (1817–1898), dubbed by historian Clarence-Smith the "Muslim William Wilberforce,"[100] argued that "in the beginning it [slavery] existed like other Pre-Islamic customs which were not repealed all at once. It [Islam] prohibited, however, the making of new slaves, and for the slaves still present many regulations were fixed with this in view that bit by bit they should be released."[101] Indeed, Sayyid Ahmad Khan published a treatise in the Urdu language entitled *Ibtal-i ghulami* (*Abolition of Slavery*) in

---

[98] Ali, *The Personal Law*, 38–39.

[99] Mahmoud Hussein, *Al-Sîra*, tome 1, 21.

[100] William Clarence-Smith, "Islamic Abolitionism in the Western Indian Ocean from c. 1800," paper presented at the 10th Annual Gilder Lehrman Center International Conference (Yale University, November 7–8, 2008), 6.

[101] J. M. S. Baljon, Jr., *The Reforms and Religious Ideas of Sir Sayyid Ahmad Khan* (Leiden: E. J. Brill, 1949), 28.

Agra in 1893. Two years later this treatise was translated into Arabic.[102] But ideas about abolition already existed in the Arab world. Tunisia, for instance, was the first country in the Islamic world to actually abolish slavery in 1846. Egyptian scholar Muhammad ʿAbdu (1849–1905) was among the pioneer Muslim Arab intellectuals who attacked in multiple legal opinions the classical institutions of subjugation such as polygyny, concubinage, and slavery.[103] He declared, for instance, in a letter to English political activist Wilfrid Blunt (1849–1922), "that the abolition of slavery is according to the spirit of the Koran, to Mohammedan tradition, and to Mohammedan dogma."[104] Unfortunately this line of thinking was confronted by the populist and literalist doctrine of Wahhabism. The Wahhabi puritanical dogma, developed by Muhammad b. ʿAbd al-Wahhab (1703–1792) in Arabia, claimed the return to the true practice of Islam and saw many rational and progressive interpretations in religious matters as illegal innovations such as the individual rights of women and ideas about abolition.[105] Hence Wahhabism reinforced mainstream eighteenth-century and nineteenth-century Islamic thought. So the moral teachings of the Qur'an were to free the slaves; just as with polygyny the goal was to establish a monogamous marriage institution and it was up to the learned community to devise the best way to apply these Qur'anic recommendations. And as in polygyny, where the right for a man to marry up to four women was legally established, the practice of slavery was also continued and institutionalized, even though both practices are against the moral teachings of the Qur'an. The Qur'an legalized manumission and did not institutionalize slavery. Why, then, did not the Qur'an abolish it outright? The Qur'an reflects the character and ethos of the Arabian people. The only reference in the Qur'an to the acquisition of slaves occurs in verses 30:50 and 47:4, where female slaves are clearly described as captives of war. The Qur'an seems to establish a rule that at the time of the revelation only captives taken in a just war could be enslaved.[106] This "just war," or *jihad*, is clearly defined in the Qur'an as self-defense: "And fight in God's cause against those who wage war

[102] See R. Brunschvig, "ʿAbd" in *The Encyclopedia of Islam*.

[103] Muhammad ʿAmara, *al-Aʿmal al-Kamila li-'l-Imam Muhammad ʿAbdu* (Beirut: al-Muʾassasa al-ʿArabiyya li 'd-Dirasat wa 'n-Nashr, 1972), 2:365. See also Muhammad ʿAbdu and Muhammad Rashid Rida, *Tafsir al-Qur'an al-Hakim* (Cairo: Dar al-Manar, 1930). For English, see William Gervase Clarence-Smith, *Islam and the Abolition of Slavery* (Oxford: Oxford University Press, 2006), 203–205.

[104] Wilfrid Blunt, *Secret History of the English Occupation of Egypt: Being a Personal Narrative of Events* (London: T.F. Unwin, 1907), 254.

[105] See Brunschvig, "ʿAbd."

[106] 8:67.

against you, but do not commit aggression – for, verily, God does not love aggressors."[107] The Qur'an recommends actually freeing the captives after the war is over.[108] In this context, Syed Ameer Ali wrote:

> The possession of a slave by the Koranic laws was conditional on a *bona fide* war, waged in self-defence, against idolatrous enemies; and it was permitted to serve as a guarantee for the preservation of the lives of the captives [...]. Mohammed found the custom existing among the pagan Arabs; he minimised the evil, and at the same time laid down such strict rules that, but for the perversity of his followers, slavery as a social institution would have ceased to exist with the discontinuance of the wars in which the Moslem community was at first involved.[109]

All verses seem to discourage the practice of slavery and aim to gradually and ultimately eliminate it. Hence, they are emancipation verses. There was indeed a precedent in the gradual steps taken to prohibit the consumption of alcohol but this model was not applied for the elimination of polygyny and slavery. One of the primary aims of the Qur'an was to gradually prohibit any unhealthy, immoral social practices among Arabs. Muhammad's faith was the foundation in the struggle for social justice. Hence, dynastic or oligarchic regimes, polygyny, the unilateral right to divorce entitled to men, concubinage, and slavery do not belong to the mission of the Qur'an. The initial message of the Qur'an was gradually eroded by the elitist regime's political and power aspirations. Muslim scholars found support for their claims regarding these institutions in selective Hadith and their own selective interpretations of the Qur'an. By the ninth century and with the compilation of the first manuals on Islamic law, concubinage and slavery were clearly defined as institutions allowed under Islamic law. The Islamic law that was the codification of the male-dominated and male-sanctioned interpretations of the Qur'an and the Hadith created a patriarchal idol-model legal discourse.

Slavery in Islamic Law

During the time of the Prophet, people referred to him in all matters of public and private life. After his death scholars assumed the task of preserving the Prophet's reports and applying those reports to the new

---

[107] 2:190.
[108] The Qur'an recommends (in 47:4) actually freeing the captives after the war is over. See Asad, *The Message of the Qur'an*, 883–884. "NOW WHEN you meet [in war] those who are bent on denying the truth, smite their necks until you overcome them fully, and then tighten their bonds, but thereafter [set them free,] either by an act of grace or against ransom, so that the burden of war may be lifted: thus [shall it be free]."
[109] Ali. *The Personal Law*, 38.

social issues of a growing Islamic society. Indeed, with the growth of the Islamic world from a small urban mercantile community to a vast empire, legal schools (*madhahib*, pl. of *madhhab*) sprang up, such as the Maliki school of Islamic jurisprudence, to address the crucial issues of the time, including slavery. The Shi'i school is generally similar to the Sunni schools but there are striking differences. The best example is that the Shi'i legal school recommended that the Muslim slave should be set free after seven years of service.[110]

The textual edifice of Islamic law and even the collections of the Hadith and the commentaries of the Qur'an were all constructed many generations after the period of the Prophet and the four rightly guided caliphs (so called because they were all elected by consensus of the *shura* Islamic system). Interpretations on crucial matters in political and gender affairs followed the course of a diverse intellectual enterprise based on cultural and ethnic diversity in the name of Islam. Islamic law was built during the time of the monarchical Islam whose elite was inspired by the Byzantine and the Sassanid Persian empires' model and was therefore imperial in its aspirations.

Malik b. Anas (died 796 in Medina) wrote an influential treatise on Islamic law entitled *al-Muwatta'*, which is the earliest book on jurisprudence, written circa A.D. 767.[111] Malik's legal formulations were based on the Qur'an, the deeds of the Prophet, and the consensus of imminent scholars of the community.[112] He examined and catalogued legal items according to the Sunna and the *ijma'* (the scholars or community leaders' consensus) in Medina in order to establish a basic manual of legal issues. In a period of new social and political developments under the early 'Abbasid rule, Malik wrote a book reacting to the new legal questions in his society meant to provide a practical manual of Islamic law, hence the title *al-Muwatta'* (*The Smoothed Path*). As J. Schacht observed, "The success of the *Muwatta'* is due to the fact that it always takes an average view on disputed points."[113]

[110] Ja'far ibn al-Hasan al-Muhaqqiq al-Hilli, *Droit musulman. Recueil de lois concernant les Musulmans Schyites*, translated by Amédée Querry (Paris: Imprimerie nationale, 1871), tome second, 109. Al-Muhaqqiq al-Hilli was an Iraqi scholar (1205/6–1277) and one of the most influential Shi'i jurists. His best influential work is *Shara'i' al-Islam* which is a legal manual for the Twelver Shi'a. See Ja'far ibn al-Hasan al-Muhaqqiq al-Hilli, *Shara'i' al-Islam fi Masa'il al-Halal wa-al-Haram* (an-Najaf: Matba'at al-Adab, 1969). The French translation was mentioned earlier.

[111] Mansour H. Mansour, *The Maliki School of Law: Spread and Domination in North and West Africa 8th to 14th Centuries C. E.* (London: Austin & Winfield, 1995), 15.

[112] Mansour, *The Maliki School of Law*, 12.

[113] See J. Schacht, "Malik b. Ana" in *The Encyclopedia of Islam*.

The spread of the Maliki system of law played an important role in shaping the concept and practice of slavery. The evolution of the Islamic form of slavery can be assessed in the following three stages: (1) the first stage began with the message of the Qur'an accepting slavery as an existing practice, but only temporarily, with the ultimate goal of abolishing the practice; (2) the second stage can be seen during the formation of the Sunni legal schools in the ninth through tenth centuries as slavery became a well-established institution; (3) in subsequent centuries, some states developed ideologies of enslavement in order to justify the needs of the state to use slaves, particularly for military service. Thus the original intention of the Qur'an, and to some extent the Hadith, to seek the abolition of slavery, was modified by later generations of Islamic legal scholars. In his study of slavery in early Islamic law, Brockoff observed that "these modifications continued for generations, to the point that the slave law found in *al-Mukhtasar al-Kabir* differed substantially from that in the Qur'an in terms of vocabulary, emphasis and scope."[114]

Indeed, by the time of Malik b. Anas, a little more than a century after the death of the Prophet, the institution of slavery seemed well entrenched. We can see from the early texts on Islamic law such as *al-Muwatta'* that the language and terms designating slaves changed manifestly from those in the Qur'an. *'Abd* (pl. *'abid*) and *ama* (pl. *ima'*) – words that the Qur'an avoided using to designate the servile conditions of humans, as these terms are reserved in the Qur'an to mean all of God's creatures and His servants – became the most common words for slaves in Islamic law. The Qur'an did not address the forms of slavery or the status of slaves; however Islamic legal scholars developed a selective vocabulary of slavery derived mainly from various Hadith, excluding the notion of the contract of freedom (*al-mukataba*), which is found in the Qur'an.[115] The key terms representing four specific categories are: emancipation (*al-'itq*), contract of freedom (*al-mukatab*), the slave promised freedom after the owner's death (*al-mudabbar*), and the female slave who bears a child for her master (*umm al-walad*).[116] Hence the early legal texts established the definition and concept of slavery in Islam.

---

[114] Jonathan Eugene Brockopp, *Early Maliki Law: Ibn 'Abd Al-Hakam and His Major Compendium of Jurisprudence. Studies in Islamic Law and Society* (Leiden: Brill, 2000), xviii. *Al-Mukhtasar al-Kabir* is a book on Islamic jurisprudence written by 'Abd Allah b. 'Abd al-Hakam (d. 829), who was a student of Malik b. Anas, the founder of the Maliki school.

[115] Ibid., 166.

[116] Ibid., 148.

With respect to the emancipation of slaves, Malik rejected any conditions made by the master when freeing a slave and commented, "If he owns the slave completely, it is more proper to free him completely and not mingle any slavery with it."[117] Malik b. Anas addressed specific issues and concrete social cases often supported by abstract reports attributed to the Prophet, such as the issue of the client relationship (*wala'*) and the debate of who has the right to the *wala'* of the freed slave. Malik said that it was not permissible for a slave to buy himself from his master on the provision that he could give the *wala'* to whomever he wished, as the *wala'* was for the one who set him free, because the Prophet forbade selling or giving away the *wala'*.[118] This means that once free, the freed slave entered into a client–patron relationship with his master, which entailed a fictive kinship. According to a Hadith attributed to the Prophet, "the *wala'* is a like a link of kinship, it cannot be sold or given away."[119] Hence, the adoption of the identity of the manumitter and taking his family name (*nisba*). Indeed, Malik defines *wala'* from the status of the slave within the family: freed slaves continue to be in a client relationship with their former masters – the freed slave would remain in a relationship of codependency created during the term of bondage.

Malik b. Anas' attention to detailed cases is an articulation of the concerns of the Muslim community regarding slavery during his time. On issues of *wala'* with regard to inheritance, he declared that if a child of a free mother and a slave father dies, the inheritance of that child goes to the mother's agnates; however, if the slave's father has a free grandfather, then the grandfather receives the inheritance.[120] Malik emphasized some interesting rights of the enslaved who entered into a contract of freedom with their owners (*mukatab*), that they would keep their property but their children might not go with them unless stipulated in the contract.[121] Regarding the slave promised freedom after the owner's death (*al-mudabbar*), Malik emphasized that it is not permitted to sell him or her, but the *mudabbar* is also allowed to enter into a contract of freedom.[122] Regarding a female slave (*mudabbara*), the master maintains the

---

[117] Malik b. Anas, *al-Muwatta'* (Beirut: Dar al-Jil and Morocco: Dar al-Afaq al-Jadida, 1993), third edition, 674–675; translated by *The Alim*, al-Muwatta, 38.2.

[118] Ibid., 682; *The Alim*, al-Muwatta, 38.20.

[119] 'Amr b. Bahr al-Jahiz, *Rasa'il al-Jahiz*, edited and annotated by 'Abd as-Salam Muhammad Harun (Cairo: Maktabat al-Khanji, 1964), vol. 2, 21.

[120] Malik, *al-Muwatta'*, 683.

[121] Ibid., 688.

[122] Ibid., 709; *The Alim*, al-Muwatta', 40.6.

right of sexual intercourse with her but he cannot sell her or give her away, and her children are in the same position.[123]

The final issue is the status of the female slave who bears a child for her master (*umm al-walad*). Malik pronounced that "if a female slave gives birth to a child by her master, he must not sell her, give her away, or bequeath her. He enjoys her and when he dies she is free."[124] Clearly, Malik b. Anas proclaims that Islam grants men the right to have sexual relations with female slaves. This license to enjoy female slave sexuality had a social impact on the rise of the *umm al-walad* status, a legal term designating a female slave who bears a child for her master. She is a concubine who acquires legal rights because of her new status and becomes, according to Islamic law, legally free upon the death of her master. Indeed, throughout Islamic history, such status became normal; for instance, even many Moroccan sultans were sons of black concubines. Malik said that if a man had intercourse with a *mukataba* of his and she became pregnant by him, she had an option: If she liked, she could be an *umm walad* and she could confirm her *kitaba* (a contract of emancipation). If she did not conceive, however, she still had her *kitaba*.[125]

The designation and status of *umm al-walad* are unknown in the Qur'an. There is only a Hadith on which Islamic jurists have made most of their juridical decrees: the story in which the Prophet liberated a slave girl named Mariya after she bore him a son. Mariya, a Christian Copt, was a slave whom the Byzantine ruler of Alexandria offered to the Prophet Muhammad. She bore Muhammad a son named Ibrahim, who died when he was only eighteen months old. According to fourteenth-century historian Ibn Kathir, "when Mariya gave birth to a child the Prophet said: 'Her son manumitted her.'"[126] According to this report, if a slave woman has borne her master a child, not only her child but she is set free. This contradicts the speculation of Joseph Schacht, who stated that "the Prophet issued no decree altering her [*umm al-walad*] position or that of her children."[127] Schacht based his conclusion on a report qualified as *salih*, meaning less than good, narrated by one of the least preferred transmitters of the Hadith: Abu Dawud, who reported: "We sold slave-mothers during the time of the Prophet

---

[123] Ibid., 708; *The Alim*, al-Muwatta', 40.5.
[124] Ibid., 677; *The Alim*, al-Muwatta', 38.6.
[125] Al-Bukhari, *Sahih*, Hadith 6749 and 6750, 1226.
[126] Ibn Kathir, *al-Bidaya wa 'n-Nihaya*, vol. 5, 304. It is also reported in Shawkani, *Nayl al-Awtar*, VII, 251.
[127] Schacht, "Umm al-Walad."

Muhammad and of Abu Bakr. When 'Umar was in power, he forbade us and we stopped."[128] A second Hadith on the issue of the paternity of the child of a slave woman is reported in the *Sahih*: "The child is for the owner of the bed."[129]

It is clear from the available reports that the Prophet insisted that the father must recognize his child with a slave but reports on *umm al-walad*'s fate are not clear. The best way to sort through the reports attributed to the Prophet Muhammad is to check them against the Qur'an. But the term *umm al-walad*, as I have argued, is unknown in the Qur'an – the Qur'an considers concubinage a prohibited sexual act. The report on the Prophet's decision that "the child belongs to the [legitimate] bed" formed the basis for legal scholars to enact a regulation to emancipate the child of *umm al-walad*. In Islamic law, however, *umm al-walad* becomes legally free only on the death of her master, contradicting Ibn Kathir's report that she should be freed upon the birth of the child. Accordingly, this legal interpretation grants the master the right to continue his entitlement to her body and her service. Nevertheless, the legal edict on behalf of *umm al-walad* offered the principal vehicle for upward mobility in the system of slavery in Islam. In order to preserve the social order, mainstream jurist Malik b. Anas advised against marriage with slaves if a man could afford to marry a free woman.[130] It is Malik b. Anas who helped identify slavery in Islam as we know it. Thus, the interpretation of Islam according to Muhammad's vision and the Qur'anic ideals was never realized. The influence of deeply entrenched cultural practices that were primarily patriarchical and benefited men, coupled with the interpretive authority of the Qur'an and the Hadith, also the sole purview of men, emphasized the internalization of sociopolitical modes of thinking as well as the assimilation of cultural strata, providing the epistemological foundation of the legal edifice constructed to permit the taking of slaves for concubinage and slavery itself.

Slavery in Maliki School in the Maghreb

It is important to note that Abbasid rulers Abu Ja'far al-Mansur (754–775) and Harun ar-Rashid (763–809) consulted and asked Malik to compile a legal text as it was known in Medina. Qadi 'Iyad b. Musa (died in

---

128 *The Alim*, Abu Dawood, 1811. Translation modified with my emphasis.
129 Al-Bukhari, *Sahih*, Hadith 2533, 459; *The Alim*, al-Bukhari, 3.710.
130 Malik b. Anas, *al-Muwatta'*, 476–477; *The Alim*, al-Muwatta', 28.29.

Marrakesh in 1149), a famous scholar of the Maliki school, reported that it was the Caliph al-Mansur who made the request in order to commit the entire empire to one legal system. Malik did not approve because he thought that the Iraqi people, who had their own version of jurisprudence based on reason by analogy (*al-qiyas*), would not accept his *fiqh* based on the consensus of eminent scholars of Medina. He recommended that people from different parts of the Islamic world follow the interpretations of their own scholars.[131] He did not see his approach as the only valid version of Islamic jurisprudence, hence his work was not meant to be certain or comprehensive. After his death in Medina, however, his teachings spread to many places in the Islamic world. His book became more influential in North Africa than in the rest of the Islamic world. Within half a century after Malik's death, the Maliki doctrine was established in all North Africa, from Egypt to Spain.[132] Ibn Khaldun, a Maliki adherent himself, mentioned two primary reasons for the success of the Malik school in the Maghreb in particular: (1) The principles of the Maliki school were straightforward, reflecting a less hierarchically rigid community, unlike the imperial cities of Damascus of Baghdad; and (2) the people of the Maghreb who traveled to Arabia on pilgrimage or to seek Islamic knowledge sojourned in the town of Medina, the seat of the Maliki school. These Maghrebian scholars looked up to scholars associated with the spiritual city of Medina and studied under the direction of Maliki scholars and consequently adopted the system of Malik b. Anas.[133] Nicole Cottart noted that:

The success of Malikism in North Africa may be explained by reference to the theory of Ibn Khaldun (d. 808/1406) according to whom Bedouin culture accounts for the predominance of this school in the Muslim West. Effectively, Malikism is loyal to the Tradition and hostile to rational explanations; it is perfectly suited to the Berber mentality of the Maghribis who refuse to accept any idea unless it can be traced back to a tradition.[134]

---

[131] Al-Qadi 'Iyad ibn Musa, *Tartib al-Madarik wa-Taqrib al-Masalik li-Ma'rifat A'lam Madhhab Malik* (Beirut: Dar al-Kutub al-'Ilmiya, 1998), vol. 1, 102; Mansour, *The Maliki School of Law*, 17.

[132] Christopher Melchert, *The Formation of the Sunni Schools of Law: 9th-10th centuries C.E.* (Leiden: Brill, 1997), 156–164.

[133] 'Abd ar-Rahman Ibn Khaldun, *Tarikh Ibn Khaldun al-Musamma Kitab al-'Ibar wa-Diwan al-Mubtada' wa 'l-Khabar fi Ayyam al-'Arab wa 'l-'Ajam wa 'l-Barbar wa man 'Asarahum min Dhawi as-Sultan al-Akbar* (Beirut: Dar al-Kutub al-'Ilimiya, 2006), vol. 1, 480–481.

[134] Nicole Cottart, "Malikiyya" in *The Encyclopedia of Islam.*

The work of Malik has inspired countless manuals, judicial commentaries, and glosses from jurists and legists around North Africa, and it continues to shape the ways in which values, social relations, and gender relations are conceptualized and practiced. I will briefly address some of the works of these scholars perpetuating the legacy of the Maliki school and its relevance to slavery issues. Among these manuals, to mention just the most influential, are:

Al-Mudawwana of Sahnun b. Sa'id (d. 855) is considered the first authority in Maliki jurisprudence (*fiqh*) after *al-Muwatta'*. Sahnun was a jurist from Qayrawan (modern-day Tunisia); he played an important role in establishing the Maliki school in the Maghreb.[135] *Ar-Risala* of Ibn Abi Zayd al-Qayrawani – a Maghrebian Muslim judge who died in 996, is one of the most popular books on Islamic jurisprudence in the Maghreb; it is a general outline of Maliki doctrine that served as propaganda for Malikism.[136] *Al-Mukhtasar* of Khalil b. Ishaq – an Egyptian Maliki jurist (d. 1366), is also an authoritative Maliki manual in the Maghreb and West Africa. *Mukhtasar* means abridgement but this book is rather a commentary of *al-Muwatta'* of Malik. Muhammad Bencheneb wrote: "This Mukhtasar, then, so obscure because of its conciseness that it can only be understood by means of a commentary, is the most renowned manual in the countries of the Muslim West, where, to some extent replacing the *Muwatta'* of Malik and the *Mudawwana* of Sahnun."[137] There are other books of legal opinions (*kutub al-fatawi* or *an-nawazil*) by Muslims jurists who interpreted Islamic jurisprudence to adapt it to the local realities; they are printed works available in bookstores but lithographed books and manuscripts are in the archives and at the royal library in Rabat. An important example is the work of renowned Maghrebian Maliki jurist and mufti al-Wansharasi (1431–1508). His major work was a huge collection of North African *fatawi* dating from the ninth to the fifteenth centuries.[138]

The *fatawi* are of crucial importance, not so much for the legal opinion formulated by the religious scholars, but rather for the questions posed by the ordinary people that represent the real practice of slavery in the society. Questions and answers reflect the kind of discourse about slavery

135 Muhammad Talbi, "Sahnun" in *The Encyclopedia of Islam*.
136 Ibn Abi Zayd al-Qayrawani, *La Risâla, ou Epître sur les éléments du dogme et de la loi de l'Islâm selon le rite mâlikite*, Texte arabe et trad. française par Léon Bercher, Bibliothèque arabe-française (Alger: J. Carbonel, 1960). See chapter 35.
137 Muhammad Bencheneb, "Khalil b. Ishak" in *The Encyclopedia of Islam*.
138 Ahmad al-Wansharisi, *al-Mi'yar al-Mu'rib wa 'l-Jami' al-Mughrib 'an Fatawi 'Ulama' Ifriqiya wa 'l-Andalus wa 'l-Maghrib* (Beirut: Dar al-Gharb al-Islami, 1981).

and the kind of slave practice of the period. In addition to these sources are official letters of the rulers concerning the acquisition of black people to the learned men and the registers of slaves. These state archives are kept at the royal library and the archives of the Bibliothèque Générale in Rabat. As of yet little exploited, they offer new possibilities in exploring Moroccan society regarding the issues of slavery.

It is clear from these legal documents that all free and freed Muslims must not be enslaved under any circumstances. According to a Hadith attributed to the Prophet Muhammad, related by Abu Dawuud, any attempt to enslave a freed person is considered a high offense to the point that God would not accept the prayers of anyone who commits such an act.[139] Thus, the condition of an enslaved person could only emerge from two main sources: captivity in war or being born into slavery to slave parents. Children born to free women are born free, even in the case when the father is a slave; however the union of a free woman with her slave is illegal. Islamic legal discourse defines the condition of slavery to denote a double nature: a slave is treated as an object and as a human at the same time. As an object a slave is subject to business regulations prescribed by the Islamic law that he or she can be bought, sold, traded, donated, bequeathed, or inherited, thus treated as a commodity such as beasts of burden. Like cattle, a child born to a slave belongs to the master and it is the domain of the *muhtasib* (controller of the market to maintain an orderly social life) who oversees the treatment of slaves. That is why slavery issues are usually classified in or next to the section dealing with sales activities in books on Islamic law. The implications of this condition have far-reaching effects on the slave as a person. Hence, the slave is uprooted from a familiar set of beliefs (a familiar language, relations, customs, places, and diet) to a different place. The initial abduction is traumatizing and the transition into bondage is shocking. Slavery is almost a social death where most civil rights of the enslaved people are extinguished, giving their owners total control over their lives.[140] Women in particular are subject to rape as is the case of taking a female slave as a concubine. As it is illegal to be involved in any sexual act out of wedlock under severe penal code, from many lashes to stoning to death, forced sexuality with an enslaved female was a device to serve men's sexual desire and fantasy.

---

[139] *The Alim*, Abu Dawood, 235.
[140] See Orlando Patterson, *Slavery and Social Death: a Comparative Study* (Cambridge: Harvard University Press, 1982).

The slave is also treated as a person with rights and duties, which are by no means equal to those of a free person. These rights and duties are: The opportunity of a formal contract with the master to gain freedom, and the right to decent living arrangements such as lodging, nourishment, and clothing. Any cruel treatment by the master may lead to selling or freeing the slave. Slaves had the right to marry but with their masters' approval, however, the slave cannot have a concubine because he cannot own a slave. A female slave who bears her a master a child gains some legal rights of *umm al-walad*; hence canceling her chattel status during the life of her master and claiming her freedom at his death; and the child, male or female, will be free. In cases of apostasy and theft, the penalty incurred by the slave resembles that imposed upon a free person, but the penalty for adultery is only half of the punishment prescribed to the free person. The slave has also certain rights of ownership. Besides these rights, there are disqualifications and exonerations that mark his or her servile status. A slave did not have legal powers. He or she could not, for instance, give testimony before a court; and masters were responsible if any fines incurred. The slave may not exercise public or private offices such as the office of a Muslim judge. The slave is not obliged to perform religious duties such as the Friday prayer and alms giving.[141]

Slavery can be translated in practice as an exploitative act utilizing to the greatest possible advantage the enslaved person's productivity, and in the case of a female slave, her sexuality and reproductive capacity. In this context my definition of slavery is more in line with Claude Meillassoux or Paul Lovejoy's than the definition formulated by Suzanne Miers and Igor Kopytoff, who mainly argued that what Western scholars referred to as African slavery was not particularly oppressive.[142] In sum, in Islamic legal terms, slavery in the words of Ehud Toledano, an expert of slavery in the Ottoman Empire: "grants one person ownership over another person, which means that the owner has rights to the slave's labor, property, and sexuality, and that the slave's freedoms were strictly limited."[143]

---

[141] On rights, duties, disqualifications, or exonerations see Brunschvig, "'Abd."

[142] Regarding the definition of slavery, see Suzanne Miers and Igor Kopytoff, editors, *Slavery in Africa, Historical and Anthropological Perspectives* (Madison, WI: The University of Wisconsin Press, 1977); Paul Lovejoy, *Transformations in Slavery: a History of Slavery in Africa* (Cambridge: Cambridge University Press, second edition, 2000), and Claude Meillassoux, *Anthropologie de l'esclavage: le ventre de fer et d'argent* (Paris: Presses universitaires de France, 1986).

[143] Ehud Toledano, *Slavery and Abolition in the Ottoman Middle East* (Seattle: University of Washington Press, 1998), 3.

In the end, slavery reflects a mental construction or rather a fantasy implying a permanent rapport depending on continuous service and fidelity provided by a human being forced into servitude for the master's desire and profit; this rapport is sanctioned by legal codes to enforce the obligations upon the slave and to ensure the privilege of the master. Thus, the use of the term "slave" that may connote a natural submissiveness or a passive dependency is inaccurate. It is more appropriate to use the term "enslaved" because it conveys that a person who was a slave became one because someone else in a more advantageous position enforced him or her into the condition of slavery.

A Comparative Mediterranean Practice of Slavery

In legal discourse, the institution of slavery in Morocco seems to be not all that different from premodern and early modern notions of slavery held in the Mediterranean basin in general. The three major religions of the Mediterranean all adhered to scriptures that could be interpreted to condone slavery; several legal aspects of the practice of slavery in the Mediterranean point to commonalties. For example, at least in the thirteenth century, Spanish slavery was nondiscriminating – slaves were described as "white, black or olive," although "most slaves in Mediterranean Europe were white."[144] Hence the usage of the term "Slav" as equivalent of slave.

In fact, slavery as depicted in the *Siete Partidas* (*The Seven Divisions*) is similar indeed to Islamic law regarding slaves and perhaps gestures to a shared Mediterranean thinking about slaves, relative to religion and relative to law. The *Siete Partidas* was the Spanish manifestation of the thirteenth-century renaissance of Roman law that swept across Europe, instituted by Alfonso X in order to replace the prevailing feudal custom law of Castile and that became the legal foundation throughout the ensuing Hispanic empire from Asia to Africa to the New World. Similar to Islam's own position vis-à-vis slaves in personal status law, in the *Siete Partidas* "slaves were not simply chattel, as in ancient Rome."[145] In Roman law, the slave is specifically an object, a possession, and not a person.[146]

---

[144] *Las Siete Partidas*, trans. Samuel Parsons Scott, ed. Robert I. Burns (Philadelphia: University of Pennsylvania Press, 2001), vol. 4, xxiii.

[145] Ibid., xxiv.

[146] Raymond Monier, *Manuel élémentaire de droit romain* (Paris: Les Éditions Domat-Montchrestien, 1938), tome I, 276–277.

Furthermore, reflecting the somewhat resigned attitude toward slavery often described as characteristic of the Islamic world, the *Siete Partidas* declared that: "Servitude is the vilest and most contemptible thing that can exist among men."[147] And "slavery is the vilest thing in this world except sin."[148] Such a statement underscores the degree to which the status of slavery was expressed as much in legal terms of status and property law as in religious terms. Additional examination of the *Siete Partidas* demonstrates further similarities between Christian and Islamic positions on slavery. The *Siete Partidas* proclaims:

> We also decree that slavery is something that men naturally abhor, and that not only does a slave live in servitude, but also anyone who has not free power to leave the place where he resides. Learned men have also declared that a party whose irons have been removed is not free, or liberated from restraint, if he is still held by the hand, or guarded in a courteous manner.[149]

The *Siete Partidas* defined three types of slaves, the first of which was "those taken captive in war who are enemies of the faith."[150] These "enemies of the faith" could emancipate themselves from their bondage through "legal baptism." This was particularly applicable to Muslims, who if enslaved could also be freed by informing on the activities of other Muslims. Masters could also liberate their slaves by drafting contracts stating such in front of five witnesses or stating that their slaves should be freed upon their deaths (i.e., the masters' deaths). An additional method of emancipation freed a slave if a judge deemed that he or she had been maltreated by his or her master. In fact, slaves in Castile "had human rights, but no civil rights."[151] Once free, the freed slave entered into a client–patron relationship with the master, which entailed "deference, public marks of honor, and other obligations."[152]

The slave codes in the *Siete Partidas*, like the Islamic slave law, were the product of a society where slavery was mainly domestic in nature. The Code Noir provides provisions similar to the *Siete Partidas* and that bear resemblance to some slave codes in the Islamic law. The Code Noir (or the Black Code), was instituted in France in 1685 by King Louis XIV. It defined the conditions of slavery in France's American possessions. Interesting, the expansion and racialization of black slavery in Morocco

---

[147] *Las Siete Partidas,* 901.
[148] Ibid., 983.
[149] Ibid., vol. 5, 1478.
[150] Ibid., vol. 4, 977.
[151] Ibid., xxiv.
[152] Ibid.

and in the adjacent Atlantic world was taking place at the same time. Mawlay Isma'il's pursuit to legalize the enslavement of black Moroccans at the same time as European leaders adopted legal measures to justify black enslavement represents an amazing independent development, stemming, however, from common roots in a Mediterranean concept of slavery and Abrahamic traditions. These similarities are the recognition of some rights for the enslaved, especially the possibility for enslaved people to regain their freedom and, more important, the provision that insisted that children follow the status of their mothers regardless of the fathers' status, hence allowing some upward mobility.[153] But in the colonies and plantations these "liberal" provisions were restricted or revoked. For instance, a 1724 code in Louisiana forbade marriage between whites and blacks. These later revisions were similar to British colonial and later U.S. slave law.[154] Here lay the differences between the Western antebellum South and the Islamic concepts of slavery. As historian Edmund Morgan stated, the laws in Virginia went further to exonerate the master who maltreated his slaves to the point of death.[155]

During the expansion of Islam, slaves were collected from among the conquered. In addition to capturing slaves to the south, west, and east of the Arabian Peninsula following the movements of Muslim armies, slaves were taken in raids on the northern shores of the Mediterranean. In fact, until the nineteenth century, slaves of various origins were brought into North Africa and the Middle East. Southeastern Europe and the northern shores of the Black Sea also proved bountiful sources for slaves. The Slavs (in Arabic, *as-saqaliba*) were one particularly exploited group. A great number of slaves were also imported from central Asia.[156] But this practice went in both directions. These sources became more and more unreliable toward the end of the Middle Ages in Europe. Slave raiding in

[153] William Renwick Riddell, "Le Code Noir," *The Journal of Negro History* 10, no. 3 (July 1925): 323. There are other similarities with the French legal codes enclosed in the Code Noir. For instance slaves can marry but with the master's consent; slaves must be supported, maintained, and treated humanely and any master who fails to do so would be punished. Masters are held responsible for any acts performed by their slaves. Slaves are not allowed to hold any private or public offices. Slaves may also be prosecuted criminally in courts like free people, and so forth. See the entire Code Noir document in Sue Peabody and Keila Grinberg, *Slavery, Freedom and the Law in the Atlantic World: A Brief History with Documents* (Basingstoke: Palgrave Macmillan, 2007), 31–36.

[154] William Cohen, *The French Encounter with Africans: White Response to Blacks, 1530–1880* (Bloomington: Indiana University Press, 2003), 50.

[155] Edmund Morgan, "Slavery and freedom: The American Paradox," *The Journal of American History* 59 (1972), (1) (June): 26.

[156] Lewis, *Race and Slavery*, 11.

western sub-Saharan Africa increased and became even more common when the slave supply of purchases and captives of war from areas of Europe such as the Iberian Peninsula, the Caucasus, and the Black Sea began to dwindle once the wars fought by Islamic sultanates died down. Islamic countries turned south to sub-Saharan Africa. North African Muslims did enslave sub-Saharan and East Africans. These were among the first sources and the last ones.

2

The Interplay between Slavery and
Race and Color Prejudice

The eternal silence of these infinite spaces frightens me.[1]

Our job is not to give pleasure or to make wrong, it is to put the pen into
the wound.[2]

In this chapter, I establish four crucial points: I argue that European travel
narratives generally represented Morocco as free of racial or color prejudice when, in fact, blacks were stigmatized and marginalized. Second, I
argue that the Hamitic myth contributed to the stigmatization or "othering" of blacks, and that even for those who rejected the myth, the connection between blacks and unbelief furthered the "othering." Third, I
explain the interplay of color and consanguinity and social function that
complicated the racial positioning of black Moroccans. And fourth, I
include a comparative discourse on race and slavery, which is necessary
and instructive in this analysis.

I begin by identifying the problem of why many scholars who focus on
the connection between race and slavery in Islam miss the mark in their
analyses. Then I turn to the question of where we might begin to see a
distinction between cultural feelings of dislike and xenophobia that do
not necessarily involve race and the evolution of ideologies and practices
that involve unmistakable racism. Many scholars who have examined
the issues related to race and racism in Morocco conclude that Islam's
color-blindness was a substantial feature in the practice of slavery. This
view asserts that such a nonracist attitude toward the practice of slavery

---

[1] Blaise Pascal, *Pensées, fragments et lettres de Blaise Pascal* (Paris: Andrieux, 1844), 224.
[2] Albert Londres, *Terre d'ébène* (Paris: Albin Michel, 1929), 6.

reduced the potential for economic and political subjugation as well as social marginalization based on skin color. In effect, this purported non-racist attitude in Islamic societies like Morocco supposedly forestalled the emergence of a more humiliating and oppressive slavery, such as the racial slavery of North America. I argue, however, that such an understanding of the politics and the practice of slavery in Morocco ignores important historical evidence and derives from gross generalizations deduced from Islamic legal treatises regarding the status and practice of slavery or from European travel accounts. Albeit of great utility, these accounts remain largely limited to towns where domestic slavery seemed a benign practice in comparison to the inhumane nature of slavery on Western plantations. In reality, slavery in Morocco was not a monolithic institution. Enslaved people participated in diverse economies and labor activities such as small-scale farming, domestic tasks, and artisanal and mercantile activities. Indeed, European travelers' accounts of social life and relations in Morocco in the late nineteenth century and early twentieth century testify to the diversity of often important roles that slaves occupied in Moroccan society as well as the absence of substantial racial prejudice as contrasted with the racist attitudes in European and American societies.[3] Based on sources such as these, one might conclude, as did French historian Evariste Lévi-Provençal (1894–1956), a scholar of Islamic studies, that, in the twentieth century, "there was no lack of mulattoes in the Muslim bourgeoisie and aristocracy, among which we must acknowledge that color prejudice has never existed, no more in the Middle Ages than today."[4] To

---

[3] For example, in the 1850s, James Richardson talked about the lack of color prejudice: "His Moorish Majesty [Mawlay 'Abd ar-Rahman], who is advanced in life, is a man of middle stature. He has dark and expressive eyes, and, as already observed, is a mulatto of a fifth caste. Colour excites no prejudices either in the sovereign or in the subject." James Richardson, *Travels in Morocco* (London: Charles J. Skeet, Publisher, 1860), vol. 2, 30. Early-twentieth-century British historian Arnold Toynbee argued that properly Islamic lands were free of racial discrimination: "White Muslims were in contact with the Negroes of Africa and with the dark skinned-peoples of India from the beginning and have increased that contact steadily, until nowadays Whites and Blacks are intermingled, under the aegis of Islam, through the length and the breadth of the Indian and the African continent. Under this searching test, the White Muslims have demonstrated their freedom from race-feelings by the most convincing of all proofs: they have given their daughters to Black Muslims in marriage." Arnold Joseph Toynbee, *A Study of History* (Oxford: Oxford University Press, 1934), vol. 1, 226. Toynbee probably relied on Islamic legal treatises and European travelers' accounts in his work. Islamic legal texts provide an abundant source of prescriptive material about slavery, and European travel literature provides a rich source of descriptive material on race and slavery in Morocco.

[4] Evarsite Lévi-Provençal, *Histoire de l'Espagne musulmane* (Paris: Maisonneuve et Larose, 1999), vol. 3, 178.

these observers, the main evidence that Morocco was not a racist society was the apparent lack of prohibitions against interracial relations, a practice that was a source of fear and anxiety in Western Europe and America. The emphasis on benign attitudes distorts the social realities of slavery and undermines its cruel effects on the enslaved person. Blacks generally occupied a marginal position in Moroccan society: they were historically racially stigmatized and occupationally segregated. I argue that the example of Mawlay Isma'il's conscription of the Haratin in the beginning of the eighteenth century clearly indicates color or racial consciousness. The illegal enslavement of the Haratin reveals the disjuncture between Islamic ideals and historical realities and between ideology and practice regarding race in Moroccan slavery. Legal texts like *Daftar Mamalik as-Sultan Mawlay Isma'il* (the register of the slaves belonging to Mawlay Isma'il) provide coherent and critical accounts of the nature of slavery in Morocco under Mawlay Isma'il.[5] It is clear from this legal register, as we shall see in Chapter 4, that slavery was associated with blackness.

The Othering of Blacks in Arabic and Islamic Traditions

I emphasize that neither the Qur'an nor the Hadith make any evaluative racial distinctions among humankind or recommend waging war to produce captives for enslavement. However, throughout the history of Islam, color prejudice was consistently embedded in the Hamitic myth and the manner that this myth was used to justify and extend Arab and Berber cultural prejudices about race that preexisted Islam. The othering of blacks goes back to the biblical Ham, son of Noah, and the Hamitic curse and discourse. Ham and the Hamitic curse do not exist in the Qur'an. The Qur'an emphasizes the fellowship of humankind:

O men! Behold, We have created you all out of a male and a female, and have made you into nations and tribes, so that you might come to know one another. Verily, the noblest of you in the sight of God is the one who is most righteous. Behold, God is all-knowing, all-aware.[6]

Racial or tribal prejudice is categorically condemned in the Qur'an. The Prophet Muhammad said, "God has removed from you the arrogance of pagan ignorance (*jahiliyya*) with its boast of ancestral glories. Man

---

[5] *Daftar Mamalik as-Sultan Mawlay Isma'il* (Rabat: Bibliothèque Générale, ms. k 394). This is a legal document addressing the acquisition of the slaves from various regions in Morocco.

[6] 49:13. Translation of Asad, *The Message of the Qur'an*, 904.

is but a God-conscious believer or an unfortunate sinner. All people are children of Adam, and Adam was created out of dust."[7] Muhammad also said: "You should listen to and obey your ruler even if he was an Abyssinian (black) slave whose head looks like a raisin."[8] Racial prejudice as it existed at the time of the Prophet was clearly culturally constructed, and such prejudice was unmistakably rejected by Muhammad. Another example of Muhammad's rejection of racial prejudice can be seen in a report given by Egyptian scholar as-Suyuti (1445–1505) that involves an incident between Bilal and Abu Dharr (both early converts to Islam at the time of the Prophet). Abu Dharr insulted Bilal by calling him: "You, son of a black woman!" When the Prophet heard of the affair, he reproached Abu Dharr severely, making a solemn declaration that one's worth has nothing to do with one's lineage and all to do with one's righteousness.[9] This incident reflects the preexisting negative perception of color among many Arabs in the new social order that Muhammad introduced and, important, the recognition of and inclusion of the "other" in the nascent era of Islam in Arabia. Thus, Muhammad's Islam was egalitarian not only among tribal Arabs but among all peoples, even those Arabs perceived as different and of lower status because of their color such as the Abyssinians. It is clear from the ancient Arab perception that Abyssinians were of low status because of their color. Hence, Muhammad insisted on human equality by declaring that there was no difference between an Arab and non-Arab,[10] nor between a white person and a black person except in righteousness, and that all humankind are children of Adam and that Adam came from dust.[11]

The evolution of the Islamic state under a profoundly Arabo-centric theocracy took a different path from Muhammad's ideals. After the death of Muhammad, the ideal of an egalitarian Islamic *umma* was more

---

[7] *The Alim*, Abu Dawood, 2425. Translation of Asad, *The Message of the Qur'an*, 904, footnote 16.

[8] This Hadith is mentioned twice in al-Bukhari, *Sahih*, Hadith 693, 137 and Hadith 7142, 1293–1294. *The Alim*, al-Bukhari, vol. 1, 662 and vol. 9, 256.

[9] 'Abd ar-Rahman Jalal ad-Din as-Suyuti, *Raf' Sha'n al-Hubshan*, annotated by Muhammad 'Abd al-Wahhab Fadl. [Cairo]: Muhammad 'Abd al-Wahhab Fadl, 1991, 276. A similar Hadith that does not include the name Bilal is found in al-Bukhari, *Sahih*, Hadith 30, 21.

[10] Many Arabic sources (and some European) refer to Arabs as white. It is important to note that even the lightest-complexioned Arabs are only light in comparison with darker people, and that many Europeans would not define them as white in European contexts.

[11] Muhammad Dawuud, *Tarikh Titwan* (Tetouan: al-Matba'a al-Mahdiya, 1963), vol. 2, 42. See also Afzalur Rahman, *Muhammad, Encyclopaedia of Seerah* (London: Muslim Schools Trust, 1992), vol. 8, 171.

illusory than real. Racial difference, discrimination, and violence followed as a consequence of the deeply entrenched cultural mores evident in the time of the Prophet and that resurfaced without much hindrance after his death. Of crucial import is the adoption of the Hamitic myth and its subsequent application with respect to how the racial constituency of societies and states were regarded. As a consequence of Arab domination and the spread of Islam, assimilation of the cultural and the scriptural traditions of Christian and Jewish populations occurred. Some confusion exists about not only whether the Hamitic curse originates in Arab culture or from the Judaic literature, but also whether the curse involves race, that is, whether the punishment conveyed by the curse is blackness. A few historians, such as Bernard Lewis, seem to attribute the racial aspect of the Hamitic curse to Arab culture and find no relation between the curse's punishment and race in the Talmud. According to Lewis, "There is, however, nothing in the text [Talmud] to indicate that the hereditary curse had been extended from servitude to blackness or that that it was transferred from Canaan, who was white, to Kush who was black. Neither Kush nor racial blackness is mentioned, nor is there anything to show that blackness as such was seen as a punishment."[12] In what follows, Lewis is clearly wrong on both counts.[13] Reference to the Hamitic curse can be found in early Judaic literature (predating Islam) and clearly brings race, that is, blackness, to the forefront as the punishment levied on Ham's descendants. English scholar Robert Graves (1895–1985) and Hungarian-Jewish historian Raphael Patai (1910–1996) reported from the Babylonian Talmud, compiled in Babylonia around A.D. 500, written partly in Hebrew but mostly in Aramaic, that Noah said:

---

[12] Lewis, *Race and Slavery*, 123, footnote 9. Lewis says earlier in his study that: "The slaves of the Arabs were not Canaanites but Blacks – so the curse was transferred to them, and blackness added to servitude as part of the hereditary burden" (55).

[13] Contemporary scholars, in addition to Lewis, such as Benjamin Braude and David H. Aaron unconvincingly suggest that there were no racist attitudes, color-based society, or racial hierarchy in the ancient Near East. See Braude Benjamin, "Cham et Noé. Race et esclavage entre judaïsme, christianisme et Islam," *Annales. Histoire, Sciences Sociales*, 57e année, N. 1, 2002, 93–125 and David H. Aaron, "Early Rabbinic Exegesis on Noah's Son Ham and the So-Called 'Hamitic Myth,'" *Journal of the American Academy of Religion* 63 (4) (Winter): 1995, 721–759. Benjamin Braude, in particular, wrote in an absurd abstract statement: "racism appears more prominently and early in Islam than in the other two traditions [Judaism and Christianity]." He laid the blame squarely and hastily on Muslim Persian historian at-Tabari (839–923), whom he labeled as racist. Benjamin Braude, "Ham and Noah: Sexuality, Servitudinism, and Ethnicity," Proceedings of the Fifth Annual Gilder Lehrman Center International Conference at Yale (New Haven: Yale University, November 7–8, 2003), 50 and 52.

"Now I cannot beget the fourth son whose children I would have ordered to serve you and your brothers! Therefore it must be Canaan, your first born, whom they enslave. And since you have disabled me from doing ugly things in blackness of night, Canaan's children shall be born ugly and black! Moreover, because you twisted your head around to see my nakedness, your grandchildren's hair shall be twisted into kinks, and their eyes red; again because your lips jested at my misfortune, theirs shall swell; and because you neglected my nakedness, they shall go naked, and their male members shall be shamefully elongated!" Men of this race are called Negroes, their forefather Canaan commanded them to love theft and fornication, to be banded together in hatred of their master and never to tell the truth.[14]

Arab culture would adopt the racial aspect of the Hamitic curse in a manner that associated race with slavery. In this chapter, I hope to show how the Hamitic curse was interwoven with social status and preexisting racial prejudices to justify racial discrimination at odds with the tenets of Islam.

Etymologically speaking, *ham* may designate dark color; it actually means "hot" in Hebrew and Arabic (both Semitic languages). One of its Arabic derivations is *yahmum*, meaning "very black," a term used mainly in connection with smoke.[15] I find it dubious that David Goldenberg, a scholar of Jewish history, denies the possible use of *ham* to mean black in Hebrew. He states: "We must also reject a derivation from the Hebrew root *hwm* 'to be black' or 'dark.'"[16] Reverend James Sloan (1817–1894) wrote a long chapter documenting the origin of color as associated with slavery and he demonstrated that the word *ham*, in the Coptic and Hebrew languages, means blackness and heat.[17] In the Babylonian Talmud, a collection of rabbinic writings that dates back to the sixth century, racial distinctions are clearly evident with respect to the sons of Noah. According to this Talmudic tradition, "the descendants of Ham are cursed by being black, and [it] depicts Ham

---

[14] Robert Graves and Raphael Patai, *Hebrew Myths; the Book of Genesis* (Garden City, NY: Doubleday, 1964), 121.

[15] Az-Zabidi, *Taj al-'Arus*, vol. 32, 10–11.

[16] David Goldenberg, *The Curse of Ham: Race and Slavery in Early Judaism, Christianity, and Islam* (Princeton: Princeton University Press, 2003), 147. According to my colleague Joel Gereboff, an expert in early rabbinic Judaism, "the word cham (ham in Hebrew) does appear in the Bible and means dark brown/black. So perhaps in time it became associated with the blacks as the cursed people." E-mail exchange on Monday, December 19, 2011.

[17] James A Sloan, *The Great Question Answered; Or, Is Slavery a Sin in Itself (Per Se?) Answered According to the Teaching of the Scriptures* (Memphis: Printed by Hutton, Gallaway & Co, 1857), chapter 4, 56–86.

as a sinful man and his progeny as degenerates."[18] The curse itself is mentioned in the Bible:

[Noah] drank of the wine, and became drunk, and lay uncovered in his tent. And Ham, the father of Canaan, saw the nakedness of his father, and told his two brothers outside. Then Shem and Japheth took a garment, laid it upon both their shoulders, and walked backward and covered the nakedness of their father; their faces were turned away, and they did not see their father's nakedness. When Noah awoke from his wine and knew what his youngest son had done to him, he said, "Cursed be Canaan; a slave of slaves shall he be to his brothers." He also said, "Blessed by the LORD my God be Shem; and let Canaan be his slave. God enlarge Japheth, and let him dwell in the tents of Shem; and let Canaan be his slave."[19]

This biblical passage does not make any reference to the race of the children of Ham but clearly and oddly condemns Canaan for the offense of his father, Ham. Historians such as William McKee Evans and Edith Sanders who have studied and commented on this issue explain that this passage is an example of the use of religion to sanction the subjugation of one people by another, in this case the Canaanites subjugated by the Israelites.[20] The *Jewish Encyclopedia* gives many variations of the Hamitic myth, among which, "Ham is represented by the Talmudists as one of the three who had intercourse with their wives in the Ark, being punished therefore in that his descendants, the Ethiopians, are black."[21] Yaakov ben Yitzchak Ashkenazi (1550–1628), an expert in the rabbinic literature, wrote: "Noah said to Ham, 'Thy children shall be dark and black.' These are the Ethiopians and the Negroes, which have descended from Ham, on account of the curse."[22] David Goldenberg contradicts himself when he argues "that in rabbinic circles, whether in the Land of Israel or in Babylonia, a dark complexion was not preferred."[23] This attitude is

---

[18] See Edith Sanders, "The Hamitic Hypothesis: Its Origin in Time" in *Problems in African History*, ed. by Robert O. Collins (Princeton: Markus Wiener Publishing, 1994), 9.

[19] Bible, Revised Standard Version, Genesis 9: 21–29.

[20] William McKee Evans, "From the Land of Canaan to the Land of Guinea: The Strange Odyssey of the 'Sons of Ham,'" *The American Historical Review* vol. 85, no. 1 (February 1980): 15–43; Edith Sanders, "The Hamitic Hypothesis."

[21] *The Jewish Encyclopedia; a Descriptive Record of the History, Religion, Literature, and Customs of the Jewish People from the Earliest Times* (New York: Ktav Pub. House, 1964), vol. 6, 186.

[22] Yaakov ben Yitzchak Ashkenazi, *Tzeénah Ureénah: "Go Ye and See": A Rabbinical Commentary on Genesis*, translated by Paul Isaac Hershon (London: Hodder and Stoughton, 1885), 55.

[23] Goldenberg, *The Curse of Ham*, 97. This book traces the origins and the evolution of the Hamitic myth in the construction of a servile race within the Judeo-Christian traditions.

consistent with the Arabs' stereotypes of blacks. Edward William Lane (d. 1876), a British specialist in Arabic language and culture, reported: "[For the Arabs] as-Sudan is said to denote [the negroes;][24] that particular people, or race, who are the most stinking of mankind in the armpits and sweat, and the more so those who are eunuchs."[25]

Evidence of the acceptance of the Hamitic story can be found in the work of early Muslim scholars and from the fact that in Arabia the majority of slaves were black Ethiopians whose subjugation was justified because of their blackness and the negative cultural perceptions that blackness held for Arabs.[26] Interesting, one of the early Arabic writers who addressed the issue of race was a scholar versed in Judeo-Christian traditions, Abu 'Abd Allah Wahb b. Munabbih (d. 728 or 732) of Persian origin from Yemen. Many biblical traditions can be traced back to his writing and influence.[27] Ibn an-Nadim (d. 990), author of a well-known book, *The Fihrist* (index of Arabic books), noted that Wahb b. Munabbih was a person of the Book who converted to Islam.[28] Ibn Qutayba (d. 889) of Baghdad wrote that Wahb b. Munabbih believed "that Ham b. Nuh[29] was a white man having a beautiful face and form. But Allah (to Him belongs glory and power) changed his colour and the colour of his descendants because of his father's curse. Ham went off, followed by his children [...]. They are the Sudan."[30]

Other Muslim scholars followed suit. I mention here only the most well known and recurrent in chronological order. Al-Ya'qubi (d. 897 in Egypt) assumed in his chronicle the same Hamitic theory:

Nuh awoke from his sleep and learnt what had happened he cursed Kan'an b. Ham but he did not curse Ham. Of his posterity are the Qibt, the Habasha, and the Hind. Kan'an was the first of the sons of Nuh to revert to the ways of the sons of Qabil (Cain) and indulged in distractions and singing and made flutes,

---

[24] Not my addition.

[25] Lane, *An Arabic-English Lexicon*, vol. 4, 1463.

[26] I am not arguing that only blacks were slaves, but that a majority of slaves were black and their blackness was commonly attributed to their being descendents of Ham.

[27] Raif Georges Khoury, "Wahb b. Munabbih" in *The Encyclopedia of Islam*; Carl Brockelmann, *Geschichte Der Arabischen Litteratur*, second edition (Leiden: E.J. Brill, 1943), vol. 1, 64 and Suppl., I, 101; and Ibn al-Nadim, *The Fihrist of Al-Nadim; a Tenth-Century Survey of Muslim Culture*, edited and translated by Bayard Dodge (New York: Columbia University Press, 1970), vol. 1, 42 and 203; vol. 2, 1121.

[28] Ibid., vol. 1, 42.

[29] Or Noah.

[30] Abu Muhammad 'Abd Allah Ibn Qutayba al-Dinawari in J. F. P. Hopkins and Nehemia Levtzion (eds.), *Corpus of Early Arabic Sources for West African History* (Cambridge, England: Cambridge University Press, 1981), 15.

drums, guitars and cymbals and obeyed Satan in vain amusements. Nuh divided the earth between his sons, assigning to Sam the middle of the earth … and to Ham the land of the west and the coasts (*sawahil*) […]. After they had crossed the Nile of Egypt the descendants of Kush son of Ham, namely the Habasha and the Sudan, split in two groups. One of these groups proceeded to the south, between the east and the west. These were the Nuba, Buja, Habasha and Zanj. The other group went to the west. These were the Zaghawa, HBSH, Qaqu, Marawiyyun, Maranda, Kawkaw and Ghana.[31]

At-Tabari (d. 923), one of the most influential and prolific Muslim scholars of his time, gave a clear racial classification of nations taken from the same source as the work of Ibn Qutayba, both adapted from the writing of Wahb b. Munabbih, with additional details based on the reports of the ancient Hebrews who gave names to their different neighbors and other peoples they encountered or heard of. The list of these names is found in the first book of the Bible (Genesis, chapter 10). The description reflects the geopolitics of the time with Canaan's inclusion under the sons of Ham:

Ham begat all those who are black and curly-haired, while Japheth begat all those who are full-faced with small eyes, and Shem begat everyone who is handsome of face with beautiful hair. Noah prayed that the hair of Ham's descendants would not grow beyond their ears, and wherever his descendants met the children of Shem, the latter would enslave them.[32]

At-Tabari adopted the chauvinistic Arabo-Persian-centered culture of his time. Ironically for a devout Muslim scholar, at-Tabari used the Torah and oral cultural traditions rather than the Qur'an as the source for racial classification. For at-Tabari, the civilized race consisted of the children of Shem: "Shem begat the Arabs, Persians, and Byzantines, in all of whom there is good."[33] The less civilized peoples form the other two races, namely the children of Japheth and the children of Ham: "Japheth begat the Turks, Slavs, Gog, and Magog, in none of whom there is good. Ham begat the Copts, Sudanese, and Berbers."[34]

'Ali b. al-Husayn al-Mas'udi (d. 956) followed suit, as found in *Akhbar az-Zaman*: "The traditionists say that Nuh, peace upon him, cursed

[31] Ahmad b. Abi Ya'qub b. Ja'far b. Wahb b. Wadih known as al-Ya'qubi in Hopkins and Levtzion, *Corpus*, 20–21.
[32] Al-Tabari, *The History of al-Tabari: Prophets and Patriarchs*, translated and annotated by William M. Brinner (Albany: State University of New York Press, 1986), vol. 2, 21. The Arabic text: Muhammad at-Tabari, *Tarikh at-Tabari*, vol. 1, 69.
[33] Ibid.
[34] Ibid.

Ham, praying that his face should become ugly and black and that his descendants should become slaves to the progeny of Sam [...]. They are the various peoples of the Sudan."[35] Muhammad an-Nusaybi, known as Ibn Hawqal (d. after 988), in his geographical work, *Surat al-Ard* (*The Picture of the Earth*), assumed the Hamitic theory and added that different shades of color resulted from the intermixing between light-skinned Berbers and blacks in North Africa. He wrote:

As for the Banu Tanamak [Berbers], the kings of Tadmakka, and the tribes related to them, it is said that they were originally Sudan whose skin and complexion became white because they live close to the North and far from the land of Kawkaw, and that they descend on their mother's side from the progeny of Ham [...]. Those who attach the Banu Tanamak to the descendants of Ham base themselves on the theory of al-Kindi that the whites, when they breed for seven generations in the land of the Sudan, take on their external appearance and black colour. Also, the Sudan, when they procreate in the country of the whites for seven generations, assume their appearance, their white colour, and the purity of their complexion.[36]

By this time, al-Mukhtar Ibn Butlan (d. 1066), an Arab Christian physician of Baghdad, published an eleventh-century manual on how to buy slaves and how to detect any physical flaws. He said, for instance, that Nubians make good slaves on account of their natural dispositions to slavery. But he attributed their character to climate rather than the curse of Ham.[37] In fact, the author divided slaves into different groups such as the people of the Caucasus region, Slavs, Armenians, Turks, Sicilians, Iranians, Indians, and black Africans: namely the Nubians, Abyssinians, and the Zanj.[38] On the basis of their ethnicity and physiognomy, the author showed which ones were suited for which activity or employment, for instance Nubians were suggested as wet nurses and maidservants, while Turks and Slavs were well suited to serve as soldiers and guards;[39] hence creating a stigmatized representation of ethnic or race-based hierarchy.[40]

[35] Al-Mas'udi (attrib), *Akhbar az-Zaman* in Hopkins and Levtzion, *Corpus*, 34.
[36] Abu 'l-Qasim Ibn Hawqal al-Nusaybi in Hopkins and Levtzion, *Corpus*, 50–51.
[37] Floréal Sanagustin, *Un Aide-mémoire à l'usage de l'acheteur d'esclaves: la Risala fi shira' ar-raqiq wa taqlib al-'abid d'Ibn Butlan (IVe-XIe)*, thèse 3e cycle Etudes arabes et islamiques (Paris 3: 1981), 52 and 235.
[38] *Az-Zanj* is a term often used in Arabic literature to designate the blacks of eastern Africa south of Ethiopia and Somalia. For more information see Alexandre Popovic, "al-Zandj" in *The Encyclopedia of Islam*.
[39] Sanagustin, *Un Aide-mémoire*, 246–247.
[40] It is important to note that this racial representation was common to many slave societies. For example, in eighteenth-century France, a similar perception was reported by historian Sue Peabody: "As everybody knows, Indian blacks, completely unlike the negroes

Racist attitudes toward black Africans were common in the southern lands of the Mediterranean, and the Talmud as well as Arabic traditions appear to describe and to justify the idea of racial divisions and power relations using a religious identity and scheme. This negative evaluation of black Africans became well established during the medieval era, and even reached Spain, which did not have any physical contact with the land of the blacks at this time. For example, the writings of the twelfth-century merchant Benjamin of Tudela in Spanish Navarre, refer to the blacks in the south of Egypt:

When the men of Assuan[41] make a raid into their land, they take with them bread and wheat, dry grapes[42] and figs, and throw the food to these people, who run after it. Thus they bring many of them back prisoners, and sell them in the land of Egypt and the surrounding countries. And these are black slaves, the sons of Ham.[43]

One of the first historians, after al-Mukhtar Ibn Butlan, to reject the Hamitic traditions was Shams ad-Din abu 'Abd Allah Muhammad ad-Dimashqi (1256–1327). He wrote:

The historians assert that the cause of the black complexion of the sons of Ham is that he had sexual intercourse with his wife while on the ship and Nuh (Noah) cursed him and prayed to God to modify his seed, so that she brought forth [the ancestor of] the Sudan. Another version is that Ham came upon Nuh asleep with his privy parts uncovered by the wind. He told this to his brothers Sam and Yafath and they rose and covered him, turning their faces backward so that they might not see his shame. When Nuh knew of this he said: "Cursed is Ham, blessed is Sam, and may God multiply [the seed of] Yafath." But in truth, the fact is that the nature of their country demands that their characteristics should be as they are [black], contrary to those connected with whiteness, for most of them inhabit the south and west of the earth.[44]

Depending on which version one accepts, Noah's wrath was incurred either by Ham having sexual intercourse with his wife while on the ark or by Ham having seen Noah's exposed genitals. According to the latter version, Noah's two other sons, Shem and Japheth, cover their father

of Africa, are ordinarily good domestics; consequently they had no difficulty finding a new position." Peabody, *There Are No Slaves in France*, 58.

[41] Or Aswan, a city in the south of Egypt at the first cataract of the Nile.

[42] Or raisins.

[43] Marcus Adler, "The Itinerary of Benjamin of Tudela (Concluded)," *The Jewish Quarterly Review* 18, no. 4 (July 1906): 678. See also Robert Hess, "The Itinerary of Benjamin of Tudela: A Twelfth-Century Jewish Description of North-East Africa," *The Journal of African History* 6, no. 1 (1965): 15–24.

[44] Shams ad-Din al-Ansari ad-Dimashqi, in Hopkins and Levtzion, *Corpus*, 212.

without viewing his shame. In either case, there are additional variations of the curse. One is that God changed the skin color of Ham to black. Another is that only the children of Ham would be born black. The progeny of Ham would become enslaved to the progeny of Shem as part of the curse. The progeny of Shem became the people of the middle temperate climates like the Arabs, Israelites, and Persians. The progeny of Japheth became the white-skinned people of the north. A good deal of discussion among medieval Arab historians about Ham focuses on his descendants. The discussions advance the thesis that African peoples with black skin color are descended from Ham, and his sons left to travel in sub-Saharan Africa where they settled and multiplied.

Many historians later disputed the genealogical claim that the black-skinned people of the Sudan are descendants of Ham. Rather, as the example from ad-Dimashqi shows, some historians rejected the Hamitic theory and attributed racial variations to environmental factors involving the intense heat of the climate in which blacks lived. Likewise, ad-Dimashqi claimed that the peoples of the north are white-skinned because of the intense cold of their particular climate. Furthermore, the strange practices and customs of these peoples were often attributed to factors and effects involving the material conditions that shaped the form of life. Blacks may be fanciful, jovial, or lazy because of the heat. Most historians of this era did not question the firmly held assumptions about the racial genealogy of populations as found regionally. Perhaps one of the most notable examples of the binary racial categories of Arab cultural arrogance can be found in the monographs of historian Ibn Hawqal in the tenth century. Ibn Hawqal traveled as far as Sijilmasa, an important caravan trading town in the south of Morocco, but never crossed the desert to the land of the blacks about whom he made trivializing remarks dismissing the region and its people as not having achieved anything worth mentioning, hence excluding the sub-Saharan Africans from human history and the world's civilization. Ibn Hawqal wrote:

We have not mentioned the land of the Sudan in the west [of Africa], nor the Buja nor the Zanj, nor other peoples with the same characteristics, because the orderly government of kingdoms is based upon religious beliefs, good manners, law and order, and the organization of settled life directed by sound policy. These people lack these qualities and have no share in them. Their kingdoms, therefore, do not deserve to be dealt with separately as we have dealt with other kingdoms.[45]

---

[45] Al-Nusaybi in Hopkins and Levtzion, *Corpus*, 44. It is useful to note that in the beginning of the nineteenth century, Hegel wrote a similar perception: "At this point we leave Africa, not to mention it again. For it is no historical part of the World; it has no

By the fourteenth century, racial stereotypes of black Africans were conspicuous in Arabic sources. The influential monographs of Ibn Battuta and Ibn Khaldun allow us to see the assumptions of cultural inferiority associated with the blackness of the people of sub-Saharan Africa. Muhammad ibn Battuta (1304–1368), a Moroccan scholar of the Medieval era whose travels are legendary, writing about his travels in West Africa in 1353, although not specifically referring to Ham's curse, made critical observations that sharply stigmatized what he considered pagan attitudes of the black populations: bare breasts, sexual freedom, and bad manners. He wrote in *Rihla* about the black people of West Africa: "These people have remarkable and strange ways. As for their men, they feel no [sexual] jealousy [...]. The women there have friends and companions among the foreign men [e.g., not a kinsperson]."[46] His reaction to local customs can be seen in examples from his descriptions: "At this I repented at having come to their country because of their ill manners and their contempt for white men";[47] or when he said: "When I saw it [their trivial reception gift] I laughed, and was long astonished at their feeble intellect and their respect for mean things."[48] Ibn Battuta implied that cannibalism was found among blacks: "A group of these Sudan [blacks] who eat human kind came with an emir of theirs to the sultan Mansa Sulayman [...]. The gold mine is in their country."[49] These anecdotes from Ibn Battuta could have been made up by black Africans themselves to discourage the Arabs and Berbers from venturing into gold mining areas as a strategy to dissuade foreign encroachment into crucial sources of economic income.[50]

movement or development to exhibit. Historical movements in it – that is in its northern part – belong to the Asiatic or European World. Carthage displayed there an important transitionary phase of civilization; but, as a Phoenician colony, it belongs to Asia. Egypt will be considered in reference to the passage of the human mind from its Eastern to its Western phase, but it does not belong to the African Spirit. What we properly understand by Africa, is the Unhistorical, Undeveloped Spirit, still involved in the conditions of mere nature, and which had to be presented here only as on the threshold of the World's History." Georg Wilhelm Friedrich Hegel, *Lectures on the Philosophy of History*, translated by J. Sibree (London: G. Bell and Sons, 1902), 103.

[46] In Hopkins and Levtzion, *Corpus*, 285.

[47] Ibid., 284.

[48] Ibid., 289.

[49] Ibn Battuta in Hopkins and Levtzion, *Corpus*, 298.

[50] It is important to note that similar tales can be found in the folklore of African Gambians, suggesting that Europeans ate human flesh and the reason they bought blacks was to eat them. Alvise Ca da Mosto, *The Voyages of Cadamosto and other Documents on Western Africa in the Second Half of the Fifteenth Century*, translated and edited by G. R. Crone (London: Printed for the Hakluyt Society, 1937), 60.

For Ibn Battuta, the ultimate criterion of a people's worth was their adherence to Islam, or lack thereof, and he sometimes rendered his judgments with respect to such adherence in terms of race. Ibn Battuta appointed himself as a moral arbiter by cataloging some of the acts of black people that he regarded with either approval or disapproval.[51] His criticisms of blacks are by and large reserved to social customs, portraying African unbelievers as savages and those who converted to Islam as civilized. 'Abd ar-Rahman Ibn Khaldun (d. 1406), one of the best-known Arab historians and thinkers, was the first to treat fully the Hamitic theory and to dispel it as myth or as a "silly story."[52] Ibn Khaldun was a truly Mediterranean figure, coming from a prominent Andalusian family and having spent his entire career along the southern shores of the Mediterranean, from Fez to Tunis to Cairo. In his book *The Muqaddimah* (introduction to his universal history) he wrote:

To attribute the blackness of the Negroes to Ham, reveals disregard of the true nature of heat and cold and the influence they exercise upon the climate and upon the creatures that come into being in it. The black skin common to the inhabitants of the first and second zones is the result of the composition of the air in which they live, and which comes about under the influence of the greatly increased heat in the south [...]. People there go through a very severe summer, and their skins turn black because of the excessive heat.[53]

Ibn Khaldun disputed the traditional claim that the black-skinned people of the Sudan are descendants of Ham. A source of traditional views that attributed skin color to the Hamitic curse may have derived from a body of Hadith known as the *isra'iliyyat*, reports taken from Jewish sources in the Arabian Peninsula during the early period of Islam, thus explaining the incorporation of the account of the sons of Ham into Arab-Islamic history. Ibn Khaldun broke with the traditionalists on this and other issues by arguing that the peoples of the Sudan were black-skinned because of the intense heat of the climate in which they lived. The peoples of the north were white-skinned because of the intense cold of their particular climate. Furthermore, the strange practices and customs of these peoples were a consequence of their climates and environmental conditions rather than the Hamitic assumption that darker skin somehow conveyed inferior human qualities considered savage or barbaric.

[51] Ibid., 296.
[52] Ibn Khaldun, *The Muqaddimah*, translated by Franz Rosenthal (Princeton: Princeton University Press, 1969), 61.
[53] Ibid., 59–60.

An important question involves why the Arabs or light-skinned North Africans did not use color to denote themselves. That is, why was being light-skinned not itself meaningful with respect to skin color given the obvious existence of variations in skin color? Ibn Khaldun explained that:

> The inhabitants of the north are not called by their colour because the people who established the conventional meanings of words were themselves white. Thus, whiteness was something usual and common to them, and they did not see anything sufficiently remarkable in it to cause them to use it as a specific term.[54]

Hence, the color labeling exists only for constructing the other. *Bilad as-Sudan*, literally "land of the blacks," was used in medieval Arabic literature to designate mainly black West Africa, an ambiguous geographic area from the Atlantic to Chad, a description found in such writers from the Maghreb as eleventh-century Andalusian geographer and chronicler Abu 'Ubayd Allah al-Bakri (d. 1094).[55] *Bilad as-Sudan* was also used randomly to refer to all black Africa, another example being that of tenth-century Iraqi scholar and bibliographer Muhammad ibn Nadim: "The races of Negroes are the Nubians, the Bijah (Beja), the Zaghawah, the Murawah (Meroe), the Istan [Zinj in Iraq], the Barbar (Berbers), and the types of blacks like the Indians."[56] The concept of land of the blacks was also used at times interchangeably with Abyssinia (Habasha). Sixteenth-century Moroccan historian al-Fishtali wrote that on the occasion of the success of the Moroccan conquest of Songhay in 1591, a poet of the sultan's court writing in celebration of the victory used the term *Abyssinians* (*Ahabish*: plural of *Habashi*) to designate the people of *Bilad as-Sudan*.[57] I argue that much of the confusion found in the literature on black culture and history stems from outsider perspectives tainted by ethnocentric and religious biases. Indeed, as David William Cohen wrote, "perhaps the major issue in the reconstruction of the African past is, and has been for some years, the question of how far voices exterior to Africa shape the presentation of Africa's past and present."[58]

---

[54] Ibid., 60–61.

[55] Abu 'Ubayd Allah al-Bakri in Hopkins and Levtzion, *Corpus*, 77–79.

[56] Ibn al-Nadim, *The Fihrist*, vol. 1, 35.

[57] 'Abd al-'Aziz ibn Muhammad al-Fishtali, *Manahil as-Safa fi Ma'athir Mawalina ash-Shurafa'*, edited by 'Abd al-Karim Kurayyim (Rabat: Matbu'at Wizarat al-Awqaf wa-'l-Shu'un al-Islamiyya wa-ath-Thaqafiyya, 1972), 163.

[58] David William Cohen, "Doing Social History from Pim's Doorway" in *Reliving the Past: The Worlds of Social History*, edited by Olivier Zunz (Chapel Hill: University of North Carolina Press, 1985), 198.

It must be noted that the Arabs were not the first to use the conventional word *Sudan* to designate black Africans south of the Sahara. Classical documents indicate that the ancient Greeks were perhaps the first people to use a similar denotation, *Ethiopia*, which meant "a burnt-faced person," to refer to dark-skinned Africans from south of Egypt.[59] The Greek concept of skin coloration was based on environmental factors, similar to the view of Ibn Khaldun. Ibn Khaldun was likely familiar with the Greeks' notion of color regarding Africans. As far as the genealogy of physical characteristics and how peoples with those characteristics came to inhabit various geographical regions, Ibn Khaldun accepted the traditional accounts of his predecessors:

These black nations of the human race are people of the Second Clime [...]. Their pedigree goes back to Ham b. Nuh, for the Habasha are the offspring of Habash b. Kush b. Ham; the Nuba (according to al-Mas'udi) are the offspring of Nuba b. Kush b. Kan'an b. Ham or (according to Ibn 'Abd al-Barr) of Nub b. Qut b. Yansar b. Ham; and the Zanj are the offspring of Zanji b. Kush. The remainder of the black people (*asawid*) are the offspring of Qut b. Ham according to Ibn 'Abd al-Barr; some say that [the true form of] his name is Qut b. Ham.[60]

In spite of his rejection of the Hamitic curse, Ibn Khaldun nonetheless accepted many of the cultural assumptions of his peers and was not concerned with correcting the negative image of blacks; in fact he held similar views to those of Ibn Battuta. Ibn Khaldun described the blacks of sub-Saharan West Africa as inferior and submissive human beings living in an inferior level of social organization: "Therefore, the Negro nations are, as a rule, submissive to slavery, because (Negroes) have little that is (essentially) human and possess attributes that are quite similar to those of dumb animals."[61] However, Ibn Khaldun's racial prejudice derived from his view that environmental factors were at work rather than from a belief in God's curse on the progeny of Ham. From Ibn Khaldun's environmental perspective, the relative level of social organization and customs came about as a consequence of geographical location and, as he explained, some blacks are more civilized than others because of their proximity to the temperate regions and their peoples:

For instance, the Abyssinians, who are the neighbours of the Yemenites and have been Christians from pre-Islamic and Islamic times down to the present; and the

---

[59] See Frank M. Snowden, *Before Color Prejudice. The Ancient View of Blacks* (Cambridge: Harvard University Press, 1991), 7.
[60] Ibn Khaldun in Hopkins and Levtzion, *Corpus*, 332.
[61] Ibn Khaldun, *The Muqaddimah*, 117.

Mali the Gawgaw, and the Takrur who live close to the Maghrib and, at this time, are Muslims. They are said to have adopted Islam in the seventh [thirteenth] century. Or, in the north, there are those Slav, European Christian, and Turkish nations that have adopted Christianity.[62]

Both Maghrebian historians, Ibn Khaldun and Ibn Battuta, seemed excessively preoccupied with color in their classification of African peoples, but not less than their neighbors, the Greeks, who recorded their perceptions of "otherness" earlier than the Arabs. According to classicist Frank Snowden, "Ethiopians became the yard stick by which classical antiquity measured colored peoples [...]. Ethiopians, the blackest; Indians, less sunburned; Egyptians, mildly dark; and the Mauri (Moors), whose name was derived from the color of their skin."[63] Snowden did not think that the Romans' classification of dark color amounted to race prejudice; however other experts on the subject such as Grace Beardsley and David Wiesen did think that blacks were perceived generally as inferior in Roman society and that they were subject to mockery.[64] But Lloyd Thompson thinks that "[t]he element of mockery and caricature evidently implies that some Romans [...] felt a sensory aversion to nigritude [*sic*], at any rate in its 'barbarian' manifestations, and to other forms of extreme distance from the Roman somatic norm image."[65]

In sum, this traditional way of classifying peoples by skin color and then evaluating their relative level of individual capacity and social achievement according to a continuum of coloration with light skin being regarded as highest or best provided the basis for how blacks were perceived among the light-skinned Arab-Berber people of North Africa. The consistent perceptions of blacks as a different people with inferior capacities and uncivilized customs promoted a stereotypical image of North African blacks that continued to exist throughout modern times. By way of analogy it is worth mentioning that the Hamitic theory was widely accepted in Western Europe and used to justify the enslavement of black Africans in the Americas. Indeed American abolitionist Frederick Douglass (1818–1895) noted that American slaveholders used the argument "that God cursed Ham" in order to excuse slavery.[66] According to

---

[62] Ibid., 59.
[63] Snowden, *Before Color Prejudice*, 7.
[64] See Grace Beardsley, *The Negro in Greek and Roman Civilization; a Study of the Ethiopian Type* (Baltimore: Johns Hopkins Press, 1929), 115–120 and David Wiesen, "Juvenal and the Blacks," *Classica et Mediaevalia* (1970), vol. 31, 132–150.
[65] Lloyd A. Thompson, *Romans and Blacks* (London: Routledge, 1989), 25.
[66] Frederick Douglass, *Narrative of the Life of Frederick Douglas, an American Slave* (New Haven: Yale University Press, 2001), 15.

James Sweet, it was from the Islamic lands and from Iberia that these racial attitudes found their way into the Americas and were instrumental in the creation of American racism.[67] Portuguese chroniclers were familiar with the Hamitic myth even before Portugal's commercial activities and slave raids in West Africa began in the first half of the fifteenth century. Portuguese scholar Gomes Eannes de Azurara (d. 1474), in service to Prince Henri the Navigator, explained the black race in terms of the Hamitic myth:

[B]lacks were Moors like the others, though their slaves, in accordance with ancient custom, which I believe to have been because of the curse which, after the Deluge, Noah laid upon his son Cain,[68] cursing him in this way: – that his race should be subject to all the other races of the world. And from this race these blacks are descended, as wrote the Archbishop Don Roderic of Toledo, and Josephus in his book on the *Antiquities of the Jews*, and Walter, with other authors who have spoken of the generations of Noah, from the time of his going out of the Ark.[69]

Not until the Western European Enlightenment and the rise of empirical science did the religious account of the origins of race start to crumble, only to give rise, unfortunately, to racist, pseudoscientific concepts of human classifications based on the unfortunate distortion of Darwin's theory, namely social Darwinism. But even the conceptual revolution of the Enlightenment did not prevent nineteenth-century European travelers to Africa from referring to the Hamitic theory in their travel accounts. As contemporary historian William McKee Evans concluded: "By studying the shifting ethnic identifications of the 'sons of Ham,' by following their journey in myth from the land of Canaan to the land of Guinea, we can perhaps learn something about the historical pressures that shaped modern white racial attitudes."[70] The use (or misuse) of the Hamitic theory and its racist essentializing is an intriguing story that involves the religious and cultural history of Judaism, Christianity, and Islam.

In the final analysis, the effect of the Hamitic myth with respect to race has no place or justification in the Qur'an or in the Hadith. However, many chroniclers and geographers referred to it, as deeply ingrained

[67] James H. Sweet, "The Iberian Roots of American Racist Thought," *The William and Mary Quarterly* 54, no. 1. Third Series (January 1997): 143–166.

[68] The author seems to conflate Cain with Canaan.

[69] Gomes Eannes de Azurara, *The Chronicle of the Discovery and Conquest of Guinea*, translated by Charles Raymond Beazley and Edgar Prestage (London: Printed for the Hakluyt Society, 1896), vol. 1, 54.

[70] Evans, "From the Land of Canaan," 16.

cultural "knowledge," in their classifications of human groups and social hierarchies, and in particular used this tacit assumption as a prescriptive analytical lens that maintained Arab superiority and justification for prejudice against black people. Muslim attitudes about black people, however, had little need of the Hamitic thesis in order to justify slavery. That is, the Hamitic story was not needed to justify slavery in Islamic societies because the only justification for enslavement in Islamic law is the condition of unbelief. Nevertheless, the Hamitic myth was part of the set of historical generalizations that contributed to the cultural ethnocentric discourse in North Africa. Historical records allow us to see that prejudice against blacks blinded light-skinned Arabs and Berbers and led them either to dismiss their darker-skinned Muslim peers' right to natural freedom as Muslims or to introduce ambiguity with respect to race that created a conflict between the teaching of the Qur'an and the entrenched cultural stereotypes about blacks, Muslims or not.

With the advance of Islam into Africa, slave raiding in western sub-Saharan Africa increased and became even more common when the supply of slaves acquired either through purchase or as captives of war in the Iberian Peninsula and the Black Sea began to dwindle once the jihads, or holy wars, fought by Islamic states in the region died down. The decrease in the European supply of Slavs to the Muslims of the southern regions was also the result of an economic imperative. Europeans obtained sugar, a commodity that medieval Europeans used to call "a product from heaven,"[71] from the Islamic lands, but soon learned to make it themselves in the late fourteenth century.[72] By the early fifteenth century, the Portuguese started sugar production in Madeira; the Castilians followed suit in the last quarter of the fifteenth century.[73] The intense labor needed was supplied in part by the Slavs from the area of the Black Sea, and this is how this slave route changed its course westward to Europe away from the Islamic lands. But this supply did not last long for either parties of the Mediterranean. With the Turks on the horizon, the Slavs became the focus of rivalry between Christians and Muslims. In fact, the Russians and the Ottoman empire competed against each other and offered to their subjects in the peripheries protection against enslavement. By the fifteenth century, the Ottomans

---

[71] Its rarity and price made it a luxury item in Europe.
[72] Charles Verlinden, *Les origines de la civilisation atlantique. De la Renaissance à l'Age des Lumières* (Neuchâtel: La Baconnière, 1966), 167.
[73] Noël Deerr, *The History of Sugar* (London: Chapman and Hall, 1949).

invaded the southern regions of Eastern Europe and converted many of the Balkan Slavs to Islam. As a result, Iberians and Maghrebians turned to Africa for slave labor. The Iberians needed Africans mainly for sugar production. This was when Christians, William McKee Evans concludes, "began to look at blacks in ways that had been characteristic of racially stratified Muslim countries for some seven centuries."[74] Islamic countries turned south to sub-Saharan Africa. North African Muslims did enslave sub-Saharan and East Africans. These were among the first sources, and the last.[75] By the sixteenth century, the enslavement of sub-Saharan Africans had become questionable because many of the West Africans had in fact embraced Islam before their enslavement. The best example illustrating this ambiguity is found in letters from ordinary Muslims, most likely merchants, from the south of Morocco, to scholars residing in proximity to regions considered providers of slaves. One jurist, Makhluf b. 'Ali b. Salih al-Balbali (d. after 1533–1534), from the western Sahel who resided in both Timbuktu and Marrakesh,[76] expressed dismay regarding the issue of enslaving black Muslims by calling it "a great catastrophe whose misfortune has had widespread effect throughout the lands in this age."[77] He insisted in his legal opinion that the only justification for enslavement was unbelief and listed the names of blacks who were Muslims and whose enslavement was therefore illegal, groups such as the Fulani or Fulbe, the Songhay, and the peoples of Kano, Katsina, and Gobir. Al-Balbali made it clear that if any of these people happened to be in slavery they must be released.[78]

A century later, letters from Sa'id b. Ibrahim al-Jirari from Tuwat,[79] and another from Yusuf b. Ibrahim al-Isi from Sus (south of Morocco), were sent to a well-known scholar in Timbuktu named Ahmad Baba (1556–1627) petitioning his opinion on the question of the enslavement of black

---

[74] Evans, "From the Land of Canaan," 39.

[75] John Hunwick, "African Slaves in the Mediterranean World: A Neglected Aspect of the African Diaspora" in *Global Dimensions of the African Diaspora*, edited by Joseph Harris, 2nd ed. (Washington, DC: Howard University Press, 1993), 296.

[76] Read his biography in Chouki El Hamel, *La Vie intellectuelle islamique dans le Sahel ouest africain. Une étude sociale de l'enseignement islamique en Mauritanie et au Nord du Mali (XVIe-XIXe siècles)* (Paris: L'Harmattan, 2002), 328–329.

[77] Ahmad Baba, *Mi'raj al-Su'ud: Ahmad Baba's Replies on Slavery*, annotated and translated by John Hunwick and Fatima Harrak (Rabat: Publications of the Institute of African Studies, 2000), 12.

[78] Ibid., 11–12.

[79] A town in the southwestern corner of present-day Algeria, a carrefour in the Saharan and trans-Saharan trade routes.

Muslims.[80] These queries seeking the legal opinion of Muslim scholars are very important because they represent the concerns of laypeople on the issue of slavery and as such reveal the tensions between cultural perceptions and the principles and the application of Islamic law. English historian Mervyn Hiskett (1920–1994) was correct to say that: "it is clear that Muslims have often found themselves in a moral dilemma in that they have been fully aware of the inhumanity of an institution which, morally, they have had to accept."[81] The legal queries and replies under discussion are not isolated cases but rather a consistent body of historical records voicing similar concerns. Al-Jirari, in his letter to Ahmad Baba, wanted to understand the meaning of the Hamitic myth and its implications:

What is the meaning of Ham's descendants being slaves to the descendants of Shem and Japheth? If what is meant is the unbelievers among them, then [being slaves] is not confined to them, nor similarly is [ownership of slaves] confined to his two brothers Shem and Japheth, since the unbeliever is allowed to be owned whether he is black or white. What is the significance of restricting slavery through conquest to the Sudan despite the fact that others share with them the status that gives rise to that?[82]

Ahmad Baba replied from Timbuktu in 1615. His reply was informative and detailed. He cited his prominent predecessors, quoting directly from scholars such as Ibn al-Jawzi and Ibn Khaldun and summarizing their opinions in refuting the curse of Ham.[83] The most important thing for Baba was that "Ham or anyone else may be possessed [as a slave] if he remains attached to his original unbelief. There is no difference between one race and another."[84] Thus, in the opinion of these Islamic legal scholars, it was absolutely illegal to enslave free Muslims under any circumstances, be they white Muslims or black Muslims.

These interpretations of Islamic law dismiss the Hamitic myth and deny any difference between the races with respect to being a Muslim,

---

[80] Mohamed Zaouit, who examined the legal opinions (*fatawi*) of Ahmad Baba regarding the legal status of black people exported as slaves to North Africa, succeeded in identifying the author of the letter. It was someone by the name of Sa'id Ibrahim al-Jirari who probably resided in Draa in southeast Morocco and the letter went by way of Tuwat to Ahmad Baba in Timbuktu. See Mohamed Zaouit, *L'esclavage au Bilad as-Sudan au XVIème siècle à travers deux consultations juridiques d'Ahmad Baba*, Thèse de Doctorat (Paris: Université Paris I Sorbonne, 1997), 66–68.

[81] Abubakar Tafawa Balewa, *Shaihu Umar: A Novel*, translated by Mervyn Hiskett (Princeton: Markus Wiener Pub., 1989), 6.

[82] Baba, *Mi'raj al-Su'ud*, 17.

[83] Ibid., 31–35.

[84] Ibid., 35.

but admit divisions and enforce or create the identity of the "enslave-able other," namely the unbeliever or infidel. This identity is validated through the insistence on differences derived from paganism, although the ideology of enslavement based on infidelity (*kufr*) does not have any foundation in the Qur'an or the Hadith. *Mi'raj as-Su'ud* by Ahmad Baba at the beginning of the seventeenth century is an example of a legal text that illustrates how identities were defined, maintained, and violated. The admission and insistence on the differences between groups of people consequently led to the affirmation of bleeding boundaries with regard to slavery. Ahmad Baba argued that the enslavement of free black Muslims in Africa was indeed unlawful. He documented that the burden of proof for rightful enslavement laid squarely on those who bought and sold slaves.[85] Ahmad Baba's view may seem forthright but it does not consider the voice of the enslaved persons to challenge their status. He deprived enslaved persons of any rights to challenge their misfortune. Some schol-ars honored the challenges from enslaved black Muslims and ordered their release. Baba himself mentioned examples of these scholars in one of his replies: "The judges of Fez ruled in like manner as did Sidi Mahmud *qadi* [judge] of Timbuktu. He would accept their word [of the enslaved] without requiring them to prove that they were from those lands."[86] Baba went so far as to make a list of lands and of people who were enslaveable and those who were not. According to Baba, the lands south of Muslim black Africa such as Kano, Katsina, Gobir, Bornu, Songhai, the majority of the Fulani (Fulbe), and the people of Mali, civilizations considered paganistic, were the only kingdoms under the threat of jihad.[87] He named the groups that Muslims could lawfully enslave without questioning like the Mossi, the Gurma, the Busa, the Borgu, the Dagomba, the Kotokoli, the Yoruba, the Tombo, and the Bobo.[88]

Ahmad Baba did not question the validity of Muslims' raids against their neighbors. This jihad seemed legitimate to him as long as it was against infidels. Conversion to Islam subsequent to enslavement did not bring salvation either, so slavery for Ahmad Baba was not justified as an opportunity for conversion, creating a dichotomy of Muslims versus

[85] Ibid., 27–28. See also Bernard Barbour and Michelle Jacobs, "The Mi'raj: A Legal Treatise on Slavery by Ahmad Baba" in *Slaves and Slavery in Muslim Africa*, edited by John Ralph Willis (London: F. Cass, 1985), vol. 1, 130.

[86] Baba, *Mi'raj al-Su'ud*, 29 and Willis, *Slaves and Slavery*, 131.

[87] Zaouit, *L'esclavage au Bilad as-Sudan*, 97–121; Willis, *Slaves and Slavery*, 125–159, and Baba, *Mi'raj al-Su'ud*, 27–29.

[88] Willis, *Slaves and Slavery*, 137 and Baba, *Mi'raj al-Su'ud*, 39–40.

"pagans," and thus providing access to a source of enslaveable human beings.[89] In Islamic law, the *kuffar* are the pagans or infidels; they are the non-scriptuaries. They usually belong to the land of the infidels (*dar al-kufr*), the "pagan" frontier of the land of Islam (*dar al-Islam*). Historically, the practice of jihad followed two principles vis-à-vis the conquered peoples: the people of the Book or *ahl al-Kitab* (Christians, Jews, and Zoroastrians) were not required to convert to Islam but were to submit to the authority of the Islamic government and pay poll-taxes (*jizya*) and land taxes (*kharaj*) in exchange for protection and safety. These groups of people, such as the Copts of Egypt, became known as *dhimmi* (the protected persons).[90] They continued to practice their religions and could not be legally enslaved. Just as the interpreters of Islamic law decided to make *Majus* or Zoroastrians "people of the book," they decided to make pagans "the enslaveable other." Pagans – any person who was not a Muslim or who was not accorded the status and privileges of a believer "of the Book" – must convert to Islam, suffer death, or be enslaved. As a criterion that justified slavery or a privileged status of tolerance and inclusion for non-Muslims, the emergence of this criterion was inconsistent with the Qur'an.[91] The Qur'an emphasized that jihad must be a just legal war in self-defense only.[92] The interpretation that became the norm from the time of the Umayyad dynasty (661–750) was that of a state-sponsored, legal conception of jihad as a holy war for the expansion of the religion of Islam rather than as a defense against unjust acts or foreign encroachment.

Ahmad Baba was neither conscientious nor sensitive to the fate of the victims of these neighborhood raids – Muslims versus "pagans." It is curious that Baba did not refer to late-fifteenth-century Soninke scholar al-Hajj Salim Suwari, who rejected engaging in war against pagan people for the sake of conversion. He declared that just war should be waged for self-defense only. He developed a set of legal principles advocating peace and coexistence among believers and unbelievers in West Africa that came to be known as the Suwarian tradition. According to historian Ivor Wilks, "al-Hajj Salim Suwari established, among Juula and Jakhanke alike, a pedagogical tradition that survives to this day despite

---

[89] Baba, *Mi'raj al-Su'ud*, 23 and Willis, *Slaves and Slavery*, 128.
[90] See Claude Cahen, "Dhimma" in *The Encyclopedia of Islam*.
[91] M. Morony, "Madjus" in *The Encyclopedia of Islam*.
[92] See the enlightening articles on jihad in John J. Donohue and John L. Esposito, eds. *Islam in Transition: Muslim Perspectives* (New York: Oxford University Press, 2007), 393–408.

the pressures of modernism."[93] Suwari drew his arguments from sources like Ahmad Baba within the Maliki teachings, but, unlike Baba, Suwari was more reflective in his interpretations regarding Muslims' relations with unbelievers.[94]

Baba did not even express doubts about the raids against the unbelievers whether or not they were carried out according to the principles of jihad recognized in the Maliki doctrine (discussed in the previous chapter). The rules provided in the Maliki doctrine with respect to captives, according to Khalil b. Ishaq (d. 1374), an Egyptian Maliki jurist, were: "death, freedom, ransom, payment of the poll-tax, or enslavement."[95] The Maliki doctrine justified waging a proselytizing campaign against unbelievers, but protocols on how to undertake such a campaign were to be strictly adhered to in applying the Maliki doctrine. There is an important Hadith in this context. When the Prophet Muhammad appointed a leader of an army to undertake a mission to fight the unbelievers within his society or against hostile entities, Muhammad insisted that those who were the focus of the campaign be given three options that would allow violent conflict to be avoided. If the hostile parties agreed to either of the first two options, the third option, war, was avoided. The first option was to convert to Islam and to join in building the nascent but growing Islamic community in Medina (Muhammad's first Islamic community). If those the Muslims fought against partially accepted this offer through willingness to convert to Islam but refused to join the Islamic community in Medina, then they would be considered like the Muslim Bedouins who converted to Islam but did not participate in the building of the Islamic community and as such would not receive any share from the spoils of war. If they refused to convert to Islam, but were followers of "the Book" – Christians, Jews, and other followers of an Abrahamic religion – then they could choose the second option of paying a poll-tax (*jizya*), another means of enlisting cooperation and support for the Islamic community in the absence of conversion. If they agreed to the tax, then their political submission to Islam was accepted. But if neither conversion to Islam

---

[93] Ivor Wilks, "The Juula and the Expansion of Islam into the Forest," in Nehemia Levtzion and Randall L. Pouwels, *The History of Islam in Africa* (Athens: Ohio University Press, 2000), 97.

[94] Ibid., 96–98; Lamin Sanneh, *The Crown And The Turban: Muslims and West African Pluralism* (Boulder: Westview Press, 1997), 214.

[95] Khalil b. Ishaq, *Mukhtasar al-'Allama Khalil* (Cairo: Dar al-Fikr, 1981), 105. See the French translation Khalil b. Ishaq, *Abrégé de la loi musulmane selon le rite de l'imam Malek*, translated by Georges Henri Bousquet (Alger: Éditions algérienne en-Nahdha, 1956).

nor subjection to a tax was accepted, then war was the last option.[96] The remaining options of the Maliki doctrine regarding captives were to kill them, enslave them, or free them. The questions posed by al-Jirari in letters to Baba expressed concern regarding the issues of jihad and slavery, and al-Jirari appeared well informed on the rules of jihad in accordance with the Maliki doctrine. In a letter from al-Jirari to Ahmad Baba, al-Jirari asks for clarification:

One of the *qadis* of the Sudan reported that the Imam who conquered them whilst they were unbelievers chose to spare them as slaves, since he had the choice, or because he did not consider the five well-known options, and that they still remain in a state of slavery, and whenever the sultan needs any of them he brings in as many as he wants. Is this true or not? How could this be so in regard to Bornu, which [is] the abode of their sultanate, and people are frequently brought to us from there. Are they also slaves or not?[97]

At issue in this letter is the question whether jihad can rightfully be conducted in order to acquire slaves and whether people enslaved as unbelievers who then convert to Islam can remain slaves. Enslaving a Muslim is forbidden in the Qur'an, and if the Maliki rules are applied, conversion to Islam should not result in continued enslavement. Ahmad Baba replied that he was not aware of the information reported by this Muslim judge from the Sudan and that the story of his setting aside the Maliki rules and conducting raids for slaves was most probably untrue. Baba confirmed that the people of Bornu were Muslims, they converted to Islam early without being conquered, but adjacent to their land lived unbelievers whom they raided, captured, and sold. Hence, he believed no further investigation was necessary. What is curious about this response is the setting aside of the issue of conducting jihad for the purpose of enslavement. Baba's response ignored the five known Maliki rules, asserting that they would not apply since the people raided in neighboring lands were not people of the Book and were also poor, hence with no hope for ransom. These are only two of the five options, outlined by the aforementioned Khalil b. Ishaq, that would have preserved the captives' freedom.

Hence, Baba failed to remind his readers that jihad for the purpose of enslaving people was illegal. Ahmad Baba's *Mi'raj as-Su'ud* not only fell short in resolving questions about when jihad was justified, but also in addressing concerns regarding the dilemma of enslaving black Muslims. By ignoring the central issues, Baba ultimately affirmed the notion of bringing

---

[96] *The Alim*, Sahih Muslim, Hadith narrated by Burayd, number 804.
[97] Baba, *Mi'raj al-Su'ud*, 14.

jihad to *Dar al-Kufr* or "pagans," hence preserving the institution of slavery. This perspective came to be applied to enslaved blacks in the Maghreb. A similar case emerged in the heartland of Morocco when Sultan Mawlay Isma'il gave his controversial order to enslave all black Moroccans to create his royal army. Here again, concerns were raised, especially by Muslim scholars of Fez who were adamantly opposed to this major violation of people's rights just because they happened to be black or former slaves. Among these scholars was 'Abd as-Salam Jassus, who issued a fatwa against the sultan's order and was murdered for his objection.

It is of considerable historic interest that many scholars of different eras expressed their objections to the negative way black Africans were portrayed and treated. Among these scholars was al-Jahiz (776–869), a famous Arab-Nubian scholar, who criticized Arabs who held what he considered fallaciously sweeping deprecatory notions about black Africans based on the few powerless enslaved blacks.[98] In his essay entitled "Fakhr as-Sudan 'ala al-Bidan" ("Superiority of the Blacks to the Whites"), al-Jahiz emphasized the positive qualities of the blacks and the validity of their culture, citing the case of Ethiopia.[99] In the same vein, Muhammad b. al-Marzuban (d. 922) wrote "Kitab as-Sudan wa Fadlihim 'ala 'l-Bidan" ("Blacks and their Superiority over Whites"). A good number of noteworthy Arab and non-Arab dark-skinned scholars emphasized the contribution of blacks to Arabic and Islamic civilization. Their scholarship represents evidence of color consciousness and a literary discourse in defense of blacks against Arab ethnocentrism.[100] There are other examples such as the famous historian and narrator of Baghdad, 'Abd ar-Rahman ibn al-Jawzi (1126–1200), who criticized the Hamitic curse as erroneous. He authored a book entitled *Tanwir al-Ghabash fi Fadl as-Sudan wa-'l-Habash* (*Lightening of Darkness on the Merits of the Blacks and Ethiopians*) in defense of black people.[101]

[98] Lewis is wrong to claim that al-Jahiz was not defending blacks but reinforcing their negative images. Lewis, *Race and Slavery*, 32. Al-Jahiz defended the blacks generally, but it is true that he portrayed one group of dark-skinned people in negative terms, the Zanj, whom he believed lived in the deep interior of Africa beyond the land of the blacks (*sudan*) and the Swahili people.

[99] Abu 'Uthman 'Amr al-Basri al-Jahiz, *Rasa'il al-Jahiz* (Beirut: Dar al-Kutub al-'Ilmiya, 2000). The essay is translated into English by Vincent Cornell, *The Book of the Glory of the Black Race* (Kitab Fakhr As-Sudan 'ala al-Bidan) (Los Angeles: Preston Pub. Co, 1981).

[100] See 'Abduh Badawi, *ash-Shu'ara' as-Sud wa Khasa'isuhum fi ash-Shi'r al-'Arabi* (Cairo: al-Hayat al-Misriyya al-'Amma li 'l-Kuttab, 1973).

[101] 'Abd al-Rahman ibn al-Jawzi, *Tanwir al-Ghabash fi Fadl as-Sudan wa-'l-Habashi* (ar-Riyad: Dar ash-Sharif, 1998).

Another example can be found in the work of the famous Egyptian scholar as-Suyuti (1445–1505),[102] who authored a book emphasizing the role and the achievements of black people in Islamic civilization. These sources focused mainly on the Abyssinians and black Muslims within Islamic societies. Moroccan scholar Ahmad an-Nasiri (1835–1897) went further by condemning his fellow citizens for the wrongs they committed against blacks, although he devoted only a few pages to this topic in his famous book on Moroccan history.[103]

In some oral traditions, blacks dismissed the absurdity of the negative portrayal of their skin color. Nina Epton, while conducting field work in Morocco in 1950s, collected an interesting narrative on the blackness of the Haratin in the Draa valley (south of Morocco); she wrote:

> The Harratin relate that they are the descendents of Noah's second son, Ham, and that once upon a time they used to be white. One day, however, Ham protected his head during a heavy rain-storm by carrying the Koran on top of it. The rain was so heavy that it washed all the characters of the holy book on to Ham's skin; these characters, being sacred, were inedible, and so they turned Ham and his offspring black forever![104]

This story illustrates the creativity of black Moroccans and it reflects their resistance and syncretism within a hostile dominant culture. They asserted that their blackness is void of any negative connotations; on the contrary, it is sacred. It is fascinating how the Haratin countered the Hamitic myth with a more favorable one within the same discourse, albeit anachronous.

These signs of questioning the institution of slavery never amounted to an abolitionist discourse similar to that argued by their European counterparts. Most of these scholars questioned the practice of slavery within the Islamic legal discourse that condoned it and did not secularize the debate until after the European colonial encounter.

The Berbers' Attitude to Blacks in Morocco

Prior to Islam's venture into Morocco, the concept of freedom was based more on the notion of protection from – freedom from – outside incursions and threats from other tribal groups than on our modern sense of

---

[102] See as-Suyuti, *Raf' Sha'n al-Hubshan* (*The Raising of the Status of the Ethiopians*).
[103] Ahmad an-Nasiri, *al-Istiqsa' li-Akhbar Duwal al-Maghrib al-Aqsa* (Casablanca: Dar al-Kitab, 1997), vol. 5, 131–134.
[104] Nina Epton, *Saints and Sorcerers* (London: Cassell, 1958). 161.

individual liberty. As such, freedom from external threats was created by bonds of alliance with a particular tribal group, on the connection and the protection that a certain tribe could provide. Freedom, then, was established through tribal solidarity. Blacks interacted with Berbers both through trade and war. Individual blacks living in the land of the Berbers occupied either a marginalized status (servants or slaves) or a dependent status (intermarriage or vassalage). Berber racial attitudes toward black people likely formed prior to the Arab conquest when the Berbers of Sanhaja and Masmuda were forced to leave their homeland because of external invasions. Berbers, victims of successive invasions by the Romans, the Vandals, and the Byzantines, were forced to move south into areas predominantly inhabited by black people. Technologically superior as a result of their contact with different cultures and the use of the camel, Berbers most likely conquered the black populations of the Sahara and assumed for themselves a superior status, subordinating blacks. Because blacks were different in their cultural and racial characteristics, a racial binary was in the making. Simultaneously, these groups of Berbers may have started to preserve their identity by rallying around family kin groups based on egalitarian concepts. The kin group was a creative way to coexist after the dispossession and the dispersal of the Berbers by external invaders.[105] Those who migrated developed a sense of kin solidarity that did not allow intermixing with outsiders. Members of the indigenous black population were not only considered outsiders with respect to kinship but also perceived as a lower class. Intermarrying with blacks was considered taboo and shameful.

By way of illustration, the following story of Abu Madyan, a North African Sufi figure (1115/1116–1198), is a particularly salient example of black–Berber social relations, in this case from the Sanhaja:

Abu Madyan used to tell his companions that ash-Shaykh abu Yi'zza foretold him that he would receive an Abyssinian female slave and that he would have a son with her and that if this son lives he would be important. Indeed, a merchant from Bijaya[106] gifted to him an Abyssinian female slave who did bear him a son whom he named Muhammad. Before long, Abu Madyan stopped having sexual intercourse with her and showed signs of discomfort. When he was asked

---

[105] Knowledge on the genesis of Berber–black interaction during Roman times is somewhat speculative, as relevant primary sources are extremely rare. See 'Abd Allah al-'Arwi, *Mujmal Tarikh al-Maghrib* (Beirut: al-Markaz ath-Thaqafi al-'Arabi, 1996), vol. 1, 109–112; Stéphane Gsell, *Histoire ancienne de l'Afrique du Nord*, 2ème édition (Paris: Librairie Hachette, 1929), tome V, 3.

[106] A city in northern Algeria.

88 *Race, Gender, and Slavery in the Islamic Discourse*

what was bothering him, he replied: "I did not have any desire for this female slave and if it was not for the prediction of ash-Shaykh abu Yiʻzza, I would not have approached her [...]. However, if I abandoned her I would have sinned, and if I married her I would be discomfited by having a son with her." Then, ʻAbd ar-Razzaq[107] told him: "I would marry her and care for your son." Abu Madyan exclaimed: "Would you do that, although marriage with an Abyssinian woman is a shameful thing among the Masmuda people?"[108] ʻAbd ar-Razzaq replied: "But, I would do it for you." So, he married her and cared for Abu Madyan's son [but at the end], the child died at a young age.[109]

It is interesting to note that the Sufi figure named Abu Yiʻzza (d. 1177) mentioned in this anecdote, who was from the Masmuda Berber, had a companion who just got married. This companion informed Abu Yiʻzza that his wife asked him for a female slave, but he did not have the means to get her one. Abu Yiʻzza proposed to him that he could take the place of the female slave. He thought that he could easily pass for a female slave when dressed up like a woman, because he was black and had no facial hair. In this way, he served the couple for a year. He ground wheat, made dough, baked bread, and fetched water; he did all this at night and in the day he practiced his devotions at the mosque. After a year when the wife found out the true identity of Abu Yiʻzza, she felt embarrassed and started to do the work herself. What is revealing in this story is the assumption among the Masmuda Berber that slavery was associated with black people. But at the same time the fact that he was an important Sufi figure suggests the opposite as well as spiritual mobility. It also seems that it was the wish of even small families to have a black maid who could do these domestic chores and more.[110]

This racist anecdote from the Masmuda Berbers is not an isolated example; we find this attitude among other Berber scholars who thought that biological intermixing with blacks would contaminate their lineage. For this reason, the Aqit, an important Sanhaja family, migrated from Masina (presently in Mali), an area whose inhabitants were mainly black Fulani, to Walata (or Biru, presently in Mauritania). Seventeenth-century Timbuktu historian ʻAbd ar-Rahman as-Saʻdi, reported:

I heard the great scholar jurist Ahmad Baba [...] saying that it was only hatred for the Fulani living in his neighborhood that made him [Muhammad Aqit] move

---

[107] ʻAbd ar-Razzaq al-Jazuli was one of Abu Madyan's disciples.
[108] Abyssinian (in Arabic *Habashiyya*) means in this context black Africans.
[109] Yusuf at-Tadili, *at-Tashawwuf ila rijal at-tasawwuf*, établi et annoté, par Ahmed Toufiq (Rabat: Université Muhammad V, Publication de la Faculté des Lettres et des Sciences Humaines de Rabat, 1404/1984), 328.
[110] Ibid., 219.

to Biru. He said that he was absolutely sure he never intermarried with them. But he was afraid that his children would do so and mix their lineage with them [the Fulani].[111]

This is an astonishing admission coming from a man versed in Islamic jurisprudence because his attitude contradicts the basic tenets of Islam. But this statement should not be taken as an unambiguous declaration about race relations because the reality was more problematic. There is historical evidence that the Aqit people did mingle with other "blacks" and Ahmad Baba himself was the product of such mixing. These brief examples, and many more exist in the historic annals, help us to understand how cultural factors were not always reconciled with the Islamic Qur'anic teaching that explicitly envisioned a color-blind society, an ideal that has never been achieved. The Berbers did not really intend to preserve ethnic purity; they intermarried with Arabs. Establishing a privileged status was in important ways central to how race entered into interpretations of the Qur'an and Hadith. The dominant culture of Islam was Arabic, the Prophet was an Arab, and therefore the association with Arabs, especially those claiming ascendance to the Prophet and to the ruling class, was seen as endowing membership in a privileged class.

The legal discourse of Islam was not always seen as overriding where social relations and alliances were in focus; legal interpretations of Islamic tenets found in the Qur'an and the Hadith were not always consistent where they might challenge deeply entrenched preexisting social mores and customs, mores and customs of an often prejudicial kind, particularly where race was concerned. Yet, as the examples in the preceding section show, some Islamic scholars objected to racist attitudes and policies that from their perspective were inconsistent with the tenets of Islam. People who professed Islam nonetheless followed local customs and traditions when considering their self-interest, regardless of the tension between what they professed as Muslims and what they practiced as members of a tribal or social group. Not only was prejudice against blacks seen as uncontroversial from the perspective of affirming Islam, but many Islamic jurists insisted that maintaining a harmonious society was an overriding social goal of Islam and as such meant that social customs with respect to interpersonal relations should

[111] 'Abd ar-Rahman as-Sa'di, *Tarikh as-Sudan*, edited and translated by Octave Houdas (Paris: Adrien-Maisonneuve, 1964), 35–36 of Arabic text and 58 of the translation. See also John Hunwick's translation, *Timbuktu and the Songhay Empire: Al-Sa'di's Tarikh Al-Sudan down to 1613, and Other Contemporary Documents* (Leiden: Brill, 1999), 49–50.

not be ignored. In this interpretation of Islam, under which social harmony was seen as an overwhelming good, social status figured prominently in how race was regarded in interpersonal relations. In a curious but not surprising way, social status, with its tacit racism intact, was used as a means to achieve social harmony at the expense of racial equality. Hence, social status (known in Arabic legal terms as *kafa'a*), or rather equivalence of social status, was the arbiter for how people formed social alliances.[112] A married couple would be matched not only in fortune but also on a racial level. Jurist al-Wazzani, for instance, said that in Fez: "a marriage with a freedman, commonly called a *hartani*, is a shameful, blameworthy act. Under no circumstances does a freedman qualify to marry a free-born woman."[113] This reasoning is within the Maliki discourse. Malik said: "A free man must not marry a slave-girl when he can afford to marry a free woman, and he should not marry a slave-girl when he cannot afford a free woman unless he fears fornication."[114] For the sake of social status racial prejudices were perpetuated. The social illegitimacy of racial intermixing overrode its legal legitimacy. Social status involved many elements such as economic wealth, titled affiliations, *sharif* descent from the Prophet's kinship, and ethnic group solidarity. As a consequence, blacks were marginalized. Berbers perceived them as a threat to their conception of social order and harmony. But at the same time masters did impart a portion of their status and class on the enslaved persons, especially those with whom they had personal ties such as concubines. Hence, the higher the class and status the less important the fact that the concubine, especially *umm al-walad*, was black. However, as women were considered inferior to men in the Moroccan gender structure their status did not affect or diminish men's position.

In the eighteenth century, in the Sus region south of Morocco, some Muslim scholars did not hide their racism when an army constituted of black soldiers created by Sultan Mawlay Isma'il (r. 1672–1727) amassed tremendous power. Al-Mukhtar as-Susi (1900–1963), a famous

---

[112] Khalil b. Ishaq, *Mukhtasar al-'Allama Khalil* (Cairo: Dar al-Fikr, 1981), 116 and the French translation: Khalil ben Ish'aq, *Abrégé de la loi musulmane selon le rite de L'imam Malek*, traduction nouvelle par Georges Henri Bousquet (Alger: Maison des livres; Paris: A. Maisonneuve, 1958), vol. 2, 28. For more information see Farhat J. Ziadeh, "Equality (Kafa'ah) in the Muslim Law of Marriage," *The American Journal of Comparative Law* 6, no. 4 (Autumn 1957): 503–517 and John Esposito, *Women in Muslim Family Law* (Syracuse: Syracuse University Press, 1982), 22.

[113] Quoted in Ennaji, *Serving the Master*, 64.

[114] Malik b. Anas, *al-Muwatta'*, 477; *The Alim*, al-Muwatta', 28.29.

Moroccan scholar, reported that another scholar, Muhammad b. Ahmad ar-Rasmuki, in a discussion with friends (all from Sus, a Berber region), derided the character of the Haratin, whom he had previously praised for their military achievements, even suggesting a poetry contest satirizing these blacks. He referred to the Haratin using three terms – *'Abid* (slaves), *Haratin* (free blacks), and *sud* (blacks) – interchangeably, a decidedly insulting admix. Ar-Rasmuki and his three friends composed a defamatory poem containing a list of negative physical and moral characteristics.[115] Some of the first verses come with a word of warning: "when one buys a slave must also get a stick."[116] In this poem, the Haratin are described as despicable, unclean, ill-fated, and vile, and ultimately no good is expected from them; praising them should be a crime and Sultan Mawlay Isma'il valuing them was shocking.[117] Even if these black soldiers had misused their power and abused their authority, not a particularly surprising occurrence for human beings in general, it is instructive that they were not criticized for such behavior, but rather because they were black, and were therefore reproached in racist terms. Even at an earlier time, a similar negative perception in popular Moroccan and Andalusian proverbs was recorded by Abu Yahya az-Zajjali (1220–1294).[118] William Sersen, who has conducted research in Arabic popular literature, observed similar proverbs among the Arabs; he reports: "Never trust a black slave (*al-'abd*); whip him well, and feed him well, and the work will be done."[119]

This cultural and racial prejudice was observed throughout the country. Moroccan scholar Ahmad b. 'Ajiba at-Titwani (d. 1809) indignantly expressed his protest of the treatment and racist attitudes toward black Moroccans. 'Ajiba, who was from the region of Tetouan, declared that he had known people who called into question their *imama* (leadership) of Friday prayer and of religious festivals. He also knew people who refused to intermarry with black people even if they were equal and free.

---

[115] Muhammad al-Mukhtar as-Susi, *al-Ma'sul* (Casablanca, Morocco: Matba'at al-Najah, 1962), vol. 18, 318–323. This work is a remarkable collection on the political and social history of the Sus region. The author was meticulous in collecting testimonies that would have otherwise been lost.

[116] Ibid., 318.

[117] Ibid., 320.

[118] See Abu Yahya az-Zajjali, *Amthal al-'Awam fi 'l-Andalus*, edited by Mohamed Bencherifa (Fez: Matba'at Muhammad V, 1975), vol. 1, 218–222.

[119] William John Sersen, "Stereotypes and Attitudes towards Slaves in Arabic Proverbs" in *Slaves and Slavery in Muslim Africa*, edited by John Ralph Willis (Frank Cass & Co. Ltd.: London. 1985), 98.

'Ajiba made a solemn statement that anybody who committed injustice against them (just because they were of a different complexion) would carry his sin to judgment day, and that anybody who read his statements and did not act in protest against the insult and injustice against the black Muslims was an accomplice.[120]

René Caillié (1799–1838), a French explorer, noted racist attitudes when he visited the south of Morocco in 1828 on his way home from a journey to Timbuktu. He wrote that in the region of Tafilalt, a region with many black slaves and some freedmen, that the blacks never intermarried with the Moors (Arabs and Berbers) and that even the children of an illegal union between a black woman and a Moor had no real status and were condemned to remain in the lower levels of society without much hope for improving their social status.[121] The late American anthropologist David Hart also confirmed and explained similar resentment toward the Haratin by the rural Berbers in the Draa region, resentments still present in the twentieth century. These Haratin tended Berber-controlled oases and were often forced into a caste system working as sharecroppers called *khammasin*. They paid one-fifth of what they produced to the Berber landowners. Hart noted the attitude of the Ait Atta Berbers of the Draa region toward the Haratin:

> In this sense the Ait Atta are without question the biggest racists in the Moroccan South. They, white tribally-organized, transhumant Berbers who traditionally always bore arms, despise the Haratin for being (1) negroid, (2) non-tribal, (3) sedentary and agricultural, and (4) inexperienced in bearing arms.[122]

The claimed superiority of the Ait Atta Berbers over the Haratin was also encoded in their pre-Islamic customary laws, which contained explicit discriminatory rules such as a prohibition of selling a house or land to the Haratin. Anyone violating this law was subject to a huge monetary fine and the penalties were imposed on the seller and on the Hartani as well.[123] The land became the basis by which a social status was defined; hence black people were excluded in order to keep them inferior. This attitude

---

[120] Dawuud, *Tarikh Titwan*, vol. 2, 42.

[121] René Caillié, *Voyage à Tombouctou* (Paris: La Découverte, 1996), tome 2, 355.

[122] David Hart, "The Tribe in Modern Morocco: Two Case Studies," in *Arabs and Berbers. From Tribe to Nation in North Africa*, Ernest Gellner and Charles Micaud eds. (London: Lexington Books, 1972), 53–54. Hart had extensive field work knowledge on the Ait Atta. He died in 2002.

[123] Larbi Mezzine, *Le Tafilalt, contribution à l'histoire du Maroc au XVII et XVIII siècle* (Rabat: Publications de la Faculté des Lettres et des Sciences Humaines, 1987), 254–255. For information on these customary laws see pages 240 to 259.

toward race, to preserve the agnatic lineage in accordance with economic privilege, can still be seen in the region of Ait Atta. Cynthia Becker did extensive field work in Morocco in 1993 among the Ait Khabbash, a Berber group who coinhabit a region with another black group descended from slaves. Becker observed that the Ait Khabbash refused to intermarry with the blacks in order to preserve the imaginary purity of their lineage. The Ait Khabbash referred to their black neighbors as *Ismkhan*, (sing. *Ismakh* or *Ismag*), a Tamazight word for "slave," which is interchangeable with black and also Haratin. As Becker noted, the Ismkhan formed a separate subgroup as a result of their being descended from slaves,[124] thus conflating the diversity of blacks in one category. As late as the 1990s, prejudice against blackness in the oasis of Aqqa led to racially divided mosques.[125]

The construction of races and racial attitudes found fertile ideological soil through various genealogies of Islamic affiliation that became an important means to establish social status and social harmony, both of which conferred justification for the imposition of political authority in lands that were occupied, and had been occupied for generations, by people who were darker skinned. When Islam came to the land of the Berbers, it transformed the land of the blacks into the land of the "infidels" or "pagans." The marginalized status of blacks was reduced further to slave status. According to the Qur'an, only "infidels" were legally allowed to be enslaved. The best place to obtain slaves was from the nearest bordering lands of the "infidels," the Sudan. The Sudan, inhabited mostly by blacks, with their contrast in physical characteristics to the light-complexioned Arab and Berber populations, contributed to the conceptual connection between skin color and enslaveability. The ancient rivalry between nomadic Berbers and sedentary blacks who occupied lands that the Berbers were forced into when they, the Berbers, were themselves threatened by foreign invaders and emigrated to lands occupied by blacks, took an Islamic form after the conversion of the Berbers to Islam during the seventh and eighth centuries.

However as a caveat, I do not claim that all Berber groups are the same in this regard; some are heavily mixed with blacks, especially the Tuareg of the Sahel region who call themselves Kel Tamasheq, emphasizing a common language.

---

[124] Cynthia Becker, *Amazigh Arts in Morocco: Women Shaping Berber Identity* (Austin: University of Texas Press, 2006), 162.
[125] Interviews with Mr. Sudani, June 2001.

A Comparative Discourse on Race and Slavery

One of the few Muslim Africans who attempted to explain the dilemma of understanding race in Arabized Africa is renowned Africanist scholar Ali Mazrui, who argued that the "Arab lineage system permitted considerable racial co-optation. 'Impurities' were admitted to higher echelons as full members – provided that the father was an Arab."[126] Thus, in Arabized societies one is either an Arab with a continuum from light complexion (like Syrian Arabs) to dark complexion (like black Arabs in Mauritania), or simply black; there is no specific category of a mixed group such as the mulattoes, mestizos, or creoles in the Americas. Ali Mazrui judged this system of race mixing against "a system of descending miscegenation like that of the Unites States, [because it] pushes 'impurities' downward into the pool of disadvantage."[127] He sees the Arab system as inclusive and tolerant. But in reality the dominant Arab culture had double standards in its treatment of non-Arabs such as black Africans, Egyptian Copts, and Berbers of the Maghreb. The Copts and Berbers were accepted into Arab society with less prejudice than black Africans, but blacks in Morocco remained the "other within." The racially mixed children of Arabs and Iberians were referred to as "new born" Muslims, al-muwalladun (plural of muwallad), a term that initially might have carried a pejorative connotation, but eventually with ensuing generations the racial distinction conveyed in the term al-muwalladun lost any negative connotation as the Moors became an homogenous group.[128] Another example of racial distinction involves the Berbers, who were classified in the early Islamic period as children of Ham,[129] but when power relationships changed and Berbers produced scholars and rulers, negative racial overtones diminished in the ensuing accounts of their achievements, which also gave their genealogy greater respect.[130]

---

[126] Ali Mazrui. "Africa and Other Civilizations: Conquest and Counter-Conquest" in *Africa in World Politics: The African State System in Flux*, edited by John W. Harbeson and Donald Rothchild (Boulder: Westview Press, 2000), 113–114. See also Ali Mazrui, *The Africans: A Triple Heritage* (Toronto: Little, Brown & Company, 1986), 90.

[127] Mazrui, "Africa and Other Civilizations," 113.

[128] *Muwallad* is derived from the root word WLD, meaning to give birth. It is the etymological origin of the English word *mulatto*, meaning a person of mixed race from white and black parents.

[129] Al-Tabari, *The History of al-Tabari*, vol. 2, 21. The Arabic text: at-Tabari, *Tarikh at-Tabari*, vol. 1, 69.

[130] Ibn Khaldun, *Tarikh*, vol. 6, 104–114. See also Abdelmajid Hannoum, *Colonial Histories, Post-Colonial Memories: The Legend of the Kahina, a North African Heroine* (Portsmouth: Heinemann, 2001).

Indeed, on the surface, following Ali Mazrui's perspective, one does not find much in the way of a discourse valorizing racial purity in Moroccan society. To illustrate Mazrui's argument I cite a typical example of Moroccan rulers: Sultan Mawlay Isma'il (1646–1727), whose mother was a black slave (*umm al-walad*) but who nonetheless perceived himself a descendant of Muhammad and therefore not black. Given that Morocco is a patrilineal and patriarchal society, the father gives to his son his *nasab* (ethnic kinship) and his religion regardless of the mother's status, whether non-Muslim, Berber, black, or slave. The Moroccan definition of race accepts the other or blacks in the Arab family as long as they possess a drop of Arab blood, seemingly ignoring their other ethnic or racial affiliations. In the name of abstract virtues, this process of assimilation camouflaged the dismissal of the natural affiliation of the "other" and manufactured Arab hegemony and political unity by insisting on the sacredness of the language of the Qur'an: Arabic. Hence, even people descended from mixed marriages did not see any ambivalence in claiming one identity, namely, their Arab lineage. This racialist discourse is deeply embedded in the assimilationist process and culture and successfully concealed or silenced other elements that were a part of the construction of one's identity. It was a curious and creative process that preserved old Arab social relations at work in the creation of a "nationalist" Moroccan Arab majority and that at the same time subjugated black ancestry, seen as having more bearing on the historical antecedents of slavery.

The Moroccan system of racial definition was clearly "racialist" and was in fact a curious inversion of the Western racist model. However, it did not have clear boundaries as found in European and American societies and was ideologically flexible enough for blacks occasionally to attain positions of power. In the antebellum American South, in the words of Frederick Douglass, "slaveholders have ordained, and by law established, that the children of slave women shall in all cases follow the condition of their mothers."[131] The adherence to the notion of racial purity as an arbiter of legal social status was shameful and racial intermixing was regarded as taboo. Repeatedly, white masters impregnated their female slaves with impunity without recognition of or obligations of paternity. But the fate of any attempt of a black male to associate with a white woman – even a prostitute – was a grave offense. Olaudah Equiano

---

[131] Frederick Douglass, *Narrative of the Life of Frederick Douglas, an American Slave* (Yale University Press, 2001), 14.

(circa 1745–1797), an ex-slave and abolitionist, witnessed a horrid event that involved torture of a black man in the British West Indies:

And yet in Montserrat I have seen a negro-man staked to the ground, and cut most shockingly, and then his ears cut off bit by bit, because he had been connected with a white woman who was a common prostitute: as if it were no crime in the whites to rob an innocent African girl of her virtue; but most heinous in a black man only to gratify a passion of nature, where the temptation was offered by one of a different colour, though the most abandoned woman of her species.[132]

The main difference between the Moroccan and Euro-American systems, rather than emphasizing racial purity (white versus black) as defined by skin color, emphasized descent: either from Arab lineage or, more prestigiously, from the Prophet or his lineage. In Morocco, unlike American slavery, the offspring of cohabitation between masters and enslaved black females gained status and legal entitlements because it was through one's father, rather than one's mother, that one acquired one's lineage (*nisba*) and racial identity. As a consequence of this substantial difference, notions of gender and race were constructed differently in Morocco and other North African Islamic societies than in the American South. This difference can be seen in that many Moroccan rulers were sons of ex-slave black women but thought of themselves as Arabs and *sharif* – descended from the Prophet Muhammad, hence of a "noble blood," which translates into an abstract virtue and a high social status. In fact it was so common to be a ruler and a son of a concubine in Morocco that Moroccan historians sometimes emphasized the free status of the mother of the sultan.[133] Sultans Mawlay Isma'il (r. 1672–1727), Mawlay 'Abd ar-Rahman (r. 1822–1859), and Mawlay al-Hasan I (r. 1873–1894) were all the offspring of black slaves who had become royal *ummahat al-awlad*.[134] These black female slaves often became the matriarchs of the sultans' households – that is, their offspring had a legal and social status that allowed them to stand as potential and indeed actual successors to the throne. For this reason, the Moroccan system of racial relations is in a way a curious kind of racialist model. It is useful to note that this kind of social structure was not unique to Morocco. The interplay of color, consanguinity, and social function that complicated

---

[132] Olaudah Equiano, *The Interesting Narrative and Other Writings* (New York: Penguin Books, 1995), 104.
[133] Historian ad-Du'ayyif (1752–1818) emphasized the mother of Sultan Mawlay Sulayman (r. 1792–1822) was a free woman. Muhammad ibn 'Abd as-Salam ad-Du'ayyif, *Tarikh ad-Du'ayyif: Tarikh ad-Dawla as-Sa'ida* (Rabat: Dar al-Ma'thurtat, 1986), 244.
[134] The issue of mother concubines will be discussed in Chapters 4 and 5.

racial positioning in Morocco was rather similar to the Brazilian racial social structure.[135]

This genealogical determinism has racialist implications because it favors one ethnic group over the other. In Moroccan society, patrilineage from the Prophet Muhammad was often emphasized and black ancestry was often stigmatized. Even the terms referring to freeborn children of concubinage sometimes carried racial connotations when they were called "*wuld al-'abda*," literally "the son of the black woman." The definition of race in the Moroccan context is fluid and flexible and resists facile analyses such as those by scholars and traveler observers. Race is scientifically a banal construct but it is crucial in power relations with serious and deadly effects. Representation of difference as conveyed through cultural symbols revolved less on the standard stereotypical physical traits and far more on social status and patrilineage. The differences were located in the power structure that patrilineage held in Islamic societies. The dominated "different" became the "racialized other." For instance, urban attitudes toward the blacks in eighteenth-century Fez were different from the attitudes in the southern oasis of Tata where their numbers were much greater and social position somewhat different. In Fez, free blacks might own lands but not in the south of Morocco among the Ait Atta Berbers of the Draa region. Nevertheless, the perceptions of Arabs and Berbers were generally similar, and even the blacks who spoke Berber and had Berber last names were not considered Berbers. The attitudes of the upper class affected the lower classes as they set up the standards for social status and relations.

The blacks in Morocco were mostly non-tribal individuals, families, and small groups. Their main occupations were sharecroppers, domestic servants, doormen, guards, porters, concubines, or artisans. There were times, though, when slaves achieved important elite status such as the black soldiers did during the reign of Mawlay Isma'il. The view that Islamic societies displayed humane attitudes toward slaves is to some extent correct. Often, close relationships of interdependence grew between masters and slaves, and affection between these asymmetric power relations was not uncommon. Concubinage was a socially acceptable practice and the children of such unions were recognized as legitimate. But such benign attitudes reflect neither the social status nor the social mobility

---

[135] See Carl Degler, *Neither Black nor White: Slavery and Race Relations in Brazil and the United States* (Madison: University of Wisconsin Press, 1971), 224 and 226. In Brazil, the mulatto class blurred the racial line and was a crucial factor in the formation of white hegemony.

of enslaved persons. In general, blacks occupied a marginal position in Moroccan society and were historically segregated somewhat by occupation. Leon Brown, examining race in North Africa, notes that, "There was, however, never anything approaching segregation based on color. North African cities, like those of the Middle East, were and still are to some extent characterized by a degree of residential and occupational segregation."[136] Thus, prejudices were more likely to be expressed as a conjunction of race and class together, with neither alone sufficient to explain segregation. Hence, economic interest and social status formed the primary basis for political and social behavior.

Applying Western concepts of race in its multiple constructs (pseudo-scientific, social, and cultural) to analyses of Moroccan history and Islam is problematic. The equivalent of the word "race" in contemporary Arabic literature is *'irq* (pl. *'uruq*). Etymologically speaking the word "*'irq*" means root. *'Irq* also has other connotations but is generally used to mean "the root, origin or source, of anything." Historically, the descriptive categories that Arabs used, similar to those used by premodern Europeans, are "people, nation, community, and tribe" for all divisions of humankind. When the word "*'irq*" was used, and only rarely, it was usually used for the purpose of highlighting the origin of the lineage but not necessarily the consanguinity of the lineage itself.[137] The collective image of black people remains that of an apparent "other" – a minority and a color often associated with the heritage of slavery. The proper Arabic term I would use for this racial conception is "*al-'Asabiyya or al-'Irqiyya*" or "*at-Ta'ssub al-'Irqi*," a social cohesion derived from lineage and patrilineal consanguinity.

To a certain extent, a Euro-American concept of race and its critique are applicable to Islamic societies as this theory itself has roots in the adjacent Islamic culture in the Mediterranean basin. It is important to note that Western theories of race and racism are polemical, incoherent, inconsistent, and contested in the Western intellectual and academic world. Bruce Hall is right to point out that: "The common problem with objections based on single terms or narrow definitions based on a modern Western idea of race is that they rest on a fiction that there is a coherent model in European racial thought with which to compare ideas about race elsewhere."[138] Hence, to analyze and assess social and racial

---

[136] Leon Brown, "Color in Northern Africa," *Daedalus* 96, no. 2 (spring 1967): 469.
[137] Lane, *An Arabic-English Lexicon*, vol. 5, 2018–2019.
[138] Bruce Hall, *A History of Race in Muslim West Africa, 1600–1960* (Cambridge: Cambridge University Press, 2011), 10.

relations in Arabized or African societies, the Western critical theory of race must take into consideration the cultural variations, social nuances, and scales of values. The fact that Arabic literature is not consistent in the terms it uses to denote race does not mean that race (for example, a racialized other) did not exist in Arabic thought and Islamic culture and history, as different terms were used to denote race such as *umma* (pl. *umam*), *sha'b* (pl. *shu'ub*), *qawm* (pl. *aqwam*), *jins* (pl. *ajnas*), *qabila* (pl. *qaba'il*), and so forth. All of these terms were used in different times selectively, randomly, or interchangeably to mean people, humankind, tribe, nation, ethnic stock, or race, except for the term *umma* that was often used to emphasize the exclusive identity of people practicing the Islamic faith. The problem is not with borrowing and benefiting from the Euro-American theory of race, racism, and slavery but with how to over-come the issue of embarrassment in engaging in profoundly tabooed sub-jects. The intersection of race and religion can be traced in Europe from historical antecedents that date back to at least late-fifteenth-century Spain. The policy of pure blood (*limpieza de sangre*) or unmixed ances-try was legally formulated and implemented in Spain during the reign of Isabella of Castile against Jews who had converted to Christianity but who were suspected of secretly observing Judaism. Eventually the Inquisition, under the command of the Spanish Dominican monk Tomas de Torquemada (1420–1498), included Muslims. This policy led to the extermination of some Jews and the expulsion of all those who were not born Christian and was therefore thought to represent a threat to the Spanish political and religious order. Similarly, in seventeenth-century colonial America, race policy was implemented when Virginia decreed a ban on interracial marriage in 1691,[139] following a decree in 1668 that the slave status of enslaved Africans converted to Christianity would remain the same.[140] In France, however, initially, The Freedom Principle, meaning that an enslaved person who set foot in France became free, was a crucial rule separating the metropole from its colonies. But French colonists continued to bring slaves back to France and contested their slaves' claims for freedom in courts. Therefore, a royal edict was enacted to in 1716 to address the issue and provided some possibilities for slave owners to bring their slaves to France. In 1759 a legal case, that of Francisque, was brought to the Parliament of Paris and enforced the

---

[139] Richard Middleton, *Colonial America: A History, 1565–1776* (Oxford: Blackwell Publishing, 2002), 303.
[140] Ibid., 302.

association of slavery with blackness. Francisque was a boy from India brought to France by his master, Brignon, and as a result of his mistreatment he decided to work for another employer. Brignon tried to claim him back through the courts but he did not succeed. The Parliament of Paris ruled in Francisque's favor, yielding to the argument of The Freedom Principle but on the premise that Francisque was not black, hence admitting the inferiority of black Africans.[141] These kinds of judgments led to a racial decree known as Police des Noirs issued in 1777 by Louis XVI. This law decreed that persons of color were not allowed in France; hence the shift from the issue of slavery to the question of race. This is not to suggest though that the French were only just beginning to connect race and slavery in 1777; this connection was much older. This decree may have been in part a reaction against the abolition movement and the liberal political reform and rhetoric coming out of the American Revolution. Indeed, twelve years later, the French Revolution, drawing inspiration from America, toppled the monarch, issued the Declaration of the Rights of Man, and, a few years later, pursued diplomatic relations with the leaders of Haiti's uprising and outlawed the slave trade and slavery altogether. However, the presence of blacks and interracial marriages seemed to disgrace the social order and were perceived as corrupting the French bloodline. This law banned marriages between whites and "blacks, mulattoes, and other people of color."[142] It was enacted partly to avoid giving blacks any idea that they were equal to whites. Sue Peabody, an American expert on slavery in France, adds: "What is more, some judges were helping slaves to escape from their masters, or they detain them in prison, prohibiting the jailers from releasing them, under the pain of exemplary punishment."[143] She concludes: "It is clear, however, that by 1782 the notion of racial purity was firmly entrenched in the minds of even the staunchest defenders of freedom."[144] While these laws were not fully successful in implementation, other laws were consequently enacted to restrict the social mobility of people of color in France.[145] Laws in France were different from those of its colonies at the start but gradually one set of laws informed the other and they finally converged together in a similar racialist discourse.

[141] Peabody, *There Are No Slaves in France*, 58–59.
[142] Ibid., 118.
[143] Ibid., 1996, 119.
[144] Ibid., 1996, 135.
[145] Sue Peabody and Keila Grinberg, *Slavery, Freedom and the Law in the Atlantic World: A Brief History with Documents* (Basingstoke: Palgrave Macmillan, 2007), 7.

Hence, by the eighteenth century, a more secular evaluation of race emerged. This was the time when influential thinkers and policy makers laid the grounds for the ideology of a racial binary and white supremacy. Even the writings of egalitarian Enlightenment thinkers such as Thomas Jefferson (1743–1826)[146] contain racially charged remarks about blacks,[147] now premised more on empirical rather than religious grounds, but which nonetheless advanced notions of racial disparities between whites and blacks.[148] Against the rising voice of the abolition movement, those who defended slavery insisted on the innate inferiority of black Africans, using theoretical constructs such as social Darwinism to justify the enslavement of blacks. This negative notion of race led to the legal segregation of races and racist policies in America. However, the concept remains quiet disorienting and illusory. For example, Jefferson was a racist, but he pursued a long-term affair with Sally Hemings (d. 1835) and ultimately freed his children by her. Similarly, at this same time, interracial marriages were apparently accepted between British people and Africans. For example, Equiano, married to an English woman, was embraced and celebrated by much of Britain during this period, and so was Phillip Quaque (1741–1816), from the Gold Coast, who was ordained in the Church of England and married an English woman.[149] Hence no matter how rigid racism was, it remained contested within the same culture and morally and philosophically unjustifiable. Slave functions in Morocco were diverse but visibly domestic in nature, and in agriculture it was small-scale economy. There was no need for mass labor, as was the case on American plantations, that necessitated rigid impersonal policies guaranteeing cheap labor and making the creation of wealth for landowners and mercantilists possible. The legal parameter for slavery in Morocco was always religious and had no secular foundation. Morocco did not undergo the conceptual revolution of the Enlightenment or experience the effect that the Enlightenment had on European elites. The Islamic textual space created by religious scholars, the critical voice of interpretation and social norms, helped prevent a rigid racial extremism.

---

[146] The third president of the United States from 1801 to 1809.

[147] Thomas Jefferson wrote in *Notes on the State of Virginia* (New York: Penguin Books, 1999), 150–151: "I advance it therefore as a suspicion only, that the blacks, whether originally a distinct race, or made distinct by time and circumstances, are inferior to the whites in the endowments both of body and mind."

[148] William Wright, *Critical Reflections on Black History* (Westport: Praeger, 2002), 31.

[149] Vincent Carretta and Ty M. Reese, *The Life and Letters of Philip Quaque, the First African Anglican Missionary* (Athens: University of Georgia Press, 2010).

The concept of race in Morocco is even more unclear because the color line is a fuzzy concept that takes religion and lineage as a salient criterion for social status, including justification of enslavement. In Morocco, there never has been legal segregation, and Islamic jurists did not legally recognize race or racism to justify either white supremacy or slavery. Hence, in Morocco, although one can find racial attitudes, the basis of race displayed in such attitudes is not premised on a rigid distinction between black and white, but rather a far more fluid distinction involving other factors such as lineage rather than skin color.

The notion of racism as a definable distinction involving skin color seems to be a modern concept. Michael Banton gives us a definition of racism as, "the doctrine that a man's behavior is determined by stable inherited characters deriving from separate racial stocks having distinctive attributes and usually considered to stand to one another in relations of superiority and inferiority."[150] Note that in this definition "behavior" is an assessment of the external object of evaluation – inherited characteristics such as skin color and facial features – and does not take into account the inherent subjective biases that are at work and that distort the analytical lens itself. Inherent bias is hardly the stuff of objective analysis. Perhaps a better definition of racism can be found in the work of George M. Fredrickson:

My theory or conception of racism, therefore, has two components: *difference* and *power*. It originates from a mind-set that regards "them" as different from "us" in ways that are permanent and unbridgeable. This sense of difference provides a motive or rationale for using our power advantage to treat the ethnoracial Other in ways that we would regard as cruel or unjust if applied to members of our own Group [...]. In all manifestations of racism from the mildest to the most severe, what is being denied is the possibility that the racializers and the racialized can coexist in the same society, except perhaps on the basis of domination and subordination.[151]

Likewise, Albert Memmi formulated a practical definition of racism that includes the intention, the idea, and the act; he elucidates that: "Racism is the generalized and final assigning of values to real or imaginary differences to the accuser's benefit and at his victim's expense, in order to justify the former's own privileges or aggression."[152] Albert Memmi argues

---

[150] Michael Banton, *Race Relations* (New York: Basic Books, 1967), 8.

[151] George Fredrickson, *Racism: A Short History* (Princeton: Princeton University Press, 2002), 9.

[152] Albert Memmi, *Racism*, translated and with an introduction by Steve Martinot (Minneapolis: University of Minnesota Press, 2000), 169.

that one can find four stages in the complex process of racist behavior that goes beyond simple attitudes and dislike of the other until it becomes embedded into social institutions and norms that sanction and validate those attitudes. He explains that racism as social conditioning involves: (1) The perception of the other as different based on physical character- istics, cultural or religious affiliations, and so forth; (2) This perception imposes negative connotations on the other as inferior in aptitude or atti- tude; (3) The perception of the other as an entire group, hence the notion of a racialized category; and (4) This perception leads ultimately to the justification of acts of exclusion, violation, or violence.[153] In Morocco, was this notion of racism ever applicable? Was it a society divided by skin color?

Historical antecedents and similar patterns of racial attitudes were evident inside and outside Europe since the medieval period, including in Morocco and North Africa more generally.[154] William McKee Evans and James Sweet argue that Mediterranean peoples preceded Western Europeans and Americans by many centuries in ideas of racially clas- sified societies.[155] In the preceding discussion, I argued that race in Morocco and Islamic societies was not given the kind of salience found in Euro-American societies. Although in Islamic societies the institu- tion of slavery was not legally and publicly drawn along racial lines to begin with and Islamic law explicitly prohibited the enslavement of any Muslim, slavery in Morocco took a racist turn under the influence of Mawlay Isma'il. Mawlay Isma'il's influence drew on cultural tenden- cies to view blacks as different and inferior, regardless of their being Moroccans and Muslims. Bruce Hall in his research on race in Muslim West Africa reached a similar conclusion on the perception of black- ness in the Sahel region. He writes: "It was blackness that rendered one vulnerable to legitimate enslavement, to political domination, and to other kinds of legal disability."[156] At the end of the seventeenth cen- tury, Mawlay Isma'il initiated a campaign to enslave all black people, whether Muslim or not, for the purpose of creating a royal army fol- lowing the Janissary model. However, the justification for this operation

---

[153] Memmi, *Racism*, xvii–xviii, 170. See also Fredrickson, *Racism*, 1–13.
[154] Fredrickson, *Racism*, 5.
[155] Evans, "From the Land of Canaan," 15–43; Sweet, "The Iberian Roots," 143–166. Bruce Hall critiqued scholars who objected to the use of the concept of race in the premod- ern era by stating that "such an objection is really just a form of nominalism." Hall, *A History of Race*, 10.
[156] Hall. *A History of Race*, 22.

of enslavement had its roots in cultural prejudices that preexisted Islam and that were not extinguished even in the face of explicit prohibitions in the Qur'an against enslaving Muslims. And here we see a kind of racism that surpassed the gray area of assimilation. Skin color became the criteria for those enslaved in service to the sultan's scheme. The irruption of a racist ideology of enslavement was a product of entrenched cultural prejudice and was a device in a game of power relations. In the end, this was color-coded religious racism because Mawlay Isma'il based his legitimization of the retention of blacks in slavery, although he knew that they were Islamized, assimilated, and integrated in the dominant culture, on their so-called slave origin status and heathen past. The sultan's scheme focused on the blacks' ancestry rather than their current religious status, hence implying their fixed race and by consequence their place in Moroccan society.[157]

Conclusion

This analysis gives sufficient warrant to my claim that racialist ideas and positions were the product of deeply entrenched cultural prejudices that were not dislodged by the egalitarian color-blind tenets of Islam. In fact, against the socially just aspirations of Islam, interpretations of the Qur'an were used to justify the continuation of preexisting cultural racial prejudices rather than to abolish them. The phenomenon of race in Morocco is old; it is as old as the Arab invasion of North Africa in the seventh century. In Morocco, the two cultures, Arabic and Berber, found ideological convergence in the sense of using Islam to justify preexisting prejudice against black Africans. At that time, such prejudice seldom amounted to a consistent and obvious racist ideology, but later as ethno-cultural distinctions became more popularly perceived as fixed, inherent, and static, the strength of these racial prejudices promoted supremacy of a certain race and established a sociopolitical order based on race.[158]

Historical events point to instances when Muslims in fact enslaved free black Muslims, the most poignant example occurring during the reign of the 'Alawi sultan Mawlay Isma'il (r. 1672–1727). The tragic events surrounding the enslavement of free Moroccan blacks were not an outgrowth of happenstance but rather a product of Arabo-Berber-centered prejudice. The enslavement of black Muslims amounts, borrowing

---

[157] I will say more about this in Chapter 4.
[158] See Frederickson, *Racism*, 5–6.

George Frederickson's definition, to a color-coded racialist attitude.[159]
Such racism played a substantial role in Sultan Mawlay Isma'il's decision
to enslave all blacks in Morocco including free black Muslims, supported
by many *'ulama'* in order to legitimize the enslavement of the free blacks
and to undermine any opposition to this project. Historian Fredrickson
stated that he would withhold the "R" word if assimilation was genu-
ine.[160] What would he say about the enslavement of free Muslim blacks?
The abrogation of their free status as Muslims into a permanent slave status in turn perpetuated and reinforced the racial attitudes of Arab-Berbers
toward blacks. In this context, social mobility was impeded for the blacks
to remain a distinctive group. The end result has been that, at least since
the seventeenth century, the Arabic term for black (*aswad*) became interchangeable with slave (*'abd*). Indeed, in the same era, Muhammad az-
Zabidi (d. in Cairo in 1791), an expert in lexicography, reported in his
voluminous dictionary *Taj al-'Arus*: "the master (*as-sayyid*) is generally
white and the slave (*al-'abd*) is usually black."[161]

[159] Ibid., 5.
[160] Ibid., 7.
[161] Az-Zabidi, *Taj al-'Arus*, vol. 8, 129.

PART TWO

BLACK MOROCCO: THE INTERNAL AFRICAN DIASPORA

3

The Trans-Saharan Diaspora

Such is the desert. A Koran which is but a handbook of the rules of the game transforms its sands into an empire. Deep in the seemingly empty Sahara a secret drama is being played that stirs the passions of men. The true life of the desert is not made up of the marches of tribes in search of pasture, but of the game that goes endlessly on. What a difference in substance between the sands of submission and the sands of unruliness! The dunes, the salines, change their nature according as the code changes by which they are governed.[1]

Tracing the Origins and Roles of Black People in Morocco and West Africa: The Autochthonous Blacks of Morocco

Moroccan Arabic sources assert that all the black people in northwest Africa were originally slaves who had been freed under different circumstances through time. However, one group of black people – namely the Haratin – might not have been of slave origin from sub-Saharan Africa, but native to southern Morocco. French anthropologist Denise Jacques-Meunié argued that the Haratin are the descendants of black people who inhabited the Draa valley since time immemorial.[2] According

---

[1] Antoine de Saint-Exupéry, *Wind, Sand, and Stars*, translated by Lewis Galantière (New York: Reynal & Hitchcock, 1940), 168. Antoine de Saint-Exupéry, *Terre des Hommes* (Paris: Gallimard, 1939), 128.

[2] Denise Jacques-Meunié, *Le Maroc saharien des origines à 1670* (Paris: Librairie Klincksick, 1982), tome I, 180–181. Interesting, even presently black people of the Draa region are called Drawa (plural of Drawi) in northern Morocco from Marrakesh to Casablanca to Fez, and *Drawi* is often used pejoratively and interchangeably with *black*. See Remco Ensel, *Saints and Servants in Southern Morocco* (Leiden: Brill, 1999), 19.

to Jacques-Meunié, the available written sources from antiquity to Jewish documents confirm that the natives of the area were black. The authors of ancient source material called the Haratin the "Ethiopians of the West"; and late Jewish sources, from rabbis who lived in the Draa region, called them "Kushites" or black descendants of Ham.[3] Charles de Foucauld (1858–1916), who sojourned in the Sahara (in Tamanrasset), remarked that the inhabitants of the oases of Bani in southern Morocco were mixed Berbers and Haratin, suggesting that the Haratin may have formed a majority in southern Morocco; he estimated that the Haratin in some areas of southern Morocco comprised nine-tenths of the population.[4]

The ancestral form of the term *Hartani* derives from the Berber word *ahardan*, which is connected with skin color. It means "dark color," and the earliest known usage of the term was among the Berbers of Sanhaja and Zanata before the great Arab migration of Banu Hassan in the thirteenth century.[5] The Berber-speaking Tuareg people inhabiting the western and central Sahara and Sahel use a similar word to designate a person of both black and white parentage: *achardan*.[6] Among the mountain-dwelling Berbers of Sanhaja origin, the term designates a person with a black skin, *Ahardan*, in contrast with white, *Amazigh*. In fact, the Berber term *ahardan* (pl. *ihardin*) was used by Berber-speaking people not only in Tafilalt but also in the High and Middle Atlas and in Mauritania.[7] Hence the term *Haratin* was in use long before the arrival of the Arabs (especially the Ma'qil) in the region in the thirteenth century. The Arabic-speaking population of Tafilalt used the term *Hartani* to designate black slaves. Although the term *Haratin* has no significance in the Arabic language, it has produced diverging interpretations: for some it is an Arabic word with two possible meanings. Certain scholars suggest that *hartani* is a combination of two words: *hurr* and *thani*, literally "the second free man," but more likely meaning "a free person

3 Denise Jacques-Meunié, "Notes sur l'histoire des populations du sud marocain," *Revue de l'Occident musulman et de la Méditerranée*, 1972, vol. 11, no. 1, 140.
4 Charles de Foucauld, *Reconnaissance au Maroc 1883–1884* (Paris: Challamel, 1888), 122.
5 Mezzine, *Le Tafilalt*, 193, footnote 34. See also Gabriel Camps, "Recherches sur les origines des cultivateurs noirs du Sahara," *Revue de l'Occident musulman et de la Méditerranée*, 1970, vol. 7, no. 1, 44.
6 Charles de Foucauld, *Dictionnaire Touareg-Français* (Paris: Imprimerie Nationale de France, 1951), tome I, 134. "Mulâtre: né d'un père blanc et d'une mère négresse, ou d'une mère blanche et d'un père nègre."
7 See Camps, "Recherches sur les origines," 44.

of a second class."[8] It has also been suggested that it derived from the Arabic verb *haratha*, which signifies "to cultivate." This suggestion may have seemed plausible because the Haratin were known to be cultivators in the south of Morocco, mainly in the Draa region, thus lending credence to this inaccurate etymological argument.[9] Incidentally, this fact alone rebuts the commonly held opinion that the nature of slavery in Morocco was mainly domestic in nature. The famous Moroccan historian an-Nasiri (1835–1893) accepted the first meaning. He argued that the word *Hartani* meant in the common Moroccan language "freed," in opposition to a person of a free origin, hence connoting a legal status. Through a long usage of the two words *hurr* and *thani* together, they were transformed into *Hartani*.[10] There is also a commonly used term, *asuqi* (black), especially widely used among the Berbers in the Sus valley region in southern Morocco. Berbers generally used three terms to designate black people: *asuqi, ismakh* or *ismag*, and *aharadani* (Hartani).[11] Each term was associated with regional Berber dialects in the Moroccan south,[12] but at times and currently they are used interchangeably (especially with the increase rural exodus to metropolises, such as Marrakesh and Casablanca, in recent decades). It is clear that by the seventeenth century there was a differentiation between *Hartani* (a black person or a free black) and *asuqi* or *ismakh* (a black slave).[13]

According to scholar Gabriel Camps (1927–2002), the founder of the *Berber Encyclopedia* (*Encyclopédie berbère*) in 1984,[14] the first inhabitants of the Moroccan Sahara were of a dark complexion but distinct from the so-called blacks of the Sahel or Savannah regions, albeit descendants of the same Neolithic Ethiopians,[15] which evinces the diversity among blacks in the region. The story of their displacement goes back to the Roman era. With the advance of the Romans into the Moroccan interior, the Jazula Berbers may have been forced to move toward the south

---

[8] Mezzine, *Le Tafilalt*, 193–194, footnote 34.

[9] See Hart, "The Tribe in Modern Morocco," 27.

[10] An-Nasiri, *al-Istiqsa'*, vol. 7, 58.

[11] Ad-Du'ayyif (d. 1818) noted that *Ismgan* means Haratin in the tongue of the Berber people of Sus. Ad-Du'ayyif, *Tarikh ad-Du'ayyif*, 89.

[12] See René Basset, "Les noms des métaux et des couleurs en Berbère" in *Mémoires de la Société de linguistique de Paris* (Paris: Impr. Nationale, 1895), tome 9, 87.

[13] On *Ismkhan* see Cynthia Becker, "'I am a real slave, a real Ismkhan': Memories of the trans-Saharan slave trade in the Tafilalet of southeastern Morocco," *The Journal of North African Studies*, 2003 (4): 97–121.

[14] An encyclopedia, in the French language, dealing with Berber or Amazigh culture in North Africa.

[15] Camps, "Recherches sur les origines," 44–45.

and compete with the blacks in the oases of the Draa. Using the camel and other advantageous weapons, the Berbers most likely conquered the native populations of the Sahara and assumed for themselves a superior status, placing the natives in lesser, subordinate status. Trans-Saharan trade developed essentially with the spread of the camel in the Sahara. It is largely accepted that camels were introduced into North Africa (and by extension to the western Sahara) by the Romans during the first century.[16] As Stéphane Gsell suggests in *Histoire ancienne de l'Afrique du Nord*: "Thus these fugitive Berbers became conquerors."[17] They may have entered into an interdependent or clientele relationship with the Haratin, the Berbers assuming the patron's role. This claim is also congruent with the local oral traditions of the Tata area in southern Morocco: that the Haratin were in the region as natives and had been free. Mohammed Ennaji made a similar observation when he reported that "[the Haratin] claim precedence as the valley's first inhabitants and say that the whites, originally nomads, came later to abuse their hospitality and treat them as slaves."[18] That is to say that they were in this region long before the arrival of the Berbers and later the Arabs, who were the real outsiders, consequently the Arabs further altered the social and political structure of the southern oases.[19] They added the *sharif* status (descent from the Prophet Muhammad), another layer, to the racial prejudice and the economic privilege in the social hierarchy, hence increasing the otherness of the Haratin.[20] Indeed, like the Berbers, the Arabs ridiculously supposed themselves superior and came to own most of the land in the Moroccan oases and, in the words of Moroccan historian Larbi Mezzine, forced the

---

[16] See Richard W. Bulliet, *The Camel and the Wheel* (New York: Columbia University Press, 1990), 111–140.

[17] Stéphane Gsell, *Histoire ancienne de l'Afrique du Nord*, 2ème édition (Paris: Librairie Hachette, 1929), tome V, 3.

[18] Mohammed Ennaji, *Serving the Master: Slavery and Society in Nineteenth-Century Morocco* (New York: St. Martin's Press, 1999), 62.

[19] For more information on this subject, see Hsain Ilahiane, *The Power of the Dagger, the Seeds of the Koran, and the Sweat of the Ploughman: Ethnic Stratification and Agricultural Intensification in the Ziz Valley, Southeast Morocco*, PhD dissertation (Tucson, Arizona: University of Arizona, 1998); Georges Colin, "Hartani," in *The Encyclopedia of Islam*; Camps, "Recherches sur les origines," 35–45 and D. Jacques-Meunié, "Notes sur l'histoire," 137–150. In June 1998, I met a historian from Tata, an oasis region in the Moroccan Sahara south of anti-Atlas between the western Bani and Oued Draa, who told me: "I am a Hartani and I live in the area of Tata and all my villagers are completely black and the Haratin were not imported from Black West Africa but they were always native of this great region of Draa." This is an expression of self-perception and a self-affirmation of the black community of this village.

[20] For more information on this subject see Ensel, *Saints and Servants*.

Haratin to work for them in a system similar to social systemic strata found in Western serfdom.[21] They all lived in a separate walled rural community called *qsar* (pl. *qsur*) in a quasi-caste system.[22]

These different interpretations concerning the term *Haratin* are important because they indicate the difficulties in defining the identity of obviously diverse blacks in Morocco.[23] They also reflect the perception of blacks in the Arabized Moroccan society that stigmatized the slave status associated with all Moroccan blacks, hence the construct of a racial category. In addition to the lack of good sources documenting the history of the indigenous Haratin and all the black people in Morocco, blackness was homogenized, obscuring the origin of the Haratin and undermining the diverse origins and historical migration of black Africans.

The Arab Conquest and Black Africans

At the time of the birth of Islam, North Africa was under the Byzantine yoke but the Romanization and the adherence to Christianity was mainly felt in the coastal Mediterranean, except Egypt and Ethiopia. The third caliph in Medina, 'Uthman b. 'Affan (644–656), approved the first attack against Ifriqiya (Tunisia) in 647. The Muslim armies defeated the Byzantines at the battle of Subaytila. The first means by which slaves were acquired in North Africa at the beginning of Islamic conquest in the seventh century was through the conquest itself, or *as-saby*.[24] Muhammad Ibn 'Idhari, a Moroccan historian who lived in the second half of the thirteenth century and who wrote one of the most important sources of the history of North Africa from the Arab conquest to the Almohad dynasty, described the process of *as-saby* – that is, the acquisition of slaves from the vanquished people made captives.[25] *As-Saby* was a state affair. After the conquest of Egypt in 641, the Arabs launched incursions against Nubia, the land and people south of Egypt, which ended with 'Abd Allah b. Sa'd b. Abi Sarh, governor of Egypt (d. 656–658), signing a treaty with Nubia in 652. By

[21] Mezzine, *Le Tafilalt*, 269.
[22] See Ilahiane, *The Power of the Dagger*, 121–127 and Ross Dunn, "The trade of Tafilalt: Commercial Change in Southeast Morocco on the Eve of the Protectorate," *African Historical Studies* 4, (2) 1971: 271–304.
[23] Mezzine, *Le Tafilalt*, 193, 198 and 210, footnote 10.
[24] Muhammad Ibn Manzur, *Lisan al-'Arab* (Cairo: Dar al-Hadith, 2003), vol. 4, 487; Lane, *An Arabic-English Lexicon*, vol. 4, 1303.
[25] Muhammad Ibn 'Idhari al-Marrakushi, *Kitab al-Bayan al-Mughrib fi Akhbar al-Andalus wa 'l-Maghrib*, Georges Séraphin Colin and Evariste Lévi-Provençal, eds. (Beirut: Dar ath-Thaqafa, 1967), vol. 1, 9.

this treaty the Nubians were to deliver annually 360 slaves to the Arabs, a custom that lasted until the advent of the Mamluk in the thirteenth century.[26] Indeed, this can be seen in an official letter from the governor of Egypt, Musa b. Ka'b, sent to the king of Nubia in 758, complaining that the Nubians failed to honor the treaty, among other infringements, by sending unhealthy slaves. The letter said on this issue: "you are liable to the baqt [pact] of [several] years, which you have not fulfilled; as for that which you have sent in accordance with the baqt, you have sent that in which there is no good – the one-eyed, or the lame, or the weak old man, or the young boy."[27] This letter is a confirmation of the continuity of the treaty. It is not known how many of these slaves ended up in the army but as early as the ninth century Egyptian ruler Ahmad b. Tulun (d. 884) had forty-five thousand blacks in his army.[28]

'Uqba b. Nafi', who pursued the invasion of the entire Maghreb and purportedly founded a military camp called Qayrawan in 670, imposed a similar levy of 360 slaves when he conquered the region of Fezzan in 667 (located on a crucial route from sub-Saharan Africa to the Mediterranean).[29] At this time, Arabic sources point to a famous Berber leader named Kusayla. This powerful leader of Awraba, an alliance of Berber tribes in the area of what is Algeria today, converted to Islam under the conciliatory new governor, Abu 'l-Muhajir (r. 674 to 681). But 'Uqba, the hardliner, was reappointed as governor of the Maghreb upon the death of Mu'awiyya, the founder of the Umayyad dynasty in Damascus. He was belligerent and determined to subdue the Berbers and humiliate their leaders. Indeed he treated Kusayla as a captive even though he converted to Islam. Arabic sources mention an anecdote when 'Uqba sought to humiliate him: he asked him to skin a sheep for him but Kusayla pushed it to his slaves to do it.[30] Here, the Arabic sources point also to the practice of slavery among Berbers. In this conflict, Kusayla found a way to side with the Byzantines and kill 'Uqba and his army in 683.

[26] Taqiyy ad-Din al-Maqrizi, *al-Mawa'id wa 'l-'Itibar bi-Dhikr al-Khitat wa 'l-Athar* (Beirut: Dar Sadir, 1974), vol. 1, 200–202.
[27] See also J. Martin Plumley, "An Eighth-Century Arabic Letter to the King of Nubia," *The Journal of Egyptian Archaeology* 61 (1975): 242–244. See also al-Maqrizi, *Al-Mawa'id*, vol. 1, 200.
[28] Ar-Rashid Ibn az-Zubair, *Kitab adh-Dhakha'ir wa 't-Tuhaf*, edited by Muhammad Hamid Allah and Salah ad-Din al-Munajjid (Kuwait: Da'irat al-Matbu'at wa 'n-Nashr, 1959), 227.
[29] 'Abd ar-Rahman Ibn 'Abd al-Hakam (d. 871), *Futuh Ifriqiya wa 'l-Andalus* (Cairo: Maktabat ath-Thaqafa ad-Diniyya, 1995), 222.
[30] Ibn Khaldun, *Tarikh*, vol. 6, 172–173.

'Uqba's deputy, Zuhayr b. Qays, fled Qayrawan, most likely to seek Arab reinforcements, and Qayrawan came under the rule of Kusayla, who continued to practice Islam and did not harm the Arabs who remained there. Indeed, Zuhayr b. Qays came back with a huge army and reoccupied Tunisia in 689. Kusayla was killed in this battle, as was Zuhayr b. Qays. The next major raid was led by Hassan b. an-Nu'man in 695, with an army of forty thousand from Egypt. His campaigns were decisive in consolidating the Arab conquest in North Africa, especially after defeating al-Kahina or Dihya, the Berber "queen," who led strong resistance to the Arab invaders in northeastern Algeria in 697. But it was Musa b. Nusayr, governor of Tunisia in 705, who set out to subdue and to convert the last Berber tribes in order to bring the rest of North Africa under Arab rule. Musa b. Nusayr had more war captives than all his predecessors. Arabic sources mention that in the course of his raids his captives reached three hundred thousand.[31] Some of these captives had been recruited into the army, others taken as gifts to rulers in Egypt and Damascus, and others sold. The abundance of captives in the slave market affected the price of slaves in the region of Ifriqiya (Tunisia). Musa b. Nusayr himself, who played a momentous part in this human tragedy, witnessed the devaluation of human beings in the slave market to the point where a man, his wife, and his children were sold for a mere fifty dirhams.[32] Indeed, as Mohamed Talbi remarked: "Musa ibn Nusayr had dazzled his superiors in the Orient by his supply of slaves. Under his rod, it was the slaves who had carried out the huge works necessary for the construction of the arsenal in Tunis, modeled on the one in Tyre."[33]

There is evidence that some of the black Africans were recruited into the army and participated in the conquest of Iberia (what the Arabs called al-Andalus) led by Tariq b. Ziyad in 711 on behalf of Musa b. Nusayr. Tariq was himself a Berber with a status similar to his predecessor Kusayla: a *mawla* or a vassal to the governor of Ifriqiya, Musa b. Nusayr. North African scholar Ibn ash-Shabbat, who died in 1282 in Ifriqiya or Tunisia, reported that when Tariq invaded Cordova, its inhabitants sought refuge in its cathedral. This cathedral was like a fortress and had an underground passage. Tariq sent a black man to explore this

---

[31] Ibn 'Idhari, *Kitab al-Bayan*, vol. 2, 23.

[32] Ibid., 22.

[33] Mohamed Talbi, "Law and Economy in Ifriqiya (Tunisia) in the Third Islamic Century: Agriculture and the Role of Slaves in the Country's Economy" in *The Islamic Middle East, 700–1900: Studies in Economic and Social History*, edited by Abraham L. Udovitch (Princeton: Darwin Press, 1981), 214.

passage to the cathedral; he was discovered by the Spaniards, who were stunned by his appearance and wondered if his dark color was natural or dyed to the point that they rubbed his skin with a rope, only to realize that his color was surely natural.[34] According to Ibn ash-Shabbat, he was purportedly the first black person encountered by the local Spaniards.[35] At the end, this man succeeded in escaping and returning to the Islamic army that subsequently captured everyone in the cathedral.[36] The intention to acquire slaves, especially female slaves, was part of the conquest, and this was made clear in Tariq b. Ziyad's speech to his soldiers upon their arrival in Spain. *As-Saby* was one of the motivating goals to incite these soldiers to fight in the name of Islam. Historian Ahmad al-Maqqari (d. 1632) reported that Tariq declared:

You have heard that in this country there are a large number of ravishingly beautiful Greek maidens, their graceful forms are draped in sumptuous gowns on which gleam pearls, coral, and purest gold, and they live in the palaces of royal kings [...]. The one fruit which he [ruler al-Walid ibn 'Abd al-Malik] desires to obtain from your bravery is that the word of God shall be exalted in this country, and that the true religion shall be established here. The spoils will belong to yourselves.[37]

As the conquest continued in the south of Morocco, according to historian ar-Raqiq al-Qayrawani, Habib b. Abi 'Ubayda b. 'Uqba b. Nafi' raided the Sus area and reached the land of the blacks, reportedly having collected so much gold and so many slaves that he caused great dismay among the natives. Al-Qayrawani emphasized the gender preference among the captives by saying that the Arab general acquired beautiful women from the Berber tribes of Masufa; he even mentioned some sexual fantasies that among the captives were two female slaves who

[34] It is interesting to note that this was exactly what happened when the Gambians first met the Portuguese. Alvise Ca da Mosto wrote: "These negroes, men and women crowded to see me as though I were a marvel [...]. Some touched my hands and limbs, and rubbed me with their spittle to discover whether my whiteness was dye or flesh." Ca da Mosto, *The Voyages*, 49.

[35] But it does not mean that the Iberians did not know about black Africans. They must have been familiar with black people in antiquity during Roman and Carthaginian times.

[36] 'Abd al-Malik b. al-Kardabus and Muhammad b. 'Ali Ibn al-Shabbat, *Tarikh al-Andalus li-Ibn al-Kardabus wa-wasfuhu li-Ibn ash-Shabbat*, annotated by Ahmad Mukhtar al-'Abbadi (Madrid: Instituto de Estudios Islámicos, 1971), 144.

[37] Ahmad ibn Muhammad at-Tilmisani al-Maqqari, *Nafh at-Tib min Ghusn al-Andalus ar-Ratib*, edited by Ihsan 'Abbas (Beirut: Dar Sadir, 1988), vol. 1, 241. The translation is of Charles F Horne, *The Sacred Books and Early Literature of the East: With Historical Surveys of the Chief Writings of Each Nation* (New York: Parke, Austin, and Lipscomb, 1917), vol. 6, 242.

had only one breast.[38] Conversion to Islam did not prevent the Arab rulers from *as-saby* and treating the Berbers as vassals. Historians such as ar-Raqiq al-Qayrawani reported that the governor of the western Maghreb (Morocco), 'Umar b. 'Abd Allah al-Muradi, wanted to subject the Berbers to a tax of one-fifth of their possessions despite their conversion to Islam, which resulted in the Berbers revolting and assassinating him around 739.[39] Indeed, Ibn Khaldun reported that the Berbers went through many revolts protesting the Arab conquests. In one report, he said that they revolted twelve times and that eventually Islam became established among them only during the governorship of Musa b. Nusayr.[40] However, many Berbers adhered to the religio-political sect known as al-Kharijiyya because its teaching was puritanical in its ethical principles and egalitarian in its political appeal. Through this movement the Berber Kharijites expressed their resistance against the political domination of the Arabs and their abuse of power. They succeeded in establishing their own rule under the Rustamids (778–909), following a form of a Khariji doctrine known as Ibadism in Tahert (modern Algeria). Ironically, the Ibadi Berbers increasingly participated in the trans-Saharan slave trade, yet another new avenue for bringing the enslaved people from West Africa to the western and the eastern markets of the Islamic world.[41]

Throughout the Islamic conquests during the Umayyad and the Abbasid dynasties, slaves arrived in great numbers at the slave markets in the growing cities of the Middle East, to the point that a physician of Baghdad named Ibn Butlan (d. 1066) wrote a manual on how to buy slaves and how to detect any physical flaws, providing evidence about the perception, treatment, and roles of an enslaved person of both sexes in Islamic societies. The manual was not specific to the people of Iraq but was intended for all Arabic or Arabized Islamic societies. These societies relied a great deal on slave labor from the field to the house. In Islamic societies many families had slaves. Even some poor families could purchase at least one slave. Ibn Butlan, an expert in medicine and physiognomy, felt compelled to provide a written set of recommendations for any potential buyers of slaves to warn them against the business schemes and scams of the slave merchant (*jallab* or *nakhkhas* in Arabic) and to

[38] Ibrahim b. al-Qasim ar-Raqiq, *Tarikh Ifriqiya wa-'l-Maghrib* (Beirut: Dar al-Gharb al-Islami, 1990), 72.
[39] Ibid., 73. See also Ibn Khaldun, *Tarikh*, vol. 6, 140.
[40] Ibn Khaldun, *Tarikh*, vol. 6, 129.
[41] See E. Savage, "Berbers and Blacks: Ibadi Slave Traffic in Eighth-Century North Africa," *The Journal of African History* 33, no. 3 (1992): 351–368.

reveal the full potential of the enslaved persons according to their ethnic origins.[42]

The hostilities on the frontiers of the Islamic lands produced captives who ended up in slavery. These captives were of different ethnicity and complexion, but my study focuses on the blacks.[43] Beginning in the seventh and eighth centuries, many Muslims coming from North Africa became involved in the Saharan trade, similar to the Ibadites who moved to the Sahara and settled in caravan centers like Ghadames and Awdaghust. North African Muslims who traded or settled in the western Sahara established a cultural, a human, and an economic link between North and West Africa. From the beginning, the Arabs at the time of the Islamic conquest of North Africa were aware of the gold of West Africa, resulting in many expeditions to attack Ghana. These early attempts to establish Arab control over the southern terminus of trans-Saharan trade were, however, unsuccessful. Arabo-Berber Muslims established trade routes with the powerful kingdom of Ghana and drew great benefits from them. Commercial centers or entrepôts were founded on Saharan routes like Sijilmasa, Awdaghust, and others.[44] The main commodities that marked the Saharan trade were salt, horses, textile, gold, and slaves.

The spread of Islam in sub-Saharan West Africa was mainly a result of trade, rather than conquest, though there were several attempts by the Arabo-Berber Islamic forces to conquer the region, what the Arabs called *as-Sudan*, aiming at its gold; these attacks were all unsuccessful except for the Sa'di invasion in the late sixteenth century. During the tenth century, many Sanhaja leaders attempted to unify the nomads of the western Sahara for the purpose of ensuring better control over the trans-Saharan trade routes and of building a strong army to conquer the Sudan, but no single confederation was able to retain supremacy in the desert. As Nehemia Levtzion stated: "Even in the Western Sahara, where important trans-Saharan trade routes created conditions conducive to the development of more centralized forms of political organization, authority over

---

[42] Sanagustin, *Un Aide-mémoire.*

[43] The primary sources for this period, which are virtually all in Arabic, ignored the social conditions and the concerns of the enslaved people. Although these sources provide only scattered information on slaves and the practice of slavery, it is nonetheless possible to glean from them some notations in order to reconstruct the opaque history of the blacks in Morocco. The sources talk about the acquisition of slaves from among the vanquished people that have been made captives or by purchases. They usually talk about female slaves and issues related to domestic servitude, concubinage, or male slaves in the army.

[44] For more information, see Raymond Mauny, *Tableau géographique de l'Ouest africain au Moyen Age: d'après les sources écrites, la tradition et l'archéologie* (Amsterdam: Swets & Zeitlinger N.V., 1967), 367–380.

the Sanhaja was loose and went through periodical crises."[45] Until the third quarter of the tenth century, the Sanhaja confederacy controlled the very important salt mines at Awlil and held the monopoly of the salt trade going through Awdaghust to Ghana. The city of Awdaghust was a flourishing commercial center inhabited by Sanhaja, Zanata, Arab traders from North Africa, and black West Africans. Historian al-Bakri (d. 1094) reported: "They owned great riches and slaves so numerous that one person from among them might possess a thousand servants or more."[46] He provided some details on the practice of slavery in Awdaghust mostly concerning female slavery. He said that there were "Sudan [black] women, good cooks, one being sold for 100 mithqals or more."[47] Al-Bakri also mentioned white female slaves desired for their beauty and sexuality; he described them as: "pretty slave girls with white complexions, good figures, firm breasts, slim waists, fat buttocks, wide shoulders, and sexual organs so narrow that one of them may be enjoyed as though she were virgin indefinitely."[48] On the basis of their physiognomy, the author illustrated which ones were suited for which role in society. The origins and ethnicity of these women were not mentioned, but they might have been either Berber or of mixed origin. Intermixing with black women was not uncommon in the highly polygynous society of the Saharan Sanhaja. Ibn Hawqal (died after 988), the Arab geographer and chronicler who visited Sijilmasa and probably Awdaghust too, the earliest to arrive near the frontiers of the Sudan, explained in his geographical work, *Surat al-Ard* (*The Picture of the Earth*), that the different complexions resulted from the intermixing between light-skinned Berbers and blacks. He even provided a list of these tribes called Banu Tanamak (also known as Tuareg) from Tadmakka, north of Gao, who were partly black from their mother line.[49] Within the Saharan region, Ibn Abi Zar' (d. circa 1315 in Fez) observed that although the Sanhaja were Muslims they practiced unlimited polygyny; there were "men who had married six, seven or ten wives, or whatever number they desired."[50] Andalusian scholar Ahmad ash-Sharisi (d. 1222) left an account based on information from merchants who traveled to Ghana in which he said that many merchants from the Maghreb who came to Ghana bought slaves for concubinage. He wrote: "God had endowed the slave girls there with laudable characteristics, both physical

[45] Nehemia Levtzion, *Ancient Ghana and Mali* (London: Methuen & Co Ltd, 1973), 8–9.
[46] Al-Bakri in Hopkins and Levtzion, eds., *Corpus*, 74.
[47] Ibid., 68.
[48] Ibid.
[49] Al-Nusaybi in Hopkins and Levtzion, eds., *Corpus*, 50.
[50] Ibn Abi Zar' in Hopkins and Levtzion, eds., *Corpus*, 239.

and moral, more than can be desired: their bodies are smooth, their black skins are lustrous, their eyes are beautiful, their noses well shaped, their teeth white, and they smell fragrant."[51] One of the first Sanhaja leaders of the Almoravid dynasty, Abu Bakr b. 'Umar, had a black wife. Ibn 'Idhari did not mention the name of this woman but he said that her son Ibrahim had black skin.[52] Abu Bakr b. 'Umar became the second leader of the Almoravid movement after his brother Yahya b. 'Umar was killed in 1056. Both leaders were faithful disciples of the spiritual leader and founder of the Almoravid movement, 'Abd Allah b. Yasin. It was Yahya b. Ibrahim, who on his return trip around 1035 from the pilgrimage to Mecca, sought out 'Abd Allah b. Yasin al-Jazuli (from the Sus area in the south of Morocco). Ibn Yasin accepted Yahya b. Ibrahim's invitation to travel with him to promote conformist Maliki Islamic beliefs and practices among the Sanhaja people. However, Ibn Yasin reportedly faced many difficulties in his initial attempts to implement the basic teachings of Islam within the Sanhaja community. He even thought of giving up his mission, and according to historian Ibn Abi Zar', "He wished to leave them and go to the land of the Sudan who had adopted Islam."[53] According to this text Islam had made its appearance in the Sudan before the rise of the Almoravid movement, even before the complete conversion of the people of the western Sahara to Islam. Al-Bakri emphasized that the people of the kingdom of Takrur (along the lower Senegal River valley) were Muslims under the rule of the king Warjabi b. Rabis, who died in the year 1040–1041.[54] Ibn Yasin decided to lead a small group of followers into a remote area of the desert where he could effectively promote his teachings. As his discipleship grew to some one thousand in number, he dubbed his disciples Murabitun (or the Almoravids as they came to be known through a Spanish mispronunciation), in agreement with the strict Maliki doctrine of his religious center in the area of Sijilmasa called "Dar al-Murabitin." Ibn Yasin was soon leading his followers on a holy war in the western Sahara, aspiring to form an Islamic community ruled by the practices of Islamic law. Under the Ibn Yasin's leadership, the Sanhaja people ultimately succeeded in forging a political community. While the teaching of Islam can be seen as the organizational base of the

---

[51] Al-Sharisi in Hopkins and Levtzion, eds., *Corpus*, 153.

[52] Ibn 'Idhari, *Kitab al-Bayan*, vol. 4, 17.

[53] Ibn Abi Zar' in Hopkins and Levtzion, eds., *Corpus*, 239. In the kingdom of Takrur (north of what is Senegal today), King Warjabi b. Rabis, who died in the year 1040–1041, was Muslim.

[54] Al-Bakri in Hopkins and Levtzion, eds., *Corpus*, 77.

Almoravid state, it was Islamic militarism that succeeded in extending the Almoravid community throughout the Sahara in the eleventh century. As the Almoravids established control over the desert, they also gained control over trans-Saharan networks of trade. Control of trade routes further bolstered the Almoravid treasury, which in turn allowed for continued support of troops and weapons and the further extension of the Islamic community through jihad. After unifying the people of the Sahara, the Almoravids wanted to expand their political interest beyond the desert, so they waged war against their neighbors in the north (Morocco) and the south in the Sudan (black West Africa).

The Almoravid movement ensured the definitive Islamization of Saharan Berbers and greatly affected the southern Sahel region in the propagation of Islam among the black people beyond Takrur, not only by sporadic militant activities but more importantly by contact, trade, teaching, and intermarriage. It also marked the shift of power of the Sahel region from the Ghana rulers to the Muslim Berber rulers. Awdaghust was at this time still nominally subject to the ruler of Ghana, but in 1054–1055 Ibn Yasin launched a violent attack supposedly as a punishment against its inhabitants' alliance with the ruler of Ghana. Al-Bakri reported that: "The Almoravids violated its women (*harimaha*) and declared everything that they took there to be the booty of the community."[55] In 1058, Ibn Yasin was killed in a battle in the south of Morocco, which happened after he had conquered the whole Sus region (southern Morocco). Abu Bakr continued the conquest of Morocco but he received news of discord that had broken out between Lamtuna and Masufa in the desert. He departed for the desert, leaving his cousin Yusuf b. Tashfin governor over Morocco. Ibn Tashfin continued his successful conquest of Morocco until Tlemcen and the region of Algiers (in Algeria today).

The Almoravids were the first ruling dynasty in Morocco to use a large number of black slaves in the army during the Islamic era, in the eleventh century. Many succeeding dynasties would also rely on black soldiers to maintain their power. Archival sources indicate the use of blacks in the armies of the Moroccan authority, and in many cases, entire garrisons consisted solely of black soldiers. During the Almoravid period, ruler Yusuf Ibn Tashfin purchased many black slaves in order to increase his personal power. Ibn 'Idhari wrote:

In this year [1071–1072] the might of the emir Yusuf increased. He bought a body of black slaves and sent [them] to al-Andalus, where there was bought for

---

[55] Ibid., 74.

him a body of *a'laj* [white slaves]. He gave them all mounts and finally he had a total, paid for with his own money, of 240 cavaliers. Of the slaves, also bought with his own money, he had about 2,000 and mounted them all. He made himself more difficult of access and his authority waxed mighty.[56]

It could be that Yusuf Ibn Tashfin's preference for black slaves was based on their non-tribal affiliation, which meant their loyalty could be most trusted. The black bodyguards became a tradition in the Moroccan regime and formed an elite corps whose task was to protect and enforce the power of the sultan. At this time, Spain was divided into about twenty statelets, known as *Muluk at-Tawa'if* ("party kings," and in Spanish *Reyes de taifas*). These statelets were unable to resist the northern Christian states, especially after the Castilians conquered Toledo in 1085. Fearing the danger of the total absorption of all the Muslim states, the 'Abbasid ruler of Seville, al-Mu'tamid, invited the Almoravids to rescue them. The Almoravid army under Ibn Tashfin crossed the Straits of Gibraltar in 1086. With additional troops provided through the slave trade, the Almoravids defeated Alfonso VI of Castile in 1086 at the crucial battle of Zallaqa (near Badajoz). Arabic sources indicate that four thousand black soldiers participated in this famous battle. They were armed with shields, swords, and spears; one of them purportedly stabbed Alfonso VI with a dagger in the thigh during the battle.[57] By 1094, the whole of Muslim Spain was annexed to the Almoravid empire. The Almoravid dynasty ruled over all of Morocco, Muslim Spain, and the eastern part of Algeria until 1147 when it was overthrown by the Almohads, another ethnic Berber group. The Masmuda of the Atlas Mountains expressed their resentment against the centralized Almoravid authority of Morocco and challenged the regime during the 1120s by rallying around Ibn Tumart, a spiritual scholar from the Masmuda tribe. Ibn Tumart preached a new doctrine based on the principles of the unity of God, or *tawhid*. His followers, referred to as the *al-muwahhidun*, literally the Unitarians, came to be known as the Almohads through a Spanish mispronunciation. With reforming zeal and puritanical teaching, the movement filled the vacuum left by the declining Almoravid empire. So zealous and aggressive was Ibn Tumart in his teachings that he once assaulted the sister of the Almoravid ruler 'Ali b. Yusuf (d. 1143) in Marrakesh for not wearing the veil in public,[58] and as a consequence he was banished from the city. Ibn Tumart

[56] The fourteenth-century historian of North Africa, Ibn 'Idhari, in Hopkins and Levtzion, eds., *Corpus*, 229 or Ibn 'Idhari, *Kitab al-Bayan*, vol. 4, 23.

[57] An-Nasiri, *al-Istiqsa'*, vol. 2, 47.

[58] Muhammad Ibn Tumart and Ignace Goldziher, *Le Livre de Mohammed Ibn Toumert, Mahdi des Almohades*, texte Arabe accompagné de notices biographiques et d'une

combined ideas from Sunni legal schools as well as Sufi orders in a doctrine written between 1121 and 1124 in which he focused on faith, worship, social behavior, and human relations. In declaring himself a *mahdi* (e.g., a divinely guided one) Ibn Tumart combined Sunni preaching, messianic vision, and, later, militancy to mobilize Muslims to revolt against the laxity of the Almoravid rulers. He preached rigorously to reform his society and direct its people down what he saw as the Islamic straight path. His doctrine consisted of a crucial Islamic principle: to command good and to forbid evil. This was a political message directed to ordinary people as well as to the ruling class. Ibn Tumart chose Tinmel in the Atlas Mountains as his headquarters for his campaign against the Almoravid rule. He organized his followers into quasi-military ranks consisting primarily of two councils, one of ten and the other of fifty. The council of ten represented his closest companions including 'Abd al-Mu'min and Abu Hafs 'Umar. Leaders and representatives from the different tribes and towns comprised the council of fifty. The first Almohad attack against the Almoravids was organized and staged in 1129 in Marrakech. It ended in defeat. Shortly afterward, in 1130, Ibn Tumart died, but he left behind a strong movement. The Almohads chose 'Abd al-Mu'min, originally of Algeria, as successor, or *khalifa*, to Ibn Tumart. He became known as the commander of the faithful (*Amir al-Mu'minin*). Historians such as Ibn 'Idhari reported that one of the decisive battles that the Almohads launched under the leadership of 'Abd al-Mu'min against the Almoravids was in Aghmat (a Berber town in southern Morocco, east of Marrakesh) in 1130, in which they killed three thousand people, most of them black.[59] Hasan ibn al-Qattan, another Moroccan historian, who lived around the middle of the thirteenth century, reported that in this battle three thousand blacks from Jnawa (also spelled Gnawa) were killed.[60] According to az-Zuhri (who lived in the 1140s), Jnawa designated the land of the blacks whose capital was Ghana. He placed the territory of Jnawa, which represented the southern terminus of Moroccan caravans, at the end of the land of the Sanhaja (Berber people).[61] These historical references provide no further details, but those blacks killed in the battle were presumably

traduction par Ignace Goldziher (Alger: Gouvernement Général de l'Algérie, 1903), iv–v.

[59] Ibn 'Idhari, *Kitab al-Bayan*, vol. 4, 84.

[60] Hasan ibn al-Qattan, *Nuzum al-Juman li-Tartib ma Salafa min Akhbar az-Zaman*, annotated by Mahmud 'Ali Makki (Beirut, Dar al-Gharb al-Islami, 1990), 158.

[61] Muhammad Az-Zuhri in Hopkins and Levtzion, eds., *Corpus*, 98. See also the Arabic version: Muhammad Zuhri, *Kitab al-Jughrafiyya*, edited by Muhammad Hajj Sadiq (Dimashq: al-Ma'had al-Faransi bi-Dimashq, 1968), 182.

soldiers in the service of the Almoravids. At the same time blacks were in
the Almohad army in considerable number. In fact it appears, as it was
reported by twelfth-century historian Abu Bakr al-Baydhaq, who wrote
a book on the beginnings of the Almohad dynasty, that Ibn Tumart was
probably the first to officially label the black slaves captured during the
raid on Tazagurt (or Zagora, a town in the south of Morocco) "*'Abid
al-Makhzan,*" meaning servants to the government.[62] *'Abid al-Makhzan*
participated in the attack on Marrakesh led by ruler 'Abd al-Mu'min,
who put an end to Almoravid rule in 1147.[63] 'Abd al-Mu'min extended
his power over the whole of the Maghreb in 1149. He died in 1163 as he
was preparing for war in Spain. In 1172, under the rule of his son, Yusuf
abu Ya'qub, Muslim Spain came under Almohad control. It was during
Ya'qub's rule that the Almohad empire reached its height. It is important
to note that Ya'qub was a son of a concubine (*umm al-walad*) given as
a gift to his father; this was a common practice in Morocco. The empire
was strengthened by Ya'qub's defeat of the Castilians in the famous battle of Alarcos in 1195,[64] in which blacks also participated. The Almohads
seemed to have had blacks in the army throughout their rule,[65] including
blacks who served as special guards responsible for the physical safety of
the Almohad rulers.[66] By the time Muhammad an-Nasir came to power
in 1198, he had a special body of thirty thousand blacks armed with jav-
elins or spears in his huge army.[67]

The Almohads were the most extensive empire achieved by Morocco
in the twelfth century. The Almohad empire enjoyed great prosperity,
manifested in its economic, architectural, intellectual, and artistic achievements. Monuments such as the mosque of the Kutubia in Marrakesh,
near the spectacular plaza called Jamaa el-Fna, which can still be visited
today, bear witness to such achievements by the Almohads. The Almohad
empire lasted for about a century until conquered by the Marinids,
another ethnic Berber group of the Zanata, in 1269. The Marinids also
used blacks in their army.[68]

[62] Abu Bakr b. 'Ali as-Sinhaji al-Baydhaq, *Akhbar al-Mahdi Ibn Tumart wa-Bidayat Dawlat
      al-Muwahhidin,* edited by 'Abd al-Wahhab b. Mansur (Rabat: al-Mataba'a al-Malakiyya,
      2004), 38.
[63] Ibid., 64.
[64] 'Ali Ibn Abi Zar' al-Fasi, *al-Anis al-Mutrib bi-Rawd al-Qirtas fi Akhbar Muluk al-Maghrib
      wa-Tarikh Madinat Fas* (Rabat: al-Matba'a al-Malakiyya, 1999), 283–303.
[65] Ibid., 273–316.
[66] Ibid., 280–282.
[67] Ibid., 316.
[68] 'Ali Ibn Abi Zar', *adh-Dhakhirah as-Saniyya fi Tarikh ad-Dawla al-Mariniyya* (Rabat:
      Dar al-Mansur li 't-Tiba'a wa 'l-Waraqa, 1972), 88.

During the rule of the Marinid dynasty, a gradual shift took place in the dynamics of the Moroccan commercial diaspora as the geopolitics of the frontiers of Islam were changing in Andalusia on behalf of the Christians and in the Sudan on behalf of the Muslims. This change affected the sources of slavery. Slaves coming from Europe would gradually diminish and slaves coming from sub-Saharan Africa would increase. This happened especially after the Muslims were severely defeated at the Battle of Rio Salado by a Portuguese–Castilian coalition in 1340. The Marinids, like their predecessors, understood that to ensure their power they had to dominate the Saharan trade or conquer the south in order to control the trans-Saharan trade, a vital income to the state. Mali succeeded Ghana at the southern termini of the trans-Saharan caravan trade routes. Unlike Ghana, Mali was located in a more advantageous position. It was situated in the Savanna belt close to the gold-producing regions of Bure and Bambuk. Whereas Ghana could not rightly be considered an Islamic society, Islam was an important factor that contributed to the rise of the Mali empire.[69] Under the rule of Sundiata (1235–1255), Mali emerged as a strong kingdom composed of many Malinke chiefdoms. Sundiata, who was from the Keita clan, acquired the title "Mansa." The Keita claimed descent from Bilali Bounama, called in classical Arabic Bilal ibn Hamama or Bilal ibn Rabah (died in Damascus circa 641), the black companion of the Prophet and the first muezzin in the history of Islam. Bilal is a famous historical figure in Islam. Al-Jahiz (776–869), an illustrious Muslim thinker, reported that the second caliph, 'Umar (d. 644), once said that Bilal was one-third of Islam.[70] The Mali oral traditions related by its griots claim that Bilal "had seven sons of whom the eldest, Lawalo, left the Holy City and came to settle in Mali."[71] Bilal was born into slavery and was originally from Ethiopia. He converted to Islam while still in captivity and he was tortured for that by his master, Umayya b. Khalaf. When Abu Bakr as-Siddiq (d. 634), a good friend of the Prophet Muhammad, heard about Bilal's heroism he bought him and liberated him in the name of Islam. Bilal became the personal assistant of the Prophet. Bilal's special relationship with the Prophet was a prestigious connection. The Keita used the Bilal factor to add another element to their identity in Islamic terms. With Sundiata, Islamic influence expanded in the Savanna, which made Mali a great partner in the Islamic world. Indeed, his nephew,

---

[69] Ibn Khaldun in Hopkins and Levtzion, eds., *Corpus*, 333–334.
[70] Al-Jahiz, *Rasa'il*, vol. 1, 179–180.
[71] D. T. Niane, *Sundiata: An Epic of Old Mali* (England: Longman, 1965), 2.

Mansa Musa,[72] who performed the pilgrimage to Mecca in 1324, would become a legendary king in the Islamic world. The rule of a Muslim king in Mali made the region more open to all Muslim merchants. Under Mansa Musa's rule, Walata, a crucial commercial and religious center in the western Sahara situated along the trans-Saharan trade route between Morocco and Mali, came under Mali's power. Walata exposed Mali to even greater Islamic diffusion. Ibn Khaldun wrote: "[The Malian] authority became mighty and all the peoples of the Sudan stood in awe of them. Merchants from the Maghreb and Ifriqiya traveled to their country."[73] Arab-speaking writers commented with great detail on Mansa's wealth and interest in Islamic learning. According to the Damascene Arab historian Ibn Fadl Allah al-'Umari (d. 1349):

[Mansa Musa] brought together [the land of the Sudan] by conquest and added [it] to the domains of Islam. There he built ordinary and cathedral mosques and minarets, and established the Friday observances, and prayers in congregation, and the muezzin's call. He brought jurists of the Malikite school to his country and there continued as sultan of the Muslims and became a student of religious sciences.[74]

Ibn Khaldun commented on the wealth of Mansa, illustrated in the amount of gold and number of slaves he owned. Just like in any other part of the Islamic world, slavery was part of the social norm in West Africa. Ibn Khaldun wrote:

He made the pilgrimage in 724/1324 [...]. At each halt he would regale us [his entourage] with rare foods and confectionery. His equipment and furnishings were carried by 12,000 private slave women (*wasa'if*) wearing gowns of brocade (*dibaj*) and Yemeni silk [...]. Mansa Musa came from his country with 80 loads of gold dust (*tibr*), each load weighing three *qintars*. In their own country they use only slave women and men for transport but for distant journeys such as the Pilgrimage they have mounts.[75]

Egyptian historian Taqiyy ad-Din al-Maqrizi (d. 1442) remarked that descriptions of the king of Mali's wealth gave more insight into the wide practice of slavery in the Islamic world across ethnic lines: He wrote:

It is said that he [Mansa Musa] brought with him 14,000 slave girls for his personal service. The members of his entourage proceeded to buy Turkish and

---

[72] Ibn Khaldun called him Mansa Uli and translated Uli as 'Ali. Historian J. Ki-Zerbo corrected Ibn Khaldun that in the Mande language Uli meant red complexioned. J. Ki-Zerbo, ed., *Methodology and African Prehistory. General History of Africa* (Berkeley: University of California Press, 1989), vol. 1, 6.

[73] Ibn Khaldun in Hopkins and Levtzion, eds., *Corpus*, 334.

[74] Al-'Umari in Hopkins and Levtzion, eds., *Corpus*, 261.

[75] Ibn Khaldun in Hopkins and Levtzion, eds., *Corpus*, 334–335.

Ethiopian slave girls, singing girls and garments, so that the rate of the gold dinar fell by six dirhams.[76]

The fame of this king reached Europe and was well illustrated in the 1375 Catalan map drawn by Abraham Cresques of Mallorca. The section on West Africa described Mansa Musa as the richest and most noble king in all the land. It showed him holding a nugget of gold and on his left a merchant apparently coming from Morocco.[77]

Indeed, Ibn Battuta, who visited the region in 1353, apparently commissioned by the sultan of Morocco, Abu 'Inan Faris (d. 1358), to do so, gave a vivid testimony to the security, justice, respect of travelers, and prosperity of Malian society. He described Mali as a rich partner in the Islamic world. His journey, which lasted for more than a year, took him, following the caravan trade route, from Fez to Gao and passed through many caravan market centers and towns such as Sijilmasa and Walata. He also commented on the diplomatic relations between Mali and Morocco. This important alliance is well illustrated in the memorial that Mansa Sulayman offered for the deceased sultan of Morocco, Abu 'l-Hasan.[78] At this time the caravan trade routes were very prosperous. The West Africans exported gold, ivory, ostrich features, hides, and slaves in exchange for North African products such as salt, horses, textiles, books, and paper. The income of the trade allowed the Malian rulers to increase their military power and acquire more horses for their cavalry, which in turn triggered more raids for slaves.[79] Historian al-'Umari (d. 1349) reported: "The king of this country [Mali] imports Arab horses and pays high prices for them. His army numbers about 100,000, of whom about 10,000 are cavalry mounted on horses and the remainder infantry without horses or other mounts."[80] The Malian king must have certainly been very rich to afford ten thousand horses. Ibn Battuta, who visited the area, did notice that the price of horses was expensive. He reported that a horse was worth 100 mithqals of gold.[81] Horses were also

---

[76] Al-Maqrizi in Hopkins and Levtzion, eds., Corpus, 351.

[77] See Edward W. Bovill, *The Golden Trade of the Moors* (Princeton: Markus Wiener Publishers, 1995).

[78] Ibn Battuta in Hopkins and Levtzion, eds., *Corpus*, 289.

[79] On the subject of raids and acquisition of slaves in West Africa see Georges Niamkey Kodjo, "Razzias et développement des Etats du Soudan Occidental," in *De la traite à l'esclavage: actes du Colloque international sur la traite des noirs*, edited by Serge Daget (Bibliothèque d'histoire d'outre-mer, 7–8. Nantes: Centre de recherche sur l'histoire du monde atlantique, 1988), vol. 1, 19–35.

[80] Al-'Umari in Hopkins and Levtzion, eds., *Corpus*, 266.

[81] Ibn Battuta in Hopkins and Levtzion, eds., *Corpus*, 297.

bartered for slaves. Leo Africanus, who visited West Africa around 1512, gives us more details on this trade and the value of horses in West Africa a century and half later. These primary sources confirm the trade pattern that had been normalized for Sahelian African rulers to exchange slaves for horses.[82] The account of Ibn Battuta, who visited the kingdom during the reign of Mansa Sulayman, confirms the main features of Malinke Islam in the fourteenth century.[83] However, Ibn Battuta rendered many negative judgments on Malian society that reflected rather the point of view of a Moroccan Arabo-Berber centrist. He disapproved of many acts of black people because of his prejudice and lack of understanding of local customs such as the roles of griots or *djeli* (bards). The griots were a caste that provided oral scholars who conserved the culture and the constitutions of their societies. They held an important and crucial status in society and developed a strong and sophisticated oral tradition of songs, stories, historical accounts, proverbs, and tales. For this reason renowned modern Malian scholar Amadou Ba stated, "with the death of each old man, a library is burnt."[84]

Except for the nudity of the enslaved women in Mali that Ibn Battuta objected to as a negative feature of Malian society, his description of slavery is in large part similar to that of descriptions of slavery in Morocco. He reported that in Mali slaves were of both sexes, young and adult. They performed all kind of tasks: they were guards, soldiers, messengers, domestic servants, and concubines; they worked in salt or copper mines, as merchants' assistants and porters. They could be sold, punished, and gifted. Before he reached Mali, Ibn Battuta noticed the hardship of the enslaved people in the Sahara and reported that, "[n]obody lives there [in Taghaza] except the slaves of the Masufa tribe [Sanhaja Berbers] who dig for the salt. They live on the dates imported to them from Dar'a and Sijilmasa, on camel-meat, and on *anili* [millet?] imported from the land of the Sudan."[85] The salt produced by the enslaved Africans was in great demand in West Africa. It was a necessary mineral for preserving and seasoning food. If one load of it was sold in Walata for ten mithqals, it was sold in Mali for more than double that and sometimes for forty mithqals. At times, its value was so high that it was used as a currency just

[82] For more information see the excellent study of Robin Law, *The Horse in West African History* (Oxford: Oxford University Press, 1980).

[83] See Ibn Battuta in Hopkins and Levtzion, eds., *Corpus*, 279–304.

[84] Quoted in John W. Johnson and Fa-Digi Sisòkò, *The Epic of Son-Jara* (Bloomington: Indiana University Press, 1992), 4.

[85] Ibn Battuta in Hopkins and Levtzion, eds., *Corpus*, 282.

like gold or silver.[86] The most fortunate slaves were those in the service of the court. Ibn Battuta reported that king Sulayman had about three hundred slaves and that they assembled whenever the king gave a public audience. He described them "carrying in their hands bows and others having in their hands short lances and shields."[87] This body of "slave" soldiers (or rather soldiers recruited from the enslaved people) is similar to the regiment of bodyguards of some of the aforementioned Moroccan rulers. A mutual trust was necessary and implicitly negotiated in order for them to bear arms and for the king to trust them with his own life. The famous incident of Wuld Kirinfil provides a well-illustrated example of what could happen when that trust was broken. Wuld Kirinfil was an enslaved person of the court of Askia Ishaq, and because he angered the king he was exiled in Taghaza. Wuld Kirinfil ran away and assisted the Moroccans in their famous conquest of Songhay.

Officers of the court also had slaves and this is usually mentioned in the written sources in connection to their harems. Ibn Battuta described, for instance, the harem of the interpreter Dugha (the king's spokesman and master of ceremony) during a Muslim holy day in the court. He wrote: "Dugha the interpreter comes with his four wives and his slave girls (*jawari*). There are about a hundred of these, with fine clothes and on their heads bands of gold and silver adorned with gold and silver balls."[88] Far from the king's court in a town in Mali, while visiting its governor, who offered Ibn Battuta a slave boy, he noticed that the governor had an Arab slave girl from Damascus who spoke Arabic to him.[89] It is important to note that acquiring white servants in this region was not that uncommon. Some rich West Africans on their return from pilgrimage to Mecca did purchase light-skinned slave girls, as documented in al-Maqrizi's text.[90] Ibn Battuta himself participated in slavery, as it was his custom to purchase a slave girl on his different long journeys. In Takadda, west of Mali, he wished to buy an educated slave girl and he did indeed find one for whom he paid a sum of twenty-five mithqals.[91] It is important to note that prices for enslaved persons throughout medieval times ranged from around 10 to 200 mithqals, and in some cases

---

[86] Ibid.

[87] Ibid., 290.

[88] Ibid., 292–293.

[89] Ibid., 300.

[90] Al-Maqrizi in Hopkins and Levtzion, eds., *Corpus*, 351.

[91] *Mithqal* is a standard of weight equal to about 4.72 gm, usually used for gold. See Hopkins and Levtzion, eds., *Corpus*, 481.

even more, depending on their skills, sex, and physiognomy. Ibn Battuta
probably wanted to use the female slave he purchased as a scribe and a
concubine at the same time. The fact that Ibn Battuta asked specifically
for an educated enslaved girl, even in a town far away from large urban
centers, implies that his was likely not an uncommon demand. The dramatic anecdote that Ibn Battuta recounted regarding the regret felt by the
person who sold him the girl reveals not only that young women with
such skills were expensive and highly sought after but also the emotional
attachment that the masters forged with their enslaved females and the
effect of the enslaved females on their masters. Ibn Battuta probably felt
sorry for the seller and agreed to return her but on the condition that a
replacement was found. Indeed, he found someone else who could sell
him his female slave, a Moroccan by the name of 'Ali Aghyul.[92] This latter slave merchant also repented the sale and almost died of grief lest Ibn
Battuta refused to cancel the sale, as the story was told.[93]

According to Ibn Battuta, the town of Takadda, ruled by Berbers, was
a crucial junction connecting two main trans-Saharan trade routes: one
to Morocco by way of Tuwat and the other to Egypt by way of Ghat. The
town also had a Moroccan community that facilitated the trade bidding
with its homeland. He wrote:

> The people of Takadda have no occupation but trade. They travel each year to
> Egypt and import some of everything which is there in the way of fine cloth (*thi-
> yab*) and other things. Its people are comfortable and well off and are proud of
> the number of male and female slaves (*al-'abid wa-'l-khadam*) which they have.
> The people of Mali and Iwalatan [Walata] also are like this. They sell educated
> slave girls but rarely, and at high price.[94]

Ibn Battuta provided other information that indicated the town had
actually other occupations beside trade – including a copper mine that
employed male and female slaves. The copper was smelted into bars
and traded in the region as far as Bornu (the area northeast of modern Nigeria and south of Chad), "from this country they [the people
of Takadda] bring handsome slave girls (*jawari*) and young men slaves
(*fityan*) and cloth dyed with saffron."[95] This is a clear testimony that
enslaved women were forced to do a variety of tasks just as enslaved men

---

[92] I am not sure if "Aghyul" was the man's real name, because *aghyul* means a donkey in the
    Amazigh language.
[93] Ibn Battuta in Hopkins and Levtzion, eds., *Corpus*, 302.
[94] Ibid., 301–302.
[95] Ibid., 302.

did, hence dispelling the stereotype that women were used for domestic work and sexual exploitation only. It is interesting to note, as indicated by Edmund Morgan, a scholar of American history, that enslaved women in America were forced to work in the field just like men. He wrote: "In an enslaved labor force women could be required to make tobacco just as the men did."[96] While in Takadda, Ibn Battuta received a message from the sultan of Morocco, Abu 'Inan Faris, summoning him back to Morocco; the sultan was probably eager to hear Ibn Battuta's report on Mali. The message came with a slave boy, apparently a messenger working for a Moroccan merchant from Sijilmasa. The mission of Ibn Battuta in West Africa was not disclosed, but the trans-Saharan trade was so beneficial and crucial to the Moroccan ruling dynasty that it might have compelled the sultan to send Ibn Battuta to investigate, or rather spy, on the sources of the gold in the area. Ibn Battuta returned to Morocco from Takadda in the company of a big caravan on September 11, 1353. He reported that there were 600 slave girls in the caravan of some rich Maghrebian merchants.[97] It is important to note that whenever slaves were mentioned in Ibn Battuta's account, the gender preference in the trans-Saharan slave trade was female. Ibn Battuta did not provide any other particular information regarding this trade, but it might have been a regular annual trans-Saharan trade. It could be that 600 was the average annual number of slaves per caravan and per route at the time of Ibn Battuta. The *caravaniers* usually spent at least two months traveling from Morocco to Timbuktu and the same on the return. They may also have stayed a month or two to rest, get provisions, and manage their commercial transactions.

In Morocco, Abu 'Inan Faris' (d. 1358) success in uniting the country after his conquest of Algeria and Tunisia was short-lived. He fell sick and was strangled by his own vizier, al-Fududi, in 1358. So whatever his ambitions regarding West Africa were, they died with him. After Abu 'Inan Faris' death, the country came under the control of the Wattasis (Zanata Berbers), who exercised effective power in the empire as viziers but were unable to secure the empire. This marked the beginning of a new shift in the geopolitics of trade: a new world trade era with new players emerging to compete over the trade in sub-Saharan Africans. The Portuguese started to assault the Moroccan Atlantic shores. The

---

[96] Edmund Morgan, "Slavery and freedom: The American Paradox," *The Journal of American History* 59 (1972), (1) (June): 26.
[97] Ibn Battuta in Hopkins and Levtzion, eds., *Corpus*, 303.

establishment of the Portuguese presence along the West African Atlantic coast after the passage of Cape Bojador (on the coast of western Sahara) in 1434 was an historical turning point that opened up lucrative Atlantic routes for Europe but had a severe impact on the trans-Saharan routes.[98] In their advance in the northwest African Atlantic, the Portuguese, as well as the Castilian rulers, sought to disrupt all contact between the Moors of Granada and their North African coreligionists, thus thwarting any efforts to recreate an Islamic empire such as the Almoravids did during the eleventh century. Hence, the Portuguese and their use of new sea routes would circumvent the Moroccan middleman and affect Morocco's economy in such a way that it would displace the trans-Saharan desert system, a significant factor in empire building for many earlier Moroccan and West African dynasties.[99]

Expanding the Diaspora: Exchange of the Atlantic and the Saharan Trade Networks

The connection of Islam and trade in sub-Saharan Africa is a well-established fact. The process of Islamization profoundly affected the culture, society, and economy in West Africa. Islam became an element for many groups in redefining their ethnic identity among the Fulani, the Soninke, the Bambara, and later the Hausa. The religious beliefs provided another vital definition of who they were. The traders and the ruling elites were among the first to convert to Islam when they came into contact with Muslim merchants and preachers. In the words of Nehemia Levtzion and Randall Pouwels, experts on Islam in West Africa, "As early as the eleventh century, Manding-speaking traders, ancestors of the Juula, traveled between the termini of the Saharan routes and the sources of the gold. They created a 'commercial diaspora,' [...]. Conversion to Islam became necessary for those who wished to join commercial networks."[100] These local merchants opened the remote rural areas to the influence of Islam.

---

[98] See Bailey Diffie and George D. Winius, *Foundations of the Portuguese Empire, 1415–1580.* (Minneapolis: University of Minnesota Press, 1977), 57–73.

[99] Among the most recent study on Saharan trade networks is the work of Ghislaine Lydon, *On Trans-Saharan Trails: Islamic Law, Trade Networks, and Cross-Cultural Exchange in Nineteenth-Century Western Africa* (Cambridge: Cambridge University Press, 2009). The work reveals a great social dynamism in the western Sahara and the Sahelian region by exploring the history of alliances among diverse groups within and outside the region.

[100] Nehemia Levtzion and Randall Pouwels, *The History of Islam*, 3.

Muhammad Fasi and Ivan Hrbek offer a good analysis of this "commercial diaspora":

The explanation of this phenomenon is to be found in social and economic factors. Islam as a religion born in the commercial society of Mecca and preached by a Prophet who himself had for a long time been a merchant, provides a set of ethical and practical prescripts closely related to business activities. This moral code helped to sanction and control commercial relationships and offered a unifying ideology among the members of different ethnic groups, thus providing for security and credit, two of the chief requirements of long-distance trade.[101]

The Saharan desert has proven to be a space of connections and interactions. What's more, unlike territorial borders that connect neighbors with at least some common features, the Sahara connected distant, diverse communities. French historian Fernand Braudel (d. 1985) wrote in his famous masterwork on the Mediterranean world, "Mediterranean civilization grew up under the determining influence of the emptiness of the sea: one zone peopled by ships and boats, the other by caravans and nomad tribes. Islam, like the sea and like the desert, implies movement."[102] In a similar way that trade across the Atlantic Ocean was influenced by Mediterranean traders and explorers, Braudel commented, "The Atlantic learns from the Mediterranean [...]. It is worth repeating that history is not made by geographical features, but by the men who control or discover them."[103]

Indeed, the early Atlantic encounter and trade between Portugal and Morocco served the Europeans as a training ground for trade with sub-Saharan Africa and across the Atlantic. When the Portuguese journeyed into the Atlantic Ocean in the fifteenth century, during the reign of Prince Henry the Navigator (d. 1460), to circumnavigate Africa and to acquire the Indian commodities, Morocco was an unavoidable stepping stone. The labeling of these Portuguese forays into the Atlantic as voyages of discovery and exploration is misleading in this context because these voyages were not motivated by scientific curiosity but rather by the economic imperative of Western Europeans to overcome their remoteness by reaching the gold sources and slaves of Africa and

---

[101] Muhammad Fasi and Ivan Hrbek, *General History of Africa. Africa from the Seventh to the Eleventh Century*, (London: James Currey, 1992), vol. 3, 39.
[102] Fernand Braudel, *The Mediterranean and the Mediterranean World in the Age of Philip II*, translated from the French by Siân Reynolds (New York: Harper & Row, 1976), 187, 225.
[103] Ibid., 225.

gaining access to the Indian Ocean and its markets, long dominated by
the Islamic world. Pierre Chaunu, French professor of European modern history, considers the acquisition of slaves on the African coasts the
primary motive behind the Atlantic voyages.[104] In 1441, when Prince
Henry the Navigator sent Captain Antam Gonçalvez on a voyage to
acquire skins and oil; Gonçalvez thought it would be a good idea to get
some slaves. Portuguese chronicler Gomes Eannes de Azurara (d. 1474)
quoted him as saying: "O How fair a thing it would be if we, who have
come to this land for a cargo of such petty merchandise, were to meet
with the good luck to bring the first captives before the face of our
Prince."[105] Indeed, Gonçalvez captured some of the natives from the
area of Rio de Oro, whom he took back to Portugal. Rio de Oro, or
River of Gold, was the name that the Portuguese gave to the river on the
southern coast of Morocco with a narrow inlet in the Atlantic Ocean,
because it was, according to Valentim Fernandes, the first place where
the Portuguese started to buy gold and blacks.[106] One of the captives in
the area of Rio de Oro was a Sanhaja Berber named Adahu who succeeded in convincing the Portuguese to "buy" him back in return for
a ransom, declaring that "he would give for himself five or six Black
Moors; and also he said that there were among the other captives two
youths for whom a like ransom would be given."[107] De Azurara said that
Adahu also provided information on black people and the West African
interior trade networks. Consequently, the Berber perception of black
people and their land was transmitted to the Portuguese.[108] After a few
months Gonçalvez took Adahu back to the Rio de Oro along with the
other two captives, but Adahu ran away, after which Gonçalvez warned
his men "not to trust [any] one of that race except under the most certain
security."[109] Nevertheless, he succeeded in exchanging the other two captives for "ten blacks, male and female [...], a little gold dust and a shield
of ox-hide, and a number of ostrich eggs."[110]

[104] Pierre Chaunu, *L'expansion européenne du XIIIe au XVe siècle* (Paris, Presses
Universitaires de France, 1969), 141.
[105] Gomes Eannes de Azurara, *The Chronicle of the Discovery and Conquest of Guinea*,
translated by Charles Raymond Beazley and Edgar Prestage (London: Printed for the
Hakluyt Society, 1896), vol. 1, 40.
[106] Valentim Fernandes, *Description de la Côte d'Afrique de Ceuta au Sénégal (1506–1507)*
(Paris: Librairie Larose, 1938), 45.
[107] De Azurara, *The Chronicle*, vol. 1, 54.
[108] Ibid., 55.
[109] Ibid., 56.
[110] Ibid., 57.

This marked the beginning of an eruption of commercial activities and slave raids in West Africa.[111] At these encounters, de Azurara reported, the Moors of Rio de Oro promised the Portuguese blacks in a large number, gold, and other commodities in which they could make a large profit.[112] Indeed, the Portuguese started to take goods from Morocco such as cloth, horses, and wheat and exchanged them in Arguin (an island off the West African coast near Mauritania) and sub-Saharan Africa for slaves and gold. Horses and cloth were much appreciated in Arguin and throughout the Sahelian region.[113] As Robert Ricard, a specialist in Portuguese studies, explains: "It is plausible to think that in the eyes of the Portuguese diplomacy, the land of Morocco and the land of Guinea constituted some kind of economic unity."[114] Morocco by the end of the fifteenth century lacked political stability under the rule of the Berber Wattasi dynasty. The weakness of this dynasty was witnessed by early-sixteenth-century traveler Leo Africanus who said: "The king of Fez has a large kingdom, but his revenues are small, which hardly reach three hundred thousand ducats,[115] and not even the fifth of which arrives at his hands."[116] This weakness prevented this dynasty from establishing a fleet or a strong army to protect the Moroccan littoral and made the Portuguese conquest of strategic coastal towns relatively easy.

Internally, the authority of the Wattasi was challenged by a new rival, the Sa'di, who emerged in the region of Sus in the south to wage a war against the Christians who had taken Moroccan coastal towns. Morocco had also lost much of its influence in the Mediterranean after the fall of Granada in 1492, and it had to fend off the Ottomans who bordered Morocco on the east and controlled most of the Middle East and North

[111] In fact, before the regular slave trade, the Portuguese attacked the small villages along the Atlantic coast, ravaged the land, and kidnapped men and women and carried them to Portugal for sale. See Ca da Mosto, *The Voyages*, 18.

[112] De Zurara, *The Chronicle*, vol. 2, 194.

[113] Robert Ricard, *Études sur l'histoire des Portugais au Maroc* (Coimbra: Universidade de Coimbra, Acta Universitatis Conimbrigensis, 1955), 100–101.

[114] Ibid., 104.

[115] Ducat is used here as the equivalent of mithqal.

[116] Al-Hasan al-Wazzan al-Fasi, known in English as Leo Africanus and French as Jean-Leon l'Africain, *Description de l'Afrique*, nouvelle édition traduite de l'Italien par Alexis Epaulard (Paris: Adrien-Maisonneuve, 1956), tome 2, 238. I have also used the Arabic translation, which I believe is more accurate, especially as the two Moroccan translators have made many annotations where Leo Africanus' memory has failed him. The Arabic translation by Muhammad Hajji and Mohammed Lakhdar is entitled *Wasf Ifriqiya*, (Beirut: Dar al-Gharb al-Islami, 1983), vol. 1, 288.

Africa. As a result, by the 1530s, the Portuguese controlled strategic Moroccan Atlantic ports from Tangier to Agadir. The fifteenth- and early-sixteenth-century Portuguese explorer Duarte Pacheco Pereira noted, "All these four places Cepta, Alcacere, Tanger and Arzila, belong to this kingdom of Portugal, and to its royal crown, for it is now about ninety years since Cepta was captured by force from the Moors by King John I."[117] The Portuguese established a new trade route for themselves; they connected Morocco to sub-Saharan Africa and their products through the Atlantic Ocean link. For instance, Moroccan horses were used in the early trans-Saharan slave trade. James Webb in his study of the ecology and the economy of the western Sahel area noted that:

The imported horses were generally exchanged for slaves, and the link between imported horses and exported slaves was direct. Horses were used in state warfare, which produced large numbers of prisoners of war, who were then sold into the Atlantic, Saharan and North African markets.[118]

This trade of horses and slaves was already known along the trans-Saharan routes from Morocco to West Africa. Alvise da Cà da Mosto (1432–1488), a Venetian merchant and explorer who confirmed the commercial patterns, reported that a horse was worth ten or fifteen black slaves and that at Arguin, the Portuguese carried back home a thousand slaves a year.[119] He also added that further south on the Senegalese coast "[Christians] have begun to trade [directly] with these blacks."[120]

Valentim Fernandes (died circa 1518), a commercial agent, printer, and writer originally from Moravia, Germany who lived in Lisbon, collected much information on the expansion of Portuguese interests in Africa. He reported that Sanhaja traders imported horses from as far as Safi (Morocco) to exchange for slaves from the area of Jolof (Senegal). With the appearance of the Portuguese on the Atlantic shores in Arguin, they represented a third party that came into play and affected the dual north–south transactions. Some slaves were sold in Arguin to the Portuguese at a price of between six to fifteen mithqals[121] or in exchange for wheat and cloths, and so forth, and some were sold to Morocco in exchange for

---

[117] Duarte Pereira, *Esmeraldo de Situ Orbis*, translated and edited by George H. T. Kimble (London: Printed for the Hakluyt Society, 1937), 39.
[118] James Webb, *Desert Frontier. Ecological and Economic Change along the Western Sahel 1600–1850* (Madison: The University of Wisconsin Press, 1995), 69.
[119] Ca da Mosto, *The Voyages*, 17.
[120] Alvise da Cà da Mosto, 1937, 30.
[121] In the early sixteenth century, a mithqal was worth 445 reis in Portugal. See Fernandes, *Description de la Côte*, 60–61.

horses.[122] A contemporary of Valentim Fernandes, Duarte Pereira, noted the same trade pattern in Arguin. He also noted that the black slaves were imported by the Arabs and the Sanhaja from "Jalofo [Senegal] and Mandingua [Mali]."[123] According to Duarte Pereira, even a poor horse was worth ten or twelve slaves.[124] He also reported that "[a]t the time when the bartering was good four hundred slaves were obtained yearly from this river [that is, the Senegal River] (but sometimes less by half) in return for horses and other merchandise."[125]

The Portuguese, and later the Western Europeans, established their commercial itinerary along a preexisting African trade network. They started only gradually to replace the North African middleman by focusing on long maritime voyages and getting closer to the sources by connecting the existing commercial Atlantic coastal towns. In their advance in the northwest African Atlantic, the Portuguese sought to thwart any efforts to recreate an Islamic empire like that of the Almoravids, whose dynasty dominated Muslim Spain as well as Morocco and the eastern part of Algeria during the eleventh century. The expansion of the new Islamic dynasty of the Sa'dis in Morocco implied a threat to the Iberian Peninsula. Therefore, they took an apprehensive approach toward Morocco while doing trade with its people. The European merchants who came to deal in the Moroccan Atlantic littoral, in towns such as Arzila and Safi in the fifteenth and sixteenth centuries, were mainly from Portugal, Cadiz, Jerez, Genoa, and later on from England. References to slaves imported from the Moroccan Atlantic littoral, especially from Azemmour, are frequently found in Iberian documents.[126] The slave trade was actually a state affair in Portugal. Belgian medieval historian Charles Verlinden wrote: "Since 1459, Alphonse V had exempted the Portuguese merchants of Ceuta of the payment of the tenth part on the Moors whom they imported in the kingdom. This privilege was extended in 1502 to the merchants of Alcacer, of Arzila and Tangier."[127] Even the Portuguese

---

[122] Ibid., 70–71, footnote a. The text is in Portuguese accompanied with a French translation by P. de Cenival and Th. Monod.
[123] Pereira, *Esmeraldo*, 72–73.
[124] Ibid., 78.
[125] Ibid.
[126] See Marcos Jimenez de la Espada (1831–1898), *La guerra del moro: a fines del siglo XV* (Ceuta: Imprenta Africa, 1940) and Bernardo Rodrigues, *Anais de Arzila: crónica inédita do século XVI*, Publicada por ordem da Academia das Sciências de Lisboa e sob a direcção de David Lopes (Lisboa: Academia das Sciências de Lisboa, 1915–1919).
[127] Charles Verlinden, *L'esclavage dans l'Europe médiévale* (Brugge, Belgium: De Tempel, 1955), tome 1, 630.

governor Simao Correia (1516–1517), of the occupied Azemmour, was involved in the slave trade and selling Moors in Castile.[128] In the same region, the number of slaves increased during the famine and plague of 1521–1522. Many Moroccan inhabitants of the area of Azemmour came to the port to sell their family members, including wives and children, to the Portuguese for a very cheap price, as little as a basket of figs or raisins.[129] There were also reports that they were sold for as little as ten to twenty testons.[130] Young Moroccan women, known in Portugal for their beauty, usually sold for a bit more, and the most beautiful ones were priced at forty testons.[131]

A few years earlier, in the early sixteenth century, Leo Africanus offered a different picture of the routes, type of merchandises, and prices for the time. Leo Africanus (born in Granada between 1483 and 1495) was a Moroccan scholar and traveler. He traveled to Timbuktu and Egypt on diplomatic and commercial missions and while still a young man was captured by Christian corsairs on the Mediterranean Sea. After his capture he demonstrated his scholarly skills and subsequently was offered to Pope Leo X who influenced him to convert to Christianity. Around 1526, he wrote his famous book on Africa. In this book he described a gift presented to the sultan of Fez that consisted mainly of commodities from the well-established trade with the land of West Africa:

Fifty black slaves, and fifty female black slaves, ten eunuchs, twelve camels, one giraffe, ten ostriches, sixteen civet-cats, one pound of fine musk, one pound of civet, a pound of ambergris, and almost six hundred skins of a certain animal *al-Lamt* [oryx], of which very light shields are made, every skin being worth in Fez eight ducats. The black slaves were valued at twenty ducats per head, female slaves cost fifteen each and each eunuch costs forty. Camels were valued at fifty each; civet-cats at two hundred ducats, a pound of musk, civet and ambergris costs sixty ducats.[132]

---

[128] Ricard, *Études sur l'histoire*, 156.

[129] Bernard Rosenberger and Hamid Triki, "Famines et épidémies au Maroc aux XVIè et XVIIè siècles," *Hespéris-Tamuda* (Rabat: Éditions Techniques Nord-Africaines, 1973), vol. 14, 129. See also Diego de Torres, *Relación del origen y suceso de los Xarifes y del estado de los Reinos de Marruecos*, Fez y Tarudante (Madrid: Siglo Veintiuno, 1980), 101.

[130] A teston was the equivalent of five vintems. One vintem was a piece of copper of twenty reals. This means that one teston is equal 100 reals. See Rosenberger and Triki, "Famines," 132, footnote 73.

[131] Ibid., 132 and Rodrigues, *Anais de Arzila*, tomo, I, 329.

[132] Leo Africanus, *Description*, tome 1, 139–140. The Arabic translation by Hajji and Lakhdar, vol. 1, 174.

This gift from a chief in the Draa region, a crucial link in the trans-Saharan caravan routes, is a great example illustrating Sudanese products and their values in Morocco. It is interesting to note that some of the enslaved people succeeded in gaining some of the most trusted official positions, as was the case of the messenger who carried this gift to the sultan. Leo Africanus wrote that the sultan treated him with the honors fit for any ambassador.[133]

At the other end of this trade network, in the land of the Sudan, Leo Africanus described the value and nature of commodities imported from the Mediterranean region. He remarked that in the West African locations of Timbuktu, Gao, and Bornu, horses and slaves were fundamental in the trans-Saharan trade. His trip to Timbuktu around 1512 was during the apogee of the Songhay empire. He described the affluence of the court of the governor of the city of Timbuktu:

Their good horses are brought from the land of the Berbers. They arrive with a caravan and, ten or twelve days later, the horses are brought to the king who takes the number of horses he desires and pays the merchants properly [...]. Many manuscripts from the land of the Berbers are also sold in this city. They bring more profit than any other merchandise. Instead of coins, pieces of pure gold are used and, for small purchases, cowry shells brought from Persia,[134] four hundred of which are worth one ducat. One Roman ounce of gold is worth six *mithqals* and two third.[135]

During his visit to Gao, the capital of the king of Songhay, Askia Muhammad (r. 1493–1528), and one of the oldest commercial towns in West Africa, he reported:

Many blacks come with a big amount of gold to the city of Gao in order to buy objects imported from the land of Berbers and Europe [...]. There exists a certain place where an endless number of slaves, male and female, are to be sold during the days of the market. A young girl of fifteen years of age costs about six ducats, so does a young man and the little children roughly half that price [...]. The incomes of the kingdom are high but its expenses are even more costly. In fact, a horse bought in Europe for ten ducats, is sold here for forty and sometimes for fifty ducats.[136]

[133] Ibid.
[134] On the exchange rate, Edward Bovill reports: "at the end of the sixteenth century a *mithqal* or *mitkal*, approximately 1/8 oz. of gold, was worth 3,000 cowries in Timbuktu; by 1912 its value had risen to about 12,000 cowries." Edward Bovill, *The Golden Trade of the Moors* (Princeton: Markus Wiener, 1995), 161.
[135] Leo Africanus, *Description*, tome 2, 468–469. Arabic translation, vol. 2, 166–167.
[136] Ibid., 471. Arabic translation, vol. 2, 169–170.

Africanus mentioned that when Askia Muhammad conquered Gobir, he had its ruler killed and his children castrated and forced to serve in his palace. This is an indication of how eunuchs were produced but it could also be a method of punishing hostile or rival powers.[137]

He also visited Bornu and described its ruler as very powerful, commanding three thousand cavalry and a huge infantry. The entire population was at his service because he was continuously at war with his neighbors. The ongoing regional conflicts were the main source for acquiring slaves in West Africa.

This king encourages merchants from the land of the Berbers to bring him horses to trade for slaves, at the rate of fifteen or twenty slaves for each horse. With these horses, he made a raid on his enemies and the merchants were obliged to await his return. They were at times delayed of two or three months and they lived at the king's expense. When he returned from the raid, he would sometimes have enough slaves to pay back the merchants, but at other times, the merchants were obliged to wait until the following year because the king did not have a sufficient number of slaves with which he could pay them, for the raid is dangerous and so can only be one a year. When I was in the kingdom, I met with many desperate merchants who wanted to end this commerce and to never come back, because they have been waiting a year without payment.[138]

We note from these accounts that the North-South trans-Saharan commodities were similar to those exchanged when the Portuguese intervened in the African West Atlantic, as I have already discussed. However, it is important to note that the Portuguese also bought light-skinned Moroccans from Moroccans themselves, usually during extraordinary times of plagues and famine. Sixteenth-century chronicler Bernardo Rodrigues gave us an eyewitness description in *Anais de Arzila* of the slave trade that took place in the Moroccan Atlantic town of Azemmour; he himself took part in it and bought five slaves. According to him, the town of Azemmour was full of merchants. At the port there were about 100 ships whose crews were engaged in this trade. The offers were so abundant that they were buying only girls and young women and at a ridiculous price.[139] The situation was so dire in the region of Safi and Azemmour that according to Rodrigues, during these years (beginning of 1520s) there were times when a thousand people were sold each day in Azemmour. The same commerce took place in other Moroccan Atlantic cities such as Agadir and Safi. Spanish merchants were also involved in

[137] Leo Africanus, *Description*, tome 2, 473. Arabic translation, vol. 2, 171.
[138] Ibid., tome 2, 480–481. Arabic translation, vol. 2, 176–177.
[139] Rodrigues, *Anais de Arzila*, tomo I, 328.

the trade. A Spanish account from Jerez de la Frontera (a city of south-west Spain northeast of Cadiz) dated in 1523 stated that sixty thousand Moroccan slaves were sold in Spain.[140] The Spaniards might have taken advantage of this opportunity to replace the shortage in the labor power caused by the gradual expulsions of Iberian Muslim workers in the years after the fall of Granada in 1492.

A few years earlier, Leo Africanus had described a completely differ-ent picture of Azemmour. He portrayed it as a fairly populated, peaceful, and prosperous town on the Atlantic shore that produced a lot of wheat. He added that this port town was known for its abundance of fish; for this, the city received an annual income of six to seven thousands ducats, derived mainly from the Portuguese who came every year to buy a large amount of fish. But soon the Portuguese, allured by the richness of the town, began planning to take it over. Leo Africanus reported the tragedy inflicted on the Azemmouri people by the Portuguese invasion: "The king sent another navy of two hundred vessels, of which sight the [Azemmouri] people lost all courage. They started to flee in so much panic that more than eighty people died of suffocation as a result of the pressing crowd at the entrance of the gates [...], and so the Christians took over the city of Azemmour."[141] This was in the year 1513.

In the beginning of the 1520s, things appeared to worsen for the city of Azemmour as a consequence of a series of calamities. The first quar-ter of the sixteenth century was a time of famine and plague, and many Moroccans chose slavery over privation, starvation, and certain death. The consequence of this "voluntary" servitude was a migration that had negative demographic consequences in Morocco. The dislocation of healthy young people on farms to cultivate the land and to take care of cattle disrupted economic growth. But the migration was advantageous to the Iberian people.[142] Some of these Moroccan slaves even ended up in the Americas. A Franciscan missionary of New Spain, Toribio Motolinia, stated that, "In these mountains there is a lot of wax and honey, espe-cially in the area of Campeche; it is said that one finds there as much honey and wax and as good as those in Safi in Africa."[143] It is interesting

---

[140] Ricard, *Études sur l'histoire*, 157, note 3. Ricard read this information in a Spanish account entitled "Estracto de las ocurencias de la peste que aflixio a esta ciudad," pub-lished by Hipolito Sancho in *Sociedad de estudios historicos jerezanos*, 1re série, n. I, 1938.
[141] Leo Africanus, *Description*, tome 1, 125–127. The Arabic translation, vol. 1, 157–159.
[142] Rosenberger and Triki, "Famines," 124 and 144.
[143] Ricard, *Études sur l'histoire*, 325.

to ask how the Moroccan reputation for honey and wax reached this priest, who lived in Mexico until his death in 1568. Ricard suggests that among the "New Christians" pursued by the Mexican Inquisition, two were contemporaries of Motolinia. The first was Francisco Millan who was born in Andalusia of Jewish Portuguese background and came to Azemmour to sell cloth and acquired a Moorish concubine. The other was Francisco Tejera, who was for many years a captive in Morocco. His trial was in 1563–1564.[144] The reputation of the honey and the wax of Safi spread through commercial trade in slaves and goods.

The most illustrious and well-documented example of Moroccans in the Americas in the sixteenth century was a man named Estebanico, an enslaved black person from Dukkala region, in which Azemmour and Safi were the most important coastal towns. Estebanico was brought to North America in the company of Spanish explorers. Estebanico de Azamor, also known as Estebanico the black or Estevanico the Moor (d. 1539), became a respected explorer and was purportedly the first black man to enter Florida or for that matter North America. In 1539, Estebanico was a member of another expedition from Mexico searching for the mythical city of Cibola in Arizona. John Terrell, who wrote about the life of Estebanico, described the event: "On a May day in the year 1539, Estevanico the Black unlocked for the world the gateway to the Southwest of the future United States."[145] Spanish explorer Cabeza de Vaca (died between 1556 and 1564) was probably the first to mention Estebanico in his travel account written in 1542. He dedicated the last chapter to four explorers who encountered many misfortunes in the "Indies," including de Vaca himself. The other three includes Andres Dorantes, Alonso del Castillo, and, "The fourth is named Estebanico, he is a black Arab and a native of Azamor."[146] Motolinia knew Alvar Nunez Cabeza de Vaca and his companions, including Estebanico, from whom he might have received knowledge about the honey and the wax of Safi.[147]

The presence of the Portuguese in the Moroccan Atlantic cities had a huge impact on the internal politics of Morocco. It stimulated the country's community sentiment to wage jihad against the Portuguese and

[144] Ibid., 327.

[145] John Terrell, *Estevanico the Black* (Los Angeles: Westernlore Press, 1968), 109.

[146] Alvar Núñez Cabeza de Vaca, *The Account: Álvar Núñez Cabeza de Vaca's Relación*, an annotated translation by Martin A. Favata and José B. Fernández (Houston: Arte Público Press, 1993), 121.

[147] Ricard, *Études sur l'histoire*, 330.

inspired criticism of the frail Wattasi rule. The first important political figure in the Sa'di movement, which originated in the Draa valley south of Morocco, was Muhammad b. 'Abd ar-Rahman al-Qa'im bi-Amr Allah. He was a pious adherent of the al-Jazuli Sufi order and was known for his outspokenness and advocacy of liberating the Moroccan Atlantic ports from Portuguese occupation; he became a leader in the war against the Portuguese in 1511. When he died in 1518, his two sons, Ahmad al-A'raj, the designated heir in Marrakech, and his younger brother, Muhammad ash-Shaykh, in the Sus region, carried on their father's mission. The principal objective of these leaders was to wage war against the encroaching Portuguese and the incapacitated Wattasi regime. The sultan of Morocco in Fez, Mawlay Ahmad (of the Wattasi dynasty), tried to forge a political alliance with the king of Portugal, Jean III, in order to undermine the immediate threat of the emerging power of the Sa'di in Marrakech. As a result, a truce was signed in 1538. The Wattasi ruler was willing to forge an alliance with the Portuguese against his own fellow Muslims. In the end, the attempt by Mawlay Ahmad to maintain political power by allying with the Portuguese failed. As Ricard noted, Mawlay Ahmad "didn't have at his disposal any real force, he had no army, no money, no supplies and the anarchy that reigned in his country damaged him even further."[148]

Meanwhile, from Sus (the Moroccan south), Muhammad ash-Shaykh became an inspiring leader bringing unity and order to the country. His forces defeated the Portuguese in the southern Moroccan Atlantic by taking back Agadir in 1541.[149] A struggle over leadership and power ensued between the two Sa'di brothers. Muhammad ash-Shaykh became the unchallenged leader of the Sa'di dynasty and pursued the struggle against the Wattasi rule of Fez, and by 1549 he succeeded in becoming the ruler of all Morocco. When Muhammad ash-Shaykh died in 1557, he was succeeded by his son, Mawlay 'Abd Allah al-Ghalib bi-llah. Meanwhile, two brothers and political rivals, al-Mansur and 'Abd al-Malik, took flight to Algiers in fear of their sultan brother. When the latter died in 1574, the succession fell to his son, Muhammad al-Mutawakkil. But 'Abd al-Malik, one of the sons of Muhammad ash-Shaykh, had been plotting to gain the support of the Ottomans to consolidate his power after the death of his father in 1557. Effectively, two years later, with the help of the Ottomans, he defeated Muhammad al-Mutawakkil (his nephew) in 1576. Muhammad al-Mutawakkil sought refuge in Peñon de Vélez and forged

[148] Ibid., 307.
[149] Ibid., 308.

an alliance with the Spaniards and the Portuguese. Subsequently, 'Abd al-Malik was assisted by the Muslim Ottomans, whereas Muhammad al-Mutawakkil sought help from the Christians, mainly from the king of Portugal, Don Sebastian, who was planning to invade Morocco as his contribution to the crusades in the land of Islam.

The motivation for the involvement of Portugal and Spain stemmed from the fear that the Atlantic routes would be threatened by the Moroccan–Ottoman alliance. Portugal and Spain feared that 'Abd al-Malik would allow the Ottomans to occupy the Portuguese forts on the Moroccan Atlantic.[150] Against the advice of his uncle Phillip II, Don Sebastian led a large Christian army of twenty thousand men, including a very small Moroccan contingent under the command of al-Mutawakkil, and embarked on a war against Morocco in 1578. The battle took place at Wadi al-Makhazin, near the town of Qasr al-Kabir (Alcazarquivir) in the northwest of Morocco. The Portuguese army was badly defeated, the king was killed, and many people of rank were taken captive. Muhammad al-Mutawakkil was also killed and 'Abd al-Malik died suddenly during the battle, hence its name, the "Battle of the Three Kings." Ahmad (the brother of the departed sultan) was nicknamed al-Mansur ("the victorious") and was declared sultan. English traveler John Windus, who visited the area of the battle in 1720, reported a traditional story, not recorded in history books, attributing the victory of Morocco to the heroic actions of a slave called Marwan who concealed the death of Sultan 'Abd al-Malik, who had been sick for some time, and gave out orders in his name until the battle was won. However, al-Mansur killed Marwan, claiming all the glory for himself. Windus wrote:

Muley Moluc ['Abd al-Malik] was a Prince very much beloved by his People, but infirm, and at the time he left *Morocco* [Marrakesh], to defend his Country against Don *Sebastian*, was so ill, that he was forced to be carried in a Litter, and when he came to *Alcassar*, (about six Miles from the place where the Battle was fought) he there died; upon which a Slave of his called *Mirwan*, (whose Name the *Moors*, to this day, mention with great regard, because of the Gallantry and Service of the Action) wisely considering the Consequence of keeping secret the Death of a Prince so well beloved by his People, at a time when the two Armies every day expected to join Battle, contrived it so, as to give out Orders for the King, as if he had been alive, making believe he was better than he used to be, 'till the Battle was over; when the said Slave (thinking he merited a better Reward

[150] For more information see Dahiru Yahya, *Morocco in the Sixteenth Century: Problems and Patterns in African Foreign Policy* (Atlantic Highlands: Humanities Press, 1981), 66–85.

than what he met with) wished the Successor Joy, both of the Victory and Empire; but the ungrateful Prince caused him to be immediately put to death, saying, *He had robbed him of the Glory of the Action.* The *Portuguese* who were dispersed in the Battle, would not believe (for a long time) that their King was slain, but ran up and down the Country, crying out, [D]*Onde esta el Rey* (i.e.) *Where is the King?* the *Moors* often hearing the word *Rey,* which in *Arabick* signifies *good Sense;* told them, *That if they had any* Rey, *they had never come thither.*[151]

Although this story cannot be verified, it represents the royal political intrigues in the public discourse, real or imagined. During the Sa'di era, Morocco did not achieve political stability until the arrival of Ahmad al-Mansur, who became the sixth ruler in the Sa'di dynasty. His reign, which lasted twenty-five years, was one of the most important in the history of Morocco. He also appeared to be of a mixed lineage, because according to Timbuktu historian 'Abd ar-Rahman as-Sa'di (1596–1656?), al-Mansur was the son of a Fulani concubine, whose name was Lalla 'Awda;[152] a point that seemed important to the Sudanese historian but not to his Moroccan counterparts.

The Battle of the Three Kings had far-reaching effects on Morocco as well as Europe; it brought Morocco unity, prestige, slaves, and gold. On the other hand, it was a terrible tragedy for Portugal; it deprived the Portuguese people of their king and their influential leaders who were among the prisoners of war. In Braudel's words:

The last Mediterranean crusade was not Lepanto, but the Portuguese expedition seven years later which was to end in the disaster of Alcazarquivir (4th August, 1578) not far from Tangier [...]. King Sebastian, still a child at twenty five, a visionary with the child's irresponsibility, was obsessed with the idea of a crusade. Philip whom he had met before the *Jornada de Africa* had tried in vain to dissuade him from carrying war into Morocco [...]. Against it, Morocco had "risen up in the mass." The Christians were overwhelmed by numbers [...]. Between ten and twenty thousand Portuguese remained in the hands of the infidel. [... This battle] was heavy with consequences. It reaffirmed the power of Morocco, now so enriched with the ransoms of the Christians that its ruler Ahmad, the brother of 'Abd al-Malik, was named not only "the victorious," al-Mansur, but also "the Golden," al-Dahabi.[153]

151 John Windus, *A Journey to Mequinez. The Residence of the Present Emperor of Fez and Morocco. On the Occasion of Commodore Stewart's Embassy Thither for the Redemption of the British Captives in the Year 1721* (London: J. Tonson, 1725), 74–75.

152 'Abd ar-Rahman as-Sa'di, *Tarikh as-Sudan,* trad. de l'arabe [et éd.] par Octave Houdas; avec la collaboration de Edmond Benoist (Paris: E. Leroux, 1898), 315 of the French text and 206 of the Arab text.

153 Braudel, *The Mediterranean,* vol. 2, 1178–1179.

Braudel was clearly accurate in his assessment about this decisive bat-
tle but mistaken that it procured al-Mansur the nickname "the Golden."
Al-Mansur was actually named "the Golden" after his conquest of the
Sudan.

Morocco seized this opportunity to assert itself as a powerful force
in the Atlantic world. Although the Moroccans won the battle on land,
they realized that they wouldn't dare to confront the Portuguese or the
Spaniards upon the sea. Therefore they deemed it necessary to build a war
fleet that could stand against the Portuguese and Spanish. And indeed, it
was in foreign affairs that al-Mansur stood out as a unique ruler.[154] He
understood the power of the Ottoman empire and avoided confronting
it, recognizing its authority in the Islamic world without submitting or
being part of its dominion.[155]

In his relations with Spain, he succeeded in circumventing all overt
conflicts. With England he made an ally, and as result of this alliance, a
"Barbary Company" was founded by British merchants in 1585 that had
the biggest share of Moroccan external trade. The British sold firearms to
Morocco in exchange for saltpeter.[156] This weapons deal was conducted
secretly to avoid incurring the antagonism of the Pope or the Catholics in
England. Although England was a Protestant country, it saw in Muslim
Morocco an ideological ally against a mutual enemy, Catholic Spain.
British weapons brought a crucial advantage that enabled the Moroccans
to invade and to win the battle against the Songhay.[157] Al-Mansur was
so ambitious in his foreign policy and motivated by imperial aspirations
to control the salt mines in the Sahara and the gold of West Africa that
he undertook a massive military campaign against a southern Islamic
neighbor: the Songhay empire (in present-day Mali) in 1591. But he had
been planning for it since at least 1583 when he sent a diplomat to report
on Songhay internal affairs.[158] Timbuktu historian as-Sa'di reported that
in 1589, a slave of the royal court named Wuld Kirinfil angered Askia
Ishaq and as a result he was sent to prison in the Saharan mining town

---

[154] For more information see Henry de Castries (ed.). *Les sources inédites de l'histoire du
Maroc*, 1. Série: Dynastie sa'dienne, Archives et bibliothèques d'Angleterre (Paris: Paul
Geuthner, 1925), tome II.

[155] See Yahya, *Morocco*, 105–110.

[156] Saltpeter, a translucent mineral composed of potassium nitreade, was used as
gunpowder.

[157] Yahya, *Morocco*, 131 and 151–152.

[158] 'Abd al-'Aziz al-Fishtali, *Manahil as-Safa' fi Ma'athir Mawalina ash-Shurafa'*, edited by
'Abd al-Karim Kurayyim (Rabat: Matbu'at Wizarat al-Awqaf wa 'sh-Shu'un al-Islamiyya
wa 'th-Thaqafa, 1972), 117–120.

of Taghaza.[159] Wuld Kirinfil succeeded in escaping to Marrakesh from where he wrote a letter to al-Mansur providing him with intelligence on the Songhay empire and encouraging him to invade it. However, according to al-Fishtali (1549–1621), the official chronicler of Sultan al-Mansur, Wuld Kirinfil was in reality a prince named 'Ali son of Askia Dawud, the brother of Ishaq, and was once the ruler of Songhay but Ishaq deposed him and banished him to Taghaza.[160] It is more likely that Wuld Kirinfil represented himself to Moroccans as a prince, but as-Sa'di knew his true identity. It could be that he assumed the fake identity in order to be more persuasive and to seek revenge for his mistreatment at the hands of his former master.

When Askia Ishaq refused the demands of al-Mansur for control of the revenues of the Taghaza salt mines, he sent a well-equipped army under the command of Jawdar, his loyal eunuch from Spain, to invade Songhay. According to 'Abd ar-Rahman as-Sa'di, the Moroccan army consisted of three thousand musketeers, both cavalry and infantry,[161] but the authors of *Tarikh al-Fattash* reported three thousand or four thousand musketeers.[162] Four thousand was also the number recorded by al-Fishtali.[163] An anonymous Spaniard writer who visited Marrakesh in 1591 provided more details. He wrote that the soldiers who participated in this expedition were:

1,000 renegade musketeers, and 1,000 Andalusian musketeers who had migrated from the kingdom of Granada [to Morocco]. Also taking part were 500 spahis, who are mounted musketeers, many of whom were also renegades, and 1,500 lancers from among the local people. The total number of men, including 1,000 service personnel, could have amounted to 5,000 men.[164]

After the fall of Granada in 1492, as a result of the Reconquista, the Iberian Muslims were forced to migrate to North Africa. Some of these Moriscos who settled in Morocco became corsairs on the Atlantic Moroccan

---

[159] John Hunwick, *Timbuktu and the Songhay Empire: Al-Sa'di's Ta'rikh Al-Sudan down to 1613 and Other Contemporary Documents* (Leiden: Brill, 1999), 186. See also as-Sa'di, *Tarikh as-Sudan*, 215 of the French text and 137 of the Arab text.

[160] Al-Fishtali, *Manahil*, 120–125. See also the account of the Sa'dian conquest of Songhay written in 1591 by an anonymous Spaniard. This account is translated by John Hunwick, *Timbuktu*, 318.

[161] As-Sa'di, *Tarikh as-Sudan*, 217 of the French text and 138 of the Arab text.

[162] Mahmud Ka'ti and Ibn al-Mukhtar, *Tarikh al-fattash fi akhbar al-buldan wa 'l-juyush wa akabir an-nas*, éd. et trad. par O. Houdas et M. Delafosse (Paris: E. Leroux, 1913), 263 of the French text and 146 of the Arabic text.

[163] Al-Fishtali, *Manahil*, 137.

[164] Anonymous Spaniard in John Hunwick, *Timbuktu*, 319.

coast fighting against Europeans and some became mercenaries in the service of the rulers. Sa'di sultan al-Mansur seemed to favor this group of soldiers because of their advanced skills in European firearms. And it was with these Iberian mercenaries that al-Mansur invaded the great Songhay empire in 1591. The historical sources do not mention whether there were any blacks in this expedition, however this does not mean that there were none in the army. Spanish chronicler Luis del Marmol Carvajal (1520–1600) did observe in the 1550s that there were blacks in the Sa'di army.[165] Italian scholar Giovanni Lorenzo Anania (born in 1545 and died between 1607 and 1609) was more specific in reporting that Sa'di sultan Mawlay 'Abd Allah (1557–1574) had eighty thousand cavalry relying on the Granatini (Andalusians) and Gialofi (Wolof from the region of Senegal),[166] among whom twelve thousand formed his personal guards.[167]

It was an easy victory for Jawdar Pasha, whose army employed the arquebus and English cannons against the bows and spears of the Songhay army.[168] According to al-Fishtali, Ishaq gathered an army of around one hundred thousand fighters in defense, which seems a great exaggeration of the enemy force.[169] Indeed the number that as-Sa'di gave was "12,500 cavalry and 30,000 infantry."[170] Al-Fishtali's testimonies were likely influenced by his high position in the court. He glorified the Sa'di dynasty and ridiculed the Songhay people. He often called Askia Ishaq, king of the Songhay, by a derogatory term, "al-'abd Askia." The "'abd" which means "slave" was used to refer to him condescendingly. Moreover, he derided their Islam because of their belief in and practice of witchcraft and magic. Al-Fishtali added that they were stupid to think that magic would save them.[171] He also confirmed that this conquest brought great prestige and wealth to the Moroccan ruler.[172] Al-Mansur even acquired

---

[165] Luis del Mármol Carvajal, *L'Afrique de Marmol*, traduction de Nicolas Perrot d'Ablancourt (Paris: Chez L. Billaine, 1667), tome II, 179–180.

[166] Wolof is used here from Portuguese sources in the context of black West Africans.

[167] Dierk Lange and Silvio Berthoud, "L'intérieur de l'Afrique Occidentale d'après Giovanni Lorenzo Anania (XVIe siècle)," *Cahiers d'Histoire Mondiale*, Neuchâtel (Switzerland): Editions de la Baconnière, 14 (2), 1972, (299–350), 311. This article is the Italian text and the French translation of the third chapter on Africa from Giovanni Lorenzo Anania's book *L'Universale fabrica del mondo, overo cosmografia*.

[168] See the study of Ismael Diadié Haidara, *Jawdar Pasha et la Conquête Saâdienne du Songhay (1591–1599)* (Rabat: L'Institut des Etudes Africaines, 1996).

[169] Al-Fishtali, *Manahil*, 137.

[170] Hunwick, *Timbuktu*, 189.

[171] Al-Fishtali, *Manahil*, 137.

[172] Ibid., 139.

a new epithet – "adh-Dhahabi," meaning "the Golden," because of the amount of gold gained from the conquest. On the other hand, the invasion was devastating and shocking to the Songhay people, as Moroccan historian Muhammad al-Ifrani (died in 1743 or 1745) reported:

The swords of Jawdar and his forces held judgment over their necks until the people of the Sudan cried out, "We are Muslims. We are your brothers in faith," as the swords were doing their work among them [...]. When Ishaq fled, Jawdar pursued him after taking possession of Timbuktu and all its surrounding towns and villages. He wrote to al-Mansur informing him of the victory and sent him a large gift, including, amongst other things, 10,000 mq. of gold and two hundred slaves.[173]

As-Sa'di informed us that when Askia Ishaq was defeated near Tondibi north of Gao, he "sent word to him [Jawdar Pasha] offering peace on the following terms: 100,000 [mq.] of gold and 1,000 slaves, which he would personally hand over to the *amir Mulay* Ahmad."[174] One would wonder why exactly one thousand slaves. Could it be that it was the average number that exported annually to Morocco? Some scholars of slavery speculate, based on scant sources, that the average number of slaves transported to Morocco during medieval and early modern times was about one thousand on each route and per caravan.[175] The estimate of the slaves who crossed the Sahara to North Africa is about four times that number. John Wright, who has written about the trans-Saharan slave trade, estimated the total number of medieval Saharan slave transits from 600 to 1499 at 3,450,000, with an annual average of 3,833.[176] He also compares his estimate to those of two preceding historians: Raymond Mauny, whose total estimate for the medieval period was the highest at 5,700,000 with an annual average of 6,333,[177] and Ralph Austen, whose total estimate for the same period was 4,320,000 with an annual average of 4,800.[178]

Jawdar Pasha returned to Timbuktu and conveyed the terms of surrender to Sultan al-Mansur, but to his surprise the sultan was disappointed

---

[173] Al-Ifrani in Hunwick, *Timbuktu*, 313.
[174] Hunwick, *Timbuktu*, 191.
[175] Lovejoy, *Transformations*, 25–26.
[176] John Wright, *The Trans-Saharan Slave Trade. History and Society in the Islamic World* (London: Routledge, 2007), 39.
[177] Raymond Mauny, *Les siècles obscurs de l'Afrique noire; histoire et archéologie* (Paris: Fayard, 1970), 240–241.
[178] Ralph Austen, "The Trans-Saharan Slave Trade: A Tentative Census" in Henry Gemery and Jan Hogendorn, *The Uncommon Market: Essays in the Economic History of the Atlantic Slave Trade* (New York: Academic Press, 1979), 66.

at his general's compromise and replaced him with Mahmud b. 'Ali b. Zarqun with the order to continue the conquest until complete domination was gained. Al-Ifrani stated that: "When Mahmud was in firm command of the situation there, he sent half of the army with a gift for al-Mansur. It contained untold treasures, including 1200 slaves, both male and female, forty loads of gold dust, four saddles of pure gold, many loads of ebony, a jar of galia, civet cats, and other highly priced valuables."[179] As-Sa'di reported that al-Mansur was unsatisfied with the spoils of war. He proclaimed angrily his disappointment that his officers had amassed enormous wealth from the conquest but sent him only one hundred thousand mithqals (pieces of gold). He then summoned his treasury officer, Hammu, to his court and commanded him to show the records, which showed an enormous amount of money. When the sultan inquired about the discrepancy, Hammu replied that the rest of the money was depleted by Mahmud b. Zarqun. However, the sultan discovered through his informants that Hammu himself had diverted fraudulently twenty thousand pieces of gold to his property in the Draa region. Hammu was imprisoned and replaced by Naffas to exercise the function of treasurer in Jenne. The stolen gold was discovered and restored to al-Mansur.[180]

After defeating the Songhay army and seizing Gao, Mahmud b. Zarqun, the military commander of the Moroccan army, settled in Timbuktu. When he noticed the influence of prominent scholar Ahmad Baba, who openly opposed the illegal invasion of his country, on his countrymen, he arrested him and exiled him with all members of his family in Morocco in 1593. Moroccan scholar al-Ifrani reported that:

[Mahmud b. Zarqun] arrested the imam, the erudite, the high-minded, the eminent among scholars, Abu 'l-'Abbas Ahmad Baba and his kin, and dispatched them in chains to Marrakesh, together with their womenfolk, plundering their goods, their treasures, and books. The author of *Badhl al-munasaha* said: "I heard [Ahmad Baba] say: 'I had the smallest library of any of my kin, and they seized 1,600 volumes.'" The scholars were arrested at the end of Muharram 1002, and reached Marrakesh in Ramadan of the same year. They remained in prison with their families until the period of tribulation ended for them, and they were released on Sunday 21 Ramadan 1004/9 May 1596, and the hearts of the believers rejoiced at that.[181]

---

[179] Hunwick, *Timbuktu*, 315.
[180] As-Sa'di, *Tarikh as-Sudan*, 266–267 of the French text and 174–175 of the Arab text. Or Hunwick, *Timbuktu*, 225–226.
[181] Al-Ifrani in Hunwick, *Timbuktu*, 315.

According to Mahmud Ka'ti and Ibn al-Mukhtar, the authors of *Tarikh al-Fattash*, the number of prisoners "was a little more than seventy people. None of them did return ever, with the exception of Ahmad Baba."[182] Ahmad Baba's scholarship was recognized throughout Morocco and when he finally was able to speak in person to the sultan of Morocco, he asked him why he invaded Songhay, which was an Islamic country – articulating his countrymen's indignation. The sultan replied, for "the unity of the lands of Islam." It was clear that this rationale of forced unity brought Morocco access to more gold and black slaves.[183] With this conquest, Morocco became a vast empire spreading from the Mediterranean to the Niger River. "The Moroccan customs," writes historian Michel Abitbol, "were henceforth stationed, not only in Sus, in Draa and in Tafilalt [and far south of Morocco], but also [...] in Timbuktu and Jenne."[184] The colony that the Sa'di invasion created in the Niger bend was called the Pashalik of Timbuktu. Although they continued to pay allegiance to the sultans in Morocco until the 'Alawid period, the Pashalik had a degree of internal autonomy.

The total of enslaved blacks brought to Morocco after the Sa'di invasion was high. According to az-Zayani, when Mahmud b. Zarqun returned to Morocco in 1598, he brought back with him ten thousand male slaves and ten thousand female slaves, all having reached puberty. He also brought with him 400 loads of gold dust. Al-Mansur gave half of the slaves to the chiefs of the navy to work as a crew in the vessels. This information adds confirming evidence that the sultan wanted to build a strong fleet to compete with the Europeans in the Atlantic. He assigned the other half of the slaves to the army and equipped them with weapons and horses, allowing them to marry female slaves.[185] The anonymous author of *The History of Marrakesh* also spoke of ten thousand slaves that al-Mansur conscripted into the army. Additional historical documents from the era of Sultan Mawlay Isma'il (1672–1727) confirm that al-Mansur did enlist a large number of blacks in the army.[186] Regardless of the accuracy of

---

[182] Ka'ti and Ibn al-Mukhtar, *Tarikh al-fattash*, 307 of the French text and 174 of the Arabic text.

[183] See Al-Fishtali, *Manahil*, 152–154.

[184] Michel Abitbol, *Tombouctou et les Arma* (Paris: Maisonneuve et Larose, 1979), 78.

[185] Roger Le Tourneau, "Histoire de la dynastie sa'dide. Extrait de al-Turguman al-mu'rib 'an duwal al-Masriq wal Magrib d'Abû al Qâsim ben Ahmad ben 'Ali ben Ibrahim al-Zayyânî. Texte, traduction et notes présentés par L. Mougin et H. Hamburger," *Revue de l'Occident musulman et de la Méditerranée* 23, no. 1 (1977): 7–109, 53.

[186] See Anonymous author, *Tarikh Marrakesh* (Rabat: Bibliothèque Générale, ms. K 970), 369.

reports about how many were enslaved, it is clear that thousands of slaves were taken to Morocco and that many of them were recruited into the army. What is not clear is what happened to the rest of the enslaved people. It is possible that some were used in the production of sugar cane. Michel Abitbol and Paul Berthier suggest that an economic motive for al-Mansur's invasion of Songhay was to import slaves to work on sugar cane plantations.[187] Although the sources are not explicit about this, there are strong indications that al-Mansur did indeed use slaves for this purpose. Historical precedents confirm such practices. Leo Africanus reported that slaves were used in farming in the south of Morocco. In other Moroccan sources, slaves are mentioned in social settings only incidentally. Leo Africanus wrote that there was so much unrest in Haskura, a region in southern Morocco, that only slaves and women could move around and go to the fields.[188]

Moroccan historian and statesman az-Zayani (1734–1833) reported that among the first things Sultan al-Mansur did after his great victory in the Sudan was to build "sugar refineries like pyramids."[189] According to al-Fishtali, al-Mansur built many sugar refineries in Haha and Shishawa in the south of Morocco.[190] With gold from the Sudanese campaign and cheap labor (black slaves obtained from the Sudan), the sultan must have been inspired to restart the sugar industry on a large scale – a lucrative product with a ready market in Europe. Al-Ifrani (died in 1743 or 1745) reported that Italian marble was exchanged for Moroccan sugar weight for weight.[191] Paul Berthier, drawing from primary sources that discuss the use of slave labor in sugar production, identified a set of toponyms associated with the regions in which sugar was produced: Dyur al-'Abid (the houses of slaves) and Rawdat al-'Abid (cemetery for slaves) in Mogador (Essaouira); Qsur al-'Abid (the villages of slaves) and Sur al-'Abid (the aqueduct of slaves) in Shishawa. In Sus, a largely Berber-speaking area, the toponym in close proximity to the sugar refinery of Tazemmourt was called Agrur Ismgan (pl. of *ismag*, slave) meaning the gathering place for slaves.[192] Spanish chronicler Luis del Marmol Carvajal (1520–1600)

[187] Paul Berthier, *Les anciennes sucreries du Maroc et leurs réseaux hydrauliques* (Rabat: Impr. Françaises et Marocaines, 1966), 243; Abitbol, *Tombouctou*, 42–43.

[188] Leo Africanus, *Description*, tome 1, 131. The Arabic translation, vol. 1, 164.

[189] Le Tourneau, "Histoire de la dynastie sa'dide," 46.

[190] Al-Fishtali, *Manahil*, 209.

[191] Mohammad Esseghir ben Elhadj ben AbdAllah Eloufrani, *Nozhet-elhadi. Histoire de la dynastie saadienne au Maroc (1151–1670)*, traduction française par Octave Houdas (Paris: Ernest Leroux, 1889), 180.

[192] Paul Berthier, "Les plantations de canne à sucre et les fabriques de sucre dans l'ancien Maroc," *Hespéris-Tamuda* (Rabat: Editions techniques nord-africaines, 1962), vol. 7, 37. See also Berthier, *Les anciennes sucreries*, 239.

noted in the 1550s that European captives were used in the Sus to produce sugar.[193] European slaves appeared to be less numerous than enslaved black Africans.

The sugar produced in these areas was of high quality and exported to European countries such as Italy and France but especially to England because during this period Morocco had an alliance with England.[194] Al-Mansur's foreign affairs with England under Queen Elizabeth were intriguing. After the initial commercial alliance, Queen Elizabeth was interested in a military collaboration with al-Mansur. In a letter to Queen Elizabeth in 1601, al-Mansur proposed that Morocco and England together conquer the West Indies, expel the Spaniards, and occupy the land under a joint authority. The queen was well disposed to attack the Spaniards in their colonies but not in their homeland. Consequently, she asked the sultan of Morocco to provide one hundred thousand pounds for their joint scheme.[195]

Al-Mansur envisioned the occupation of the West Indies in the following letter that he wrote to the queen:

Besides, we must treat of your armie and of our armie, which shall go to those countries, of peopling the land, after that – with the help of God – we shall have subdued it. For our intent is not onely to enter upon the land to sack it and leave it, but to possesse it and that it remayne under our dominion for ever, and – by the help of God – to joyne it to our estate and yours. And therefore it shall be needful for us to treat the peopling thereof, whether it be your pleasure it shall be inhabited by our armie or yours, or whether we shall take it on our chardg to inhabite it with our armie without yours, in respect of the great heat of the clymat, where those of your countrie doo not fynde themselfes fitt to endure the extremitie of heat there and of the cold of your partes, where our men endure it very well by reason that the heat hurtes them not.[196]

The letter continues to emphasize that this will be a joint venture in which the two parties will equally share in the profits of the West Indies by dividing it so that every party would know its share. The letter calls the queen's attention to the benefit of such an alliance by stating:

And your high estate shall knowe that, in the inhabiting of those countries by us and yow, yow shall have a great benefite: first for that those countries of the East are adjoyning to many Kinges Moores and infinite nations or our religion; and further, if your power and command shall be seene there with owre armie,

[193] Carvajal, *L'Afriqve de Marmol*, tome II, 30–31.
[194] See Berthier, "Les plantations," 37 and de Castries (ed.), *Les Sources inédites de l'histoire du Maroc*, tome II, 200.
[195] De Castries (ed.), *Les sources inédites de l'histoire du Maroc*, tome II, 206.
[196] Ibid., 208.

all the Moores will joyne and confederate themselves – by the help of God – with us and yow.[197]

Coincidentally, both rulers died in 1603, and their alliance regarding the colonization of the West Indies did not materialize. These great achievements of al-Mansur were not followed up after his death as Morocco fell into political disarray due to the struggle for power between the sons of al-Mansur. Furthermore, the European mass production of sugar in the Americas and in the West Indies meant that Europe was no longer interested in importing this commodity from Morocco. The competition from these new sources of sugar was a factor in the decline of the sugar industry in Morocco. The sixteenth century marked the beginnings of European dominance on the African continent. British historian Basil Davidson explained:

From 1500 onwards the western seas were increasingly traced by sailing ship routes linking western Africa to Western Europe, and soon afterwards to the eastern seaboard of the Americas and the Islands of the Caribbean. In this new trading community West Africans played almost from the first an indispensable part. This was not as ship-builders or ship-masters, for they had none of the necessary skills, experience or incentive to impel them in that direction; and the carrying trade remained a European monopoly of skill and ownership. With rising European technological supremacy, this was the period in which the foundations for Africa's future dependence on Europe, whether economic or political, began to be laid.[198]

The events in Morocco as they related to the dynamics of Atlantic trade were crucial in shaping and defining the path and future of a globalized Atlantic world. The diverse people of the Atlantic regions and the Saharan borders created a world of cosmopolitanism, forged in the crucible of cultural exchange, biological hybridity, and political alliances as well as violence, enslavement, colonization, and war.[199]

Indeed, it was in the southern part of Morocco where most slaves and even free blacks were collected and enrolled in the army of Mawlay Isma'il (1672–1727) and the subsequent ruling 'Alawi dynasty. This unique episode in the history of blacks in Morocco will be discussed in the following chapter.

---

[197] Ibid., 209.
[198] Basil Davidson, *Africa in History: Themes and Outlines* (New York: Touchstone, 1995), 205–206.
[199] See Paul Gilroy, *The Black Atlantic: Modernity and Double Consciousness* (New York: Verso, 1993).

4

"Racializing" Slavery

The Controversy of Mawlay Isma'il's Project

When you make men slaves, you deprive them of half their virtue, you set them, in your own conduct, an example of fraud, rapine, and cruelty, and compel them to live with you in a state of war; and yet you complain that they are not honest or faithful! You stupify them with stripes, and think it necessary to keep them in a state of ignorance.[1]

The main legal schools of Islam sanctioned the enslavement of non-Muslims, regardless of skin color, race, or ethnicity, through legitimate means such as a "just war," a purchase, or a gift.[2] The restriction of enslavement to the context of "just war" meant that Muslims were forbidden to enslave free Muslims or to enslave non-Muslims outside the context of jihad. Historical events and records, however, point to instances when Muslims did in fact enslave other Muslims. The enslavement of freed black Moroccans and Haratin during the reign of Mawlay Isma'il (1646–1727) is one particularly poignant example. The enslavement of free blacks by the sultan for the purpose of forming an army exclusively loyal to him, consisting solely of "black slaves," and the debate that it provoked in Morocco marked a crucial incident in the history of relations between social groups defined by different skin colors, with racial questions becoming implicitly embedded in the legal discourse.

During the reign of Mawlay Isma'il, Morocco was a complex society that could be divided according to a variety of overlapping social categories. Linguistically, Morocco consisted of Arabic speakers and Berber

[1] Olaudah Equiano, *The Interesting Narrative and Other Writings* (New York: Penguin Books, 1995), 111.
[2] For more details see Chapter 2.

speakers.[3] Religiously, Morocco was composed of an overwhelming Muslim majority and a Jewish minority. The leader of the Jewish community during Mawlay Isma'il's reign was Abraham Maymuran. The Jews followed their own law administered through their synagogues, but they did not have the right to bear arms. They generated their income mainly from commerce and from trades such as tailoring and jewelry making.[4] Among Muslims, there were followers of various Sufi orders (*zawaya*, plural of *zawiya* or *turuq*, plural of *tariqa*), some of which conflicted openly with the teachings and practices of others. There were the descendants of and those who claimed descent from the Prophet Muhammad, the *shurafa'* (sing. *sharif*), who possessed certain privileges, which might relate to material or political benefits. Indeed, many ruling dynasties and leaders of religious brotherhoods claimed a sharifian descent to the point that this kinship became sine qua non for authority. There were the religious scholars (*'ulama'*) and Sufi masters (*shuyukh*); sometimes the two were one and the same. There were also the transhumant pastoralists, nomads, sedentary agriculturalists, urban merchants, and artisans. And then there were the social groups known as Haratin and slaves (sing. *'abd*; pl. *'abid*). Physical characteristics and other means of categorizing the latter subaltern groups constituted another cluster of markers used in defining Moroccan society.

The Isma'ili Project

In the middle of the seventeenth century, Morocco's central government was in turmoil. The Sa'di dynasty was in decline and could not resolve the political disorder and anarchy that infested the country. Powerful individuals, often at the head of Sufi orders (for example, the Dila'iyya order) or tribal groups (for example, the Shabanat tribe), took control of their own regions and often tried to challenge the authority and legitimacy of the Sa'di dynasty. As a consequence of this political instability, the army once relatively united and well organized under the rule of al-Mansur became

[3] I have explained in the previous chapter that the Arab people of Arabia were ambitious to extend their sphere of influence in the name of Islam. They invaded North Africa in the 640s and from then on North Africa grew vastly linguistically and biologically arabized and Islamized. Berbers are the first inhabitants of North Africa and are linguistically identified as an ethnic group.

[4] Chantal de La Véronne and Joseph de León, *Vie de Moulay Isma'il, roi de Fès et de Maroc: d'après Joseph de León, 1708–1728: étude et édition*. Documents d'histoire maghrébine, v. 2. (Paris: P. Geuthner, 1974), 68 of the French translation and 156–157 of the Spanish text.

fragmented. In Morocco, the weakness of the central authority affected the "national" political cohesion. Loyalties fluctuated and devolved into regional, tribal, ethnic, or religious orders' interests, strengthening corporate communities. Some soldiers returned to join their tribal groups. As for black slaves, they gradually claimed their freedom and settled in different parts of the country, doing all kinds of work in order to support themselves and their families. In addition, Western European countries, such as Spain, took advantage of Moroccan internal political divisions and occupied more towns along Morocco's coast, such as Larache, Ceuta, and Melilla. The Sa'di dynasty grew inept at protecting the sovereignty of its territorial borders.[5] The internal strife was also harmful to commerce, especially long-distance trade routes such as those between Marrakesh, Tafilalt, Tuwat, and Timbuktu. The inhabitants of the oasis of Tafilalt called upon the 'Alawi family to assume an ambitious political role in order to pacify the country. The 'Alawi family came from Arabia to Tafilalt in the thirteenth century and enjoyed special social prestige because of their connection to the house of the Prophet – they were known as *shurafa'* because they claimed descent from the Prophet Muhammad through his grandson, Hasan. They also controlled a great deal of the trade and the land in the region of Tafilalt, especially date plantations.[6] The first leader was Mawlay ash-Sharif and he was succeeded by his son, Mawlay Muhammad in 1635. Among Mawlay Muhammad's first acts in building his power base was to seize control of the trans-Saharan trade. Historian 'Abd al-Karim ar-Rifi (fl. 1740–1786) reported that in 1645, this emerging 'Alawi leader attacked key areas across the southern trade routes such as Tikurarin and Tuwat and required their inhabitants to pay tribute. In this way he amassed a fortune in gold, silver, and slaves.[7] His brother, Mawlay ar-Rashid, further expanded 'Alawi power in the eastern part of Morocco. In 1666, he seized Fez and proclaimed himself sultan. He attacked Marrakesh in 1669 and named his nephew Ibn Mahraz its governor.[8] Mawlay ar-Rashid continued his territorial conquest with an army that included a good number of black slaves.[9] However, he died in 1672 before completing the unification of Morocco and consolidating

[5] Eloufrani, *Nozhet-elhadi*, 321.
[6] Windus, *A Journey to Mequinez*, 190.
[7] 'Abd al-Karim b. Musa ar-Rifi, *az-Zahr al-Akamm*, ed. by Asia Ben 'dada (Rabat: Matba'at al-Ma'arif al-Jadida, 1992), 112. Ar-Rifi's exact date of death is unknown. He died between 1740 and 1786.
[8] See Eloufrani. *Nozhet-elhadi*, 501–503.
[9] Ar-Rifi, *az-Zahr al-Akamm*, 138–139.

'Alawi rule. The task of extending 'Alawi rule fell to his brother, Mawlay Isma'il, who inherited his brother's treasury and took command of the 'Alawi establishment from the city of Meknes. Mawlay Isma'il's intention was to move from Fez to Meknes, the mark of a new political era associated with his personal autonomy.

When he came to power in 1672, Mawlay Isma'il faced a fragmented society and political instability in many areas of Morocco. The southern provinces that controlled the trans-Saharan trade routes frequently revolted against the central authority. In the north, the towns also desired to keep some, if not all, of the autonomy they had gained during the decline of the Sa'di dynasty in the middle of the seventeenth century. In central Morocco, the Sufi group of the Zawiya Dila'iyya challenged the young 'Alawi dynasty and its claim of sharifian descent. In addition, the European occupation of coastal towns such as Larache by the Spaniards and Mogador by the Portuguese, and the threat of the Ottomans from Algeria, urged the sultan to strengthen the authority of the Makhzan (Moroccan central government) in order to achieve unification of the territory.[10] Traditionally, the strength of royal political power was negotiated and relied upon a clientele system – the political support of tribal groups and Sufi orders in return for royal favors. Accordingly, sultans mustered soldiers from specific tribal groups, rural Sufi orders, and mercenaries in return for exemption from taxes and rights to land controlled by these sultans. Mawlay Isma'il, however, was convinced that this clientele system was not reliable enough for the maintenance of a strong central government and the unity of the country. The soldiers that came from various tribes were not completely free of their obligations toward their tribes, and those conscripted from Sufi orders pledged their allegiance to the heads of their orders.

As for the black soldiers, after the decline of the Sa'di rule, there were those who stayed in the army and those who served officials and their families. There were also those who claimed their freedom where they were garrisoned and ended up working in agriculture, digging wells, tending cattle, and so forth. Consequently, black Moroccans, in addition to the Haratin and other freed blacks from the private sector, formed endogamous social groups and isolated families, owning properties and managing their lives just like other free Muslims.[11] The state

---

[10] See Mohammed Kenbib (ed.), *La Grande Encyclopedie du Maroc: Histoire* (Rabat: GEM, 1987), 121–126.

[11] This is confirmed even by Ibn Naji who delivered a fatwa against the Haratin. I own a copy of this document of forty-eight pages which came from a private collection in

slave registers from the time of Mawlay Isma'il's rule attest to the fact that some blacks were indeed affluent and possessed important assets such as land and livestock.[12] Some former slaves ended up in the urban streets and markets as casual laborers doing menial work, acquiring a pejorative label: "the slaves of the streets" (*'abid az-zanqa*).[13] But many Moroccan blacks had been free since long before the Sa'di dynasty (which ruled from the 1550s to circa 1659); they were autochthonous like the Haratin, who were mostly sharecroppers in southern Morocco, or others who came to Morocco as slaves and were manumitted through various means: serving in the central authority or as a result of the commendation of the *mukataba* contract or the status of *umm al-walad* (mother of the child) or running away.[14] A minority of West Africans traveled to Morocco as seekers of Islamic knowledge or for other opportunities.[15] Hagiographical literature mentions that some of the blacks were scholars and mystic figures (Sufis).[16] Collectively, though, black Moroccans formed an economically underprivileged class and hence a marginalized social group. Allan Meyers, whose dissertation focuses on the slave soldiers of Mawlay Isma'il, points out that most of the blacks in Morocco "were landless, vulnerable, and despised, and therefore, they had neither sentimental nor material commitments to groups with interests independent of the Mahzan's [central authority]."[17]

Mawlay Isma'il understood that as sultan it would be impossible to consolidate his rule and unite the country without a permanent, organized, and loyal army. Indeed, traditionally, as Moroccan historian Laroui concluded, "the military role of the army was secondary in comparison

---

Rabat. Ahmad b. Muhammad b. Naji (d. 1710), *Fatwa Ibn Naji*, 7. It is cited in the catalogue of Muhammad al-Mannuni, *al-Masadir al-'Arabiyya li-Tarikh al-Maghrib* (Rabat: Publications de la Faculté des Lettres et des Sciences Humaines, 1983), 212.

[12] Unknown author, *Jany al-Azhar wa Nur al-Abhar* (Rabat: Bibliothèque Royale, ms. 11860), 9.

[13] See Ahmad Ibn al-Hajj (d. 1898), *ad-Durr al-Muntakhab al-Mustahsan fi Ba'd Ma'athir Amir al-Mu'minin Mawlana al-Hasan* (Rabat: Bibliothèque Royale, 12184), vol. 6, 111.

[14] See Chapter 2.

[15] See for instance Hassan Sadqi, "Manuscrits Marocains relatifs à Fès et l'Afrique" in *Fès et l'Afrique: Relations Economiques, Culturelles et Spirituelles* (Matba'at an-Najah al-Jadida, 1996), 22–24.

[16] See for instance al-'Abbas ibn Ibrahim as-Samlali, *al-'I'lam bi-man Halla Marrakush wa-Aghmat min al-A'alam*, edited by 'Abd al-Wahhab b. Mansur (Rabat: al-Matba'ah al-Malakiyya, 1993) and Yusuf b. Yahya at-Tadili, *at-Tashawwuf ila Rijal at-Rasawwuf*, établi et annoté, par Ahmed Toufiq (Rabat: Université Muhammad V, Publication de la Faculté des Lettres et des Sciences Humaines de Rabat, 1984).

[17] Allan Meyers, *The 'Abid 'l-Buhari: Slave Soldiers and Statecraft in Morocco, 1672–1790*, PhD Dissertation (Ithaca: Cornell University, 1974), 114.

to its administrative and political function."[18] At first, and in addition
to the Arab Ma'qil troops he inherited from the Sa'di dynasty, Mawlay
Isma'il recruited Arab troops mainly from the Udaya and stationed them
in a camp outside the walls of the city of Fez. The mother of Mawlay
Isma'il, Mubarka bint Yark al-Maghfiri, was born a black slave in the
Arab Mghafra tribe, a division of the Udaya. Mawlay Isma'il referred
to them as the tribe of his uncles, claiming the fictive kinship tied with
his mother's birthplace, albeit unrelated by blood, in order to seek their
loyalty, and invited them to live in Fez.[19] They were, however, small in
number.

Moroccan chronicler Muhammad al-Kardudi (d. 1851) commented
that when Mawlay Isma'il was in the process of organizing his army, initially recruiting Arabs from the Udaya tribe, he consulted with an influential Muslim scholar, Muhammad b. al-'Ayyashi, one of his loyalists,
asking which tribe would be best suited to provide recruits. Al-'Ayyashi
suggested that the slaves who came (through *saby*) from West Africa after
the 1591 Sa'di invasion of Songhay and who formerly had been in service
to the Makhzan might serve well as they were still slaves belonging to the
state. The sultan regarded the idea so highly that he made al-'Ayyashi a
supreme judge (*qadi al-qudat*) acting on his behalf in all the legal matters related to their collection. He also named Pasha 'Alilish as his official
representative in this affair.[20] According to another story found only in a
European account by Joseph de León, a Spanish officer who spent twenty
years in captivity in Morocco (1708–1728), at the beginning of his reign,
Sultan Mawlay Isma'il escaped an assassination attempt committed by
white Moroccans during the celebration of a religious holiday and from
then on he swore that he would trust no one except blacks.[21]

It also appears that Mawlay Isma'il was inspired to establish a black
army when he went to Marrakesh around 1673 to confront the revolt of

[18] Abdallah Laroui, *Les origines sociales et culturelles du nationalisme marocain (1830–
1912)* (Casablanca: Centre Culturel Arabe, 1993), 83.

[19] See 'Abd ar-Rahman b. Zaydan, *al-Manza' al-Latif fi Mafakhir al-Mawla Isma'il
ash-Sharif*, edited by 'Abd al-Hadi at-Tazi (Casablanca: Librairie Idéale, 1993), 43–44;
Abu 'l-Qasim Ahmad az-Zayani, *Le Maroc de 1631 à 1812, extrait de l'ouvrage intitulé
Ettordjemân elmo'arib 'an douel elmachriq ou 'lmaghrib*, published and translated by
Octave Houdas (Paris: Leroux 1886), 5 of the French translation and 3 of the Arabic
text.

[20] Muhammad al-Kardudi, *Kashf al-Ghumma fi Bayan anna Harb an-Nizam Wajib 'ala
Hadhihi al-Umma (The Dissipation of Grief in Revealing that the War of the Regime is
a Duty of the Nation)* (Rabat: Bibliothèque Générale, ms. D 1584), folios 171a–172a.

[21] De La Véronne and de León, *Vie de Moulay Isma'il*, 55 of the French translation and 140
of the Spanish text.

his nephew, Ibn Mahraz.[22] Nineteenth-century Moroccan historian an-
Nasiri described the encounter in the following passage:

The government official Abu Hafs 'Umar b. Qasim al-Murrakushi known as
'Alilish[23] presented [Mawlay Isma'il] with a register that contains the names
of black slaves who served in the army of the Sultan al-Mansur as-Sa'di [r.
1578–1603]. The sultan asked him if there has been anybody left among them,
he answered him that they were numerous and with their children scattered in
Marrakech, in its vicinity and among the Dir tribes. Then he added: "if my lord
ordered me to bring them to him I would do it."[24]

Moroccan chronicles reported that the Sa'di slave register was written
by the father of 'Alilish.[25] Since Sultan al-Mansur as-Sa'di died in 1603,
it appears likely that the grandfather of 'Alilish had served the Sa'di
dynasty. Also, it appears unlikely that the black slaves who had served in
the army of Sultan al-Mansur as-Sa'di were even alive to serve Mawlay
Isma'il. 'Alilish proceeded, however, with gathering these so-called slaves
(*'abid*). Criers announced in the markets, in the cities, and in the countryside that the slaves who wanted to serve the sultan should come forward.
This initial call brought the sultan five thousand men from the streets
(*'abid az-zanqa*) who were given clothes, horses, weapons, and a salary.
This particular group of people appeared voluntarily to join the army
likely because the offer was more promising than living in hardship on
the margins of society. But their number was not sufficient. So the officials coerced more black people to join the army.[26] English traveler John
Windus, who visited Morocco in 1720, wrote on the events that preceded
his visit by a couple of decades:

For in the Year 1698, the Emperor appointed all the Records of the Country to
be searched, that the Discovery might be made of such as were descended from
Slaves and Renegadoes. In this Search were committed a great many Cruelties;
and many thousands of poor People [...] being of a duskier Complexion than
ordinary, if they could not produce long Scrowls [*sic*] of Genealogies, notwithstanding their having lived free for Ages, and enjoyed comfortable Fortunes,

[22] Ar-Rifi, *az-Zahr al-Akamm*, 153.

[23] Historian Mohammed El Fasi pointed out that his real name was Muhammad b.
al-Qasim rather than 'Umar b. Qasim, "Lettres inédites de Moulay Ismaël," *Hespéris
Tamuda* (Rabat: Editions Techniques Nord-Africaines), 1962, 15.

[24] An-Nasiri, *al-Istiqsa'*, vol. 7, 56.

[25] Mohammed El Fasi, "A special issue on the Sultan Mawlay Isam'il," *Hespéris Tamuda*
(Rabat: Editions Techniques Nord-Africaines), 1962, 15. See also Muhammad Akansus,
al-Jaysh al-'Aramram al-Khumasi (Rabat: Bibliothèque Générale, ms. 965), folio 53a.

[26] Muhammad al-Kardudi, *Kashf al-Ghumma fi Bayan anna Harb an-Nizam Wajib 'ala
Hadhihi al-Umma* (Rabat: Bibliothèque Générale, ms. D 1584), folio 172a.

were declared Slaves, their Estates and Persons seized for the Use of the Emperor.[27]

Believing that they were free Muslims, Moroccan blacks were shocked at the way they were singled out and treated like slaves by government officials and protested this illegal procedure. Even among slaves there were those who had established bonds with their masters and simply refused to leave their quarters. 'Alilish agreed to accompany those who protested to the supreme judge's office, knowing very well that their fate had already been decided. The judge was the sultan's collaborator in this affair. Consequently, Mawlay Isma'il commanded his officials to enslave all blacks, even those who were free, including the Haratin. Recall that the word *Haratin* is a complicated name that encompasses different meanings or different categories such as free blacks and freed ex-slaves, but that signified a common trait: they were legally entitled to their freedom.

Complying with the sultan's order, 'Alilish succeeded in collecting all black people in the area of Marrakesh whether they were slaves, free blacks, or Haratin, married with a family or single. He gathered three thousand blacks in a single year. 'Alilish noted their names in a register and sent it to the sultan, who was pleased with the initial success of the mission. The sultan then asked 'Alilish to buy female slaves for the unmarried enslaved recruits, to provide them with clothing, to pay off their owners from the Marrakesh city revenue, and to then send them to him in Meknes. 'Alilish proceeded to carry out the sultan's directive. All tribes and individuals were forced to cooperate with the sultan's officials in this project if they wanted to remain on good terms with him. Blacks who were in someone's possession were bought at the price of ten mithqals per person, male or female, and free blacks or Haratin were collected with no payment to anybody. This process became the pattern in collecting blacks in the rest of the country. All recruits were finally taken to a massive military camp called Mashra' ar-Ramla (sand dam), near the Tiflet River, west of Meknes in the Salé region. In this special enclave, the sultan's new conscripts were trained to serve the sultan and his Makhzan.[28] Among the names given to this army of black people, military and civilians, were *'Abid ad-Diwan* (slaves of the royal court), *Jaysh al-Wisfan* or *Jaysh al-'Abid* (the slave army), and *Wisfan* or *'Abid as-Sultan* (the sultan's slaves),

---

[27] Windus, *A Journey to Mequinez*, 215.

[28] This entire paragraph is taken with my emphasis from az-Zayani, *al-Bustan az-Zarif fi Dawlat Awlad Mawaly 'Ali ash-Sharif* (Rabat: Bibliothèque Royale, ms. D 1577), 31–32.

but the most famous and the commonly used name was *'Abid al-Bukhari,* especially when referring to black soldiers.[29] The origin of this name is explained as follows:

When the Sultan had gathered all the blacks and succeeded in his mission in achieving complete loyalty and abandoned his reliance on the tribes [...]. He gave them a copy of the Imam al-Bukhari's book and said you are now slaves of the Prophet; you follow what he said and avoid what he forbade. He gave each one of the leaders a copy of the book to keep. This is how they have become to be known as *'Abid al-Bukhari.*[30]

According to an-Nasiri, Mawlay Isma'il gathered the chiefs among the blacks and told them: "You and I are now servants of the *Sunna* [traditions] of the Prophet Muhammad (peace be upon him) and his law contained in this book [of al-Bukhari]. We practice what he prescribed and we abstain from all that he forbade and upon that we fight."[31] By this, Mawlay Isma'il legitimized and cemented his command of the black army through an oath or a solemn declaration calling on a sacred object: the book referred to as *Sahih al-Bukhari,* the second fundamental source for Islamic law after the Qur'an, as witness. Mawlay Isma'il instructed them to keep copies of *Sahih al-Bukhari* and to carry them in battle, similar to the arc of the covenant carried by the people of Israel when going into battle. In this way the black army came to be known as *'Abid al-Bukhari.*[32]

The color of their skin and their slave origin status were the grounds for enslavement, regardless of the blacks' long integration in Moroccan society. Such prejudice played a substantial role in Sultan Mawlay Isma'il's decision to buy and enslave all blacks. But this prejudice was fluid, albeit locked in patrilineal lineage, as we shall see. Mawlay Isma'il treated the black army as conscripts and not as slaves. The soldiers could have been motivated by "racial solidarity" even if the sultan was not. Indeed, Africanist scholar Baba Ibrahima Kaké argued that blacks pledged loyalty to Isma'il because his mother was a black slave. But he seemed to conflate the motivation of the soldiers with those of the sultan. The color and origin of the slave army was just a coincidence as a

[29] Black soldiers saw their status as something other than slaves as the ensuing analysis will show. Henceforward, I will to refer to the *'Abid al-Bukhari* or the "black army" simply as "the army."
[30] Ahmad Ibn al-Hajj, *ad-Durr al-Muntakhab al-Mustahsan fi Ba'd Ma'athir Amir al-Mu'minin Mawlana al-Hasan* (Rabat: Bibliothèque Royale, ms.12184), vol. 6, 116.
[31] An-Nasiri, *al-Istisqa',* vol. 7, 58–59.
[32] Ibid., 59.

significant marker. What was crucial to the sultan was the servile status of these people. Incidentally, the intimate reliance of the rulers on slaves was a common practice in Africa. This was clear even within societies where color was not a marker as in the Hausa case. Sean Stilwell, who studied slavery in the nineteenth-century Sokoto Caliphate, commented that: "for the ruler, slaves were the perfect antidote to relying on unpredictable kin or clients."[33] Indeed, Mawlay Isma'il's main concern was to establish a strong army by any and all means. Kaké argued that the "bi-racial status" of Mawlay Isma'il was a factor in conscripting all black Moroccans into his army and hence the sultan was motivated by "black racial solidarity."[34] Abu Hassun as-Susi, a Berber Sufi leader of a religious order of Iligh in the Sus region, gave a female slave who was born in slavery among the Arab Mghafra tribe to Mawlay ash-Sharif, the first 'Alawi leader in the Tafilalt region, in order to serve him while he held him temporarily captive in Sus during a regional conflict. Her name was Mubarka bint Yark al-Maghfiri (d. 1668); she was a servant/concubine of Mawlay ash-Sharif. When she bore him children, her status became *umm al-walad* and she acquired certain legal rights. Her two children, Mawlay Isma'il and Mawlay al-Mahdi, were considered free as a consequence of being fathered by a free man.[35] Under Islamic law, patrilineal descent constitutes the arbiter of one's Arabic identity. Thus Sultan Mawlay Isma'il, although a son of a black woman, thought of himself and was perceived to be an Arab, and referred to himself as *sharif* rather than black (that is, of African descent).[36]

---

[33] Sean Stilwell, *Paradoxes of Power: The Kano "Mamluks" and Male Royal Slavery in the Sokoto Caliphate, 1804–1903* (Portsmouth: Heinemann, 2004), 39.

[34] Baba Ibrahima Kaké, "L'aventure des *Bukhara* (prétoriens noirs) au Maroc, au XVIIIe siècle," *Présence Africaine*, No 70 – 2nd quarterly, 1969, 67–74.

[35] See Ibn Zaydan, *al-Manza' al-Latif*, 43–44; az-Zayani, *Le Maroc de 1631 à 1812*, 5 of the French translation and 3 of the Arabic text. It is important to note that Ibn Zaydan insisted that Mawlay Isma'il mother was a slave (*ama mamluka*) and not related to the Udaya by blood or milk.

[36] Ensel concludes that this distinction between blacks and Arabs in reference to the *sharif* status in Draa region contributed to perpetuate the subordinate status of the blacks. Remco Ensel, *Saints and Servants in Southern Morocco* (Leiden: Brill, 1999), 25–29.
It is also interesting to note that African American scholar Joel Augustus Rogers (1883–1966) had a special entry for Mawlay Isma'il in his book *World's Great Men of Color*. He presented him as a son of "a full-blooded Negro slave." See Joel Augustus Rogers, *World's Great Men of Color* (New York: Collier Books, 1972), vol. 1, 257. Rogers' categorization of Isma'il as a "man of color" is arguably more reasonable than defining him as "white." Hence this is clear evidence that all these racial designations are arbitrary and culturally constructed.

The controversy over the enslavement or conscription of all black Moroccans provoked a heated debate and overt hostility between some of the *'ulama'* (religious scholars) and Mawlay Isma'il. This was a sharp violation of the most salient Islamic legal code regarding the institution of slavery, which stated that it was illegal to enslave any adherent to Islam. The discourse and needs of the state as advanced by the sultan as a political authority and the discourse and interpretation of the tenets of Islam as advanced by the religious scholars, custodians of Islamic law, collided. And this collision had racial implications questioning the legal status of only one group of Moroccans who happened to be black.

An annually renewed oath of investiture (*al-bay'a*), a contractual agreement between the ruler and the people, was an important ritual through which the sultan was recognized as a legitimate ruler. However, the religious scholars were also crucial in legitimizing the authority of the ruler and ensuring that he remained within the scope of accepted Islamic codes and practice. Consequently, the sultan had no choice but to take the religious scholars seriously and consult with them in his initiative concerning the enslavement of black Moroccans. Mawlay Isma'il corresponded with the most influential religious scholars in Morocco, trying his best to convince them of the need and legitimacy of his recruitment project already under way. In one of the first letters dated July 31, 1693, the sultan requested one of the leaders among these scholars, Muhammad b. 'Abd al-Qadir al-Fasi (d. 1704), to deliver his legal opinion regarding 'Alilish's enslavement of black Moroccans. The scholar unequivocally declared that it was illegal to reduce free people into bondage and that the sources of Islamic law, the Sunna, and the consensus of the Muslim community all agreed on this.[37] But he affirmed that those whose slave condition was confirmed were subject to business regulations prescribed by Islamic law: they could be bought, sold, and recruited into the army or used for any other benefit.[38]

The Legal Debate

The sultan was aware of the implications of his project but he wanted to find an exception to the rule allowing him not only to legitimize what he had done so far but also to continue the enslavement of free black Moroccans. By 1678, thousands of people had already been gathered

[37] El Fasi, "A special issue," 17, 19, and 45.
[38] Ibid., 29.

from different parts of Morocco – from Marrakesh, Tetouan, Fez, and
Meknes.[39] Mawlay Isma'il had personally overseen one of the early campaigns to gather a great number of the Haratin in the move to consolidate
his power. In 1678, he ordered an expedition to the south of Sus and to
the Sahara (Aqqa, Tata, Tishit, and Shinqit) requesting the inhabitants of
the Sahel region such as the Mghafra, Dalim, Barbush, Mta', Jarrar, and
others from the Ma'qil tribes to send their deputations and declare their
allegiance to him. Among the leaders of these deputations was Bakkar
al-Mghafri, who offered his daughter Khanatha to the sultan. The sultan
admired this woman and married her because she was beautiful and cultivated: she was versed in many sciences. Khanatha became the mother of
Sultan Mawlay 'Abd Allah. He also imported from this region two thousand Haratin with their children and sent them to the camp in Mashra'
ar-Ramla.[40]

In a letter dated July 15, 1697, to the aforementioned scholar
Muhammad b. 'Abd al-Qadir al-Fasi, the sultan insisted on the necessity
of creating an efficient professional army, albeit at the expense of coercing a segment of the Moroccan population to serve a higher purpose,
claiming that the soldier among the free Arabs or Berbers did not forget
where he came from. He could not wait to go back to his herd or his field,
and if the opportunity was offered he would leave the army and join his
tribe again after receiving payment for his unfinished job. In addition,
the sultan argued, Arabs such as those in Fez were disposed to idleness;
they lacked physical strength and preferred leisure, unlike the slaves who
were brave, gritty, competent, and patient.[41] The sultan used the term
'Abid as interchangeable with *black*. His intention was to emphasize the
slave origin of free black Moroccans. This was stated clearly in his letters to religious scholars. In a letter dated May 21, 1698 from the sultan
to Fez scholars that was read in the mosque of Fez, the sultan requested
the scholars to sign the registers of the Haratin and hence approve their
collection.[42] In a letter dated January 26, 1701 to Muhammad b. 'Abd
al-Qadir al-Fasi, Mawlay Isma'il wrote that no matter how the blacks,
especially the brown-skinned Haratin (*ahmar al-jilda*), had been urban-
ized, had become prosperous practicing all kinds of crafts and managing their own properties, they nonetheless remained slaves. That they

---

[39] Az-Zayani, *al-Bustan az-Zarif*, 32.
[40] An-Nasiri, *al-Istisqa'*, vol. 7, 58 and az-Zayani, *al-Bustan az-Zarif*, 32.
[41] El Fasi, "Lettres inédites de Moulay Ismaël," 48–50.
[42] Ahmad Ibn al-Hajj, *ad-Durr al-Muntakhab*, vol. 6, 389.

gradually had severed all ties with their masters and had even forgotten that they were originally slaves did not alter the fact that in Isma'il's view, they were still slaves. The sultan argued that some of the Haratin might have known that they were slaves or descendants of slaves but pretended not to know in order not to degrade themselves, and would surely invoke Islamic law to prove their free status.[43]

It is clear that Mawlay Isma'il did not intend to have a dialogical debate with the scholars of the city of Fez to resolve the Haratin legal question. Rather, his intention was to persuade them to concede to his request. According to Moroccan historian Muhammad al-Kardudi, the scholars of Fez were more indignant when 'Alilish tried to force the Haratin of Fez to accept the condition of slavery. Some scholars and their leaders resisted the arguments of the sultan concerning the enslavement of free black people, and they overtly expressed their disagreement with the sultan. In response, Mawlay Isma'il ordered these scholars to have an audience with him.[44] The divergent views between the sultan and the scholars infuriated the sultan. When Shaykh Jassus, who appeared to be the most outspoken, expressed his dismay and condemned the sultan's slavery project, the sultan was even more infuriated and left the meeting. Muhammad al-Kardudi stated that, "Jassus experienced great affliction and the cause of it was the devil's work of 'Alilish who gathered the Haratin and brought forcefully these free people unjustly into servitude and confiscated their wealth."[45] Mawlay Isma'il dismissed the outcry of the scholars and continued to insist that the crucial need of a strong army to unite and defend the country overrode the objections of the religious scholars. He was convinced that the gap could only be filled by slaves and he argued that the slave origin of the Haratin justified their re-enslavement for forced conscription. He insisted on the legality of the compulsory buying of slaves from their masters and the enslavement of the Haratin. He claimed that every register of slaves was annexed by a long list of names and signatures of the scholars, notaries, and witnesses. The sultan communicated to the scholars of Fez that he was deeply displeased with them for not complying and sent them harsh warnings informing them that they would be subjected to fines, humiliation, torture, and even death in order to intimidate and to coerce them to

---

[43] El Fasi, "Lettres inédites de Moulay Ismaël," 56.
[44] Muhammad al-Kardudi, *Kashf al-Ghumma fi Bayan anna Harb an-Nizam Wajib 'ala Hadhihi al-Umma* (Rabat: Bibliothèque Générale, ms. D 1584), folio 173b. Muhammad al-Kardudi provided the names of some of these scholars.
[45] Ibid., folio 174a.

endorse his project. Jassus was probably the most outspoken in defense of the free black Muslims, but other scholars also refused to concede to these threats. Jassus issued a fatwa against this operation because he saw a great violation of Islamic law in the collection of the Haratin and believed that it was the moral duty of every Muslim to object and stop this transgression immediately.[46] He also questioned the authority's methods and the documentation of slave registers. Jassus explained that the Haratin were born free and argued further that, even if the Haratin conceded to the sultan's request of their own free will and acknowledged their slave origin, their enslavement would still be illegal because they had been acknowledged as free Muslims for generations. Their free status was unquestionable. Jassus was appalled to witness such a scandalous injustice against the Haratin in his own city, the capital of Islamic learning in Morocco, and was filled with consternation in the way he was coerced along with colleagues to conform to the sultan's demands. He exclaimed:

As for those who are today marked out for enslavement and who are our immediate concern, we grew up together in the same town (Fas). We know them well. We know their free status and nothing pertaining to their condition is hidden from us. But now we have been coerced to retract our firm beliefs and what we are certain of. On the whole the evils that are associated with this issue are indeed innumerable.[47]

Jassus' heroic defiance landed him in prison. 'Abd Allah ar-Rusi, governor of Fez, executed the order. He tortured Jassus, imposed fines on him, harassed his entire family, and confiscated all their possessions. When ar-Rusi was unable to induce him to embrace the legality of the actions against the Haratin, he ordered Jassus executed by strangulation on July 2, 1709, setting an example to all who dared to challenge the authority of the ruler.[48] Besides Jassus, the moral hero of the tragedy of the blacks, there were other outspoken leading scholars ostracized by the government, such as al-'Arabi Burdulla (d. 1721), who delivered legal

---

[46] The English translation of this fatwa is in Aziz Abdalla Batran, "The *'Ulama'* of Fas, M. Isma'il and the Issue of the Haratin of Fas," *Slaves and Slavery in Muslim Africa*, edited by John R. Willis (London: Frank Cass, 1985), vol. 2, 9–13.

[47] Ibid., vol. 2, 13.

[48] The information regarding the great scholar Jassus is taken from three sources: Muhammad ibn 'Abd as-Salam ad-Du'ayyif, *Tarikh ad-Du'ayyif: Tarikh ad-Dawla as-Sa'ida*, edited and annotated by Ahmad al-'Ammari (Rabat: Dar al-Ma'thurtat, 1986), 83–86; al-Kardudi, *Kashf al-Ghumma*, folios 173b-174a and an-Nasiri, *al-Istisqa'*, vol. 7, 94–95.

opinions against the sultan's project. But unlike Jassus, they were not as forceful in reproving the sultan; they cast the blame upon his representative 'Alilish, whom Burdulla called "the wicked."[49] Nevertheless, Burdulla was dismissed many times as a judge of the city of Fez for not fully cooperating. Other scholars were more compromising and avoided any open conflict with the sultan. They approached the issue in an elusive and abstracted way, discussing the requirements enjoined by Islamic law without explicit reference to the Haratin. Renowned scholar Muhammad b. 'Abd al-Qadir al-Fasi seemed to object in principle in his correspondence but eventually conceded to the sultan's request, stating in an official legal opinion in 1705 that he did not see any objection to the enslavement (*tamlik*) of the brown-skinned Haratin (*ahmar al-jilda*) for the sultan's army, serving the greater good. He also agreed with the sultan that the Haratin were more patient than others and more content,[50] going even further by sanctioning the sultan to take as many concubines from among the Haratin young women as he desired.[51] It is clear from this fatwa that in legal discourse enslavement of the Haratin meant forced conscription.

Some scholars who dared not confront the authorities decided to flee to nearby mountains in order to avoid witnessing these dreadful events or being forced to endorse the slave registers.[52] Conscientious scholars from other parts of Morocco expressed their condemnation as well. There was, for example, the scholar and Sufi Ahmad b. 'Ajiba at-Titwani (d. 1809), who declared vehemently his objection to the enslavement of black Muslims.[53] He condemned the scholars' community for its silence against the repulsive and unjust acts against black people. He condemned specifically those venal scholars who delivered legal opinions in support of the sultan's project to enslave all blacks in Morocco. He implicitly condemned the sultan himself for deviating from Islamic law and ordering his most trusted official, 'Alilish, to coerce the religious scholars to endorse his project. He declared that "anybody who expresses prejudice

[49] The fatwa of al-'Arabi Burdula was entitled: *Ifsha' al-Qawa'id al-Madhhabiyya wa 'l-Aqwal al-Mardiyya fi Ibtal an-Nihla al-'Alilishiyya, al-Lati Asha'aha al-Mulhid fi al-Aqatar al-Maghribiyya* (Bibliothèque Générale, ms. D 163). See al-Mannuni, *al-Masadir al-'Arabiyya*, 211–212.
[50] Unknown author. *Jany al-Azhar*, 20.
[51] Ibid.
[52] Ibn al-Hajj. *Ad-Durr al-Muntakhab*, vol. 6, 389.
[53] See Ahmad b. Muhammad b. 'Ajibah. *The Autobiography (Fahrasa) of the Moroccan Sufi Ibn 'Ajiba*, translated by Jean-Louis Michon and David Streight (Louisville: Fons Vitae, 1999).

and refuses to marry them and have children with them is a haughty ignorant [...]. And anybody who witnesses any injustice committed against them and accuses them of being slaves and does not do anything to change this evil act is disobeying God and his messenger."[54] There was also 'Ali b. 'Isa al-'Alami, who submitted his letter of resignation from the office of judge in the city of Chefchaouen to the governor of the region. He complained that some officials had been causing anarchy in society and compelling people to deviate from the right path by providing false testimonies and enslaving free people.[55]

The scholars' protest was not solely about defending an Islamic tenet against enslaving a fellow Muslim; personal economic hardships factored into their objections as well. Many scholars came from rich mercantile and landowning families and did own slaves and/or hired free black servants, males and females, to work in their homes, to manage their businesses, or to tend their farms and cattle. Their forced conscription meant a severe blow to their social and economic status.

The sultan tried in vain to convince the majority of scholars to grant him an unreserved approval. Discontented with the Moroccan scholars, especially those of Fez, he sent a letter to the scholars of al-Azhar in Cairo, a renowned center of Islamic scholarship, seeking their legal opinion regarding his desire to establish an army of black slaves (The full text of the letter in Arabic along with the translation is placed at the end of the book).[56] In order to convince the scholars of al-Azhar to issue a favorable legal opinion, he prepared his text carefully. The sultan opened his letter by stating his purpose:

To most eminent scholars, honorable jurists and men of legal advice and wisdom of the Islamic land in the East, living in Egypt; may God preserve it; and especially among you the muftis and teachers of the al-Azhar mosque [...]. The essential of the matter [...] concerns the states of the Maghreb. These states are in reality borderline areas and fortified places neighboring the infidel enemy and therefore needing, up and down the border, the presence of combatants and defenders fighting with perseverance in the name of Islam. There is therefore no doubt that the ruler of these lands is in need of a strong army consisting of united and prudent soldiers in order to defend the security of the Muslim community.

He stated in his letter that free Arab and Berber Muslim men were irresponsible, lazy, weak, envious, and opportunistic, but slaves, and he

[54] Muhammad Dawuud. *Tarikh Titwan*. Tetouan, 1963, vol. 2, 41.
[55] Ibid., vol. 2, 40.
[56] "Kitab Mawlana Nasarahu Allah ila 'Ulama' Misr" ("Letter from Mawlay Isma'il to the Learned Men of Egypt") (Rabat: Bibliothèque Royale, ms. 12598), 60–63.

emphasized black slaves, were different. They were content, satisfied, patient, and strong. These were necessary qualities to have in a person trusted to defend the coastal cities and to protect the land of Islam.

Not having found upon our arrival in power an organized and available army on which we could rely and which could inspire confidence and security, we turned to God, imploring his help in the choice of convening and building up an effective army. We then realized that free men and the inhabitants of the Maghreb at this time would not be suitable for a military engagement and this for multiple reasons. Slothfulness and laziness were established in their habits, and the force of want as well as greed had become a character trait [...]. It was then that we shifted our interest to slaves whom we bought from their owners, this having been done after searching for them and conducting investigations on them following the law and in respect for the tradition [...].

We have chosen these slaves to make soldiers and to make up the shield of Islam because they possess distinctive traits not found in others, such as the fact that this stock is not very costly, that it is content with little, and that it is very satisfied with whatever is offered to it. In addition, this group of slaves is better qualified for the blessed task for which it has been chosen, and especially the surveillance of the frontiers and the combat fronts and the protection of the land of Islam. They are sufficiently strong and patient to put up with the movements and voyages imposed by this function. Because of this fact, they are worthy and can accomplish their task in the best way.

Mawlay Isma'il avoided entering into an open debate about the current religious status of the black people – whether they were Muslims or not at the time of their re/enslavement. He explained that these black people originally came to Morocco through the slave trade from sub-Saharan Africa, thus indicating that they were of slave origin. His emphasis on their past slave and heathen condition was his pretext for the forced conscription of the enslaved blacks and the free black Muslims. He continued to say that, at the time being, if some blacks were free, it was because they had been separated from their masters either by running away or because their owners were obliged to abandon them during disastrous times such as drought and famine, and later on, after years and even centuries, they created their own families.

In reality, even in the case of the runaway slaves, blacks had become so habituated into Moroccan culture and integrated as free citizens in society, regardless of the blackness stigma, that it was difficult to sort them out on the basis of unbelief and slave origin. But, he continued to say:

We have noticed that the majority of these slaves had become fugitives and that their masters no longer had power over them. There was not a single one who was not a runaway slave. They have become accustomed to running away for many generations. They are aware of this insubordination and they would not refrain from it. At the first chance, they deserted their master and rebelled against him. Each one left his master and adopted a new one; allied himself with a tribe or had recourse to a sheikh or the head of a clan in order to go against his legitimate master to whom he owed his loyalty. In this way they were dispersed in the countries and regions, especially when the drought and disorder had plagued the country and the power of the caliphate had weakened, may God forever preserve the Muslims from this experience [...]. These slaves are originally pagans from the Sudan [...]. For a long time, these slaves were permitted to marry and to have children and it is not unlikely that this procreation was done in an illegitimate, sinful manner and through crime, particularly in perilous rural areas. The situation stayed this way for long periods of time.

He added somewhat disingenuously that he had already consulted the Moroccan scholars and that they had given him their full support and the support of the *shari'a*. He explained that the economic and political crisis in Morocco was so disastrous that the only means of salvation and staving off further European incursions on Islamic lands was to build a strong professional servile army.

We carefully examined the question in all its aspects by researching the interest and usefulness of the investment in owning these slaves for making a shield of Islam out of them. In this matter we got together with scholars, jurists, judges, muftis, teachers, eminent notaries, and virtuous religious men and especially noteworthy persons from among the people of the Maghreb, may God preserve them. We explained to them the life and past experience of these slaves, before ordering their round up, the insubordination in which they were, and the repulsive wrongdoing which they committed, and among them lives the outlaw, the pillager, the embezzler, the bandit, the perfidious and the usurper. We explained all this to the jurists and scholars, until they understood it and have witnessed themselves some of it. They then gave us their immediate response, without hesitation or stammering; these are written responses according to the Maliki legal school just as those we bring to you through our messenger, if God wills it.

According to an-Nasiri, Mawlay Isma'il did receive the support of the scholars of the Orient, hence gaining more legitimacy to enforce his authority in this affair.[57] Regardless of the importance of the scholars' reply on this matter, the sultan's message conveyed a negative image of blacks as restless, thieves, and rebels in order to legitimatize their subjugation. These characteristics seemed contradictory to those qualities stated in his letters, but in fact, they were not. Rather, the sultan implied that

---

[57] An-Nasiri, *al-Istiqsa'*, vol. 7, 88. An-Nasiri is the only evidence I have of any response from al-Azhar. One would think that if Mawlay Isma'il received this written support, he would have widely publicized the fatwa.

blacks had natural, good qualities as long as they were in a servile status. Once free, they would return to their natural state of corruption and irreligion. This text therefore tacitly implied that blacks were natural slaves.

The conflation in the meanings of the term *Haratin* could have developed with Mawlay Isma'il's project. At the very least the definition of the Haratin as "former slaves" or "freed slaves" was certainly reinforced at that time and the belief that they were originally free and autochthonous was damaged. This new meaning was an ideological construct to justify the subjugation of the free/freed blacks and was buttressed by documents that sought to advance the Makhzan's agenda by demonstrating that the Haratin were of slave origin, therefore creating a racialized caste. The fatwa of religious scholar Ahmad b. Muhammad al-Filali, known as Ibn Naji (d. 1710), which represented the Makhzan's official opinion during the reign of Mawlay Isma'il, affirmed the slave status of the Haratin, and hence was set against the dissenting opinion of the scholars of Fez. Fez was the most important intellectual center in Morocco owing to its famous al-Qarawiyyin Mosque-University. Its leading scholars challenged the order of the sultan to re/enslave the freed slaves and the Haratin. But there was also a great deal of correspondence between some scholars of Fez and the sultan that demonstrated the scholars' approval for the sultan's proposal to conscript all blacks into his army. These letters represent the official opinion and are preserved in the archives of Morocco.[58] The "Jany al-Azhar wa Nur al-Abhar" ("The Gathering of Flowers and the Dazzling Light"), compiled in 1705 under the order of Mawlay Isma'il to proclaim the legality of his project and to summarize the documents concerning the acquisition of slaves, provides a list of about eighty-one scholars, including Muhammad b. 'Abd al-Qadir al-Fasi, who endorsed the forced recruitment of blacks in Morocco.[59] These scholars, who traditionally benefited from the patronage of the rulers in exchange for the legitimacy they offered them, backed his project. This official document claimed that the operation of acquiring slaves was embraced willingly by slaves as well as slaveholders.[60] It also claimed that the sultan's decision to make an army of soldiers out of them was an effective way to discipline "these Haratin" who had marooned.[61]

---

[58] Some of these letters were compiled and published by Mohammed El Fasi, the president of Qarawiyyin University during the 1940s and 1950s. See El Fasi. "Lettres inédites de Moulay Ismaël," 1962.

[59] Unknown author, *Jany al-Azhar*, 30–33.

[60] Ibid., 2.

[61] Ibid., 7.

The official document, *Jany al-Azhar wa Nur al-Abhar*, reports that a total of 221,320 slaves (*mamalik*, plural of *mamluk*), male and female, old and young, child and infant, were gathered in Morocco. It provides the list of tribes and places from which blacks were gathered. They are as follows: Banu Malik and Banu Sufyan (21,000 persons), Khlut (12,500), Tliq (13,000), a1-Fahsiya, al-Habtiya, and their allies (10,000), Awlad ʿIsa (2,900), Sbih ar-Ramliyyin and at-Tirsiyyin (2,000), Awlad Jamaʿ (2,730), Shraqa (3,300), al-Mhamid, Awlad al-Hajj, and al-Mlalqa (1,800), al-Hyayna (10,000), the tribes of Taza and their allies (10,000), al-Yazghiya, al-Mukhtariya, and their allies (5,000), al-Hasnawiya (4,000), al-Mukhtariya (2,250), al-ʿAmriya, as-Sahiriya, as-Sahliya, al-Hsiniya, ar-Raʿmiya, as-Sbahiya, as-Sabtiya, and al-Hartiya (5,040), the Berber tribes of Fazaz and their allies (6,000), Zʿir and the adjacent Arab tribes (6,000), at-Tadlawiya (10,000), at-Hasnawiya and al-Maskiniya (26,000), ad-Dukkaliya (14,000), as-Sarghiniya, and al-ʿAmiriya (7,000), ad-Damnatiya, al-ʿItabiya, al-ʿIyatiya, and the adjacent Berber tribes (5,000), Zamran, Harbil al-Mnabha, ʿAkkara, Awlad Mtaʿ, and the Banu Idrasin (3,000), ad-Diriya (4,000), al-Hahiya and ash-Shyadmiya (18,000), the tribes of the Sus region: al-Khaliliya, ash-Shabaniya al-Yahyawiya, and al-Haksimiya (4,000), ar-Rhamna (2,500), al-Majatiya, al-Ablaliya, and an-Nakniya (2,800), religious centers from this region (2,500), other religious centers or *zawaya* (3,000). The total is 219,320 people enslaved.[62] There is a discrepancy of two thousand from the total of 221,320 provided in the document. The list does not seem to mention the two thousand persons gathered by Mawlay Ismaʿil himself during his expedition to the region south of Sus,[63] which could explain the discrepancy. The document also reports that the amount of money that was compensated to the "owners" was one thousand quintals of silver.[64] The document's main goal was to emphasize strongly that the acquisition of "slaves" was conducted legally and justly according to Islamic law.[65]

The Registers of Slaves Belonging to
Sultan Mawlay Ismaʿil and the Haratin's Protest

The archival sources inform us that Mawlay Ismaʿil's enslavement of blacks triggered a "national" discord;[66] however, few details are provided.

[62] Ibid., 15–16.
[63] An-Nasiri, *al-Istisqa'*, vol. 7, 58 and az-Zayani, *al-Bustan az-Zarif*, 32.
[64] Unknown author, *Jany al-Azhar*, 16.
[65] Ibid., 14.
[66] Dawuud, *Tarikh Titwan*, vol. 2, 38.

The information of the agency of the enslaved people is scant. Many black people refused their re-enslavement and sought refuge and help among different communities. The Haratin, conscious of their social identity, refused to accept the servile status attributed to them and refused to submit to the order of the sultan. Some of them sought refuge in the religious sanctuaries and others went into hiding in the midst of their Berber or Arab communities; some ran away with scholars to nearby mountains. There were also blacks who were slaves and who established certain bonds with their masters or patrons and preferred not to join the army and wished to hide with their masters or patrons who could not imagine life without their service. There were also those who were mistreated by their masters and saw in Mawlay Isma'il's actions an escape and possible emancipation. The reaction of the Haratin did not result in any kind of united movement, but some groups succeeded in organizing an effective protest. The protests of the Haratin of Fez in the year 1699 are well documented.[67] The people of Fez sympathized with their cause and expressed their outcry in the historic Mosque al-Qarawiyyin by repeating: "We are all free Muslims and servants of God."[68] This protest must have been effective because the sultan ordered an end to the collection of the Haratin of Fez. Similarly in other regions, the Haratin of Tetouan to the north of Fez contested the conscription project of the sultan and took refuge in the sanctuary of Ibn Mashish in Mount 'Alam. The *shurafa'* of the area pleaded to the sultan on their behalf.[69] Here as well, the sultan finally ordered the governor of the region to leave them in peace. These pockets of resistance may have spared some blacks in some regions from being enslaved, but also reinforced the system of domination and pushed the establishment to think and to work rigidly to legitimize the project in order to gain more influence in public opinion and among religious leaders. The famous rule of Islamic law that religion is the factor in determining slavery was discarded in this context even though it was evident that nobody could question black Moroccans' claims to have adopted Islam and lived as pious Muslims.

The forced conscription of Moroccan black people by Mawlay Isma'il in the late seventeenth century was documented in the official registers. These registers are significant and original because they reveal the system and the process through which the Muslim Moroccan blacks and

---

[67] Ibn al-Hajj, *ad-Durr al-Muntakhab*, vol. 6, 339 and 396. For more information about the *Haratin* of Fez see the scholarly article of Batran, "The *'Ulama'* of Fas," 1–15.

[68] Ibn al-Hajj. *Ad-Durr al-Muntakhab*, vol. 6, 339.

[69] Dawuud, *Tarikh Titwan*, vol. 2, 38.

those of black origin were enslaved or re-enslaved. The officials, namely Muslim judges and notaries in service to the sultan, established techniques for classifying blacks. The techniques consisted of two kinds: a class dealing with slave status and another dealing with physical features. The construction of and marking of this group as different from all other free Moroccans asserted control of the ruling class to classify and eventually enforce an inferior status and a slave condition on all blacks in Morocco. Blackness in this discourse became an ambivalent category excluded from the community of Muslims and therefore denied freedom. The enslavement of these Moroccans – their forced conscription for life in the service of Sultan Mawlay Isma'il – was illegal under Islamic law.

While conducting the research for this chapter, I was able to consult two registers concerning the acquisition of slaves in northern Morocco. Both registers are called *Daftar Mamalik as-Sultan Mawlay Isma'il* (*The Registers of the Slaves of Sultan Mawlay Isma'il*);[70] they are both conserved at Bibliothèque Générale in Rabat, Morocco.[71] I will closely examine one register *'Abid al-Manatiq ash-Shamaliya* (*The Slaves of the Northern Region*) as a case study representing a census of a partial number of slaves, generally of black origin,[72] in Morocco at the beginning of the eighteenth century. This register describes the acquisition of slaves from the northern part of Morocco, from areas such as Tangier, Larache, Asilah, Tetouan, and Chefchaouen. The date of this document, 1710, is mentioned throughout the text. The text was written

---

[70] A version of this section on slave registers has been published: Chouki El Hamel, "The Register of the Slaves of Sultan Mawlay Isma'il in Late Seventeenth Century Morocco," *Journal of African History*, 51 (1), 2010, 89–98.

[71] *Mamalik as-Sultan Mawlay Isma'il* (Rabat: Bibliothèque Générale, ms. k 394), it consists of 110 pages and ms. j 5, it consists of 548 pages.

[72] *Mamalik as-Sultan Mawlay Isma'il:'Abid ash-Shamal* (Rabat: Bibliothèque Générale, ms. k 394). It consists of 110 pages (fifty-five folios). The writing is Moroccan simple and clear in the entire manuscript. The paper is of the size of 48 x 33 cm. The number of lines per page is generally thirty-eight and sometimes it varies between thirty-six and forty. The paper is of white yellowish color as a result of time and the folios are separated from their binding. It is generally in a good condition except for a small part, about five pages, from which the edges and sometimes the third of the folios are damaged by termites. The manuscript is tricolor; the text is black, the titles of biographical chapters are of a red color in bold characters, and the name of Sultan Mawlay Isma'il and the formula *hamdala* ("praise be to God") at the beginning of the manuscript are written in gold. The scribe or scribes, as the case may be, have written in a clear hand. One is tempted to say that several scribes worked on this project because the script varies in size and style. There are several sections in which the script is reduced in size, yet there are also sections written in a larger script. The text does not have any colophon.

under the direction of the leading Muslim judge (*Qadi al-jama'a*) in the city of Qsar al-Kabir, whose name is given as Muhammad followed by an illegible signature on the manuscript. English traveler John Windus visited Morocco in 1720 and mentioned these registers in his travel notes:

> There was a Register made of the unfortunate People found, or forced to be Slaves, signed by all his [Mawlay Isma'il's] Cadies, who are the Judges of all Causes both Ecclesiastical and Civil, so that they and their Children are become Slaves by a Form of Law.[73]

The association of blackness and slavery was being developed to justify the subjection of free Muslim black Moroccans in order to persuade the populace and their influential Muslim leaders of the legality of this enterprise.[74] These slave registers were carefully written to document and to provide the appearance of legality of the sultan's directive that all blacks be conscripted into his army regardless of being Muslim and free or not. These registers also are valuable sources that reflect the political discourse of power.

The text of the *Daftar* is divided into sections under the rubric of the former owners. Within each of these sections is a list of conscripts according to the slaves' tribal affiliations, for example, Awlad al-Hajjam, and so forth. Conscripts are listed in the form of a short biographical record containing their names, slave labels or categories, and descriptions of their physical characteristics (tall, fat, thick bearded, dark skinned, etc.), as well as the names, labels or categories, and descriptions of their spouses, children, and grandchildren, if any. Individual identification is further detailed by inclusion of their genealogies. These genealogies appear to go back several generations and indicate the type of servant that the contemporary individual descended from. In certain cases, when ancestors of the male conscript are unknown the genealogy is according to the mother's line. These short biographical records represent both sexes (about half are women) of all ages; there are mostly families and often extended families, which include grandparents, parents, siblings, spouses, children, and grandchildren (ranging from adults to teenagers to infants). This register represents a census of less than a thousand black "slaves" in Morocco at the beginning of the eighteenth century. At the end of the section are

---

[73] Windus, *A Journey to Mequinez*, 216.
[74] For more information on Mawlay Isma'il's project refer to my article: "Blacks and Slavery in Morocco: The Question of the Haratin at the End of the Seventeenth Century," in *Diasporic Africa: A Reader*, ed. by Michael Gomez, New York University Press, 2006.

signatures of witnesses followed by signatures of notaries (*'udul*) attesting to the veracity of the information contained therein, followed by a transaction deed attesting to the purchase of the slaves by the representative of the sultan, whose name is Ahmad b. Haddu. The text lists the price of each servant at ten silver ouqiya, and, finally, signatures of judges confirm the transaction.

The following is a translation of a sample of biographies given in the first section of the slaves of the tribe Awlad al-Hajjam in the property of Ahmad ibn Muhammad al-Marini in the Qsar al-Kabir region:

Al-Wasif (the slave) Muhammad b. *al-wasif* Musa b. *al-wasif* 'Isa b. *al-wasif* 'Ali al-Hajjam (the barber). His description: Light brown or copper-colored (*safari*), medium height (*marbu 'al-qadd*) and grey thick bearded.

His mother is *al-wasifa* Amina bint *al-wasif* al-Hasan al-Hajjam; she died in slavery (*matat fi ar-riqq*) in the property of the owner aforementioned in the tribe aforementioned.

His grandmother is *al-ama* (the slave woman) Mas'uda bint *al-wasif* Mubarak al-Hajjam. The mother of his grandmother is *al-wasifa* Fatima bint *al-wasif* Ahmad al-Hajjam; she died in slavery (*matat fi ar-riqq*) in the property of the owner aforementioned.

His wife is *al-wasifa* Maryam bint *al-wasif* 'Isa al-Hajjam. Her description: Light brown, tall and fat and she has (*siyyala*) a tattoo on her chin.

Her mother is *al-wasifa* Fatima bint *al-wasif* 'Umar al-Haddad (the smith).

Her grandmother is *al-ama* (the slave) Tata bint *al-wasif* Qasim Bujattu.

The mother of this grandmother is *al-wasifa* Khadija bint *al-wasif* Husayn. All of them died in slavery (*fi ar-riqq*) in the property of the owner aforementioned.

She gave birth in slavery (*fi ar-riqq*) to:

Al-'abd (the slave) 'Ali. His description: Light brown, tall and light bearded.

Who is married in slavery (*mutanakih fi ar-riqq*) to *al-ama* Fatima bint *al-wasif* Ahmad al-Jamal. Her description: Light brown and thin-limbed.

Her mother is *al-wasifa* Halima bint *al-wasif* al-Husayn al-Jamal. She died in slavery (*fi ar-riqq*) in different property rather than the one aforementioned.

Her grandmother is *al-wasifa* Mas'uda bint *al-wasif* al-Husayn al-Hajjam.

The mother of her grandmother is *al-wasifa* zaynab bint *al-wasif* 'Isa al-Hajjam. All of them died in slavery (*fi ar-riqq*) in the property of the owner aforementioned.

[And she also gave birth to] the brother of 'Ali aforementioned, *al-wasif* al-Hasan. His description: Light brown, medium height and flattened [nose].

Who is married to *al-ama* (the slave) Rahma bint *al-wasif* al-Hasan b. Dadda al-Khumsi. Her description: Light brown, short and fat. She is in the property of his highness.

She gave birth in slavery (*fi ar-riqq*) to *al-wasifa* Amina who is still nursing. [End of the first biography][75]

Below are additional examples with only the names of some biographies from different sections in order to convey an idea of the different categories (written in italic) used to designate the status of slavery:

Al-Wasif Qasim b. *al-wasif* Umar b. *al-mamluk* Musa b. *al-'abd* 'Isa Harraq al-Hafidh. His description: Brown (*ahmar al-lawn*, literally red-skinned), little gray-haired and tall and beardless.[76]

Al-Wasif Yusuf b. *al-wasif* Musa b. *al-qinn* 'Umar b. *al-mamluk* al-Hasan al-Harraq al-Hafidh. His description: Dark brown (*kabdi*, literary the color of liver), light bearded and medium height.[77]

Al-Wasif 'Iyyadh b. *al-qinn* 'Ali b. *ar-raqiq* Qasim b. *al-wasif* 'Ali al-Hajjam. His description: Tall, gray-haired and big.[78]

Different degrees of dark color of many enslaved people described in the *Daftar* range from light brown to red, dark brown, and black. Some of the light-skinned people could have been either Fulani or the product of cohabitation or concubinage (in cases when masters denied paternity of their concubines' children), and it is mentioned in the *Daftar* that they were in the condition of slavery and bought to be conscripted for life in the army of the sultan.

We notice from these typical samples that the text uses different terms to designate the status of slaves. I have catalogued these terms and they are not dropped in the text as mere synonyms for the sake of style or to avoid repetition, but rather seem to have different connotations and special meanings.[79] In this legal text, the Muslim jurists, judges, and notaries in charge of this project appear to have constructed a system to assess the status of black people and to prove that they were slaves and/or children and/or grandchildren of slaves. Their purpose was to legitimize the enslavement of all blacks as ordered by Sultan Mawlay Isma'il. In service to the sultan's initiative, they came up with a system of slave labels that provided a discursive representation of blackness.

---

[75] *Daftar*, 2.

[76] Ibid., 3.

[77] Ibid.

[78] Ibid., 19.

[79] I have referred to classical dictionaries such as *Taj al-'Arus* of az-Zabidi and modern dictionaries such as *Supplement aux Dictionnaires Arabes* of Reinhart Dozy (1820–1883) (Leiden: E.J. Brill, 1881) and *An Arabic-English Lexicon* by Edward William Lane (1801–1876) in order to find as close as accurate significance to these terms.

The meanings of the main conscripts' categories and names in the text are:

Wasif (pl. *wisfan*): It generally means a slave or a servant, depending on the context. According to the Dutch Arabist R. Dozy (1820–1883), in nineteenth-century North Africa *wasif* meant a black slave. As for *wasifa*, it generally meant a female slave.[80] In *Taj al-'Arus*, *wasif* means male servant and *wasifa* means female servant.[81] They seem to have similar meanings in the *Daftar*, as it reads in this biography: *Al-Wasif* Muhammad b. *al-wasif* Musa b. *al-wasif* 'Isa b. *al-wasif* 'Ali al-Hajjam. *Wasif* is almost always the term of choice for the first generation and is often used in infant and youth descriptions, as in the following example: *Al-Ama* (the slave) Rahma gave birth in slavery (*fi ar-riqq*) to *al-wasifa* Amina who is still nursing. In the historical context of Mawlay Isma'il, *wasif* was used as a generic term that is open to nuanced interpretations regarding the legal status of the person in question between servile and free. It certainly meant servant of the sultan. Moroccan histories distinguished between the enslaved (*wasif*) and the free (*khadim*) in the service of the Makhzan.

'Abd (pl. *'abid*): A generic term for a male slave. In *Taj al-'Arus*, the word *mamluk* is added as an adjective to *'abd* to mean a chattel.[82]

Ama (pl. *ima'*): A generic term for a female slave. According to mid-nineteenth-century Arabist E. W. Lane: "*'abd* is now generally applied to a male black slave; and *mamluk*, to a male white slave."[83] This was probably true in the Egyptian context, but in Morocco until Mawlay Isma'il's reign both terms were used to designate servitude in general but the terms reserved to a European slave were *a'laj* or captive. *'Abd* and *ama* are often used in the *Daftar* to mean a slave of a mature age born to slave parents as in the following example: "She [*al-wasifa* Maryam wife of *al-wasif* Muhammad] gave birth in slavery (*fi ar-riqq*) to *al-'abd* (the slave) 'Ali."

Mamluk (pl. *mamalik*): It generally means an enslaved possession or a chattel slave.[84] In the *Daftar* it often means a "new slave" or an

---

[80] Dozy, *Supplément aux dictionaires Arabes* (Leiden: E. J. Brill, 1881), vol. 2, 818.

[81] Az-Zabidi, *Taj al-'Arus*, vol. 24, 249.

[82] Ibid., vol. 8, 189.

[83] Lane, *An Arabic-English Lexicon*, vol. 5, 1935.

[84] Az-Zabidi, *Taj al-'Arus*, vol. 27, 216.

owned person. As in the following biography: *Al-Wasif* Yusuf b. *al-wasif* Musa b. *al-qinn* 'Umar b. *al-mamluk* al-Hasan al-Harraq al-Hafidh.

Qinn (pl. *aqinna* or *aqnan*): According to *Taj al-'Arus al-qinn* is an enslaved possession as well as his/her parents, it's a neutral term used for singular, plural, and feminine.[85] It appears to have a similar meaning in the *Daftar* that it is a slave, male or female, born to slave parents as in the following biography: *Al-Wasif* 'Iyyadh b. *al-qinn* 'Ali b. *ar-raqiq* Qasim b. *al-wasif* 'Ali al-Hajjam.

Raqiq (pl. *riqaq* or *ariqqa'*): According to Lane: "A slave, male and female, but the latter is also called *raqiqa* and slaves; for it is used as sing. and pl."[86] According to *Taj al-'Arus*: "A slave in the property of an owner [...] It can be used for plural [...] And according to Abu-'l-'Abbas, the slaves are so called *raqiq* because they are humble and submissive to their owner."[87] In the *Daftar* the meaning of *raqiq* and *riqq* is the condition of slavery as in the following examples: The mother [of *al-wasif* Muhammad] is *al-wasifa* Amina bint *al-wasif* al-Hasan al-Hajjam, she died in slavery (*matat fi ar-riqq*). The wife [of the same person aforementioned *al-wasif* Muhammad] is *al-wasifa* Maryam bint *al-wasif* 'Isa al-Hajjam, she gave birth in slavery (*fi ar-riqq*) to al-'abd (the slave) 'Ali. This latter is married in slavery (*mutanakih fi ar-riqq*) to *al-ama* Fatima bint *al-wasif* Ahmad al-Jamal.

These registers were in existence before Jassus was imprisoned. He protested that the slave registers and legal texts used to justify the enslavement of the Haratin were the result of pressure, coercion, fear, and outright fabrications:

In whose name, may we ask, are these authentic legal texts compromised and twisted? How could these abominable distortions and falsifications (of the Holy Law) and all that they engender, which are essentially improper, unsound and do not conform to any legal principle, be perpetrated, when this is known to whomever has the minimum knowledge of the Law and can see that they are used as pretexts to justify the enslavement of free men and trading in them like chattel? And we ask, in the light of the legal texts cited above, are these not alterations and distortions of the Holy Law? This ignominious (crime) has engendered evil deeds and hideous sins.[88]

---

[85] Ibid., vol. 36, 10–11.
[86] Lane, *An Arabic-English Lexicon*, vol. 3, 1131.
[87] Az-Zabidi, *Taj al-'Arus*, vol. 25, 204.
[88] Batran, "The *'Ulama'* of Fas," 11.

Jassus also wondered how the authorities could identify the free or slave status of people who lived in remote areas when they did not even know their names and their family history. He was amazed to find the signatures of Muslim judges who allowed their enslavement in the slave registers.[89] Another famous scholar of Fez, al-'Arabi Burdulla (d. 1721), first appeared to endorse the project in 1705, according to the official document *Jany al-Azhar*,[90] but by 1708 he seemed to retract his decision and protested by placing the blame on 'Alilish,[91] perhaps as a result of witnessing the torture of his colleague Jassus. Another historical document by an unknown author described the collection of the Haratin in Fez in 1708 as cruel and illegal. This document reported that 'Abd Allah ar-Rusi,[92] governor of Fez, would gather witnesses among the jurists and would bring a black person against his will and force him to admit to a slave status. Then he would ask him about his master and possibly beat him until he came up with some name. Then he asked about his wife and his children and would note this information and pass it on to the copyists.[93] This "documentation" was a clear example of the infringement of natural rights sanctioned by Islamic law but denied to a group of people who because of their color were not to be accorded the benefits of that law even though the law itself forbade such prejudice. During this period we find that some people even falsely asserted their ownership of black people.[94] As for the Haratin who owned houses, Moroccan historian Muhammad al-Qadiri (1712–1773) reported that in 1713 officer Hamdun ar-Rusi came from Meknes to sell the Haratins' houses in the city of Fez.[95]

This project perpetuated the slave status of all black people, even those who were free. In the official discourse, being Hartani became a stigma and at times, free Muslims were accused of *Hartaniyya* (slave descent)

[89] Ibid., 13.
[90] Unknown author. *Jany al-Azhar*, 21 and 38.
[91] See footnote 49; Ibn al-Hajj, *ad-Durr al-Muntakhab*, vol. 7, 189.
[92] The people of Fez seemed to have avenged their scholars by killing this governor as well as members of his entourage soon after Mawlay Isma'il's death in 1727. See Muhammad al-Qadiri, *Nashr al-Mathani li-Ahl al-Qarn al-Hadi 'Ashar wa 'th-Thani*, edited by Muhammad Hajji and Ahmad Tawfiq (Rabat: Manshurat al-Jam'iyya al-Maghribiyya li-'t-Ta'lif wa 't-Tarjama wa 'n-Nashr, 1986), vol. 3, 293.
[93] Anonymous author, *Document ms. 12595* (Rabat: Bibliothèque Royale).
[94] See Ibn Naji, *Fatwa Ibn Naji*, 6–8.
[95] Al-Qadiri, *Nashr al-Mathani*, vol. 3, 215. Muhammad al-Qadiri lived in Fez and worked as a notary and *imam*. His most important work is *Nashr al-Mathani li-Ahl al-Qarn al-Hadi 'Ashar wa 'th-Thani* (*The Diffusion of Praises of the People of the Eleventh and the Twelfth Centuries*), which is a chronicle and a biographical dictionary.

and unjustly treated like slaves even in areas where there were no blacks.[96] Hence, claims that much of the practice of slavery in Islamic societies like Morocco was benign do not explain and account for Mawlay Isma'il's enslavement of free black Muslims on an enormous scale, and serve as an injustice to the historical record. When Mawlay Isma'il ordered the conscription of black people of all ages and both sexes, the authorities proceeded with this initiative not by determining their status as slaves but on the premise of color related to African black origin, which was used to define them as outsiders, although they had been in Morocco for centuries. The recent black transplants were a small fraction of the black population compared to the overall black population that had lived in Morocco for generations. Mawlay Isma'il's project created a racial classification for enslavement that went against the tenets of the Qur'an because free black Muslims were enslaved simply because they were black, resulting in the displacement of black Moroccans outside of the community. To borrow the words of Richard Brown: "Such classifying and such naming not only are ways to make others do what one wants, but also to get them to be what one wants."[97] Hence, the construction of "other" was closely connected to power and the ends to which that power served. The discourse of power used typifications and generalizations that made blacks "others" – that they were inherently different from the rest of the free Moroccans. The French consul in Morocco, Louis de Chenier (1722–1795), observed: "The words negro and slave are synonymous among the Moors, and indicate dependence and a state of humiliation incompatible with the ideas they have of their own freedom. Is it not astonishing that people, who have not the liberty of thinking, and who are only distinguished from those they call slaves by their colour, should hold the idea of servitude in such abhorrence?"[98]

In the end, Mawlay Isma'il usurped and circumvented the political domain of the scholars; those who ostensibly interpreted and regulated Islamic codes and practice and to whom the sultan was to answer for his actions as the leader of the nation. He did not use the scholars' council to discuss state affairs or the welfare of people but rather to guarantee the legitimacy of his authority. Mawlay Isma'il created his own bureaucracy

[96] Dawuud, *Tarikh Titwan*, vol. 2, 35–41.
[97] Richard H. Brown, "Cultural Representation and Ideological Domination" in *Social Forces*, March 1993, 71 (3), 659.
[98] Louis de Chenier, *Recherches historiques sur les Maures, et histoire de l'empire de Maroc* (Paris: Chez l'auteur [etc.] 1787), tome III, 425. The English translation: *The Present State of the Empire of Morocco* (New York: Johnson Reprint Corp., 1967), vol. 1, 280.

to carry out his orders to build his empire. He even undermined the Makhzan in its traditional sense by replacing it with his palace-centered government and warrior establishment. By creating an army legally loyal only to his authority and person, Mawlay Isma'il affected a separation between the sultanate and the community of Muslims he ruled. He also helped create a new collective vocabulary for black Moroccans as is apparent in the term *wisfan* (sing. *wasif*), which simply meant servants in the official documents. The term connoted the new status of blacks as a military caste, analogous to the Egyptian Mamluk, now in the service to the sultan. It also implied freedom as the black soldiers were treated as conscripts and received regular payments. Indeed black soldiers saw their status as free and gradually behaved accordingly. Despite the legal status implied in the terms applied to the conscripts in the official documents, the Haratin and all the army were treated publicly as conscripts and servants of the government. Hence, a mutual trust was tacitly negotiated in order for them to bear arms and for the sultan to trust them with his own life.

5

The Black Army's Functions and the Roles of Women

Mawlay Isma'il was inspired by the Ottoman Turkish army system; he created an army similar to their Janissaries (specially trained troops organized in the fourteenth century and abolished in 1826). Turkish soldiers and bodyguards were supremely loyal supporters of the ruler. Historian an-Nasiri provides a detailed account about life for the conscripted in the main camp of Mashra' ar-Ramla. He reported that by 1688 the black population was increasing as children were born. Mawlay Isma'il requested that the children of slaves ten years old or older be delivered to him. The girls were divided among the various wings of the palace and were entrusted to head servants for their training in preparation for domestic tasks in the service of the palace and its harem and as future wives for the soldiers. As for the boys, they were distributed among masons, carpenters, and other craftsmen in order to learn their trades and to be trained to tend and mount donkeys. At the end of the first year, they were employed to drive the mules loaded with bricks, tiles, wood, and so forth. The following year, they helped in construction sites. After a year, they were promoted to the first class in the army and were given clothes and weapons and started training for military service. After another year, they were trained to ride horses without saddles and when they learned how to master their horses, they were provided with saddles; then they were taught the art of war – forms of attack and retreat, of fighting and shooting. Finally, at the end of the sixth year, at the average age of sixteen, they were deemed sufficiently trained to join the regular ranks of the army. Mawlay Isma'il also arranged marriages among the males and females. He would give each man ten mithqals as a dowry for his wife, and to each young woman five mithqals for her wardrobe. Then he placed them under the command of one of their elders and sent them to reside in *al-Mahalla* (the camp) after being recorded in the register of the army.[1] In the Mashra' ar-Ramla camp, they were given land to cultivate and to build houses and were exempt from taxes.[2]

The training program was regimented in order to ensure the upbringing of obedient slave boys and girls. The girls learned literature, cookery, tailoring, and all domestic tasks as well as the etiquette of service in the palace.[3] These girls were conditioned to adhere to practices and to forms prescribed by the authority of Mawlay Isma'il in order to cement the allegiance of his slave army by marrying them to his soldiers and to reproduce loyal servants. The sultan even sent some of the girls to wealthy families to live with them in order to gain education and to acquire skills useful for the palace. For example, he sent a letter to a notable man in Salé as a royal decree to the entire city, commanding him to assist with the formation of the female slaves. The sultan was stern in his demands, threatening execution to all who failed to assist in the formation and the development of these girls or anyone who abused or neglected them.[4] John Windus wrote:

[The sultan] takes care to lay the foundation of his tawny nurseries, to supply his palace as he wants, into which they are admitted very young, are taught to worship and obey this successor of the Prophet, and being nursed in blood from their infancy, become the executioners and ministers of his wrath, whose terrible commands they put in execution with as much zeal and fury [...]. [The sultan places] much of his safety in them.[5]

Thomas Pellow (1704 – ?), an Englishman who spent twenty-three years in captivity in Morocco (from 1715 to 1738), noted how the sultan conducted marriage ceremonies:

This short way of marrying his guards the Emperor frequently put in practice, by often ordering, great numbers of people before him, whom he marries without any more ceremony than pointing to the man and woman and saying, "Hadi yi houd Hadi," that is to say, "That take That;" upon which the loving pair join together, and march off as firmly noosed as if they had been married by a Pope.[6]

---

[1] An-Nasiri, *al-Istiqsa'*, vol. 7, 71.
[2] See de La Véronne and de León, *Vie de Moulay Isma'il*, 55 of the French translation and 141–142 of the Spanish text.
[3] See Ibn Zaydan, *al-Manza' al-Latif*, 131.
[4] Ibid., 132.
[5] Windus, *A Journey to Mequinez*, 1725, 138–139.
[6] Thomas Pellow, *The Adventures of Thomas Pellow, of Penryn, Mariner: Three and Twenty Years in Captivity Among the Moors* (London: Fisher Unwin, 1890), 78. This is also one

Pellow himself was involved in one of these ceremonies:

One day, the Emperor being on the merry pin, ordered to be brought before him eight hundred young men, and soon after as many young women, who also instantly appearing (as being, no doubt, before ordered to be ready at hand), he told the men, that as he had on several occasions observed their readiness and dexterity in obeying him, he would therefore, as in some part of recompense, give every one of them a wife; and which, indeed, he soon did, by giving some by his own hand (a very great condescension), and to others by the beckoning of his head, and the cast of his eye, where they should fix. After they were all coupled and departed, I was also called forth, and bid to look at eight black women standing there, and to take one of them for a wife. At which sudden command, I (being not a little confounded, as not at all liking their colour) immediately bowing twice, falling to the ground and kissing it, and after that the Emperor's foot (which is the custom of those who desire to be heard, as well as a very great favour and condescension to be permitted to do), humbly intreated [*sic*] him, if, in case I must have a wife, that he would be graciously pleased to give me one of my own colour. Then, forthwith sending them off, he ordered to be brought forth seven others, who all proved to be Mulattoes; at which I again bowed to the ground, still entreating him to give me one of my own colour; and then he ordered them also to depart, and sent for a single woman, full dressed, and who in a very little time appeared, with two young blacks attending her, she being, no doubt, the same he and the Queen had before particularly designed for me. I being forthwith ordered to take her by the hand and lead her off, which she holding out to me, I perceived it to be black also, as soon after I did her feet; at which I started back, like one in a very great surprise, and being asked what was the matter, I answered him as before; when he smiling, ordered me to lift up her veil (it being the custom of the country for women to go veiled) and look at her face; which I readily obeying, found her to be of a very agreeable complexion, the old rascal crying out, in a very pleasing way, in the Spanish language, "Bono! Bono!" which signifies, "Good! Good!" ordering me a second time to take her by the hand, lead her off, and keep her safe. This artificial blackness of her hands and feet was laid on by a certain grass, first made into powder and mixed with water, alum, and the juice of lemons, and is called el bhenna [henna].[7]

According to these sources and other primary sources such as the writings of az-Zayani, Ibn al-Hajj, and an-Nasiri, the officers or heads of the military units were black too.[8] Joseph de León (Spanish captive in Morocco from 1708 to 1728) wrote that the camp of the black army became a vast agglomeration and that the officer Mbarak Semorán was

---

of the passages he borrowed verbatim from English traveler John Windus, who visited Morocco in 1721; see Windus, *A Journey to Mequinez*, 138.

[7] Pellow, *The Adventures of Thomas Pellow*, 75–76.

[8] Az-Zayani, *al-Bustan az-Zarif*, 36–37; Ibn al-Hajj, *ad-Durr al-Muntakhab*, vol. 6, 113; an-Nasiri, *al-Istiqsa'*, vol. 7, 71.

their captain general.[9] The soldiers were divided into companies of 100, 200, or 400 and commanded by captains nominated by the sultan. The captain general was also in charge of the judicial system of the army, except for grave cases, which were presented to the sultan.[10]

The document *Jany al-Azhar wa Nur al-Abhar* reports that the total number of slaves gathered in Morocco was 221,320.[11] This total included both sexes and all ages. It is important to note that by the time this document was written in 1705 the gathering of blacks was still going on. Hence, the ultimate total was probably between two hundred thirty thousand and two hundred forty thousand black Moroccans, including women and children. The collection of blacks had started shortly after 1673, so the collection process had been going on for about thirty years. The slave register mentioned in Chapter 4, entitled *'Abid al-Manatiq ash-Shamaliya*, concerning the enslaved people from the northern region of Morocco, was not included in this census because it was completed in the year 1710. Some Moroccan sources reported that in the year 1713 'Alilish and two other officers were still roving the area looking for more black slaves and Haratin in order to add them to the army.[12] Hence, there seem to have been significant numbers of blacks who had avoided conscription up to 1713. Other records provide different conscript counts. According to Abu al-Qasim az-Zayani (1734–1833), one hundred fifty thousand men (adults and youth) were recruited into the sultan's army:[13]

The military register of the black army recorded a total of 150,000 men, of which 70,000 were at Machra' ar-Ramla, 25,000 at Wajh 'Arus in Meknes and the rest were spread out in the fortresses which the Sultan, as it is known to everyone, have built in Morocco from Oujda[14] to Oued Noun [15].[16]

An-Nasiri says that Mawlay Isma'il personally pursued the formation of the black army until its number reached one hundred fifty thousand. This was a great achievement on a scale far beyond any other armies

---

[9] It is possible that this was the same person as the black officer Mbarak al-Fulani, who was the chief of the Rabat garrison in 1728.

[10] De La Véronne and de León, *Vie de Moulay Isma'il*, 56 of the French translation and 142 of the Spanish text.

[11] Unknown author, *Jany al-Azhar*, 8 and 18–19.

[12] Dawuud, *Tarikh Titwan*, vol. 2, 36–38.

[13] Az-Zayani, *Le Maroc de 1631 à 1812*, 31 of the French translation and 16 of the Arabic text. See also An-Nasiri, *al-Istiqsa'*, vol. 7, 191.

[14] Oujda is a city at the very northeast of Morocco near the actual Algerian borders.

[15] Oued Noun is at the very southern part of Morocco near the Atlantic.

[16] Az-Zayani, *Le Maroc de 1631 à 1812*, 31 of the French translation and 16 of the Arabic text.

in Moroccan history. There were seventy thousand cavalry and fusiliers. The number of the *inkishariya* corps was twenty-five thousand; they were all fusiliers except for their leaders who mounted horses and were under the leadership of the black pasha Msahil. An-Nasiri also says that there were five thousand officers (called *quwwad ru'usuhum*, the plural of *qa'id ra'sahu*) in the area of Meknes.[17] Thomas Pellow mentions that his [Moroccan] wife's brother in-law had under his command fifteen hundred of these young officers called "Kiadrossams" (*quwwad ru'usuhum*).[18] French priest Germain Beguin, commander of the monastery of Mercy in Paris,[19] stated in a document dated April 24, 1728, one year after the death of Mawlay Isma'il, that these officers, who numbered eighteen hundred, were young black sons of the principal officers of the sultan's army, and he compared them to the guards of the king of France.[20] The rest of the army, some fifty thousand, were distributed in garrisons all over the country in order to guard the major trade routes, to protect the frontiers, and to confront any potential hostility.

European sources' estimates of the sultan's army were lower than those found in Moroccan documents. The reason for the discrepancy is partly because Europeans focused mainly on the number of fighting soldiers in the camp of Mashra' ar-Ramla and in the capital city of Meknes. Beguin, on a mission to redeem the Christian captives in Morocco, in a document dated April 24, 1728, stated that at the end of February 1728, the sultan's army had sixty thousand black soldiers at the camp of Mashra' ar-Ramla.[21] This number did not include the black soldiers stationed in Meknes and those scattered all over the country. Moroccan historian Muhammad al-Qadiri (1712–1773) reported a similar estimate, that there were "at least 60,000 fighting men, counting only those stationed in Mashra' al-Ramla and not including those scattered throughout the regions of Morocco."[22] Joseph de León noted that the black army in time of peace numbered fifty thousand standing soldiers, thirty thousand cavalry, and twenty thousand infantry.[23] He was talking about the

---

[17] An-Nasiri, *al-Istiqsa'*, vol. 7, 191. For more information see Allan R. Meyers, "Note sur les qa'id ras-hu," *Hesperis Tamuda* (Rabat: Editions Techniques Nord-Africaines), vol. 17, no. 1, 1976–1977, 85–96.

[18] Pellow, *The Adventures*, 76.

[19] He was one of the 'Pères Rédempteurs' whose mission was to redeem the Christian slaves in North Africa.

[20] De La Véronne, *Documents inédits*, 44.

[21] Ibid.

[22] Al-Qadiri, *Nashr al Mathani*, 59 of the Arabic text and 168 of the English translation.

[23] De La Véronne and de León, *Vie de Moulay Isma'il*, 54 of the French translation and 140 of the Spanish text.

cavalry of Mashra' ar-Ramla,[24] and he did not provide any details on the soldiers scattered throughout the country. Louis de Chenier (1722–1795) reported that at the time of the death of Mawlay Isma'il, about one hundred thousand blacks served him as soldiers.[25] If the overall total of collected black Moroccans was two hundred and thirty thousand to two hundred forty thousand persons, of which about one hundred fifty thousand could have been adult men and teenaged boys, then the total number of the conscripted is consistent with the estimate of one hundred fifty thousand black soldiers reported in Arabic sources. Eventually, the numbers would decrease after the death of Sultan Mawlay Isma'il, the result of uncertainty surrounding the political succession of power as well as the failure to pay the soldiers. The army also included other ethnicities such as European renegades, but a small number. In Thomas Pellow's account, he said that fifteen hundred renegades served in the army, but only 600 remained after many battles.[26] The army of Mawlay Isma'il also had small numbers from the traditional units such as the Shraga, the Udaya, and Awlad Jarrar.

Ibn Zaydan (1873–1946), historian of the 'Alawi dynasty, provided a detailed account of the deployment of the black army, ranging from 100 to 2,000 soldiers depending on the exigencies of the post, in seventy-six garrisons and posts in Morocco, and stated that the soldiers were often deployed with their families.[27] Every garrison was financially supported by a local tribe. Each tribe provided its tithe for the subsistence of the soldiers and fodder for their horses. These garrisons were spread out mainly along the trade routes and along the area of dissidence known in Arabic as *bilad as-siba*, mainly populated by Berber tribal groups. These autochthonous ethnic groups often resided in rural areas; they shared a common locality and a patrilineal descent. Thus, these garrisons served as a buffer zone to control the tensions between the Arabs and the Berbers; these old tensions that have traditionally contributed to the "national" political disequilibrium were usually manifested in the conflict between the dwellers of urban areas and the rural folks. The garrisons also helped to extend

[24] Ibid., 56 of the French translation and 142 of the Spanish text.
[25] De Chenier, *Recherches historiques*, tome III, 226. The English translation: *The Present State*, vol. 1, 297.
[26] Pellow, *The Adventures*, 81 and 188. Historian Magali Morsy estimated the number of European Christian captives at three thousand detained in Meknes at the time of Mawlay Isma'il. Magali Morsy, "Mawlay Isma'il et l'armée de métier," *Revue d'histoire moderne et contemporaine* (Paris: Presses universitaires de France, 1967), 14, 102.
[27] See Ibn Zaydan, *al-Manza' al-Latif*, 333–339; Az-Zayani, *Le Maroc de 1631 à 1812*, 31 of the French translation and 16 of the Arabic text.

the sultan's administrative apparatus and enforce the collection of taxes, particularly from the area known as the "land of dissidence."

The black army provided the means to realize the dream and the vision of the sultan to bring security and unity to the country. But it took two decades to accomplish the task.[28] This demonstrates the political and social divisions within Morocco at the time of Mawlay Isma'il's ascendancy. John Windus described the outcome of the sultan's initiative in the safety and ease of travel:

At the beginning of his reign, the roads were so infested with robbers, that it was dangerous to stir out of the town, without being well guarded; but he has so well cleared them, that now it is [anywhere] safer traveling. He maintains his large Empire (which consists of several kingdoms joined together) in peace and quietness.[29]

Az-Zayani confirms Windus' observation on the security that prevailed in Morocco, that even a non-Muslim (*dhimmi*) or a woman could travel anywhere in Morocco and had nothing to fear from interlopers or robbers. The security and prosperity that the country enjoyed allowed the sultan to exhibit his power by building palaces and gardens.[30] Mawlay Isma'il lived lavishly in his palaces. Windus described the palace of Meknes: "This Palace is about four Miles in circumference, and stands upon even Ground, in form almost square, and no Hill near to overlook it."[31] Pellow remarked that the "palace or castle is the stateliest of any in Africa, it being of a prodigious extent, some of the rooms of which have large fish-ponds in them, and the fishes may be seen swimming in the looking-glasses, with which the ceilings are covered."[32] Az-Zayani reported that the sultan himself supervised the construction of his palaces; no sooner had he completed one than he started on another. He also built a new mosque in the casbah in order to accommodate the growing population. The new sultan's casbah had twenty fortified gates entrusted to twelve hundred black eunuchs and was topped by bastions equipped with canons and mortars. Inside the casbah he also built a large ornamental pond large enough for a boat. There were granaries and water tanks. The sultan set up a three-mile-long stable to shelter his twelve thousand

---

[28] See de La Véronne and de León, *Vie de Moulay Isma'il*, 54 of the French translation and 139 of the Spanish text; and an-Nasiri, *al-Istiqsa'*, vol. 7, 71–88.

[29] Windus, *A Journey to Mequinez*, 119.

[30] Az-Zayani, *Le Maroc de 1631 à 1812*, 52 of the French translation and 28 of the Arabic text.

[31] Windus, *A Journey to Mequinez*, 112.

[32] Pellow, *The Adventures*, 87.

horses. The casbah contained about fifty palaces.[33] The sultan used his army not solely for military purposes. He also used it in the construction of his palaces. Joseph de León reported that Mawlay Isma'il continually put fifteen thousand men to work. Some of them came from the infantry in time of peace. Additionally, according to Magali Morsy, there were three thousand European Christian captives at Meknes at the time of Mawlay Isma'il.[34] The sultan also used these Christian captives as construction workers and forced the inhabitants of Meknes to provide additional men to work on construction projects. None of the laborers were compensated for their work. Even the material used in the construction cost nothing to the sultan. All suppliers and workers were exempted from paying taxes.[35] Some of the palaces housed hundreds of concubines whose company the sultan enjoyed. By definition, concubines were female slaves forced to fulfill the sexual desire of their master. Pellow commented:

a very large spacious building (as indeed are all the Emperor's houses), and certainly prodigious strong, the walls twelve feet thick, and five stories high, built only of fine earth and hot lime, mixed and well incorporated by a vast number of slaves kept for that purpose; for it is thrown, as I may say, into a mould, being first boarded up on each side, so that being very well rammed together, it becomes, in a very little time, harder and more durable than stone. It is covered on the top with blue tiles, ceiled in the inside, and finely painted, and hath in it several hundred separate apartments for his concubines and eunuchs, besides those set apart for his favourite queen and her retinue. All his other wives (in number no less than four thousand) being closely shut up in several other sumptuous houses allotted for them; though all, as I may say adjacent, and all within the same enclosure.[36]

The number of concubines would likely be large, but the real number remains unknown. Numbers provided by writers like Pellow are uncorroborated speculation. The author mistakenly labeled all women in the harem as wives. The sultan had four legitimate wives as prescribed by Islamic law. The rest were concubines and maids. Moroccan sultans usually chose their wives from *sharif* and notable families. But Mawlay Isma'il's favorite wife and queen of the palace was a black woman who started her relationship with Isma'il as his concubine. Her name was Lalla 'Aisha Mubarka (or Zaydana, the new name she acquired after her firstborn

---

[33] Az-Zayani, *Le Maroc de 1631 à 1812*, 28–29 of the French translation and 14–15 of the Arabic text.

[34] Magali Morsy, "Mawlay Isma'il et l'armée de métier," 102.

[35] De La Véronne and de León, *Vie de Moulay Isma'il*, 57 of the French translation and 144 of the Spanish text.

[36] Pellow, *The Adventures*, 59.

son Zaydan). She was a powerful woman and held great influence with the sultan. She was the mother of one of the sons whom she designated as Isma'il's successor, named Mawlay Zaydan, the first of the sultan's sons.[37] Dominican priest Dominique Busnot, who traveled to Meknes three times to redeem Christian captives, described Zaydana, saying: "This woman is black, and of an enormous height and size. She was slave to Mawlay ar-Rashid, from whom Mawlay Isma'il bought her for sixty ducats, and none can conceive by what means she has endeared herself to the Sultan, that she has power over his mind, and often manages him as she pleases."[38] Busnot reported that some Moroccans attributed her influence on the sultan to magic.[39] This report reflects the negative perception held among men of women who did not behave docilely and intervened in political affairs, hence belittling them and attributing their achievements to superstition. Indeed, magic was often associated with women in Morocco. This perception made its way into the historical narratives and undermined women's agency and the power of their intelligence. It was not uncommon for female servants and especially concubines to become quasi-free, free, or even legal wives. The status of a concubine or "woman of the bedroom," once she bore a child from her master changed to that of *umm al-walad*. Whenever concubines succeeded in forging emotional bonds with their masters or patrons they were able to survive, thrive, and negotiate better conditions. In Islamic law, the man had a license to enjoy a female slave's sexuality, but he also had the obligation to assume the legal consequences when his slave bore him a child. Zaydana's bond with Mawlay Isma'il seemed to go further, to the point that he freed her and made her his prime wife. The mother of Mawlay Isma'il himself seemed to have had a similar experience with his father. Zaydana was involved in many intrigues in order to secure her son's right to succession. The succession was usually based on a first come, first choice policy, so the son who got the first *bay'a* (oath of allegiance from most notables in the country) would be sultan. Zaydana succeeded in making her son heir presumptive to the kingdom.[40] A potential rival, Mawlay Muhammad al-'Alim, a

[37] François Pidou de Saint-Olon, *Relation de l'empire de Maroc où l'on voit la situation du pays, les moeurs, coutumes, gouvernement, religion et politique des habitans* (Paris: Vve Marbre-Cramoisy, 1695), 65–66. Pidou de Saint-Olon (1646–1720) was the ambassador of France to Morocco in the year 1693.

[38] Dominique Busnot, *Histoire du règne de Mouley Ismael, roy de Maroc, Fez, Tafilet, Souz, &c* (Rouen: G. Behourt, 1714), 52.

[39] Ibid.

[40] Ibid., 106.

son of a European concubine, was a victim of Zaydana's intrigues. She
convinced the sultan to condemn Muhammad al-'Alim, the viceroy of
the south, on the basis that he intended to proclaim himself sultan of
Morocco. According to Ibn Zaydan, the sultan appointed his son al-'Alim
governor of Marrakesh for his natural leadership qualities. This visibility
made him a strong potential future sultan but caused envy in the sultan's intimate circle. Members of this circle such as Zaydana sowed seeds
of mistrust between the sultan and al-'Alim. And as a result, the sultan
removed him from his position as governor of Marrakesh. But as soon
as he realized al-'Alim's innocence the sultan appointed him governor of
Tarudant, though three years later the sultan once again dismissed him.
This time, al-'Alim rebelled against this treatment and claimed back the
governorship of Marrakesh. The sultan sent Mawlay Zaydan to defeat
him and eventually captured and replaced him in 1706. For his punishment the sultan ordered al-'Alim's opposite hand and leg amputated in
order to send a message that any disobedience would mean severe punishment or death, even for his favorite son. Al-'Alim died as a result of
bleeding in 1706.[41] Mawlay Zaydan, unlike his brother, was not fit to
rule; he soon showed contemptuous behavior against his father and gave
himself over to drunkenness. He ended up being strangled by his wives
in the year 1708.[42] Joseph de León claimed that Mawlay Isma'il sent
two beautiful young women as a present to his son and instructed them
to kill him but he kept it a secret from Zaydana in order to avoid her
resentment.[43] But according to Louis de Chenier, Zaydana was aware of
this plot and avenged her son by ordering the breasts of these women severed before having the women strangled.[44] Indeed, it is interesting to read
the comments of Robert Brown, the editor and annotator of Thomas
Pellow's book, that Mawlay Isma'il's palace "was a hot-bed of intrigues –
the rival wives struggling to advance themselves and their sons, and to
ruin the children of their rivals. Thus Muley Mohammed, the best of the
many sons of the Emperor, by the machinations of Lala Zidan[a], a negro
queen, was first driven into rebellion and then butchered."[45]

[41] Ibn Zaydan, *Ithaf A'lam*, vol. 4, 61–65.
[42] Windus, *A Journey to Mequinez*, 121.
[43] De La Véronne and de León, *Vie de Moulay Isma'il*, 1974, 21 of the French translation
   and 95 of the Spanish text.
[44] De Chenier, *Recherches historiques*, tome III, 418. The English translation: *The Present
   State*, vol. 1, 224.
[45] Pellow, *The Adventures*, 349.

When Zaydana died in 1716, she was succeeded to the first rank in the harem by Lalla Halima. This sultana (queen) was reportedly the first lady to come out of the harem in open court and plead to the sultan for clemency for her brother. The public spaces in the palace as well as in society in general were dominated by men and private spaces were reserved for women. But this sultana, like others, remained within limited freedom. She interacted mainly with the women in her service and the women of great families, and usually no male stranger could see her face, except for the eunuchs. Although she was the first lady and the mistress of the palace, her authority was manifested in the deference that other women showed her. Although the sultan provided for her, she owned property managed by an officer who communicated with her through other women. She had money that was entrusted with the Jews to be invested on her behalf.[46]

All women of the harem practiced seclusion (*hijab*), as was common for Moroccan middle urban families of that era. They used the belvederes to peer into the outside world since their houses had no windows. Unlike the women in the palace, the women of the city could go out to run different errands, but always completely veiled except for their eyes.[47] Concubines were of varied complexions but mostly black, and a few were of European and Eastern origin. It was a custom for the governors of the provinces to send beautiful young women to the sultan. Dark-skinned women were more numerous because they were usually easily acquired from the local markets as a result of the continuous yearly supply from the trans-Saharan slave trade. The sultan also chose his concubines, sometimes from free women. There were notable people who considered it an honor to send their daughters to join the harem.[48] Some concubines could ascend to a status close to that of the legitimate wives as in the case of the mother of Muhammad al-'Alim. John Windus reported that "[Mawlay Isma'il] seldom bestows his favours to a woman more than once, unless she proves with child, for then she becomes in greater esteem, and stands fair to partake of his bed again."[49] Concubines were aware that if they bore children from their master their progeny would inherit the father's

---

[46] See de La Véronne and de León, *Vie de Moulay Isma'il*, 28 of the French translation and 100–101 of the Spanish text.

[47] Ibid., 34 of the French translation and 108 of the Spanish text.

[48] De La Véronne and de León, *Vie de Moulay Isma'il*, 28 of the French translation and 100 of the Spanish text.

[49] Windus, *A Journey to Mequinez*, 188–189. See also Budgett Meakin, *The Moorish Empire, A Historical Epitome* (London: S. Sonnenschein & Co., 1899), 150.

legal status, and they would secure a better position for themselves. They were forced to trade sexual pleasures for social benefits. Some of these women were rich, had properties managed by people they trusted, and were exempt from taxes.[50] The sultan gave some of his concubines in marriage to pashas (governors of provinces) and crucial officers in his government on the condition that they did not have any children. It was a way to buttress his alliances with powerful people in society. As for the concubines who no longer pleased the sultan or lost his respect, they were sent to live the rest of their lives in a nearby residence outside the harem. At the sultan's death, his successor offered some of the concubines who had no children to some of the officers and pashas. Those who wished to do so could go to Tafilalt and live there with their children; others remained in Meknes and lived on pensions. After the death of Mawlay Isma'il, until the election of the new sultan, it was incumbent upon the city of Meknes to support the harem.[51]

Mawlay Isma'il's long life and reign allowed him the opportunity to create a large harem. He fathered several hundred children. Morocco had a long tradition of female seclusion; hence it is difficult to determine the real number of Mawlay Isma'il's wives and concubines or his children. The lack of information on the living arrangements of the harem filled the European writers with wonder and speculation. The primary sources that provide an estimated number of the sultan's harem are mainly European. The estimates ranged from hundreds to thousands. Dominique Busnot reported that at the time of his visit to Morocco (1704–1708), the harem of the sultan contained about 500 women of all nationalities.[52] John Windus reported that, "The Emperor (by his four Wives, and many Thousands of Women, whom he has had in his *Seraglio*, during the time of his long Reign) has got a numerous issue."[53] Thomas Pellow's estimate was the highest: eight thousand wives.[54] As for the children, the number ranged from 500 to 900 sons and about 300 daughters. Thomas Pellow, who drew upon information from sources such as his contemporary, French scholar Adrien Maurice de Mairault,[55] also estimated 900

---

[50] De La Véronne and de León, *Vie de Moulay Isma'il*, 27 of the French translation and 100 of the Spanish text.

[51] Ibid., 28 of the French translation and 100 of the Spanish text.

[52] Busnot, *Histoire du règne de Mouley Ismael*, 1714, 50.

[53] Windus, *A Journey to Mequinez*, 189.

[54] Pellow, *The Adventures of Thomas Pellow*, 147.

[55] This writer had never been to Morocco and did not seem to have any expertise on the subject. He might have used informants who visited Morocco.

sons and about 300 daughters.[56] Busnot reported that some Moroccans assured him that there were at least 600 hundred living sons but did not mention the number of daughters.[57] The Arabic sources on the number of children, the earliest being that of az-Zayani, reported that according to popular accounts Mawlay Isma'il had 528 sons and an equal number of daughters; that some of his descendants occupied 500 houses in Sijilmasa. He affirmed that he knew the names and faces of twenty-eight of the sons of Mawlay Isma'il and twenty-eight of his daughters.[58] Windus provided some insights on the fate of his children:

They say he has seven hundred Sons able to mount Horse; the number of his Daughters is not known, because they never appear; for as they grow marriageable, he sends to *Taffilet*, for some of the Family of *Xeriphs*, to whom he marries them himself in his Palace, and dispatches them away with their Husbands to that Province.[59]

Through his daughters, some of them from black concubines, he cemented an intimate link with the political and economic base of his origins in the south. As for his sons, they presented a major challenge for the sultan. The black army provided the bodyguards who insured the safety of the princes and carried out the biddings of some capricious princes. The sons of the sultan were distinguished by wearing an earring of gold ornamented with a pearl that the Jews were accustomed to offer as a gift to the sultan's newborn sons.[60] They lived with their mothers until they came of age, when they moved to an adjacent residence; then they would be on their own, except for the ones whose mothers had some influence in the palace – they would be sent to Tafilalt "where the Emperor [gave] them a Plantation of Dates, on which they live[d]."[61] Hence, the role of mothers was crucial in securing a better position for their sons:

But to some of his eldest and best beloved, he has given the Government of large Provinces, nevertheless limits them in the Command of Troops, over whom he

---

[56] Pellow, *The Adventures*, 147; Adrien Maurice de Mairault, *Relation de ce qui s'est passé dans le royaume de Maroc, depuis l'année 1727 jusqu'en 1737* (Paris: Chaubert, 1742), 41.

[57] Busnot, *Histoire du règne de Mouley Ismael*, 54.

[58] Az-Zayani, *Le Maroc de 1631 à 1812*, 54 of the French translation and 28–29 of the Arabic text.

[59] Windus, *A Journey to Mequinez*, 189.

[60] De La Véronne and de León, *Vie de Moulay Isma'il*, 26 of the French translation and 98 of the Spanish text; Claude de Massac, *Relation en forme de journal, du voiage pour la redemption des captifs, aux roiaumes de Maroc & d'Alger, pendant les années 1723. 1724. & 1725* (Paris: Sevestre, 1726), 160.

[61] Windus, *A Journey to Mequinez*, 190.

places Alcaydes; for, since the Rebellion of his Son *Muley Mahomet*, he cares
not to trust any great body of Forces in the Hands of his Sons; three of which
are most remarkable, being lookt upon as Competitors for the Empire; they are
Muley Hamet Deheby, *Mulyey Xeriph*, and *Muley Abdelmelech*.[62]

Thus, legitimate wives and concubines all practiced their suppressed
agency within the limits of a male-dominated society, as it was in society
at large, using schemes and detours to improve their conditions and those
of their children.

The sultan's harem was inconceivable without eunuchs. The harem
included many concubines who lived in a walled space supervised by
eunuchs who performed many tasks such as guarding the gates of the palace, keeping security, providing a link to the outside world, and serving
as intermediaries between the master and his wives and concubines. Most
Moroccan rulers had eunuchs and, depending on the size of the sultan's
harem, the number ranged from hundreds to thousands of eunuchs who
served the sultan and his harem. Az-Zayani reported that Mawlay Isma'il's
eunuchs numbered up to twenty-two hundred.[63] The eunuchs' unique position and movement between highly restricted spaces allowed them to have
powerful positions in the palace. They conspired with women in their plots
and were involved in politics, an example being the role of Ibn Marjan in
state politics. The most senior position among the eunuchs was that of the
office of *al-hajib* (literally the doorkeeper, but it is used here in the sense of
the chamberlain). Joseph de León reported that the eunuchs were imported
from Tuwat and Guinea (black West Africa) and they were the only male
slaves admitted into different parts of the palace. Eunuchs themselves had
slaves to serve them.[64] According to English writer William Lemprière (d.
1834), Moroccan rulers seemed to have a monopoly over the eunuchs.
When William Lemprière was in the army medical service in Gibraltar in
1789, he responded to an invitation by Sultan Sidi Muhammad to come
to Morocco and treat his son, who was suffering from a cataract. After he
successfully cured him he was forced to stay for a while to attend the medical needs of some ladies in the sultan's harem. He wrote:

It but seldom happens that any eunuchs are brought away, unless by a particular commission from the Emperor for some of the princes, no other person
in the country being permitted to keep them. It is indeed extremely difficult to

---

[62] Ibid., 190–191.
[63] Az-Zayani, *Le Maroc de 1631 à 1812*, 29 of the French translation and 15 of the Arabic
text.
[64] De La Véronne and de León, *Vie de Moulay Isma'il*, 28 of the French translation and 100
of the Spanish text.

procure them at all. The place whence they are usually brought is the kingdom of Bambara. In Muley Ishmael's reign the number of eunuchs in the empire of Morocco was supposed to amount to seven hundred.[65]

From these reports it appears that the eunuchs were not part of the black army but imported from the land of Bambara and Tuwat. The emasculation procedures were possibly done in that region. In addition to eunuchs there were also 'arifa roles in the harem. The 'arifa was the overseer or the woman who administered the concubines' affairs; she was in charge of the most discreet assignments such as escorting the concubine to the sultan's chamber.[66]

Mawlay Isma'il's reign lasted fifty-five years and is probably the longest documented reign in Moroccan history. Moroccan historians such as az-Zayani and an-Nasiri recorded that he died due to sickness in 1727,[67] but according to Captain John Braithwaite (circa 1700–1768), who accompanied John Russel Esq., the British consul-general to Morocco, who was in Morocco at the time, Mawlay Isma'il died two months before his death was officially announced to the public:[68]

The Great Emperor *Muley Ismael,* during his Illness, foreseeing his Death, gave Orders to his Chief Eunuch to conceal it for some time, for fear of Insurrections in the City, until *Muley Hamet*'s Interest was sufficiently established, and his Enemies secured. All agree it was concealed two Months, and the monthly Presents were received from the *Alcaides* as usual: But the People who suspected something, not having seen the Emperor for some time, began to murmur, and gather about the Palace, in a very tumultuous Manner, desiring to see their King.[69]

Two important points emerge from this eyewitness report – that the sultan trusted the black servants of his palace with his sickness and his death

---

[65] William Lemprière, *A Tour from Gibraltar to Tangier* (London: printed for the author; and sold by J. Walter, J. Johnson, and J. Sewell, 1791), 346–347.

[66] See de Massac, *Relation en forme de journal,* 199.

[67] Az-Zayani, *Le Maroc de 1631 à 1812,* 55 of the French translation and 29 of the Arabic text; an-Nasiri, 1997, vol. 7, 100.

[68] Joseph de León reported that Mawlay Isma'il was possibly strangled by one of his concubines, perhaps the mother of the prince Mawlay Ahmad adh-Dhahabi, Zaydana. This rumor is false because Zaydana died eleven years before Mawlay Isma'il died. Information on the harem is generally rumors and guess work at best, since no man, let alone a foreigner, had access to the sultan's harem, but it definitely reflected a glimpse of the intrigues and rivalries among wives and concubines in the sultan's harem. See de La Véronne, *Documents inédits,* 3. See also de La Véronne and de León, *Vie de Moulay Isma'il,* 14–15.

[69] John Braithwaite, *The History of the Revolutions in the Empire of Morocco, upon the Death of the late Emperor Muley Ishmael* (London: printed by J. Darby and T. Browne, 1729), 5.

and that he was aware of the problems of the politics of succession and the insurrections that might ensue.

The alliance and the mutual trust between the sultan and the black army benefited not only the sultan but also eventually the black army, in spite of the manner in which soldiers were forcibly conscripted. The membership in the ranks of the black army had legal and social implications for the status and conditions of ex-slaves and blacks in general. The term *wisfan* (sing. *wasif*), meaning servants, replaced the term *'abid* in the vocabulary of the official (Makhzan) discourse to designate the back soldiers. As in the words of Ennaji: "Their *de facto* liberty came outside the usual channels of emancipation; service to the State granted them this dispensation. The Makhzen, furthermore, very pragmatically made use of the terms 'freedman' and 'wazif' for many of its servants."[70] Hence blacks occupied many offices typically assigned to free men such as tax collectors, treasury heads, and so forth. But most of all, they occupied positions of trust. Indeed, Ibn Marjan as-Saghir, who occupied the post of treasury chief, signed his name in an official letter dated May 28, 1728, sent to the French cardinal Fleury, as: "wasif ad-dar al-'aliyya bi-llah, Marjan as-Saghir," or "the servant of the house elevated by God, Marjan as-Saghir."[71] Ibn Marjan was also the head of the black servants in the palace. Mohammed Ennaji notes that "[S]tate correspondence almost never uses the word *'abd*, calling the slave a *wazif* (pl. *wazfan*) instead. At least in the nineteenth century, the Makhzen used this term generally for all male servants of slave origin, regardless of their rank in the official hierarchy."[72] However, the term commonly used for state officials of free condition is *khadim*. The legal terms that were commonly used to refer to a male slave were *'abd* and *mamluk*; for a female slave *ama*, *jariya*, and *mamluka*. So the use of *wasif* (masculine) and *wasifa* (feminine) in the Makhzanian context of Mawlay Isma'il was a deliberate attempt to distinguish those in the service of the Makhzan from others who were free as well as from those who were in private servile condition. The institutional and legal rearrangement was necessary in order for the Makhzan's servants to carry out their work; unlike privately owned slaves (not in service to the state), they could not be sold. The commoners had to respect them as representatives of the Makhzan and not as slaves. While the Makhzan servants behaved like free people

---

[70] Ennaji, *Serving the Master*, 95.
[71] De La Véronne, *Documents inédits*, 55–57.
[72] Ennaji, *Serving the Master*, 94.

and gradually claimed their freedom, nevertheless the stigma of being of slave origin persisted.

One of the crucial responsibilities of the black army was the physical safety of the sultan. Germain Mouette (1652–1691), who was captured in Morocco in 1670 and spent eleven years in captivity, observed that the bodyguards of the sultan were young blacks. He wrote that: "The blacks [in his army] were so imposing, because of the confidence that the sultan has placed in them, that the Moroccans tremble in front of them, and they treated them like lords."[73] Joseph de León reported that young men from ten to sixteen years of age formed the personal guards of the sultan. They were armed and well dressed. They followed the sultan everywhere he went. And when they became older they were transferred to the army. The sultan was demonstrating by using personal bodyguards who were clearly young that the best protection was the affection of his subjects.[74] The sultan succeeded in being perceived as a father figure. His preference for blacks extended their training by teaching young blacks professions normally the purview of Arabs and Berbers in order to entrust them with the responsibilities of the palace.[75] Windus confirmed the sultan's preferential treatment of the blacks by saying that:

Altho' the Natives of his Dominions are Whites, yet they are not so much esteemed by him as the Blacks, and the Copper-coloured, to whom he commits the Guard of his Person, and is so fond of their Breed, that he takes care to mix them himself, by often ordering great Numbers of People before him, whom he marries [...]. He always yoaks his best-complexioned Subjects to a black Help-mate, and the fair Lady must take up with a Negro.[76]

This preferential treatment was contingent upon complete allegiance to the sultan and any deviation was not tolerated: it was met with severe punishment as in the case of 1714 when the sultan ordered the execution of seventeen black soldiers and four officers in Mashra' ar-Ramla.[77] Hence it was in the interest of the blacks that they did not seek any autonomy or compromise their loyalty to the sultan. The alliance between

---

[73] Germain Mouette, *Histoire des conquestes de Mouley Archy, connu sous le nom de Roy de Tafilet; Et de Mouley Ismaël, ou Seméin son frère, & son successeur à présent Regnant, Tous deux Rois de Fez, de Maroc, de Tafilet, de Sus, etc.* (Paris: Couterot, 1683), 409.

[74] De La Véronne and de León, *Vie de Moulay Isma'il*, 57 of the French translation and 145 of the Spanish text.

[75] Ibid., 59 of the French translation and 147 of the Spanish text.

[76] Windus, *A Journey to Mequinez*, 138.

[77] Az-Zayani, *Le Maroc de 1631 à 1812*, 51 of the French translation and 27 of the Arabic text.

the sultan and his racialized army helped create centralized power and simultaneously undermined the alliance between the central government and the tribal groups who traditionally provided manpower in return for tax exemptions and rights to land. The sultan did indeed annihilate the power of the Berbers and Arabs in the Makhzan. He intended these consequences; from his first year in power he was critical of the dual loyalty and unreliability of the soldiers provided to the state by some Berber and Arab tribes.

The formation of a black army and the building of the empire were costly. To minimize the costs, Mawlay Isma'il kept his government simple and made it more palace-centered than Makhzan civil service-oriented. The palace has always been central to the Makhzan in "traditional" Morocco and, as contemporary Moroccan historian Mohamed El Mansour wrote, "the so-called 'Makhzan service' was basically made up of the palace domestic organization, the administrative hierarchy and the army."[78] According to Windus, the sultan's administrative staff at the court was made up of five standing officers:

> the Grand Mufti for Affairs of Religion; the chief Eunuch to take Care of the Seraglio; a Treasurer for his Revenue; the Superintendant of his Buildings and the Basha of Mekness, who is the first Minister, or the supreme Akcayde, of which there are three forts; the first and chief are those who, in the nature of Vice-Roys, are sent to govern the Provinces; to whom, for their greater Honour, is sometimes given the Title of Bashas [...]. Another fort are the Generals of his Armies, and Commanders over small Parties of Horse of Foot. The Third fort are Governours of Cities, or Towns, and are either made by the Emperor himself, as are the Alcaydes of Morocco [Marrakesh], Fez, Sally, and other great Cities; or by the Governours of the Provinces, over small Towns and Cities; a fourth fort may be added, which are titular only, and therefore called *Alcaydes of their Heads*.[79]

Although he ruled as an absolute monarch over the lives of his subjects and their possessions, the sultan appeared in modest attire, as Windus described, "not much different from what his Bashas wear,"[80] unlike his counterparts' regalia as seen with Turks in Algiers or Louis XVI of France. In his entourage were many secretaries, including religious scholars versed in Islamic law, to whom he consulted and entrusted his correspondence. According to Joseph de León, one of the sultan's personal secretaries was a concubine who was highly trusted in reading his correspondence.[81] He

---

[78] Mohammed El Mansour, *Morocco in the Reign of Mawley Sulayman* (Wisbech, England: Middle East & North African Studies Press, 1990), 19.

[79] Windus, *A Journey to Mequinez*, 122–123.

[80] Ibid., 100.

[81] De La Véronne and de León, *Vie de Moulay Isma'il*, 51 of the French translation and 133 of the Spanish text.

was a charismatic ruler whose presence required great deference and obedience from all his officers and subjects.[82] His methods to establish social
stability and unity among his subjects were extreme, but they were effective in preventing plots against him.

Mawlay Isma'il did not have a minister of foreign affairs, but he had
ambassadors to Western European countries, mainly important players in
the Atlantic such as England and France. He felt that the immediate threat
would come from his subjects and the Turks, so he relied on his army to
make him feared among his subjects and to discourage the Turks who
ruled the neighboring country of Algeria.[83] His conscription initiative,
which assembled the largest army in Moroccan history as of his reign,
allowed the sultan to exert great authority through which he was able
to undermine the power and influence of tribal groups in the sultanate.
The sultan went even further by requesting that the tribes turn over their
weapons and horses to the black army.[84] Al-Hasan al-Yusi (1631–1691),
an eminent Sufi scholar, articulated the concerns of the tribes in a letter
addressed to the sultan in which he criticized the sultan for disarming the
Moroccan tribes.[85] The black army's strong loyalty to the sultan and the
prerogatives they enjoyed threatened the interests of the Moroccan tribes
and caused resentment and jealousy. The tribes' resentment also focused
on the army and revived and reinforced the negative perception of black
people. Although the success of the army in unifying Morocco against
internal dissidence and external hostilities was impressive, the army did
not try to win the trust of the Moroccan people. On the contrary, they
were generally cut off from society and formed isolated communities in
their garrisons and posts. They were feared as an instrument of the monarchy but not admired, which deepened the binary between the Makhzan
and the Moroccan tribes.

John Windus noted that the army accompanied the sultan almost
everywhere he went. He described their hierarchy: "they are of all ranks
and degrees, some are the sons of his chief alcaydes, others picked up by
chance, or taken from a large Negro Town joining to Mequinez,[86] which
the Emperor has filled with families of Blacks and Tawnies for his use."[87]

---

[82] Windus, *A Journey to Mequinez*, 124–125.
[83] See de La Véronne and de León, *Vie de Moulay Isma'il*, 52 of the French translation and
137 of the Spanish text.
[84] See Ibn Zaydan, *Ithaf A'lam an-Nas*, vol. 2, 69–70.
[85] Jacques Berque, *Al-Yousi. Problèmes de la culture marocaine au XVIIème siècle* (Paris:
Mouton, 1958), 92.
[86] Mashra' ar-Ramla. Mequinez was the English spelling of Meknes.
[87] Windus, *A Journey to Mequinez*, 140.

This royal reliance benefited blacks, enabling many to attain high positions in the central government. Windus reported that at his time they
numbered about 800 officers:

[S]everal have the Names of Alcaydes, as the chief of them who wait on the
Emperor's Person; others are made Overseers of some Task or Work the Emperor
has ordered them to finish; some he makes perpetual Alcaydes over a certain
Number of his Companions, and such a one is to answer for the rest, as to their
Diligence, cleanly and good Deportment in all particulars; and it is wonderful to
see the Insolence, State and Gravity of these young Rogues, and how they ape the
old Emperor[88] in their way of Government.[89]

These officers fulfilled multiple functions according to the will of the sultan. Some officers were appointed to the staff of a pasha or a great officer to ward off any encroachment of the Christians or the resistance of
the Berbers in the mountains. Mawlay Isma'il kept some officers in his
entourage as his special emissaries for delicate missions. Windus reported
that they were "intrusted [sic] with all important Messages as to carry
the Emperor's Letter of Thanks to any Officer who serves him well, or to
call him Cuckold, spit in his Face, give him a Box on the Ear, spangle, or
cut off his Head."[90]

These officers also performed the role of tribute collectors. Windus
wrote that this kind of officer "remains by him [the sultan] without any
Employment (after performing this service) he is called Alcayde of his
Head [in Arabic, *qa'id ra'sahu*], which is a sort of an Alcayde titular or
Reforme."[91] Such officers were called *quwwad ru'usuhum* (plural of *qa'id
ra'sahu*), usually chosen from the sons of high-ranking officers of the
black army. The literal meaning of *qa'id ra'sahu* is "an officer of himself,"
but technically the term designated a title for an officer or a clerk in the
palace without a specific duty and whose job might entail military or civil
affairs. Windus continued:

The first Mark of their Preferment, after they grow too big to serve the Emperor
in this nature, is giving them a Horse (a Horseman being in the highest Esteem
imaginable amongst them [...],) then the Emperor either recommends them to
some of his Bashas or great Alcaydes employed against the Christians, or the

[88] The Sultan was about seventy-five years old at the time of John Windus' visit to Morocco.
Windus estimated the age of the sultan at eighty-seven years old. It was a wrong estimate
because he died at the age of eighty-one. See the description of the sultan in Windus, *A
Journey to Mequinez*, 99.
[89] Ibid., 142.
[90] Ibid., 143.
[91] Ibid., 144.

Berbers that inhabit the Mountains, or keeps them near him, and they are ready to be intrusted with all important Messages.[92]

The principal fiscal officers in charge of the treasury were chosen by the sultan from among his most trusted blacks such as Ibn al-Ashgar, 'Ali b. Yashshur, and Ibn Marjan.[93] Indeed, one of the highest positions in the government was entrusted to a black person, Ibn Marjan as-Saghir. Ibn Marjan had been an influential figure in the palace for at least a decade during the latter years of Mawlay Isma'il's life and soon after his death.[94] The decision to favor certain black individuals in the palace, some of whom had reached a very high status in power, caused the Arabs and Berbers to envy them. The power of some blacks surpassed that of some Arab dignitaries.[95]

The building of the empire and the upkeep of the army demanded large expenses. It was not in the capacity of the state treasury (*bayt al-mal*) to absorb the expenses that the recruitment and the upkeep of this huge army required, hence Mawlay Isma'il resorted to enforcing and increasing taxes. The range of legal taxes levied was not inconsiderable: *zakat* (alms tax), *'ushr* (a tenth part) on productive property or *kharaj* (land tax), which was one-tenth of the produce; *jizya* or poll-tax imposed on "people of the Book," called *dhimmi* – this status allowed Moroccan Jews to hold land, to practice their religion, and to maintain their culture in exchange for payment of poll-taxes to the central government; and customs duties on imports and exports set from ten to twenty-five percent of the value of the goods transported.[96] The sultan established other taxes such as *an-na'iba* (affliction), which was a supplementary fixed sum imposed on each family and was considered as a family's contribution toward jihad against European encroachment; and a sales tax (*maks*, pl. *mukus*). The imposition of these additional taxes, arguably illegal under Islamic law, was strengthened by historical precedents. For example, the Sa'di regime imposed one dirham on each person of the region of Sus during its fight against the Portuguese.[97]

---

[92] Ibid., 143.

[93] Az-Zayani, *Le Maroc de 1631 à 1812*, 56 of the French translation and 30 of the Arabic text.

[94] See de La Véronne, *Documents inédits*, 44–59. Windus mentioned that the treasurer of the sultan was a black eunuch called as-Saghir. Windus, *A Journey to Mequinez*, 109.

[95] For more information on the story of the black army, known as 'Abid al-Bukhari, and its role in the success of Mawlay Isma'il's efforts to reform the state, see Meyers, *The 'Abid 'l-Buhari*.

[96] See Kenbib (ed.), *La Grande Encyclopedie*, 105.

[97] Eugène Aubin, *Morocco of to-Day* (London: J.M. Dent & Co, 1906), 194.

The sultan assigned members of his army to collect taxes from different regions in Morocco. This was a dangerous task during times of hostility, Thomas Pellow wrote that in 1722, in the region of Mhamid al-Ghuzlan, there was "a wild sort of people, coming thither from the coast of the deserts for dates, killing sixteen of the Emperor's blacks sent there with his credentials to receive and bring to Mequinez their accustomed tribute."[98] Aware of the crucial importance of the trans-Saharan trade for the Moroccan economy, the sultan sent his army to take control of the main Saharan routes and the salt mines. To establish security in the Saharan region, he sent a contingent of the black army to support his allies the Trarza against the Brakna.[99] He also built an important *qsar* (a fortified village) called Rissani near Sijilmasa in the Tafilalt region, about ten days by caravan from Fez, and twelve from Marrakesh, to serve as a center for the trans-Saharan caravan trade.[100] The authority of Mawlay Isma'il extended as far as Timbuktu. The Moroccan army had a presence in Timbuktu from the time of the Sa'di dynasty, during which a vassal regime in northern Mali known as the Arma Pachalik was established. With the arrival of the 'Alawi dynasty, the Arma rulers of Timbuktu region pledged their allegiance to Mawlay ar-Rashid in 1670.[101] Although this allegiance was nominal, Mawlay Isma'il demanded taxes from the rulers of Timbuktu. Joseph de León reported that an officer of the sultan was in charge of collecting these contributions from what is now northern Mali. This officer was accustomed to gather a troop of twenty to thirty thousand men, conscripted from the tribes adjacent to the Sudan (black West Africa), for this mission. This way, he succeeded in collecting from the inhabitants of the region whatever he could in the form of gold dust and slaves, mainly eunuchs and women. The journey to the Sudan took four months but the return took six months. The officer might stay for two to four years in the area collecting gold and gathering slaves. On the way back, he left his troops with their respective tribes. After two or three months, the journey was repeated under the same conditions. Most of these slaves ended up in the palace and among the people of

---

[98] Pellow, *The Adventures*, 110–111.

[99] Paul Marty, *L'émirat des Trarzas* (Paris: Ernest Leroux, 1919), 68–69.

[100] See Budgett Meakin, *The Land of the Moors: A Comprehensive Description* (London: S. Sonnenschein & Co., Lim, 1901), 399. Rissani is also the place of the tomb of the founder of the 'Alawi dynasty.

[101] The *arma* is a deformation of the word *ar-rumat* (pl. of *ar-rami*), which means "rifleman" or "gunner"; it is the principal force of the Moroccan army that conquered the northern region of Mali.

the court.[102] In addition to these tax-collecting expeditions, Windus also mentioned that Morocco sent yearly caravans, departing from Fez to the Sudan, specifically Timbuktu. "From thence they return richly loaden [*sic*] with Gold-dust, Ostrich Feathers, Elephants Teeth, and Negroes, who are the Emperor's Property."[103] From Windus' account, the emperor (sultan) had a monopoly over trade in black slaves.

The sultan harvested all sources of revenue, including the corsair activities, which became a state affair. European hostilities on the Moroccan Atlantic shores spurred corsair activities to secure the Moroccan shores. European captives were used as slaves in the Moroccan palaces or held hostage in expectation of ransom.[104] Thomas Pellow, himself a European captive who witnessed such activities, reported that the corsairs of the Atlantic city of Salé received fifty ducats for each captive, but the sultan got back one-third as his share and a tenth as a customary tax.[105] Mawlay Isma'il also used the expertise of the Jews in commerce and financial affairs. The Moroccan Jews had international business deals with Europeans as far as Holland.[106] The sultan depended on them. For example, Abraham Maymuran, chief of the Jews, was a banker and consultant to the sultan. His monetary support was crucial to Mawlay Isma'il's war of accession to the throne.[107] Pellow mentioned one particular figure among the Jews, Ben 'Attar, to whom the sultan assigned the task of managing the affairs of the Christian captives.[108] These European captives were very useful to the sultan in arsenal and military skills, ship building, and masonry. Mawlay Isma'il had amassed considerable wealth by the time of his death. Ibn Marjan's accounting given to the sultan's first successor stated that the treasury contained eighty-six quintals of gold, twenty-five hundred quintals of silver, sixty-five saddles embroidered with gold and gems, 400 rifles damascened with gold, and other precious items.[109]

Moroccan historians such as 'Abd al-Karim ar-Rifi and an-Nasiri praised the efficiency of the army in achieving security in the country

---

[102] De La Véronne and de León, *Vie de Moulay Isma'il*, 63–64 of the French translation and 152 of the Spanish text.

[103] Windus, *A Journey to Mequinez*, 212.

[104] Pellow, *The Adventures*, 27.

[105] Ibid., 53.

[106] See Germain Mouette, *Relation de la captivité du Sr. Moüette dans les royaumes de Fez et de Maroc* (Paris: Chez Jean Cochart, 1683), 31.

[107] Windus, *A Journey to Mequinez*, 117. See also de La Véronne and de León, *Vie de Moulay Isma'il*, 68 of the French translation and 157 of the Spanish text.

[108] Pellow, *The Adventures*, 53.

[109] De Mairault, *Relation de ce qui s'est passé*, 54.

after participating in many battles against the tribes and Sufi orders who rebelled against the sultan's authority. The sultan established an internal defensive posture – in any area where restive tribal groups had shown resistance, he stationed black troops.[110] However, historical chronicles suggest that the black army played only minor roles in the battles fought to recapture coastal cities under European occupation. Apparently, liberation of these ports relied more on local people and volunteers than the participation of the black army, although the main legal rationale, as discussed, for the formation of the army was to wage jihad against intrusions of the Christians on Islamic soil. It seems that the sultan's real priority for his army was to impose and to protect his authority after decades of continual political disorder. Hence, he was very cautious not to run the risk of compromising it in any potentially huge battle where the costs might deprive him of such a formidable police power.[111]

Mawlay Isma'il did not create a state army but a personal one. At his death in 1727, both the central authority and the black army were in crisis. This was a clear indication of the shortfalls of the Moroccan political system – that the centralization of the society was impossible without a strong military base.

---

[110] See an-Nasiri, *al-Istiqsa'*, vol. 7, 61–70; ar-Rifi, *az-Zahr al-Akamm*, 178 and Ibn Zaydan, *Ithaf A'lam an-Nas*, vol. 2, 69–70.
[111] See ar-Rifi, *az-Zahr al-Akamm*, 166–188.

6

The Political History of the Black Army

Between Privilege and Marginality

The black army originated with enslaved people but became a major political force – making and unmaking rulers – for much of the eighteenth century, and even retained influence, albeit reduced, well into the nineteenth century. Its power fluctuated, mirroring and reacting to the abilities, qualities, and rivalries of the rulers. Its influence was gradually reduced as various rulers brought in Arab and Berber soldiers to offset the influence of the black military, especially during the reign of Sidi Muhammad when the army became largely mixed in the 1780s and its position was finally eroded after the reign of Mawlay 'Abd ar-Rahman (1822–1859). This chapter follows the remarkable journey of the rise and gradual decline of the black army over these successive periods.

After the death of Sultan Mawlay Isma'il in 1727, the army had to make a difficult decision to choose among the many sons of the sultan who competed to inherit the throne.[1] Moroccan sources are not consistent regarding whether or not the sultan designated his heir. Some sources claimed that Mawlay Ahmad adh-Dhahabi was designated by his father to inherit the throne, but most sources insist that it was the army who proclaimed him sultan.[2] Historian an-Nasiri wrote that the army played a major role in his election.[3] But the new sultan relied mainly on the contingent of infantry in Meknes that was under the leadership of the black

[1] I note that most of the Arabic sources called the black army by the term *'Abid. Blacks* or *slaves* were used interchangeably.
[2] See an-Nasiri, *al-Istiqsa'*, vol. 7, 100–101.
[3] Ibid., vol. 7, 115.

pasha Msahil,[4] and failed to pay the army in Mashra' ar-Ramla their salary, already six months late. The three officers from Mashra' ar-Ramla went to the palace to register their complaint before the new sultan, but the sultan scolded them for not being useful to him and rejected their request. At the same time, the officers (*quwwad ru'usuhum*) of the palace of Meknes were dissatisfied with the sultan's odious behavior and disastrous rule.[5] The officers realized that no good could be expected from him; they approached Ibn Marjan as-Saghir for advice. This event marked a shift of political influence from the pasha Msahil to the treasurer Ibn Marjan. Ibn Marjan managed the palace during the last days of Mawlay Isma'il's life and was in charge of the treasury during his life.[6] Ibn Marjan did not support the new sultan or his loyal supporter pasha Msahil. French priest Germain Beguin reported that Ibn Marjan told these officers:

> I very much fear that you are not men; our law will be destroyed because of your fault. Knowing a man [that is, Ahmad adh-Dhahabi] unfit to reign, you have been the first to enthrone him. If you want to believe me, you will overthrow him and replace him by his brother 'Abd al-Malik whom you know; he is a good warrior and a good Muslim.[7]

The officers replied that they would follow his counsel. Ibn Marjan, an astute diplomat, added: "The situation is delicate. You are not powerful enough to succeed in this venture; examine the moods of the notables and the people of Meknes, and then we will take the necessary measures."[8] The palace officers reported to Ibn Marjan that most notables were in favor of his plan and ready to execute it. Ibn Marjan replied that they should first join forces with the three officers from Mashra'

---

[4] This high officer of the black army was apparently a crucial figure in politics but Arabic sources do not provide any details about him.

[5] Louis de Chenier described Ahmad's rule: "Indolence and neglect pervaded the court. The debauched life of the king, the contempt in which his inactive government was held, and the murmurs of the people, rendered discontent so universal that it ended in revolt." De Chenier, *Recherches historiques*, tome III, 425. The English translation: *The Present State*, vol. 1, 234. Similarly, Muhammad al-Qadiri (d. 1773) wrote that "the Sultan was engrossed in his excesses of food, drink, [fine] clothes, women and music. Raids between the Moroccan tribes became widespread, as did plunder, highway robbery, fear and oppression of the weak by the strong, while roads were cut, and the blood of Muslims was spilled." Al-Qadiri, *Nashr al Mathani*, 58–59 of the Arabic text and 167–168 of the English translation.

[6] Az-Zayani, *Le Maroc de 1631 à 1812*, 56 of the French translation and 30 of the Arabic text.

[7] Chantal de La Véronne, *Documents inédits sur l'histoire du Maroc: sources françaises* (Paris: Geuthner, 1975), 44.

[8] Ibid., 44–45.

ar-Ramla and urge them to mobilize the army to support their plan. The three officers enthusiastically dispatched letters to the army headquarters in Mashra' ar-Ramla and urged officers there to put an end to the decadence of this ruler. At the army headquarters, officers agreed to deploy four thousand soldiers to Meknes and to admonish the sultan for his mistreatment of the army. On Friday morning, March 18, 1728, 600 of the leading officers gathered at one of the main gates of the palace, at the site of the apartment of Ibn Marjan, and screamed: "Long live the truth! Long live the law of Muhammad and death to anyone who will oppose it."[9] This slogan reflected the aspiration of reforming the institution of the central authority (Makhzan) according to the Islamic law. After consulting Ibn Marjan, 200 of the officers stayed at the gate to protect him and the rest took control of another palace gate. Soon, the people of Meknes joined the eighteen hundred officers (*quwwad ru'usuhum*) and 600 pages of the late Sultan Mawlay Isma'il in a coup against Sultan Ahmad, who was trapped in his palace with his generals and 200 pages. Fearing death, he did not want to come out. Ibn Marjan intervened and persuaded the sultan to leave the palace and move back to the house in Meknes where he lived before becoming sultan. The following day, Saturday, March 19, the four thousand soldiers from Mashra' ar-Ramla arrived and were informed of what had happened the day before. They quarreled with the local officers about the way they had proceeded and reproached them for not waiting. The army officers appeared divided between those supporting the removal of the sultan and those opposing his removal and wishing to see him reinstated. The general of the army intervened, concerned that the division among the army would not help its cause and that the officers should take measures that would satisfy the whole army.[10] So representatives from different parties met in the palace to deliberate the course of action. They made three different propositions: 1) reinstate Mawlay Ahmad, 2) replace him with his brother 'Abd al-Malik, 3) replace him with another of his brothers. But Ibn Marjan was successful in swaying the assembly in favor of Mawlay 'Abd al-Malik, insisting that no other was fit to bring safety and prosperity to the country. And so the army proclaimed 'Abd al-Malik sultan. Then the general of the army renewed the demand to compensate the army. At first, Ibn Marjan was reluctant to comply with the demand,

---

[9] De La Véronne, *Documents inédits*, 1975, 45
[10] Beguin's document does provide the name of this general. It is possible that he was Salim ad-Dukkali.

using the pretext that Mawlay Ahmad had given the duty to guard the treasury to another person, a eunuch called Ba 'Allal. The general did not accept this and replied by noting that Ibn Marjan was the master of the palace and threatening not to support Ibn Marjan's political position if the army was not paid. Subsequently, Ibn Marjan issued an order to provide the general with 220 quintals of silver, double the six months of salary due to the army. He also distributed 120 quintals to the palace officers and the people of the city of Meknes.[11]

Ibn Marjan was one of the few diplomats who had political leverage to conduct state affairs. He tried to preserve his prestigious role in the palace through his involvement in the coup d'état. His actions in concert with the army, his preference for Mawlay 'Abd al-Malik as sultan, his desire to alienate pasha Msahil (a key supporter of Mawlay Ahmad adh-Dhahabi) and thus undermine the pasha's power and influence were critical and earned him more power and influence in state affairs. There is considerable evidence found in his correspondence with French diplomats and a group of priests referred to as "Pères Rédempteurs" who visited Morocco to free European Christian captives that he had assumed the role of viceroy. In a letter dated April 27, 1728 that he wrote to a black officer, Mubarak al-Fulani, chief of the Rabat garrison,[12] Ibn Marjan informed the officer that the new sultan, 'Abd al-Malik, had not arrived at the palace, and instructed al-Fulani not to allow the Pères Rédempteurs to leave Salé and come to Meknes under any circumstances, even if he received a letter from the sultan himself unless the sultan's letter was accompanied by his own letter and delivered by one of his friends.[13] Ibn Marjan wrote to King Louis XIV of France requesting an official royal letter regarding the redemption of the captives in Morocco, informing him that any redemption could be done only by a royal order. In a letter addressed to the Pères Rédempteurs, dated May 2, 1728, Sultan 'Abd al-Malik himself instructed the Pères Rédempteurs that all negotiations had to be conducted solely with Ibn Marjan.[14]

Given the involvement of the army in the coup, the new Sultan Mawlay 'Abd al-Malik distrusted and feared the power of the army, which he thought represented a threat to the institution of the monarchy. He decided to terminate any compensation as a means to create dissension and undermine the cohesiveness and resolve of the officers and ranks. The army felt

[11] De La Véronne, *Documents inédits*, 1975, 47–48.
[12] Ibid., 61.
[13] Ibid., 49.
[14] Ibid., 50.

betrayed and secretly planned for his deposal. 'Abd al-Malik, aware of the army's plan, embarked on his own plan to create alliances with different tribes, warning them against the oppression of the army. The sultan planned to break the power of the army by sowing discord between them and the Berbers. However, the army discovered his counterplot and deposed him, sending for his brother, Mawlay Ahmad adh-Dhahabi, who was in exile in Sijilmasa to become the new sultan. The deposed sultan sought refuge among the people of Fez. Mawlay Ahmad adh-Dhahabi went to Meknes and was proclaimed sultan by the army of Mashra' ar-Ramla and other notables of the country. As the new sultan, Ahmad adh-Dhahabi eliminated many people involved in the previous coup who might be a threat to his rule, including the judge of the army and Ibn Marjan, killed in late 1728. Muhammad al-Qadiri reported that: "He went after them systematically, forced them out of their houses, and had them executed in prison, after which they were crucified."[15] And the bitter struggle between the two brothers ended with the execution of 'Abd al-Malik by strangulation under the order of Mawlay Ahmad adh-Dhahabi, who in turn fell sick and died shortly after, in 1729.[16] The army became in effect free agents and "sultan makers," and were in this case a complete analogy to the Mamluks in Egypt. The army and other powerful groups comprising the notables and scholars of Fez elected Mawlay 'Abd Allah, another son of Mawlay Isma'il, to the throne. French scholar Adrien Maurice de Mairault (1708–1746) believed that the army's support of this particular son was generated by Mawlay 'Abd Allah's mother, Lalla Khanatha (d. 1742), who formed a strong cabal in order to put her son on the throne. For this purpose she distributed three hundred thousand ducats among the army and fifty thousand among the principal officers.[17] But this ruler was also unable to bring peace and stability to the country. Under the pretext of pursuing those involved in killing his brother 'Abd al-Malik, he killed many influential people. With such acts, discord arose among the people of Fez, who regretted having enthroned him. The sultan's wrath was severe – he ordered his army to ravage all the land surrounding Fez including constructions, trees, and farms and to deprive the city of water by blocking river flow. The people of Fez had no choice but to endure, giving up their rich farms to the authority of the sultan.[18] The sultanate was no longer providing security for the people; on the contrary, it was

[15] Al-Qadiri, *Nashr al Mathani*, 63 of the Arabic text and 174 of the English translation.
[16] An-Nasiri, *al-Istiqsa'*, vol. 7, 119–124.
[17] De Mairault, *Relation de ce qui s'est passé*, 156–157.
[18] See an-Nasiri, *al-Istiqsa'*, vol. 7, 129–131.

a growing source of anxiety among the populace. The anxiety was exacerbated beyond the area of Meknes and Fez as a result of the imposition of additional taxes and the brutal ways by which they were collected. The resentment of the Moroccan tribes turned into violence. The people of Lahyayna (north of Fez) protested by killing the sultan's officer, Abu 'l-'Abbas Ahmad al-Kaydi, sent by the sultan to collect taxes.[19] With a growing sense that the army was becoming a threat rather than a loyal ally, as well as rancor against those within the army involved in the killing of his brother, 'Abd al-Malik, the sultan began to forge alliances with other Arab tribes such as the Udaya, a resort to the traditional supplier of military manpower to the sultanate. The strategy of Mawlay Isma'il to amass a formidable and loyal army used to unify and maintain his rule was being undone by his son. Salim ad-Dukkali, general of the army, was apprehensive and conveyed to his ranks that Mawlay 'Abd Allah's intention was to have their officers killed and subject the blacks to the domination of the Arabs and Berbers and sell them as slave labor.[20] When the army saw that he had killed many of its leaders, it decided to depose and kill him. But the sultan discovered its plan through his mother, Khanatha bint Bakkar, and ran away from the capital city of Meknes and went into hiding in the south of Morocco in the company of 600 cavaliers and with a great fortune from the treasury – about sixty thousand golden ducats – leaving his mother and family at the mercy of his enemy.[21]

With the flight of Mawlay 'Abd Allah, the army enthroned his brother 'Ali al-A'raj as the new sultan in 1734. Some sources mention that this sultan was submissive to the will of the army and that he was forced to illegally find money to pay them, an example being the arrest of Khanatha, the mother of his half brother and previous sultan 'Abd Allah, and whom he robbed of her wealth.[22] Muhammad al-Qadiri reported that during a conflict between the people of Fez and Sultan 'Ali al-A'raj, the army under the leadership of Salim ad-Dukkali refused to obey the sultan's order to besiege the city of Fez and persuaded him to renounce his threat against the notables of Fez.[23] The army also encouraged the sultan to attack Ayt Umalu, a group of Berbers, in revenge for conspiring with the previous sultan, 'Abd Allah, against them. This attack did not end well for

[19] Kenbib (ed.), *La Grande Encyclopedie*, 212.
[20] De Mairault, *Relation de ce qui s'est passé*, 221.
[21] Ibid., 223–224.
[22] An-Nasiri, *al-Istiqsa'*, vol. 7, 138.
[23] Al-Qadiri, *Nashr al-Mathani*, 74–75 of the Arabic text and 188–189 of the English translation. See also an-Nasiri, *al-Istiqsa'*, vol. 7, 139.

the army. It ended with a defeat that affected their confidence, and when they heard that the previous, deposed sultan, 'Abd Allah, who had settled in the Sus area, was on his way back, they grew anxious. A group of them talked about re-enthroning him. But Salim ad-Dukkali and his followers disagreed, reminding the officers of their complicity in his deposal and the election of his brother 'Ali as sultan. When the support of 'Abd Allah intensified, Salim ad-Dukkali, among other army officers, fled to the city of Zarhum to seek refuge in a Sufi center, and 'Ali fled to the city of Taza. The majority of the army and the Udaya group renewed their allegiance to 'Abd Allah. But Salim sent a letter from Zarhun to the notable scholars of Fez informing them that the army council agreed to enthrone yet another son of Mawlay Isma'il, Muhammad b. Isma'il, known as Ibn 'Arbiya. But when the army heard of Salim's scheme, they captured him and his loyal officers and sent them to Sultan 'Abd Allah, who was in the town of Tadla. The re-enthroned sultan ordered the local judge to prosecute them. The judge issued a death sentence against them and the sultan ordered them killed. In the meantime, Ibn 'Arbiya, who was in Tafilalt, received the erroneous news that he had been named sultan, so he hurried to reach the capital, but when he arrived in the city of Sefrou (about eighteen miles south of Fez), he learned that 'Abd Allah had already been declared sultan. He then traveled incognito to the city of Fez and stayed in the house of his friend, Abu Zayd ash-Shami, a notable resident.

'Abd Allah's reign was turbulent. His brutal extermination of opponents turned the people of Fez against him. In 1737, a great number of them decided to renounce their oath of allegiance to him and give it to his brother, Muhammad ibn 'Arbiya, and wrote to the army requesting approval. The army agreed and Ibn 'Arbiya became the new sultan. He moved to Meknes and compensated the army for its services from his own money. When 'Abd Allah heard this news, he fled to the mountains to reside among the Berbers. The reign of Ibn 'Arbiya proved a disaster for the country because he inherited a bankrupt government that could not be easily fixed as well as an army that demanded its salaries. The need for money to pay the army for continued support of his sultanate led the sultan to plunder people's wealth. He proceeded to confiscate all granaries and silos that the people of Meknes owned. He also seized the grain of rural residents, who normally brought their goods to sell in the city. These brutal tactics greatly exacerbated civil discord.[24] When the army realized

---

[24] Az-Zayani, *Le Maroc de 1631 à 1812*, 80–81 of the French translation and 43–44 of the Arabic text. See also Ar-Rifi, *az-Zahr al-Akamm*, 245–248.

the inefficiency of this ruler they revolted against him in 1738; they captured him and the governor of Fez and put them both in chains.[25] Then,
they wrote to his brother al-Mustadi' b. Isma'il, who lived in Tafilalt,
requesting his presence in order to enthrone him. But this latter sultan
proved even worse than his predecessors; he encouraged pillages and
increased taxes as a quick maneuver to secure his throne. The army did
not seem to agree with his repressive conduct. When this sultan ordered
his brother Zin al-'Abidin tortured and sent in chains to prison in Tafilalt,
the army sent a special envoy to intercept the convoy and release him. In
the end, the army tried to depose him and reconsider for the third time
his brother 'Abd Allah, who was living among the Berbers of Ayt Idrasan.
'Abd Allah was re-enthroned and al-Mustadi' fled to Marrakesh. The
army wrote to the people of Fez and the Udaya and petitioned for their
approval. The people of Fez responded by sending an envoy from among
their *shurafa'*, notable scholars and merchants, in order to present 'Abd
Allah, who was still in the fortress of Alsam among the Berbers, with their
oath of investiture (*al-bay'a*). In the meantime, the army was in charge of
the central government in Meknes. The army nominated one of its officers, Abu Muhammad 'Abd Allah al-Hamri, governor of Fez.[26] As soon as
'Abd Allah got back to Meknes he started to kill officials who previously
had acted against his rule. He was unable to unite the people or the army.
He tried to increase state income by imposing heavy taxes, an act that
intensified the resentment of the tribes against the central power.

Political disorder, confusion, and restiveness became the norm in
Morocco. The army found itself weak and divided in a cycle that shifted
its political loyalty among the three sons of Mawlay Isma'il: 'Abd Allah,
al-Mustadi', and Zin al-'Abidin. Zin al-'Abidin declined the sultanate and
lived far away from the political machinations until he died. 'Abd Allah
attempted to consolidate his power by forging alliances with the Berbers
in Ayt Idrasan and the Arab Udaya. He faced an alliance forged by his
brother al-Mustadi' and the governor of Tangier, Ahmad b. 'Ali ar-Rifi,
and with their supporters from the army engaged in successive battles. In
1741, the governor of Tangier declared his independence and some of the
black officers deserted to him. Al-Qadiri reported:

The ruler of Tangier was lavish in honoring the *'abid* deserting to him, and the
latter wrote to their companions in al-Raml and strove to induce them to break
their oath to the Sultan and to return to the ruler of Tangier. They reached an

---

[25] Al-Qadiri, *Nashr al-Mathani*, 84 of the Arabic text and 201 of the English translation.
[26] See an-Nasiri, *al-Istiqsa'*, vol. 7, 152.

agreement with [al-Rifi] on salaries, since they were in a great need, as a famine has just ended, during which little of their salary had been given to them, indeed it had been totally stopped for years.[27]

The repeated letters of ar-Rifi to the army of Mashra' ar-Ramla helped secure its allegiance to his cohort. In 1742, the army declared its allegiance to al-Mustadi', but the people of Fez remained loyal to 'Abd Allah.[28]

In 1743, when 'Abd Allah met ar-Rifi in battle in the fertile lands around Fez, his army was composed of various groups from the army, from the Udaya, the Zrara, the Arabs of the Lahyayna, Shraqa, Awlad Jami', and the Arabs of the Gharb. When 'Abd Allah defeated ar-Rifi he moved on to confront his brother al-Mustadi', who succeeded in gathering ten thousand cavaliers from the army of Mashra' ar-Ramla and a similar number from the Arab tribe of Banu Hasan, located in the area north of Salé. The battle ended with the defeat of al-Mustadi', who fled from one town to the other until he finally settled in Sijilmasa until he died in 1759, renouncing his claim to the throne. In the year 1744, a group of officers of the army who had sided with al-Mustadi' were forced to return to their most powerful rival, 'Abd Allah, and ask to be forgiven and to resubmit to his authority.[29] He pardoned them and paid their long overdue salaries, but when 300 prominent members of Banu Hasan came to pay him homage, he killed them all. He inflicted the same punishment on an envoy from the Rif. Those who did not side with his rival but failed to show their support or to pay him homage were also punished. 'Abd Allah's cruel methods made everybody apprehensive among his army as well as among the populace. So, when the Berber deputation of Ayt Idrasan did not show up, 'Abd Allah sent a reprimanding letter to their leader, Muhammad Wa'ziz. Wa'ziz reacted quickly and swayed his people to designate 100 cavaliers to accompany him to the sultan's residence in the Abu Fikran fortress. 'Abd Allah said to the Berber chief that he blamed the Berbers for not respecting their sultan and his army and added: "I want to put face to face this black goat against this white ram; one of them will perish; and then I will get rid of its furies; as for the other, I will be able to contain it."[30] An-Nasiri explained that by "black goat" he meant the *'abid* (the army) and by "white ram" he meant the

[27] Al-Qadiri, *Nashr al-Mathani*, 89–90 of the Arabic text and 206 of the English translation.

[28] Ibid., 88 of the Arabic text and 209 of the English translation.

[29] An-Nasiri, *al-Istiqsa'*, vol. 7, 166.

[30] Az-Zayani, *Le Maroc de 1631 à 1812*, 106–107 of the French translation and 58–59 of the Arabic text.

Berbers.[31] When the army heard these words, it informed its leaders in Meknes and Mashra' ar-Ramla and requested their advice on the measures the army should take. To maintain his power, 'Abd Allah applied the divide and rule strategy by encouraging divisions among the existing power structures in order to hinder any alliance that could challenge his authority. To ensure his safety, he resided partly in Meknes and partly in the vicinity of Fez. Although 'Abd Allah seemed to gain some momentum, his methods to pacify the country were violent and created more factions and civil discord. In the end, the army coalition agreed to depose him again in 1748 and appoint his son Muhammad, governor of Marrakesh, as the new ruler. Sidi Muhammad, however, scolded them, refused their offer, and remained loyal and even convinced the army to renew its oath of allegiance to his father, 'Abd Allah.[32] 'Abd Allah spent the rest of his life until he died in 1757 trying in vain to gain the trust of the population.

By this time the army had lost its value as a unified military force. Many chronicles and even some contemporary publications glorified the army when it was in service to Sultan Mawlay Isma'il, but condemned it for its role in the political instability and accused it of creating anarchy after his death. Az-Zayani believed that if Mawlay Isma'il had crossed the sea with this army he would have conquered all of Spain.[33] An-Nasiri believed that the black army was the greatest army in the 'Alawi dynasty but reproached it for its part in the political upheaval, social discord, and economic disasters that ensued after the death of Mawlay Isma'il. The black army was made to bear the blame of others.[34] Ibn Zaydan (1873–1946) blamed the army for the anarchy after Mawlay Isma'il's death, accusing the soldiers of being greedy, corrupt, and malfeasants.[35] He was particularly apologetic for Mawlay Ahmad's failures, by blaming the army for coercing him to commit evil acts as the first successor to Mawlay Isma'il.[36] Some modern scholars, such as French historian Robert Montagne, perceived the army as being pernicious to the 'Alawi dynasty.[37] Contemporary Moroccan historian Thuraya Berrada wrote

---

[31] An-Nasiri, *al-Istiqsa'*, vol. 7, 172.

[32] Al-Qadiri, *Nashr al-Mathani*, 104 of the Arabic text and 228 of the English translation.

[33] Az-Zayani, *al-Bustan az-Zarif*, 37.

[34] An-Nasiri, *al-Istiqsa'*, vol. 7, 56 and vol. 8, 47–49.

[35] 'Abd ar-Rahman ibn Zaydan. *Ithaf A'lam an-Nas bi-Jamal Akhbar Hadirat Maknas.* (Casablanca: Matabi' Idyal, 1990), vol. 1, 267–271.

[36] Ibid., vol. I, 265.

[37] Robert Montagne, *Les Berbères et le makhzen dans le sud du Maroc; essai sur la transformation politique des Berbères sédentaires (groupe chleuh)* (Paris: F. Alcan, 1930), 102–103.

that the army was a great tool in maintaining security in the country as long as it was unified in the service of Mawlay Isma'il, but it became an agent of discord and tyranny after his death.[38]

The political crises that ensued after the death of Mawlay Isma'il were not solely due to the political power of the army exerted in support of one then another of Isma'il's sons, as some historians have indicated. The army's survival depended on a stable political order. It was in its interest to have consistent political stability that guaranteed its salaries. Its political activities seemed for the most part justified and often with the blessings of the populace. Historical documents attest to the fact that people rejoiced at the news when an unjust ruler was deposed by the army.[39] But as soon as some security was restored, the next ruler proved no better than the previous one until the rule of Sidi Muhammad b. 'Abd Allah in 1757. There were also instances when the army refused to execute a royal command it deemed unjust. An-Nasiri reported that the military office of Mashra' ar-Ramla wrote once to Sultan 'Abd Allah reproaching him for the unjust killing of Muslims.[40] Ar-Rifi insisted on the soldiers' role as agents of peace and restoring order to society, as the army intervened to put an end to the upheaval and pillage caused by the Berbers and Banu Hasan in the region from Meknes to Salé.[41] There were also times when the army had to conform to the rulers' demands or fight vindictive battles, as in the case of the attack on the Berbers of Ayt Umalu in order to avenge their defeat in 1735.[42]

The army became a symbol of the political conflicts in Morocco. The crisis of the Moroccan system of political succession based on patron–client groups adversely affected the unification of a Moroccan political entity and limited the effectiveness of the ruler's administrative apparatus. In this context, the army's intervention in the politics of succession was necessary in order to secure its stability and prerogatives. The setbacks in payment of the army's salary were critical. During the thirty years of political instability after the death of Mawlay Isma'il, the army received only sporadic payments rather than a fixed salary. As early as 1728, officers from Mashra' ar-Ramla complained on behalf of the army

[38] Thuraya Berrada, "'Abid al-Bukhari" in *Ma'lamat al-Maghrib* (Sale: Nashr Matabi' Sala, 1991), 1093.
[39] Al-Qadiri, *Nashr al Mathani*, 87 of the Arabic text and 205 of the English translation.
[40] An-Nasiri, *al-Istiqsa'*, vol. 7, 134.
[41] Ar-Rifi, *az-Zahr al-Akamm*, 252.
[42] Az-Zayani, *Le Maroc de 1631 à 1812*, 76 of the French translation and 41 of the Arabic text.

to Sultan Ahmad that their salary was six months late.[43] The subsequent rulers failed to establish a salary to be paid to the army on a regular basis. Their payments often came late or only to a group of them or as a reward for performing a special service to the ruler. The sources inform us that the army repeatedly reminded rulers of the necessity to pay the soldiers. It was only when the soldiers revolted that their demands were taken seriously, an example being in 1735 when they revolted against 'Abd Allah and as a result he sent them 100 quintals of silver in order to win them over again.[44] At other times, when he failed to pay them, some black leaders joined his enemy, Ahmad ar-Rifi, who promised better payment.[45] There were also times when the ruler had nothing to provide as was the case in 1736 when the army requested that Sultan al-A'raj provide them clothes, weapons, and their salary. The sultan could not provide the requested resources and as a result the army revolted against him.[46]

The salary crisis and the army's equipage had other implications that affected the black troops stationed in the posts that Mawlay Isma'il established throughout the country. Az-Zayani reported that when Mawlay Isma'il died the garrisons in different parts of the country were abandoned by his sons who ruled after him. No provisions reached the troops, who were left on their own to deal with their subsistence. They scattered among the tribes adjacent to their posts or returned to their native soil.[47] As for the fortresses left behind, they became a target of pillage at the hands of the Arab and Berber tribes who stole the wood and other useful things they found there.[48] The same fate happened to the massive camp in Mashra' ar-Ramla where the army was originally gathered by Mawlay Isma'il. Al-Qadiri reported:

> The [Arab] tribes neighboring the 'abid of al-Raml, such as the Sufyan, Bani Malik, and Bani Hasan, and the Berbers frequently plundered Mashra' al-Ramla, due to [the 'abid's] inability to repulse them, and the Sultan, who wanted to send them on a campaign, was afraid that [those who remained] after the others had marched off would be plundered. He therefore ordered them to transfer from al-Raml to quarters in Meknes.[49]

[43] De La Véronne, *Documents inédits*, 44.
[44] Al-Qadiri, *Nashr al-Mathani*, 72 of the Arabic text and 186 of the English translation. A quintal of silver was worth one thousand ducats. See de La Véronne, *Documents inédits*, 44, footnote 4.
[45] Al-Qadiri, *Nashr al-Mathani*, 89–90 of the Arabic text and 209 of the English translation.
[46] An-Nasiri, *al-Istiqsa'*, vol. 7, 140.
[47] Az-Zayani, *al-Bustan az-Zarif*, 87.
[48] An-Nasiri, *al-Istiqsa'*, vol. 7, 191–192.
[49] Al-Qadiri, *Nashr al-Mathani*, 88 of the Arabic text and 206 of the English translation.

As soon as the black soldiers moved to Meknes, during the last years of the reign of Sultan 'Abd Allah, the Banu Hasan started to pillage their area and even raided those lagging behind. They ravaged the houses and the palaces in Mashra' ar-Ramla and took all the wealth that black officers had accumulated, leaving only walls behind. They sold the doors and other wood in the markets of Salé at a cheap price. Only about half of the army reached Meknes; the rest of the soldiers scattered around the country, returning to their tribes or native villages. The relocation of the army had negative demographic ramifications on the city of Meknes that led to inflation, famine, displacement of the local poor, and political discord. In addition, the natural disaster of an earthquake that occurred in the city of Meknes in 1755 caused many casualties including, about five thousand dead among the army.[50]

Some positive changes occurred in 1757 when Moroccan leaders from different power structures, including the army, proclaimed Sidi Muhammad b. 'Abd Allah (1710–1790) the new sultan. He had gained experience in politics by serving as viceroy of the Marrakesh area. He resided in the imperial palace in Meknes and embarked on restoring central authority. He tried to reorganize the central government and modernize the country. He organized the taxation system and minted new currency and promoted trade with Europeans as a solution to generate more state income and as a way to lessen reliance on the army. He realized the importance of the Atlantic trade with the Europeans and in 1764 decided to found a new port and town on the Atlantic coast where the Portuguese had built a small fortress (known as Mogador) to be called "Essaouira."[51] He hired European architects to execute his plan. At that time, Agadir was the center for most of the maritime trade, but Sultan Sidi Muhammad, to escape the disturbances from the Berbers on this part of the coast, closed the port for foreign trade and replaced it with the Essaouira port that would be under his authority. He used the labor of the local people, Arabs and Berbers (from the Shiadma-Haha region east and south of Essaouira), and ordered a contingent of several hundred troops to be stationed in the city.[52] One finds a quarter in Essaouira that is called "al-Bawakhir," named after this contingent of black soldiers (known as 'Abid al-Bukhari).

---

[50] Az-Zayani, *al-Bustan az-Zarif*, 87 and an-Nasiri, *al-Istiqsa'*, vol. 7, 191–192.
[51] It was originally called *Souira*, meaning "the small fortress."
[52] Georg Høst, *Histoire de l'Empereur du Maroc Mohamed Ben Abdallah* (Rabat: La porte, 1998), 33.

Sidi Muhammad had to face a new-generation urban army that had a strong sense of entitlement to a steady income from the country's treasury and a commitment to urban life, unlike the troops at the time of Mawlay Isma'il when most lived in camps outside the walls of the city. He tried to restore the position of the army as a tool under the control of the Makhzan and to curb its political involvement by dividing the soldiers and officers and dispersing them throughout the country and by mixing and replacing some of them with Arab troops. At the same time, he continued to recruit newly enslaved blacks into the army. In 1768, the sultan sent his black officer al-Mahjub to gather black slaves living in the south of Morocco. Al-Mahjub collected four thousand blacks and their children from the Sus area, Tata, Aqqa, and Tishit and sent them to Marrakesh. The sultan ordered that they be provided with clothes and weapons and made al-Mahjub their leader. And when the sultan went to Rabat, he ordered the black soldiers moved to a new location with more facilities, and added another twenty-five hundred soldiers from the Udaya Arabs to their ranks. He was especially generous with them as they protected one of the important frontiers of Islam.[53] But other groups among the army were not as satisfied. The black soldiers of Meknes, aware of Sidi Muhammad's intention to undermine their political influence in the capital, revolted against him and proclaimed his son Yazid sultan. In 1775, the sultan sent ash-Shahid, an officer of the army, in the company of his chamberlain al-Mukhtar, to order the army to gather a thousand black soldiers from Meknes and send them to Tangier, where they would reside under his command. Arriving in Meknes, al-Mukhtar read the sultan's command and the soldiers seemed to obey. Ash-Shahid gave his speech and said: "By God! I will take from among these thousand men only those of my rank, i.e. having a house like mine, a garden like mine and a land similar to mine." At these words that seemed to favor selective members of the military, the soldiers were in turmoil and wanted to kill ash-Shahid and al-Mukhtar, who escaped and found refuge in the mausoleum of Mawlay Isma'il.[54]

The sultan was in Marrakesh with his son al-Yazid when he learned this news; he dispatched his son to the rebellion to restore order. As soon as the young prince arrived, the army grouped around him and proclaimed him sovereign. Al-Yazid complied and opened the treasury

[53] An-Nasiri, *al-Istiqsa'*, vol. 8, 35.
[54] Az-Zayani, *Le Maroc de 1631 à 1812*, 146–147 of the French translation and 80 of the Arabic text.

and arsenals, which contained weapons and powder. The army then wrote to the tribes asking them to recognize his authority. Muhammad Wa'ziz, chief of the Ayt Idrasan tribe, refused to join the rebellion and left Meknes. The Udaya, solicited by al-Yazid, refused to join him as well, and informed Wa'ziz of their decision. Al-Yazid, at the head of his army, marched to meet the recalcitrant tribes in battle. The Udaya were reinforced by two thousand Berbers from Ayt Idrasan and Garwan, sent to them by Wa'ziz. The battle ended in the defeat of al-Yazid and his army of Meknes. In the meantime, Sultan Sidi Muhammad left Marrakesh at the head of his army and other tribes from the Hawz (the great region of the city of Marrakesh) and before reaching the city of Meknes, al-Yazid fled and sought refuge in the *zawiya* of Zarhun.

It is important to note that by this time the black army was no longer a monolith, as the black soldiers were split between rival political leaders who recruited Arab and Berber soldiers to join the army. When the sultan entered Meknes, the *shurafa'* and the *'ulama'* came to greet him and interceded for pardon on behalf of the black soldiers and al-Yazid. The sultan forgave the rebels, on the condition that they would leave Meknes. The sultan expelled them from Meknes and dispersed them in the port cities of Tangier, Larache, and Rabat.

According to Geog Høst (1734–1794), who lived in Essaouira and was an agent of a Danish company in Africa and consul of Denmark in Morocco, "Mawlay Isma'il had used the black army to overawe the whites; now, it was all the opposite that was occurring."[55] Høst provided some details. He said that there were thirty-six hundred black soldiers in Meknes, whom the sultan ordered dispersed throughout the country. They were reluctant to give up their dwellings and habits for a life in camps on the outskirts of other towns, especially in winter. The sultan ordered all black soldiers to leave with their families for Rabat, Larache, and Tangier, one-third to each place. All together there were more than four thousand persons.[56] They were obliged to obey, as the sultan had given each soldier enough money to build a house. However, they were not satisfied with the deal and rebelled in their new bases. In 1776, the group sent to Tangier revolted against its chief, ash-Shaykh, and against the chief of the Arab and Berber troops, Ibn 'Abd al-Malik, and pillaged the city.[57] These

---

[55] Høst, *Histoire de l'Empereur*, 103.
[56] All this passage is taken from Høst, *Histoire de l'Empereur*, 103.
[57] The term that az-Zayani used was "the free troops," hence emphasizing, by contrast, the servile status of the black soldiers. Az-Zayani, *Le Maroc de 1631 à 1812*, 148 of the French translation and 81 of the Arabic text.

two officers fled to Asila and waited for the orders of the sultan.[58] With this event, in addition to mutinies in other port cities, the sultan decided to put an end to the seemingly rebellious behavior of the army and the political instability allegedly caused by its restive activities. He dissolved the large concentrations of black troops. He sent a letter to the officers in Tangier and Larache informing them that he forgave them and would allow them to return and reside in Meknes. When they received this letter, they were very pleased to return to Meknes. They left with their families and came to a place called Dar al-ʿArbi where they camped under the leadership of the officer Saʿid b. al-ʿAyyashi. This officer had come there on the order from the sultan to wait and provide food for them. The sultan then sent the Arabs of Banu Hasan, Banu Malik, Khulut, and Taliq to ambush the army in Dar al-ʿArbi and gave the Arabs the right to enslave the black soldiers and to seize their possessions. According to az-Zayani, the sultan told the Arabs:

Go and camp next to the black army[ʼs site] in a way that they are surrounded by all sides by your troops. Seize their horses and their weapons, then share these blacks between you. That each one of you takes a man, a woman and their children: the husband will plow and harvest; the woman will grind, knead, fetch water and wood and the children will keep the herds. May God ensure your prosperity! Ride then their horses, gird their weapons, put on their clothes and eat all that you will find on their premises, because you are, you, my soldiers.[59]

Az-Zayani reported that the order was carried out as planned. Had they been white they would not have ended up in slavery. In the end the black military was still the property of the palace/Makhzan. The sultan regained Rabat and dispersed the blacks who were there, sending a group to Marrakesh and others to Sus. But four years later, he forgave the army, reclaimed the soldiers from their tribes, and reinstated them in a largely mixed army and dispatched them to the various ports of the country.[60] Their number was reduced and replaced by tribal troops; hence the sultan resolved the burden of paying salaries to a huge army. The condition

---

[58] Ibid.

[59] Ibid., 149–150 of the French translation and 81–82 of the Arabic text. See also Muhammad ibn ʿAbd as-Salam ad-Duʿayyif, *Tarikh ad-Duʿayyif: Tarikh ad-Dawla as-Saʿida* (Rabat: Dar al-Maʼthurtat, 1986), 180–181 and an-Nasiri, *al-Istiqsaʼ*, vol. 7, 48–49.

[60] Az-Zayani offered no explanation for how soldiers could be enslaved by Arab troops on the orders of the sultan, then four years later be reclaimed by the sultan on the basis of their belonging to the Makhzan. But it could be that the sultan never meant that the Arabs would keep these people as slaves.

of the army became better than it had been since the death of Mawlay Isma'il.[61]

Sidi Muhammad also achieved a goal to make the city of Essaouira the most important port for European trade as well as a new destination of the trans-Saharan trade. It hosted many foreign consulates from England, France, Portugal, Denmark, and even Brazil. Some important Moroccan Jewish families were recruited by the sultan to take control of the developing international commerce in Essaouira.[62] A century after its foundation, a French botanist who visited the port in 1867 remarked that three-eighths of Moroccan maritime trade came through Essaouira; that its population was about twelve thousand inhabitants, half of them Jewish.[63] John Buffa, a physician to the British forces who resided in Morocco in 1806, estimated the Jews of Morocco exceeded one hundred thousand.[64]

The death of Sidi Muhammad in 1790 was followed by two years of political turmoil and terror under the rule of al-Yazid. By this time the political influence of the army ceased to be a crucial factor in the making of the sultan, but did play a minor role in enthroning al-Yazid, manifested mainly by the black bodyguards in his entourage. He inaugurated his rule by robbing and killing anybody perceived to be against him. He even persecuted his father's close officials, allegedly saying about them, "No good is expected from someone who hunts with his father's dogs."[65] He exploited the vulnerable status of the Jewish minority, the *dhimmi* people whom by law he was supposed to protect. Az-Zayani mentioned that when al-Yazid arrived in Tetouan soon after his enthronement, "he authorized his soldiers to plunder the Jews of this city; the soldiers invaded the houses and the shops and seized all that they could find."[66] Historian ad-Du'ayyif (1752–1818) reported an event during which al-Yazid unleashed a spiteful and violent revenge on the Jews of Meknes because of one Jewish person's audacious confrontation. All this Jewish person did was to claim his daughter back who was apparently forced

---

[61] Az-Zayani, *Le Maroc de 1631 à 1812*, 150 of the French translation and 82 of the Arabic text.

[62] See Høst, *Histoire de l'Empereur*, 33–43.

[63] B. Balansa, "Voyage de Mogador à Maroc" in *Bulletin de la Société de géographie* (Paris: Société de géographie, 1868), tome XV (312–334), 314.

[64] John Buffa, *Travels Through the Empire of Morocco* (London: J.J. Stockdale, 1810), 183.

[65] Ad-Du'ayyif, *Tarikh ad-Du'ayyif*, 210.

[66] Az-Zayani, *Le Maroc de 1631 à 1812*, 158 of the French translation and 86 of the Arabic text.

into the harem of al-Yazid before he became sultan. Al-Yazid threatened him but the Jewish father replied: "when you become the ruler then hang me." Unfortunately for him, al-Yazid became sultan and hanged him and then ordered his soldiers to plunder all Jewish households in Meknes.[67] According to a Moroccan Jewish account, blacks also took part in this pogrom.[68] The spite toward the Jews was not coming from al-Yazid alone but from many people who resented the elevated status and the freedom of mobility of Jews thanks to Sidi Muhammad who had entrusted them with the sultanate's commercial affairs with the Europeans. By the turn of the nineteenth century, the tensions between the Jewish population and the sultanate increased. Moroccan historian Mohamed El Mansour explained:

> Travel to Europe meant that many Jews had adopted European dress, names and even nationalities. Many Gibraltar Jews were in fact Moroccans who had changed their nationality while maintaining commercial links with their country of origin. For the Muslims, this represented a violation of the *dhimma* status and exacerbated tension between the two sides. The rising fears of European intervention in Morocco by the turn of the nineteenth century only worsened relations between the two communities.[69]

In the hope of consolidating more power, following his grandfather's example, al-Yazid ordered his general, Sa'id b. al-'Ayyashi, to restore the camp at Mashra' ar-Ramla in an attempt to regroup the army.[70] He died in 1792 soon after this initiative began, before realizing his goal, which would have been impossible because he had lost the support of the Berber army as a result of late payment. He left an army significantly smaller. This was apparent from his last battle against his brother Hisham, who ruled the Marrakesh area. Al-Yazid had only fifty-five hundred soldiers including the blacks who formed a contingent of fifteen hundred men.

In an attempt to bring peace and unity to the country, the learned men of Fez, the notables among the Arabs and Berbers, the generals – notably Muhammad Wa'ziz, Sa'id b. al-'Ayyashi, and other leaders of the army and the Udaya – all got together and proclaimed Mawlay Sulayman, a younger son of Sidi Muhammad and a devout Muslim, sultan in 1792.[71] Mawlay Sulayman faced a great challenge to pacify and to unite a divided

---

[67] Ad-Du'ayyif, *Tarikh ad-Du'ayyif*, 207.
[68] Georges Vajda, "Un recueil de textes historiques judéo-marorains (2ᶜ partie)," *Hespéris* 36 (1949), 146.
[69] El Mansour, *Morocco*, 15.
[70] Ad-Du'ayyif, *Tarikh ad-Du'ayyif*, 211.
[71] Ibid., 244.

country and to modernize its society and technology. Morocco was tied to the tumultuous dynamics of modern history. This was a period that coincided with the French occupation of Egypt (1798–1801), which caused many Islamic leaders to question whether the traditional order needed to be reformed to deal effectively with the modern world. At the same time the Wahhabi doctrine and movement emerged in Arabia and offered a popular ideology to solve social ills; it was a clarion call to return to the straight path of Islam in Arabia where all Islamic countries and cultures met through the annual pilgrimage to Mecca. The Wahhabi ideas reinforced Mawlay Sulayman's religious convictions against popular Sufi Islam. He struggled to regenerate Moroccan society through the teaching of a pristine Islam. To him, redemption from the decadence and the erroneous teaching of Islam propagated by the mystic religious orders was to revive an authentic Islam, a return to the Sunna and the Qur'an.

But first, in order to consolidate his power, he had to gather military strength. He selected the Udaya, which consisted of three thousand cavalry (mainly in the city of Fez), and the black troops, which consisted of both cavalry and infantry (mainly in Meknes in addition to the black garrisons stationed in many city ports). He also chose from both groups fourteen hundred men to serve him as his personal guards.[72] According to John Buffa, "the Emperor's body-guard, which consists of eighteen thousand horsemen, is chiefly composed of negroes, who enjoy every privilege that despotic power can confer, and are ready upon all occasions to enforce the royal mandate."[73] The black soldiers were a small but important contingent among others. Ad-Du'ayyif, who witnessed the events during the reign of Mawlay Sulayman, reported that in 1795 the sultan dispatched three thousand soldiers from the Berbers, the blacks, and the Udaya to gain control of Tetouan, which was under the rule of his brother Maslama.[74] It took the sultan about six years to subdue most of the defiant provinces: the northwest of Morocco that was under the control of Maslama and the southern region and Marrakesh that was under the control of his brother and rival Mawlay Hisham. He also succeeded in regaining control of the Oujda region (on the eastern border with Algeria) from the Turks. Maslama, who claimed the northwest of Morocco, gained key constituents, especially the endorsement of the Wazzaniya religious order that was known for its political neutrality. The Moroccan Sufi leaders

---

[72] Ibid., 265.
[73] Buffa, *Travels*, 135.
[74] Ad-Du'ayyif, *Tarikh ad-Du'ayyif*, 262. Or Salama, according to this historian.

resented the Sultan's Wahhabi inclinations in condemning the activities of the Sufi centers. Another challenge for Mawlay Sulayman was to forestall any further political ascendancy of the religious orders.

Throughout most of his reign, Mawlay Sulayman fought battles on multiple fronts – from dynastic feuds to religious, from regional to national conflicts. The role of the black contingent in the army remained crucial. The army descendants of those called al-Bukhari (from the time of Mawlay Isma'il) had gained many entitlements. They developed a sense of location in Meknes as a place of power and identity, and some of them were important officers and generals. They obviously wanted to remain in Meknes and it was in their interest to team up with the Berbers of the plains in support of Mawlay Sulayman in Fez against the other two pretenders in the northwest and in the south. Indeed, their role in the battle against Maslama and his Wazzani allies ensured the triumph of Mawlay Sulayman.[75]

Some blacks continued to maintain powerful positions within the palace as well as in some major cities.[76] The example of Abu al-'Abbas Ahmad b. Mubarak (d. 1819) is worth mentioning. He was a slave of Mawlay Sulayman and served him from an early age. He was formerly a slave of Mawlay Sulayman's father, Sidi Muhammad, who offered Mubarak and his father and siblings to Mawlay Sulayman. He was given an education and grew up known for his piety, wisdom, and trustworthiness. It was for this reason that the sultan was fond of him and granted his emancipation and appointed him to high office. He became chamberlain-vizier when Sulayman became sultan. Ahmad b. Mubarak was so influential that he became a patriarch of an elite line of descendants who served future sultans.[77]

John Buffa observed a great number of blacks in the Moroccan army and noted that they "[we]re reckoned very loyal, and perfectly devoted to the Emperor. This account[ed] for so many black governors being at the head of the most important districts and provinces."[78] For instance, the port of Rabat was "commanded by a black chief, and garrisoned with black soldiers,"[79] and the port of Essaouira, according to ad-Du'ayyif,

[75] See an-Nasiri, *al-Istiqsa'*, vol. 8, 90–93.

[76] Al-Mukhtar as-Susi reported that there was a black governor in this region of Sus during the reign of Mawlay Sulayman. See as-Susi, *Min Khilal Jazula* (Titwan: al-Matba'a al-Mahdiyya, 1958), vol. 6, 75.

[77] See his biography in Ibn Zaydan, *Ithaf A'lam an-Nas*, vol. 1, 367–368.

[78] Buffa, *Travels*, 108.

[79] Ibid., 49.

had three thousand blacks from the Sus region.[80] Essaouira illustrates the agency of some blacks in climbing the social hierarchy. In 1795, al-Hajj Muhammad b. 'Abd as-Sadiq al-Maskini was a black officer from Essaouira. While returning from a pilgrimage he visited Sultan Mawlay Sulayman. He informed him on the situation of Essaouira and assured him the allegiance of the black garrison stationed in the city and promised to bring the city under his control. He talked the sultan into appointing him governor of Essaouira. Ad-Du'ayyif reported that it was Mawlay 'Abd as-Salam, a brother of the sultan who was once the master of Ibn 'Abd as-Sadiq, who came up with this scheme.[81] The sultan authorized him to govern Essaouira and put his appointment in writing. But he ordered him to keep it secret until he was fully aware of the situation of the inhabitants and their tendencies. This occurred before the sultan set out on an expedition to pacify the region of Marrakesh. Essaouira was then among the areas controlled by 'Abd ar-Rahman b. Nasir (who was an ally of Mawlay Hisham in Marrakesh) and subjected to the tribal confederation of the Haha. At this time, the governor of Essaouira was Abu Marwan 'Abd al-Malik b. Bihi al-Hahi, who enjoyed a great reputation among the Haha tribes and their neighbors. When Ibn 'Abd as-Sadiq returned to Essaouira he acted simply as a man who had just finished his pilgrimage. After having a few days of rest, he went to the governor's office to resume the position of usher that he held before he left on his pilgrimage. He carried out the orders of the governor with utmost promptness and strove to please him and provide counsel as much as he could. He guarded the governor's door day and night, and acted in every way as a loyal and trustworthy servant. Soon, the governor recognized his unflinching service and appointed him his personal adviser. During this time, Ibn 'Abd as-Sadiq was conspiring with his people and waiting for the arrival of the sultan in the region of Marrakesh. When he learned that the sultan was approaching and had already taken Azemmour, he announced his appointment to his friends and allies and obtained their promise to support him in overthrowing the governor. 'Abd al-Malik suspected nothing and was accustomed to receive Ibn 'Abd as-Sadiq at any hour of the day. At a predetermined time at night, he gathered a number of his most trusted black soldiers of Essaouira and positioned them so they could hear his voice. He told them: "As soon as you hear me talking to him, you seize him in haste." He thus went to see 'Abd al-Malik

[80] Ad-Du'ayyif, *Tarikh ad-Du'ayyif*, 259.
[81] Ibid.

and asked to speak to him. When he came out and started chatting with him, black soldiers surrounded him and seized him as well as the people of Haha who were in his service and took them immediately out of the city. They gave 'Abd al-Malik his horse, and closed the gate behind him. And so Ibn 'Abd as-Sadiq succeeded in executing his bloodless coup and became governor of Essaouira. This was how Essaouira came under the authority of Mawlay Sulayman.[82] Such maneuvers in the long process of pacification allowed the sultan to extend his sovereignty over Morocco. Ibn 'Abd as-Sadiq apparently abused his power and struck a deal with the Europeans, but was arrested in 1801 under the order of the sultan, who sent him to live in Fez.[83]

Mawlay Sulayman appreciated the value of the black soldiers but he was cautious to curtail the monopoly they had in the army by counterbalancing their power. Thus, he returned to the pre-Mawlay Isma'il policy of tribal levies; he relied also on auxiliary troops from the *jaysh* (or gish) military tribes (mostly Arab tribes living in the areas surrounding the major cities such as Fez, Meknes, and Marrakesh) who traditionally provided the Makhzan with manpower. They were mobilized whenever the sultan deemed it necessary. According to John Buffa in 1806, the army grew to eighty thousand cavalry.[84] Some of the Berbers also contributed to the sultan's army. For instance, Ayt Idrasan, under the leadership of Muhammad Wa'ziz, was one of the sultan's first supporters. In a battle against a rebellion in the region of Chaouia in 1797, Mawlay Sulayman was able to mobilize sixty thousand men, most of whom were from Ayt Idrasan and the Berbers of the plains.[85]

Sultan Mawlay Sulayman was successful in curtailing the power and the political weight of the black military, but at the same time, relying on unprofessional and irregular tribal forces, he revived the old problem of tribal group social cohesion (*'asabiyya*).[86] The Makhzan or central authority had long forged alliances with the Berbers of the plains – the Ayt Idrasan, the Banu Mtir, the Guarwan, and the Ayt Immur – but the Berbers of the mountains – the Ayt Umalu – were usually more defiant toward central authority. Mawlay Sulayman generally neglected the Berbers of the plains in his military policy and as a consequence undermined their

---

[82] An-Nasiri, *al-Istiqsa'*, vol. 8, 102–104. See also ad-Du'ayyif, *Tarikh ad-Du'ayyif*, 259.
[83] Ad-Du'ayyif, *Tarikh ad-Du'ayyif*, 321 and 394.
[84] Buffa, *Travels*, 107.
[85] El Mansour, *Morocco*, 97.
[86] Ibid., 24.

traditional position as a buffer zone between lands controlled by the Makhzan and the Berbers of the mountains. In a conflict between the Ayt Idrasan and the Ayt Umalu, the sultan supported the confederation of the Ayt Idrasan, but the battle ended in their defeat, resulting in serious political problems for the sultan, who wanted to pacify the whole country. Colonial French historian Henri Terrasse viewed the Berber revolts in the middle Atlas region as being generally against all Arabic-speaking people in Morocco. From his perspective, it appeared a logical outcome of the resistance struggle of the colonized Berbers against the colonizing Arabs.[87] However, in my view, Moroccan historian El Mansour was right to dismiss Terrasse's simplistic conclusions, pointing out that "Mawlay Sulayman, in particular, tended to disregard the realities of tribal politics and often appointed his own qa'id-s [chiefs]. His attempts to impose outsider qa'id-s on the Berber tribes of the Middle Atlas were constantly rebuffed and constituted an important factor in the deterioration of Makhzan-Berber relations."[88]

With constant resistance and rebellion from so many tribes and regions, the sultan realized that he lacked the military and the financial means to fight large revolts and that the best way to increase the number of his army was to revive Mawlay Isma'il's military policy. He did indeed attempt to recruit the Haratin (the free black people), but the extent to which this order was carried out is not clear. According to ad-Du'ayyif, the sultan's order targeted mainly the Haratin of the region of Rabat-Salé. This region harbored many blacks who had been dispersed from the great camp of Mashra' ar-Ramla. In the year 1811, the local judge authorized local officers to register the Haratin of Salé, among whom was al-Hajj Muhammad as-Sammar, the timekeeper of the great mosque of Salé.[89] Whatever number of Haratin eventually were recruited in this area, it was apparently not a substantial number and did not figure in Mawlay Sulayman's vision of rebuilding a massive army. As El Mansour notes, "However the political instability which characterized the latter part of his reign, in addition to financial problems experienced by the Makhzan, rendered any efficient reorganisation [of the army] futile."[90]

---

[87] Henri Terrasse, *Histoire du Maroc des origines à l'établissement du protectorat français* (New York: AMS Press, 1975), 310.
[88] El Mansour, *Morocco*, 21.
[89] Ad-Du'ayyif, *Tarikh ad-Du'ayyif*, 354. Mohamed al-Mansour misread this passage and understood that the plan was never carried out. See El Mansour, *Morocco*, 25.
[90] El Mansour, *Morocco*, 25.

The Moroccan economy was prosperous in the early years of his reign. Wheat exports to Europe helped consolidate his power and encouraged the growth of a merchant class in the city ports.[91] But there were periods of drought, famine, and plague that represented hurdles in the course of the pacification of the country.[92] Ad-Du'ayyif reported that the great plague of 1799–1800 had devastating effects on Morocco. Most people fled the city of Fez where a countless number of people died, including many scholars. The sultan himself left with his black soldiers and other tribal groups, traveling from Meknes to Rabat and then to Safi, and every day a number of soldiers died from the plague. It was due to the sultan's movements with his retinue to avoid the plague that the plague spread in the region of Dukkala and 'Abda.[93] There were other episodes of these calamities in the years of 1812, 1817, and 1818–1820 that had severe effects on Moroccan demography, the army, and state revenue.

Mawlay Sulayman could not rely solely on local taxes to maintain his power; he allowed the export of wheat, which was much needed in Europe. He also restored the commercial position of the Jewish community but prevented it from adopting European dress, preferring that the Jews conform to the status that the Muslims were accustomed to in order to avoid any xenophobic sentiments among Moroccan Muslims.[94] Additionally, internal political agitations after the death of Mawlay Isma'il caused the trans-Saharan trade to periodically decline, although it continued in a relatively regular pattern. Mawlay Sulayman made sure to bring the south of Morocco under the fiscal policy of the Makhzan. He extended his authority to Tafilalt,[95] and sent letters to the people of Tuwat to confirm his sovereignty over the region. The letters inform how his authority was mediated in remote areas. He reminded them that every year he appointed a number of *talba* (scholars versed in Islamic law/civil servants) to come to their region to administrate, to render judgments in issues between individuals and groups in accordance with Islamic law, and to collect taxes.[96] By bringing the south under his authority and control he helped regulate the caravan trade and the flow of the customary

[91] Ad-Du'ayyif, *Tarikh ad-Du'ayyif*, 267–268, 274, 321
[92] Ibid., 314–317, 340.
[93] Ibid., 314–317, 314–315.
[94] El Mansour, *Morocco*, 16.
[95] Ad-Du'ayyif, 1986, 345.
[96] *Al-Watha'iq* (Recueils périodiques publiés par la Direction des Archives Royales), edited by 'Abd al-Wahhab b. Mansur (Rabat: Imprimerie Royale, 1976), vol. 1, 443–447. It contains two from Mawlay Sulayman dated on July 16 and July 21, 1800.

gifts that were his due. In 1797, and on the occasion of the 'Id al-Adha (the holiday of sacrifice marking the end of the annual pilgrimage to Mecca), the people of Tafilalt sent many gifts to the sultan. The governor of Draa, for instance, presented Mawlay Sulayman with a gift that consisted of thirty quintal (of gold?), sixteen female slaves, four male slaves, dates, and henna.[97] In 1807, Mawlay Sulayman led an expedition to the south of Morocco and reached Guelmim, an important link in the caravan routes. 'Abd Allah Usalim was the ruler of the people of Guelmim and commanded independently a vast region in the western Sahara. He dominated the trans-Saharan caravan trade and had an army of fifteen hundred black slaves.[98]

The number of black slaves we find in various accounts of this period marked by political disturbances indicates continuous human trafficking. In James Grey Jackson's account of the empire of Morocco and the Tafilalt region, in 1798, a caravan from Timbuktu to the Tafilalt region consisted of two thousand camels and 700 slaves.[99] Three decades later, French explorer René Caillié (1799–1838) traveled in 1828 in a huge caravan of fourteen hundred camels taking slaves, gold, ivory, gum, and ostrich feathers to Morocco. The usual route was Timbuktu, Arawan, Taghaza, and Tafilalt. He commented that traffic in human beings "exist[ed] in full vigour in this part of Africa."[100]

Mawlay Sulayman died in 1822 before achieving his goal of bringing peace and unity to the country. He designated his nephew, Mawlay 'Abd ar-Rahman b. Hisham (r. 1822–1859), the governor of Essaouira, as heir. This choice reflected the importance of the growing mercantile class as a crucial player in the advancement of Moroccan society. Mawlay 'Abd ar-Rahman continued his uncle's battle to repress the revolts of the tribes. His first order was to strengthen the army and find ways to generate state revenue. He traveled from Fez to Meknes to assess the army. He was surprised to find a small number, and when he inspected the treasury he found it empty. What is more, he learned that the army was forced to sell horses and weapons for survival. He then restored its position and reequipped the soldiers with horses, weapons, and rations. Initially, the

[97] Ad-Du'ayyif, *Tarikh ad-Du'ayyif*, 309.
[98] Ibid., 341.
[99] James Grey Jackson, *An Account of the Empire of Marocco, and the District of Suse* (London: Printed for the author, and sold by G. and W. Nicol, 1809), 287.
[100] René Caillié, *Travels Through Central Africa to Timbuctoo; and Across the Great Desert, to Morocco, Performed in the Years 1824–1828* (London: H. Colburn and R. Bentley, 1830), vol. 2, 187.

sultan relied on the *jaysh*, whose majority was the Udaya. But the Udaya
were already dissatisfied with the long political and economic instability
of the central government and revolted against the sultan in 1831. They
failed in their expedition to Tlemcen (in Algeria), but nonetheless plun-
dered the region against the order of the sultan and kept their plunder
when they returned to Fez. The sultan sent the governor of Fez, at-Tayyib
al-Bukhari, to meet them before they reached the city and arrest the leaders of the Udaya as well as the black soldiers who conspired with them in
this mutiny. The Udaya refused to obey and when they entered the city the
sultan's officers arrested some of their commanders. The Udaya revolted
against the sultan and forced him into house arrest. The black troops
were rivals of the Udaya because the Udaya considered them second-class
members of the army and perceived them as slaves of the Makhzan. This
presented the black soldiers an opportunity to assert their position and
to side with the sultan. The sultan succeeded in escaping and sent a message to the black military in Meknes to join him to repress the Udaya.
The black soldiers engaged in battle against the Udaya and many people
died on both sides.[101] The sultan finally was able to arrest the leaders of
the rebellion and ordered the Udaya dispersed. Each of the factions was
sent to a particular destination – people of the Sus region were stationed
in Rabat, the Mghafra were sent to the surroundings of Marrakesh, and
the most of the remainder of the Udaya were sent to Larache with some
remaining on the outskirts of Fez. Mawlay 'Abd ar-Rahman was so disappointed about the Udaya that he wanted to bar them from the Makhzan
forever.[102] The black military was then awarded the quarters formally
held by the Udaya. The sultan felt a pressing necessity to reinforce his
army, particularly given that the French were strengthening their colonization of Algeria. Once again, he turned to the black soldiers. In a letter
to the governor of Tangier, Mawlay 'Abd ar-Rahman, in the footsteps
of Mawlay Sulayman, advised his governor to reorganize the 'Abid al-
Bukhari corps and to recruit new ones by the same means of his predecessors, perpetuating Mawlay Isma'il's racialist policy and enforcing a
problematic image of blacks in the collective memory. He ordered the
governor of Tangier to inspect and to correct the structure of the army. A
month later, he ordered him to search the region of northwest Morocco
for the black soldiers who had deserted and for the descendants of the

An-Nasiri, *al-Istiqsa'*, vol. 9, 32–35.
Ibid., vol. 9, 40. See also Eugène Aubin, *Le Maroc d'aujourd'hui avec trois cartes en
      couleur hors texte* (Paris: A. Colin, 1904), 181.

Bukhari army who now lived among the local population.[103] As a result of the French attack on the Moroccan eastern border in 1844, the sultan also called for the Udaya to be reinstated into the army. The sultan did mobilize his forces both to assist the Muslims of Algeria against the French invaders and to meet the European threat on the Moroccan borders. The sultan's assistance to the Algerian resistance army under the leadership of 'Abd al-Qadir ended in defeat against the superior discipline and technology of the French army in Oujda at the battle of Isly in August 1844. In the same month, the French navy attacked strategic Moroccan ports; it bombarded Tangier and Essaouira. The black troops took part on all fronts; they fought with bravery and many of them died in these battles protecting Moroccan soil.[104] French scholar Jules Duval (1813–1870) testified:

In 1844, we have seen them defending themselves with a remarkable strength against our troops in the island of Mogador, where many preferred to throw themselves armed in the tides rather than giving in. In [the battle of] Isly, the black guard alone honorably sustained the shock of our troops.[105]

Morocco was compelled to sign a peace treaty with France and agreed to abandon its alliance with Algeria and to establish a commission to demarcate the border.

During the reign of Mawlay 'Abd ar-Rahman in 1842, the sultan was approached by the British consul general, Drummond Hay, with a plea to take measures against the slave trade. The response of the sultan was not what the British had hoped for. From the perspective of the sultan of Morocco, slavery was clearly acceptable under Islamic law and the British demand was deemed offensive to Islamic traditions. Sultan Mawlay 'Abd ar-Rahman's negative reply did not, however, discourage the activities of the European abolitionist movement in Morocco.[106] The increasing contact with Europeans and the defeat at Isly urged Mawlay 'Abd ar-Rahman and his successors, Muhammad b. 'Abd ar-Rahman (r. 1859–1873) and Mawlay al-Hasan (r. 1873–1894), to modernize the army – to create a standing, salaried, professional army and abandon the

---

[103] Letter from the Sultan Mawlay 'Abd ar-Rahman to 'Abd as-Salam as-Slawi, Dhu 'l-Hijja 1252 (March 1837) and Muharram 1253 (April 1837) (Rabat: Bibliothèque Royale, number 21).

[104] See Bahija Simu, *al-Islahat al-'Askariyya bi-'l-Maghrib* (Rabat: Al-Matba'a al-Malikiyya, 2000), 122–123.

[105] Jules Duval, "La question du Maroc et les intérêts européens en Afrique," *Revue des deux mondes* (Paris: Imprimerie de J. Claye, Novembre–Décembre 1859), 938.

[106] The subject of the abolition of slavery will be discussed in Chapter 7.

old model that relied on tribes who rendered military service in exchange for tax exemption.[107] It took the 'Alawi rulers a century and a half of struggle to finally dissociate the privileged military tribes and bring them submissively under the central authority. They continued to provide, in theory, the base of the authority of the 'Alawi dynasty and the principal reserve of government personnel.[108] Henceforth, the number of the blacks in the army would be reduced and blacks would serve mainly as royal guards and continued to serve faithfully all future sultans.

According to Oskar Lenz (1848–1925), a German-Austrian mineralogist and traveler, in 1880, Sultan al-Hasan's army numbered about thirty thousand men. The black guard numbered five thousand cavalrymen. They followed the sultan in all his expeditions, in times of peace as well as war. When the sultan was in the capital city of Fez, he kept permanently with him a unit of cavalrymen on active duty and the rest were sent to cultivate their lands and wait to be summoned.[109] A similar assessment was given by French scholar Henri Poisson de La Martinière (1859–1922), who traveled to Morocco in the 1880s, stating that "the numbers of the Abids and Bou Khari have been actually reduced from 100,000 to 5 or 6000 men on a peace footing, and to 15,000 to 20,000 in times of war."[110] The Udaya replaced the black troops and "[they] multiplied in number so rapidly that they could in time easily furnish 25,000 to 30,000 mounted troops, and, owing to this powerful force, the Sultans succeeding Muley Ismail were able to reduce numerous Arab and Berber tribes to submission."[111] The author made the distinction between the so-called 'Abid (black slaves) who represented all the acquired slaves gradually added into service of the Makhzan and the palace either as servants or soldiers after the formation of the 'Abid al-Bukhari, and those who were Bukhari, descendants of the initial stock of the black army.

Some black individuals continued to serve in high offices and in the palace. For example,[112] the prestigious position of the *hijaba*

---

[107] See the work of Simu, *al-Islahat al-'Askariyya*.

[108] Aubin, *Le Maroc d'aujourd'hui*, 1904, 183.

[109] Oskar Lenz, *Timbouctou, voyage au Maroc, au Sahara et au Soudan* (Paris: Hachette, 1886), 428–435.

[110] Henri Poisson de La Martinière, *Morocco: Journeys in the Kingdom of Fez and to the Court of Mulai Hassan*, with itineraries constructed by the author and a bibliography of Morocco from 1844 to 1887 (London: Whittaker, 1889), 265–266.

[111] Ibid., 267.

[112] Another good example is Faraji, who occupied the position of pasha of Fez during the reign of Mawlay 'Abd ar-Rahman (d. 1859). See Ibn Zaydan, *Ithaf A'lam an-Nas*, vol. 5, 85–86.

(chamberlain-vizier) was monopolized by one black family from the time of Ahmad b. Mubarak (d. 1819), who served Sultan Mawlay Sulayman (d. 1822).[113] Ahmad's son Musa (d. 1878) served as Sultan Muhammad b. 'Abd ar-Rahman's chamberlain-vizier, and his other son 'Abd Allah (d. 1885) was governor of Fez. He also served Mawlay al-Hasan (r. 1873–1894) as grand vizier.[114] Historian Ibn Zaydan, who had seen several official correspondences written by Musa, portrayed him as a secretary of state with great political influence. In some of these letters, Musa b. Ahmad issued orders to governors and officers in the name of the sultan. In one letter, Musa ordered his brother 'Abd Allah, governor of Fez, to investigate a case of a freed black man from Essaouira whose daughter was abducted and passed from hand to hand until she reached a family in Fez.[115] This case reflects the vulnerability of young dark-skinned women in Morocco. It also sheds light on the possibility of making a claim for justice involving illegal human trafficking. Black individuals in high offices encouraged ill-fated blacks to file complaints. When Musa b. Ahmad died, the sultan personally took charge of his funeral and buried him near the tomb of his father in the mausoleum of the 'Alawi patriarch, Mawlay 'Ali ash-Sharif, in Marrakesh. State poets sang his eulogy.[116] Musa's son Ahmad (1841–1900) succeeded his father as chamberlain of Mawlay al-Hasan until his death in 1894. Some high officers attempted to sow seeds of discord between him and Sultan al-Hasan to the point that the sultan threatened to remove him from his position and execute him. The sultan trusted Ahmad b. Musa but was uneasy with his outspokenness. Ahmad b. Musa was indeed critical of the sultan's decision to name al-Hajj al-Ma'ti grand vizier because he thought that he was unqualified for the position. When al-Hasan died, Ahmad b. Musa played a leading role in proclaiming the young prince 'Abd al-'Aziz sultan (1878–1908). His position as chamberlain and educator of the prince granted him a special connection to the prince's Circassian mother, Lalla Ruqayya, who was queen of the palace. His political scheme brought him the highest political position in the country; he became the grand vizier. Given the young age and the inexperience of Sultan 'Abd al-'Aziz, Ahmad b. Musa was the de facto ruler of Morocco. He dominated political power and to secure his position he eliminated all his potential rivals. He removed most of the viziers from their offices and replaced them with his own brothers and people he trusted; he brutally dismissed Grand

---

[113] See his biography in Ibn Zaydan, *Ithaf A'lam an-Nas*, vol. 1, 367–368.
[114] Ibid., vol. 4, 370–380.
[115] Ibid., vol. 4, 371.
[116] Ibid., vol. 4, 379.

Vizier al-Hajj al-Ma'ti and the minister of war, his brother Muhammad as-Saghir. He had their properties confiscated and sent them to prison. He ruled, in the words of American traveler Frederick Moore (who visited Morocco in 1907), "as dictator, suppressing wayward tribes by vigorous means, as well, probably, as anyone not a Sultan could, until the year 1900, when he died."[117] After his death, Sultan 'Abd al-'Aziz cultivated the assistance of foreign European advisers such as the British Harry MacLean, who was put in charge of his infantry and who attempted to modernize the county. He was fascinated with European products and spent lavishly acquiring them for his personal use. Frederick Moore observed that: "News of his European tendencies spread throughout the land. The influence of Kaid Maclean in the army was known and resented. Photographs of the Sultan had been seen by many of the Faithful. Finally, it was reported that he had become a Christian."[118]

When the country was on the verge of bankruptcy, 'Abd al-'Aziz tried to reform taxes in a more equitable way and abolish the privileges of the traditional tax system. The behavior of the sultan and his new reforms alienated the conservative notables and the populace who were receptive at this point to any rebellious message. The sultan's reforms were met with hostility that prevented their implementation. Consequently, in 1902, the sultan had to borrow money in the amount of 7,500,000 francs from the Bank of Paris and the Netherlands. A year later, he borrowed more money from English and Spanish banks. These loans were used to repay his debts and to finance his military campaigns against revolts in the country. The Moroccan government was unable to pay its debts and had to face the European powers' aggressive policies. Morocco's location between the Atlantic and the Mediterranean made it an ideal target for many competing European powers: the British, the Germans, the French, and the Spaniards. France negotiated a deal with Britain to occupy Morocco in 1904, but the Germans protested and forged an alliance with Morocco, making things difficult for France. In 1912, Morocco finally came under French rule. The direct pressure to abolish slavery came with the French protectorate regime in Morocco.

In conclusion, the status of blacks since Mawlay Isma'il fluctuated between privilege and marginalization, as slavery became associated with blackness. To be a slave in the Makhzan and in service to the sultan or other high officials afforded many individuals special access to power and

---

[117] Frederick Moore, *The Passing of Morocco* (London: Smith, Elder & Co, 1908), 163.
[118] Ibid., 169.

privilege. They provided the masters with a means to enhance their status and prestige and at times they succeeded in improving their own conditions through bonds of trust established with them. As Ennaji stated:

Everything about them [slaves] inspired fear and respect: their whispering outside the doors of princes, their comings and goings around the master on feast days, their complicitous looks, their air of sadness at the funerals, their proven devotion. They provided a weapon against the machinations of the envious and the blows of enemies open or secret. Finally, they constituted the last bulwark against treachery among one's own people, and dishonesty within the family. In nineteenth-century Morocco, power came first from one's entourage: family, slaves, henchmen, clients, and allies.[119]

The connection between master and slave continued for generations in the form of clientship (*wala'*) or a paternalistic relationship, which in a way was similar to clientship among private rich households. But a great number who were not in the service of the Makhzan or domestics in the private sector were marginalized, living in poor conditions.

In the end, the black army and their families separated themselves from the Makhzan and reclaimed their original status of freedom, as a great number of them (such as the Haratin) were indeed free before their enslavement by Mawlay Isma'il. When the majority of the army left the Makhzan they scattered all over the country and settled near and among different tribes. Al-Mukhtar as-Susi mentioned, for example, that the first inhabitants of the rural villages of Tama'it in the Sus region were blacks, descendants of those who were in the service of the government during the beginning of the 'Alawi dynasty. At times, people raised questions about the status of the black army and its descendants, wondering if they were still slaves, but religious scholars affirmed that all members of the black army were free. The late-eighteenth-century legal scholar at-Tawdi stated that "as for the slaves who were in the army of the Sultan [Mawlay Isma'il] are now free. They may serve as notaries and witnesses. Those among them who were formally freed may lead Friday's prayer; prayers other than Friday's can be led by a slave."[120] Mohammad Ennaji conceded that "For legal experts, the former soldier's freedom remained more *de facto* than *de jure*; social practice still validated it on its essential

---

[119] Ennaji, *Serving the Master*, 8.

[120] Abu 'Isa al-Mahdi al-Wazzani, *an-Nawazil al-Jadida al-Kubra fima li-Ahl Fas wa Ghayrihim mina al-Badw wa 'l-Qura*, Wizarat al-Awqaf wa 'sh-Shu'un al-Islamiyya (al-Muhammadiyya, Morocco: Mataba'at Fudala, 1999), vol. 9, 384. Al-Wazzani (d. 1923) was mufti of Fez. According to ad-Du'ayyif, *Tarikh ad-Du'ayyif*, 261, at-Tawdi b. Suda died in 1795.

point."[121] It was custom that some of them continued in the service of the government until after the French protectorate (1912–1956). For instance, some of them worked at the stables of Tarudant and others were in the service of its governor. In the late 1950s, these occupations and any position with the government were honorable and sought after.[122]

Although blacks had lived in Morocco for centuries before the reign of Mawlay Isma'il, the large-scale introduction and dispersion of a substantially new black population into and throughout Morocco was a result of Mawlay Isma'il's forced conscription program as a means to solidify his authority and control over a fractious Moroccan political landscape.

[121] Ennaji, *Serving the Master*, 95.
[122] As-Susi, *Min Khilal Jazula*, vol. 6, 75.

7

The Abolition of Slavery in Morocco

The nineteenth century was marked by European abolitionist campaigns championed by England and France, the two former greatest slave-trading countries. Given their imperial ambitions, their foreign policies and the campaigns to abolish the slave trade – and eventually slavery – became intrinsically linked. The campaign to eradicate slavery became a tool in service to colonial political interests and a crucial part of propaganda in the foreign policy of the British and the French. Advocacy of the abolition of slavery was gaining momentum in Western Europe in part because of the Enlightenment, which brought with it many humanitarian reforms, and in part because of the growth of industrial capitalism, which brought with it new labor relationships based on wages rather than servitude. This Western European economic development helped to shape the argument for the European invasion of Africa as a civilizing and modernizing mission.[1]

While the early-nineteenth-century abolition of the slave trade significantly affected the trans-Atlantic slave trade, the trans-Saharan slave trade continued to flourish throughout the nineteenth century as demand for slaves increased.[2] During this period, Western travelers to the southern

---

[1] See Frederick Cooper and Ann Laura Stoler, eds., *Tensions of Empire: Colonial Cultures in a Bourgeois World* (Berkeley: University of California Press, 1997), 31, and Eric Williams, *Capitalism and Slavery* (New York: Capricorn Books, 1966).

[2] Patrick Manning, *Slavery and African Life Slavery and African Life: Occidental, Oriental, and African Slave Trades* (Cambridge: Cambridge University Press, 1990), 73. On the abolition of slavery in the lands of Islam see the great work of William Gervase Clarence-Smith, *Islam and the Abolition of Slavery* (Oxford: Oxford University Press, 2006). See also Suzanne Miers and Richard L. Roberts, *The End of Slavery in Africa* (Madison: University of Wisconsin Press, 1988).

region of the Mediterranean documented the cruel practice of slavery and publicly condemned it. In 1839, thirty-two years after the enactment of the British law to abolish the slave trade and six years after the Slavery Abolition Act that outlawed slavery in the British empire, the British and Foreign Anti-slavery Society was officially established to launch a campaign to eliminate the traffic in human beings in the Mediterranean region. In Tunisia, ruler Ahmad Bey agreed to prohibit the export, the import, and the sale of slaves in 1842, and in 1846 he issued a decree that made slavery illegal, a decree that preceded even France's abolishment of slavery. Slavery was first abolished in France on February 4, 1794, when the National Convention voted for the abolition of slavery in all French colonies. But when Napoleon took power in France, he reinstated slavery in 1802 and it was not until 1848 that slavery was definitively abolished on French abolitionist Victor Schoelcher's initiative. Gradually, France incorporated the antislavery argument into other arguments for the conquest and colonization of Africa. In 1848, the French abolished slavery in Algeria, which they had occupied since 1830.[3] Slaves who entered any area of Algeria under French civil or military law were theoretically free. Among the Maghrebi countries, why was Morocco more defiant to European abolitionist pressures?[4] But as Mauritania is also usually included in the area of the Maghreb, it is in fact this country that was the last to abolish slavery. If the French were credited for the success in putting an end to slavery in Algeria and, to a certain extent, Morocco, they tolerated the practice of slavery in Mauritania.[5] According to historian Martin Klein, the reason that the French were unsuccessful in ushering in abolition in Mauritania is because once the French established their colonial rule they compromised their abolitionist policies to facilitate colonial

---

[3] Yacine Daddi Addoun's work exposed the ambivalence of the European powers in the application of the principles of the abolition of slavery in North Africa. He explained the complexity of the French-Algerian abolition of slavery in a coherent narrative. Unlike in Morocco, he claimed, slavery in the Algerian regency was not a racialized phenomenon as slaves were both black sub-Saharan Africans and white Europeans. But this should not suggest that Algeria was free of prejudice and racial discrimination against black Africans. He argued that while slavery of Europeans ended by a decision made after the Napoleonic wars in Europe; the abolition of slavery of black Africans took more than a century. This reluctance reveals the long history of racial prejudice of the French toward black Africans. See Yacine Daddi Addoun, *Abolition de l'esclavage en Algérie: 1816–1871*, Dissertation Thesis (Toronto: York University, 2010), 253–261.

[4] See John Wright, *The Trans-Saharan Slave Trade* (London: Routledge, 2007), 137–166.

[5] Mauritania's dominant Arab and Berber-speaking people labeled themselves in a ridiculously superior racial category called al-Bidan (literally, "the whites") in contrast to blacks (natives or immigrants, slaves or free persons).

efforts to co-opt and forge alliances with groups' representatives in a vast and arid territory. "They had limited forces, long supply lines, and as to slavery, had to accept Tuareg and Moor institutions France had long condemned."[6] Indeed Mauritania did not abolish slavery until 1980 as a result of international pressure.[7]

The first official British intervention toward the abolition of slavery in Morocco is documented in a letter dated January 22, 1842, by Drummond Hay (1816–1893), British consul general to Morocco (1845–1886), to Sultan Mawlay 'Abd ar-Rahman (d. 1859). The British consul, from his residence in Tangier, asked if the sultan had enacted any decrees for the purpose of prohibiting the traffic in slaves and, if he had done so, Hay wished to see the evidence.[8] In a letter dated February 4, 1842, the Moroccan sultan totally opposed the British recommendations to abolish slavery and responded in the following terms:

> Be it known to you, that the traffic in slaves is a matter on which all sects and nations have agreed, from the time of the sons of Adam, on whom be the peace of God, up to this day; and we are not aware of its being prohibited by the laws of any sect, and no one need ask this question, the same being manifest to both high and low, and requires no more demonstration than the light of day. But if there be any peculiar event which has occurred, inform us about it particularly, in order that the answer may be apposite to the question.[9]

Consul Hay replied in a long letter (dated February 26, 1842) informing the sultan that he was fully aware that slavery and the slave trade were not prohibited by Islamic law, any more than they were by Jewish or Christian laws. However, in the march of social progress, the practice of slavery was unacceptable in civil society and to rational people and as such, should no longer be allowed. Many nations had followed the

---

[6] Martin Klein, "Slavery and French Rule in the Sahara" in Suzanne Miers and Martin Klein, eds., *Slavery and Colonial Rule in Africa* (London: Frank Cass, 1999), 74.

[7] Ironically, the legal abolition of slavery in Mauritania, which was not implemented, recommended compensations to slaveholders. Hence the liberation of enslaved blacks was delayed. Those who claimed their freedom ended up in dire poverty in the capital city of Nouakchott with limited resources offered partly by a local nongovernmental organization called SOS-Esclaves founded by Abdel Nasser Yessa a former slave owner, and Boubacar Messaoud, a son of a slave, on February 16, 1995 in Nouakchott. Ibid., 85; Clarence-Smith, *Islam and the Abolition*, 145–146; and E. Ann McDougall, "Living the Legacy of Slavery Between Discourse and Reality," *Cahiers d'études africaines*, 2005/3 n° 179–180, 957–986.

[8] *British and Foreign State Papers. 1842–1843.* Compiled by the librarian and keeper of the papers, Foreign Office (London: James Ridgway and Sons, Piccadilly, 1858), vol. 31, 599.

[9] Ibid., 600.

example of England in abolishing the traffic in human beings, and the rulers of many Muslim states such as Egypt and Tunisia "have already exhibited a generous disposition to follow the Christian governments in the same march of beneficence."[10] The Moroccan sultan's response was:

Be it known to you, that the religion of Islam – may God exalt it! – has a solid foundation, of which the corner stones are well secured, and the perfection whereof has been made known to us by God, to whom belongs all praise, in his book the Forkan [the Qur'an] which admits not either of addition or diminution.

As to what regards the making of slaves and trading therewith, it is confirmed by our book, as also by the *Sunna* of our Prophet, on whom be the blessing and the peace of God; and furthermore there is not any controversy between the Oolamma on that subject, and no one can allow what is prohibited or prohibit that which is made lawful.[11]

For the sultan of Morocco, the question of slavery was clearly accepted in Islamic law and therefore the British demand was deemed offensive to Islamic traditions. Sultan Mawlay 'Abd ar-Rahman's negative reply did not, however, discourage the British from their efforts to convince Moroccans to end slavery.

The abolitionist campaign in the 1840s did have an effect on the slave trade across the Sahara, but this disruption was felt mainly in Algeria as a result of French colonial rule. Historian Ralph Austen has noticed the gradual decrease in slaves imported to Algeria from 3,300 in the year 1840 to 700 in 1858.[12] However, the number of slaves imported to Morocco in the 1850s reached 3,000 a year according to French historian Léon Nicolas Godard (1825–1863).[13] Godard estimated the number of all blacks in Morocco in the 1850s at 500,000 out of a total population of 8,250,800.[14] According to Graberg de Hemso (1776–1847), Swedish consul in Tangier, the number of blacks was much lower at 120,000 out of a total population of 8,500,000.[15] De Hemso's estimate does not

---

[10] Ibid., 602.

[11] Ibid., 605–606.

[12] Ralph Austen, "The Mediterranean Islamic Slave Trade out of Africa: A Tentative Census," in Elizabeth Savage, ed., *The Human Commodity: Perspectives on the Trans-Saharan Slave Trade* (London: Frank Cass, 1992), 224.

[13] Léon Nicolas Godard, *Description et histoire du Maroc: comprenant la géographie et la statistique de ce pays d'après les renseignements les plus récents et le tableau du règne des souverains qui l'ont gouverné depuis les temps les plus anciens jusqu'à la paix de Tétouan en 1860* (Paris: Ch. Tanera, 1860), vol. 1, 221.

[14] Ibid., 9.

[15] Graberg de Hemso's statistics reported in Conrad Malte-Brun, *Précis de la géographie universelle* (Brussels: Th. Lejeune, 1835), vol. 6, 148.

match the numbers evidenced by the slave registers discussed in Chapter 4. One century earlier, the official number of blacks conscripted by Mawlay Isma'il exceeded 221,320 persons.[16] This figure did not include those who escaped in many oases and remote areas or who sought refuge in Sufi centers. American historian and diplomat Stephen Bonsal (1865–1951) indicated in 1893 that the domestic black slaves in Morocco numbered around 250,000.[17] Hence, the projection of Léon Godard at 500,000 blacks (slaves and free) in Morocco in the 1850s is more credible. The continuing import of slaves fed the growing black population in Morocco. According to Jean-Louis Miège, Morocco imported about 7,000 or 8,000 slaves a year during the nineteenth century.[18] Miège's estimate concurs with Daniel Schroeter's assessment that annual slave imports toward the end of the nineteenth century were between 4,000 and 7,000.[19] This was apparently an increase from the previous century when Morocco imported between 3,000 to 4,000 slaves, according to Michel Abitbol.[20] There were at least two principal and well-established trade routes that continued to exist throughout the nineteenth century (via three main carrefours: Tindouf, Ijil, and Tuwat). An official document from the British Consulate in Mogador dated April 12, 1876, by Consul R. Drummond Hay, stated:

There are two great caravans during the year, by which slaves are brought to Morocco by the Moorish traders with Timbuctoo, and by the slave dealers from that city. It is difficult to calculate the number of slaves imported into Morocco by Tindoof. I am informed by persons who have been engaged in the Timbuctoo trade at that station, and who are therefore well acquainted with all the particulars, that as many as 3,000 slaves have been known to arrive in a caravan. This, however, was an exception to the rule; and, as far as I can learn, the average number of slaves that enter Morocco viâ Tindoof annually, by the two great caravans, does not exceed 2,000 souls. The number imported by other means and routes is insignificant.[21]

[16] Unknown author, *Jany al-Azhar*, 18–19.
[17] Stephen Bonsal, *Morocco As It Is: With an Account of Sir Charles Euan Smith's Recent Mission to Fez* (New York: Harper & Brothers, 1893), 328.
[18] Jean-Louis Miège, *Le Maroc et l'Europe* (Rabat: Editions La Porte, 1996), vol. 2, 151. He also quotes other sources with estimates from one thousand to six thousand a year.
[19] Daniel Schroeter, "Slave Markets and Slavery in Moroccan Urban Society," in Elizabeth Savage, ed., *The Human Commodity: Perspectives on the Trans-Saharan Slave Trade* (London: Frank Cass, 1992), 193.
[20] Abitbol, *Tombouctou et les Arma*, 204.
[21] *Reports from Commissioners, Inspectors and Others*, Great Britain, Parliament House of Commons (London: Printed by George Edward Eyre and William Spottiswoode, 1876), vol. 28, 113.

The annual estimate for the nineteenth century varied from 2,000 to 8,000. This discrepancy is also reflected in European accounts of the total number of blacks in Morocco, which varied drastically, from 50,000 to 500,000. These estimates are often confusing, as they mixed blacks as an ethnic group with servile conditions. It is important to note that during the abolitionist era a great number of enslaved people were not in the records because slave transactions were done discreetly in order to evade state taxation and also to avoid notice by official European representatives and observers.[22] The estimate of a total black population of half a million by the end of the nineteenth century is likely close to the actual number of blacks living in Morocco. Throughout the nineteenth century, the slave trade and slavery were legal in Morocco, and it was from Morocco that slaves were transported clandestinely to Algeria. At the beginning of the French conquest of Algeria, the French authorities were not consistent in their measures against slavery or the slave trade. In fact, as John Wright noted, "slaves taken into Algeria were reportedly bought by European immigrants and Muslims."[23] Algerian slave merchants resorted to the slave markets in Morocco to supply slaves to their Algerian customers.[24] In the nineteenth century, the Tuwat trade route provided the most slaves to Morocco. From this region slaves were supplied to Algerian towns such as Tlemcen.[25]

The Ganduzi affair is a clear example of how enslaved blacks were trafficked across the border and how the French colonial authorities dealt with the issue of slavery in Algeria. Al-Mukhtar b. 'Abd ar-Rahman al-Ganduzi, a Moroccan merchant from Figuig (a town on the border with Algeria), traded regularly in Tlemcen. In 1850, he brought ten black female slaves to Tlemcen for private sale – public sales were forbidden by the colonial authorities. But the French justice of the peace, Mr. Perez, was informed of the arrival of these slaves and without alerting General de brigade Mac Mahon,[26] he confiscated them and entrusted them to the care of the inhabitants of the city. Apparently, this action did not sit well with the military administration that intended to delay the implementation of the abolition decree. The colonial administrators did not

[22] See the excellent article of Mohamed Ennaji and Ben Srhir, "La Grande Bretagne et l'Esclavage au Maroc au XIXe Siècle," *Hesperis-Tamuda* (Rabat: Editions Techniques Nord-Africaines, vol. 29, 2, 1991), 250–251.

[23] Wright, *The Trans-Saharan Slave*, 147.

[24] See Marcel Emerit and Pierre Boyer, *La révolution de 1848 en Algérie: mélanges d'histoire par Pierre Boyer* (Paris: Éditions Larose, 1949), 31.

[25] Wright, *The Trans-Saharan Slave*, 142.

[26] Paul Estienne, *Histoire complète du maréchal Mac-Mahon, président de la République française* (Paris: A. Duquesne, 1874), 39.

want to endanger the fragile alliance with the local elites and were also concerned about the risks of creating hostility with the Moroccans.[27] The governor general reminded the attorney general in Algiers to make sure that the military and civil administrations were in agreement on such affairs and to avoid any hasty decision that might cause embarrassment to the French authorities,[28] and furthermore asked that the justice of the peace be transferred to a position less pivotal in decision making.[29] It is clear from the French state letters on the subject of slavery that the law should be enforced only when slaves filed complaints and demanded their freedom. As historian Dennis Cordell stated: "The law and the circulars abolishing slavery and the slave trade were clear, but the ambiguity in attitudes persisted until the end of the century and beyond."[30] We find documents from the year 1880 that confirm the continuous trafficking in black female slaves from Morocco to Algeria.[31]

On an unofficial front, the activities of British abolitionists continued in Morocco. James Richardson (1806–1851), a traveler in Africa and an anti-slavery campaigner, attempted to deliver a letter on behalf of the British and Foreign Anti-Slavery Society to Sultan 'Abd ar-Rahman in 1844, but the governor of the Atlantic seaport Mogador (Essaouira) refused to convey the message to the sultan. According to Donald Mackenzie: "The governor of that city would not allow it to be forwarded. 'If he did so,' he said, 'he would himself have his tongue cut from the roof of his mouth.'"[32] At this point Richardson commented that trying to convince the Moors (i.e., the Moroccans) to abolish slavery was futile. In his interview with the governor of Mogador on the abolition issues, Richardson wrote:

I then asked His Excellency if a person were to come direct from our Government, with larger powers and presents, he would have a better chance of success. The Governor replied, "Not the least whatever. You have done all that could have

---

[27] Archives Nationales de France, Centre des Archives d'Outre-Mer (CAOM), Aix-en-Provence, Gouvernement général de l'Algérie, Affaires indigenes, 12H: Réformes en faveurs des indigenes,12H50: Esclavage. See Addoun, *Abolition*, 230–232.

[28] The documents I consulted do not mention the name of the governor, but the governor general of Algeria in this year was Viala Charon.

[29] Gouverneur Général de l'Algérie to Procureur Général, Bureau des affaires politiques no 3, 17 juillet 1850.

[30] Dennis Cordell, "No Liberty, Not Much Equality, and Very Little Fraternity: The Mirage of Manumission in the Algerian Sahara in the Second Half of the Nineteenth Century" in Miers and Klein, eds. *Slavery and Colonial Rule*, 45.

[31] These documents are in the form of letters and circulars; they are preserved at Archives Nationales de France, CAOM, Aix-en-Provence, 12 H 50. I am indebted to Yacine Daddi Addoun for sending me copies of these documents.

[32] Donald A. Mackenzie, *The Khalifate of the West, Being a General Description of Morocco* (London: Simpkin, Marshall, Hamilton, Kent & co. ltd, 1911), 100.

been done. We look at the subject, not the persons. The Sultan will never listen to anybody on this subject. You may cut off his head, but cannot convince him. If all the Christians of the world were to come and take this country, then, of course, the Mussulmen would yield the question to superior force, to the decree of God, but not till then."

Myself. – "How is it, Sidi, that the Bey of Tunis, and the Imaum of Muscat have entered into engagements with Christians for the suppression of slavery, they being Mussulmen?"

The Governor. – "I'll tell you; we Mussulmen are as bad as you Christians. We are full of divisions and sects. Some of our people go to one mosque, and will not go to another. They are foolish (*mahboul*). So it is with the subject of slaves. Some are with you, but most are with me. The Bey of Tunis, and the Imaum have a different opinion from us. They think they are right, and we think we are right; but we are as good as they."

Myself. – "Sidi, does not the Koran encourage the abolition of slavery, and command it as duty to all pious Mussulmen?"

The Governor. – "No, it does not command it but those who voluntarily liberate their slaves are therein commended, and have the blessing of God on them."[33]

The British continued to put pressure until the sultan finally yielded to some demands of the British Anti-Slavery Society. In 1863, the sultan "decided that any runaway slave seeking refuge in the Makhzen (the Moroccan authority) and requesting its protection would not be sent back to his master."[34] This reform was directed only toward runaway slaves and the text did not say whether these slaves would be set free or put into the service of the Makhzan, which was in a way another 'Abid al-Bukhari (i.e., servants to the government), and ironically the trade in slaves went on. In the 1870s, when Donald Mackenzie, the manager of the North-West African Company, tried to establish a commercial center in the southern Moroccan seaport of Tarfaya, he informed the British Foreign Office about his intentions, which included his desire to end slavery in the area.[35] Mackenzie also visited Morocco in 1886 and wrote a report addressed to Earl of Iddbsleigh, principal secretary of state for foreign affairs, about the slave trade in Morocco. He commended the British and Foreign Anti-Slavery missions that achieved some success after forty years of persistent work, but the results were only partial, mostly in coastal and port towns where Sultan Mawlay al-Hasan prohibited the public sale of slaves in 1882.[36] He wrote:

[33] James Richardson, *Travels in Morocco* (London: Charles J. Skeet, 1860), vol. 2, 195–196.
[34] Ennaji and Ben Srhir, "La Grande Bretagne," 251.
[35] Ibid., 252–253.
[36] Mackenzie, *The Khalifate of the West*, 100.

The newspapers which have of late years been established in that benighted country assisted heartily in the same noble work. The result of this agitation has been that the markets have been closed in the seaport towns, so that now the business is carried on privately. The traffic still continues openly in the interior towns, and the slaves are generally sold at the following prices: Young Slaves, Males, from £8 to £10 each. Females, from £15 to £16. Adult Slaves, Males, from £4 to £6, Females, from £6 to £8 each.[37]

He continued that the British government had not made sufficient effort to persuade Morocco to put an end to this horrible trade.[38] It seems that the official remonstrations were more flexible and mild than the outcry and condemnation of the British abolition activists, travelers, and traders. Drummond Hay never pressed hard enough on the issue of slavery and at times was even apologetic on behalf of the Moroccan government. As of 1842, in a letter to his government, he expressed the difficulties encountered by people who investigated slavery lest they be suspected of prejudice against Islam. At the same time, he downplayed the abuse and cruelty of slavery in Morocco by declaring that "the slaves in this country are not numerous, and, according to all my own observation, and every report, are kindly treated by their masters, who, at their decease, frequently emancipate their slaves."[39] Throughout his tenure as general consul of Morocco from 1845 to 1886, in different reports to the British government, he repeatedly emphasized the mild nature of slavery in Morocco, and his estimates of the number of slaves imported annually to Morocco were much smaller than the ones mentioned in travel accounts, as in this report:

There is no slave trade by sea; five or six hundred slaves are brought yearly by land, I believe. The men are bought for servants in the houses of wealthy Moors, and the women as handmaids and servants. They are very kindly treated, and when their masters die are given their liberty and a portion of the estate.[40]

Hay hoped to see the abolition of slavery in Morocco, but insisted there was no brutality, that some slaves had appealed to him to intervene on their behalf so they might return to their masters after they

[37] Donald Mackenzie, *A Report on the Condition of the Empire of Morocco: Addressed to the Right Hon. the Earl of Iddesleigh, G.C.M.G., Her Majesty's Principal Secretary of State for Foreign Affairs, &C* (London: British and Foreign Anti-Slavery Society, 1886), 47.
[38] Ibid.
[39] *British and Foreign State Papers 1842–1843*, 598–599.
[40] John H. Drummond-Hay, *A Memoir of Sir John Drummond Hay, Sometime Minister at the Court of Morocco Based on His Journals and Correspondence* (London: J. Murray, 1896), 357.

were emancipated. He added: "Slaves are not used for agricultural purposes – not transported, like pigs, in vessels – and are generally the spoilt
children of the house."[41] Hay's rather forgiving view contradicted most
eyewitness accounts of the horrors of the trans-Saharan slave trade.
Morocco was the largest slave-owning society in the Maghreb at the end
of the nineteenth century. Contrary to Hay's comments, some enslaved
people were aware of the abolitionist movement and used the available
resources to improve their conditions or even ultimately to get their freedom back. In 1861 a female slave in the city of Safi claimed that her
mistress mistreated her and complained to a European Christian (by
the name of KNBR?) whom she got to know and trust. This European
gave the necessary funds for her emancipation and entrusted her to the
care of the French residents in the city of Safi. When Sultan Muhammad
b. 'Abd ar-Rahman heard of this affair from the governor of Safi he
instructed his viceroy, Muhammad Barkash, to inform the French consul
that the benevolent action of the European was not necessary because
Islamic law guaranteed her right to be emancipated as soon as she was
mistreated by her mistress.[42]

Nineteenth-century European accounts reported that a large number
of slaves were owned by several governors of provinces, officers, merchants, and so forth.[43] A singular *caïd* (chief) of Haha had 500 black
slaves in the 1860s.[44] Italian journalist Edmondo De Amicis (1846–1908)
noticed during his visit to Morocco in the 1870s that there were so many
blacks in Fez that it seemed like he was in the Sudan. He wrote:

I meet so many negroes in the streets of Fez that I sometimes seem to find myself
in the city of the Soudan, and feel vaguely between me and Europe the immen-
sity of the desert of Sahara. From the Soudan, in fact, the greater part of them
come – a little less than three thousand in a year, many of whom are said to die in
a short time from home-sickness. They are generally brought at the age of eight
or ten years. The merchants, before exposing them for sale, fatten them with
balls of cuscussu, try to cure them, with music, of their home-sickness, and teach
them a few Arabic words; which last augments their price, which is generally
thirty francs for a boy, sixty for a girl, about four hundred for a young woman

---

[41] Ibid., 357.
[42] Ibn Zaydan, *Ithaf A'lam an-Nas*, vol. 3, 385.
[43] *Report of the Commissoners, minutes of the evidence, and appendix, with general
index of minutes of evidence and appendix. Presented to both houses of Parliament by
command of Her Majesty.*, Gt. Brit. Parliament (London: Printed by G.E. Eyre and W.
Spottiswoode, for H.M. Stationery off., 1876), 113–114.
[44] B. Balansa, "Voyage de Mogador à Maroc," *Bulletin de la Société de géographie* (Paris:
Société de géographie, 1868), tome XV (312–334), 318.

of seventeen or eighteen who is handsome, and knows how to speak, and has not yet had a child, and fifty or sixty for an old man. The emperor takes five per cent. on the imported material, and has a right of the first choice. The others are sold in the markets of Fez, Mogador and Morocco [Marrakesh], and separately, at auction, in the other cities.[45]

In the 1870s, Joseph Hooker, noting an abundance of black slaves, described what he perceived as the robust role that black slaves played in Moroccan society: "The negro often possesses far more energy than the Moor [Arab and Berber], united to at least equal natural intelligence, it may be believed that the rulers of Marocco [*sic*] have shown no want of policy in favouring this section of the population."[46] Observing that a local governor in the southwest region of Morocco was black, Hooker added: "We were not then familiar with the fact that slaves frequently rise in Marocco [*sic*] to the highest posts in the State."[47] Further south in the Sus area in Iligh (an important location for the trans-Saharan trade), according to Oskar Lenz who visited Morocco in 1880, Sidi Husayn, an old black man who ruled the area as an independent prince, maintained an army of five thousand slaves, all black, from different backgrounds in West Africa, including the Fulani.[48]

In the 1880s, Henri Poisson de La Martinière (1859–1922), a member of the Geographical Society of Paris, wrote an account of his travels in Morocco. Confronted with the realization that slavery still existed in Morocco, he noted in his journal that slaves in Morocco appeared to be treated humanely and with far greater consideration and respect than slaves owned by Christians:

The black slave's experience [was] no worse a fate than that of a servant[...]. It is, indeed, regrettable that similar usages did not prevail among Christian nations in times of slavery. [... But] their treatment at the hands of the dealer is frightful and abominable. It is this phase of the evil trade afflicting the dark Continent that constitutes the gist of the question.[49]

Although La Martinière noted that black slaves in Morocco were treated humanely, he nonetheless thought that slavery was an ignoble

[45] Edmondo De Amicis, *Morocco: Its People and Places*, translated by C. Rollin-Tilton (New York: G.P. Putnam's Sons, 1882), 294–295.
[46] Joseph Dalton Hooker, *Journal of a Tour in Marocco and the Great Atlas* (London: Macmillan, 1878), 115.
[47] Ibid.
[48] Oskar Lenz, *Timbouctou, voyage au Maroc, au Sahara et au Soudan* (Paris: Hachette, 1886), 354–355.
[49] De La Martinière, *Morocco: Journeys*, 234.

institution.[50] Other European travel accounts of the late nineteenth century are consistent with La Martinière's observation that black slaves in Morocco were treated humanely. Walter Harris, who traveled to Morocco in the 1880s, wrote:

> We went very often to the slave market, but never saw such sights as children separated from their parents, though we saw both sold together in the "lot." Nor did we see many other things of which we had read; in fact, the slaves wore a wonderfully contented, even cheerful, expression while the sale was proceeding[...]. This I will say, that I would far rather be a slave in Morocco than a peasant. From what, too, I saw of slaves out of the market, they appear not to have such a bad time of it, and in many of the houses [that slaves served] enjoy more liberty than the paid servants.[51]

On the status of women, Harris alluded to the relation between wives and concubines in the sultan's harem:

> It is only very seldom that we can hear anything of the life led by his wives [the sultan's], except that it must be a tragic one, for the favorite, for the time being, lolls on cushions of velvet and gold in dimly-lit rooms full of the odours of incense and flowers, and attended by slaves, any one of whom, should she find favor in the sight of her lord and master, would usurp the place of the Sultana, who would sink to the degradation of slavery; and no doubt this is often the case.[52]

Harris's description is likely more fanciful than factual about the life of these women inside the harem because the harem was a zone closed to men, especially strangers. However, it is well established that Moroccan sultans had large harems and that wealthy men had considerable assets in slaves and concubines as well. In the 1890s, Stephen Bonsal gave a detailed description of slavery in Morocco. He estimated the number of slaves to be about a quarter of a million and described Moroccan slaves as being mostly black and having domestic duties "of a very mild character."[53] He wrote:

> Many Moors, when they come to die, manumit their slaves, an action which is highly recommended by the Koran. These freed men mingle with the population, marry and intermarry with the Moors, Arabs and Berbers, producing the numerous negroid types that astonish the traveler in Morocco. They are by no means looked down upon owing to their previous condition of servitude or because of

---

[50] Ibid., 237.
[51] Walter Harris, *The Land of an African Sultan: Travels in Morocco, 1887, 1888, and 1889* (London, Sampson Low Marston Searle & Rivington, 1889), 221.
[52] Harris, *The Land of an African Sultan*, 211.
[53] Bonsal, *Morocco As It Is*, 328.

their colour. The mother of the present Sultan was a negress, the mother of the late Grand Shereef of Wazzan was a Haussa mulatto.[54]

In 1892, two British abolitionists, Henry Gurney and Charles Allen, were sent by the committee of the B.F.A.S.S (British and Foreign Anti-Slavery Society) to North Africa to investigate slavery in the region. They spent one week in Tangier and wrote a valuable report. They stated that the slave trade in Tunisia and Algeria (mainly Algiers) had been brought to an end and that slavery itself existed only "in a very modified form,"[55] thanks to the French colonial authority. However, they said that "in Morocco, despite the long-continued efforts of British Ministers, the Slave-trade is carried on with unblushing effrontery, almost within sight of Europe."[56] They did credit Drummond Hay for his influence in putting an end to the public slave markets in coastal towns, but they expressed deep concerns for the interior. In this report, they cited their friend, Donald Mackenzie, as saying that the slave trade was still going on in coastal towns, but privately, in order to escape the attention of the colonial authorities and the Anti-Slavery Society.[57] Mackenzie thought that "Drummond Hay, no doubt on account of his long residence in Morocco – some forty-two years – was so accustomed to slavery that he was not very strongly opposed to it."[58] Mackenzie wrote on November 14, 1891, from Cape Juby:

The supply is drawn from the Soudan, by various routes, each caravan bringing about 300 Slaves. It is heartrending to see mothers and children separated, perhaps never to meet again in this world. A short time ago, the Moorish Kaids gave the Sultan and his son a present of 200 male and female Slaves, to celebrate the event of the marriage of the heir to the Moorish throne. The great markets for the disposal of Slaves are in Morocco city [Marrakesh], Fez, Tetuan, and Rabat. During the two fairs which are held every year, in 'Side Ahmed Amusa,' in Sus, about 1,200 boys and girls are sold.

Girls, from ten to thirteen years of age, fetch about £16 to £24 each, and the Slave merchants find the females more profitable from ten to twenty years of age.

I pointed out to you before that a considerable amount of Slave traffic is carried on between Senegal and Morocco by Moorish merchants.[59]

---

[54] Ibid., 332–333.
[55] Henry Gurney and Charles Allen, *Tripoli, Tunis, Algeria and Morocco. Report to the Committee of the British and Foreign Anti-Slavery Society* (London: British and Foreign Anti-Slavery Society, 1892), 17.
[56] Ibid.
[57] Ibid, 21.
[58] Mackenzie, *The Khalifate of the West*, 105.
[59] Gurney and Allen, *Tripoli, Tunis, Algeria and Morocco*, 21.

Mackenzie also mentioned French traders who profited from the slave trade, writing that "Some pretty girls are, I found, brought from Senegal in French vessels as passengers and disposed of privately to wealthy Moors."[60] At the same time, as of 1884, the French consul in Tangiers had forbidden the French and their Muslim protégés to buy or to own slaves in Morocco.[61]

Henry Gurney and Charles Allen also commented about the strategic location of Morocco in relation to Europe and the great economic potential for Morocco with trade to Europe that appeared to be hindered by lack of efficiency and onerous duties:

Simply because there is no law nor justice in the country, nor are there any roads or means of communication, so that everything has to be carried by beasts of burden or by men, and trade has thus been reduced to a *minimum*, whilst the export of wheat is either prohibited or rendered impossible by exorbitant duties. And yet Morocco could grow sufficient grain to feed half Europe.[62]

Indeed, Drummond Hay had tried to convince the Moroccan government to modernize the country. He advocated open trade between Morocco and Europe and recommended the production of commodities for export such as grain, cotton, and sugar cane.[63] As this was his primary goal, he did not want the issue of slavery to complicate British–Moroccan diplomatic relations. England was comfortable with the status quo of the geopolitics in the area – it already controlled the entrance to the Mediterranean basin (from the stronghold of Gibraltar). Its policy was to maintain that status and not allow other European nations to gain a foothold or any influence in Morocco. John Wright points out: "If any one individual protected Morocco from such pressures over many decades, it was the British Consul (later Minister), Sir John Drummond Hay. For so long as successive British governments were persuaded by him to take an indulgent view of the issue, other powers were equally unwilling to face the risks and troubles of doing otherwise."[64] Drummond Hay was probably further persuaded by Moroccan officials that slavery in Morocco was largely domestic in nature and benign in practice and that slavery had actually protected the poor from being homeless. A portion of the slave population served the big urban houses that relied heavily on the

[60] Mackenzie, *The Khalifate of the West*, 104–105.
[61] "Anti-Slavery Notes" in *Africa. A Quarterly Review and Journal* (London: S. W. Partridge and Co., May 1st, 1884), 136.
[62] Gurney and Allen, *Tripoli, Tunis, Algeria and Morocco*, 15.
[63] Ennaji and Ben Srhir, "La Grande Bretagne," 254.
[64] Wright, *The Trans-Saharan Slave*, 151.

work of maidservants on account of the seclusion of Muslim women. But there was no guarantee that these domestic servants were not maltreated or occasionally abused. Whether or not they were treated well misses the salient point that they were reduced to servitude and forced to leave their native location. The idea that the practice of slavery was benign and even "compassionate" withers in the face of such facts. A substantial proportion of slaves worked in rural areas and performed menial and harsh labor in the oases, small farms, mines, or ports. Some of the extreme European reports (such as the one written by Gurney and Allen) may not have exaggerated the harshness of slavery in Morocco, since Sultan Hasan I (r. 1873–1894) expressed indignation at the way slavery was conducted in his society, as even poor Arabs and Berbers were subjected to random enslavement. In 1882, he wrote a letter in the form of an admonishing sermon addressed to all Moroccans stating: "It is an impious act that one could not ignore or tolerate this misfortune which has occurred in this time, it is the outright reduction of free people into slavery without any legal base."[65]

Gurney and Allen suggested more aggressive British intervention in the country not only to stop the cruel practice of slavery and the despotic Moroccan regime but also for the benefit of England:

By the opening up of Morocco, with its untold wealth in agriculture, minerals, fruits, etc., to the trade of the world, England would be the first country to find fresh markets for her manufactures, and fresh fields for the immigration of many of her unemployed, whilst the making of roads and the laying of electric telegraphs would bring the now dark and hidden towns of the interior into communication with the outer world [...].

The hands of the British Minister in that country would thereby be strengthened, and he would be able to urge upon the Sultan, with more emphasis than has ever yet been done, the imperative necessity of abolishing the Slave-trade, and closing the disgraceful pens for human cattle that now exist in every town in which there is no resident European Consul, to prevent, by his presence, so great a scandal to humanity.[66]

Other travelers did not see much of the abuse. In 1893, Stephen Bonsal stressed the effects of the British and Foreign Anti-Slavery Society and the nature of slavery in Morocco:

Negro slavery is practiced in Morocco, but certainly of a very mild character. The slaves almost without exception are well treated, and would not, if they could,

---

[65] Ibn Zaydan. *Ithaf A'lam an-Nas*, vol. 2, 229.
[66] Gurney and Allen, *Tripoli, Tunis, Algeria and Morocco*, 23.

change their lot [...]. The domestic slaves in the Empire number, I should say, about a quarter of a million. Since 1880 all European Governments have forbidden their *protégés* from holding or dealing in slaves, a prohibition which has certainly not been strictly observed by all concerned [...]. It is owing in a great measure to the representations of the British and Foreign Anti-Slavery Society, and the ceaseless vigilance of its agents, that in 1883 the Sultan was induced to forbid the exposing of slaves for sale in the street. While this decree has been by no means generally observed, certainly it has resulted in a great improvement. In Fez and in the city of Morocco [Marrakesh], and, in fact, in every seaboard, as well as inland, there is a slave market. In the city of Morocco there are two or three, in Fez there is one large one, but so cautious have the Moors become, and so jealous are they of the observing stranger, that it has become almost an impossibility to witness, without assuming a disguise, the workings of the "retail" slave trade. Whenever I entered the slave market in Fez everything stopped. The slaves who were being sold were hustled away before I could make any note of their appearance and manner, and presto! the slave dealers and the slave owners who had been so boisterously busy trafficking in human flesh, sat around in a circle in the most innocent manner possible, smoking *kief* [hashish].

The prices of slaves vary from 5*l.* to 15*l.*, according to age and sex. In Marakesh the slave market is held three times a week about sunset in an open square near the Kessaria.[67]

It seems that by the 1880s the Moroccans were apprehensive in conducting open slave sales in the presence of Europeans. However, at the gate of the Moroccan Sahara, there was a daily slave market at Souk al-Ghazal. The most popular among the local slave traders was al-Hajj 'Abd ar-Rahman al-Kasri, who amassed a fortune in human trafficking. The gender preference in the market was female. According to Bonsal, the great demand for female slaves over male slaves was described in the travel journal of Dr. Adolphe Marcet, a French bureaucrat who visited Morocco in 1882 as part of an official tour.[68] Dr. Marcet wrote:

Here again is a fine, tall, young woman of eighteen or twenty, a promising mulatress with expressive features and handsome figure. A costume of red and white striped calico, fitting tight below the waist, sets off her splendid form, and harmonizes agreeably with the colour of her skin. The seller seems to have decked her out expressly to enhance her charms. There is a bid of two hundred and twenty-five francs, but, as she is the cream of the sale, she will fetch a good deal more[...]. Now comes a young woman with two small children, [...] her face wearing an expression of deep sadness and melancholy[...]. In like manner, some thirty more of these poor creatures are led round, exhibited, bargained for, and subjected without pity to the most degrading examination of any one who

---

[67] Bonsal, *Morocco As It Is*, 328–329.
[68] Ibid., 330–332.

pleases. Amongst all this human merchandise, not one male! They are all females of varied degrees of colour.[69]

The slave markets of North Africa were not places where the slaves were contented or docile, as many travelers suggested. Many women, men, and children sold into slavery did not yet know what was in store for them. At the same time, the enslaved people probably realized that they were now in a place distant from their homes, their forced migration through an ocean of sand in their minds, and may have decided to make the best of a bad situation. Other slaves being resold, who might have been living with an impersonal or abusive slaveholder, likely realized from experience that the more pleasant and amicable their appearance, the more likely they would be bought by a "better" and more humane "owner." In this meager way, slaves were able to have some agency in their future treatment and conditions of life by trying to make themselves more appealing to warm-hearted "owners."

Ahmad an-Nasiri (d. 1897), who was aware of the horrors of the trans-Saharan slave trade and slavery, protested against the immoral acts committed against this particular group of Muslims who happened to be black.[70] By 1900, the trans-Saharan slave trade dwindled drastically; the French Eugène Aubin remarked that the external sources for slavery had been eliminated thanks to the French colonial establishment in Timbuktu. But he noted during his visit to Morocco in 1902 that the Marrakesh slave market still received black slaves from the Sus area, as a result of war booties among the Saharan tribes. He also stated that the general character of slavery in Morocco was domestic.[71] He wrote in 1904: "The price of black females was very variable, from twenty to a thousand douros. A simple maid who does everything fetches a small value; the prices rise as regards a cook or a musician. The highest prices are reached for concubines."[72] Some slaveholders may have impregnated their female slaves for the purpose of selling their children into slavery, especially during hard times as during the periods of famine.[73] Moroccan historian al-Mukhtar

[69] Adolphe Marcet, *Le Maroc: voyage d'une mission française à la cour du Sultan* (Paris: E. Plon, Nourrit et Cie, 1885), 208–209. This passage is an accurate translation by Bonsal, *Morocco As It Is*, 331.

[70] An-Nasiri, *al-Istiqsa'*, vol. 5, 131.

[71] Aubin, *Le Maroc d'aujourd'hui*, 316–318.

[72] Ibid., 317–318.

[73] Jean Potocki. *Voyages en Turquie, en Égypte, en Hollande, et au Maroc*. Paris: Fayard, 1980, 233.

as-Susi (1900–1963) reported that some families in southern Morocco owned seventy slave couples,[74] who could have been used for this purpose.[75]

With the onset of a more active colonial ambition of the French in Morocco in the early twentieth century, we find substantial documents that report on how the French dealt with the issue of slavery in Morocco. In 1907, Edouard Michaux-Bellaire observed that slavery still existed freely and publicly in Morocco. Even though the slave markets no longer existed in the big cities, slavery was practiced in more clandestine forms, in places where Europeans were infrequent in order to avoid diplomatic conflicts with the European powers.[76] He also noted that female slaves were more numerous than male slaves. He observed that in rural areas, female slaves seemed to lead lives similar to those of free women.[77] French colonial official Lapanne Joinville reported that "at the dawn of the Protectorate, slaves were numerous in Morocco. They were, for the most part, blacks. The Arabic word designating slave (*'abd*, pl. *'abid*) has taken, in daily language, as the meaning of 'black.'"[78]

In 1904, England ceded its presence in Morocco to the colonial aspirations of France, ending Britain's push against slavery. Morocco under Mawlay 'Abd al-'Aziz (r. 1894–1908) and Mawlay 'Abd al-Hafid (1908–1912), who had tried to position Morocco as an international partner by playing off European powers, came to an end in 1912 when the Treaty of Fez with France and Spain marked the end of Moroccan independence. Spain controlled a small portion of the northern part of Morocco (the lands around Melilla and Ceuta from Larache to Nador) until 1956.[79] France ruled over most of the territory until 1956. With

---

[74] Muhammad al-Mukhtar as-Susi, *al-Ma'sul* (Casablanca: Matba'at al-Najah, 1962), vol. 17, 275. See also Mohamed Naji, "A propos de l'esclavage au Maroc précolonial" in *Colloque, travail et société* (Fez: Publications de la Faculté des Sciences Juridiques, Economiques et Sociales, 1983–1984), 5–16.

[75] See Mohamed Naji, "A propos de l'esclavage," 12–13.

[76] See Edouard Michaux-Bellaire, "L'esclavage au Maroc," *Revue du Monde Musulman* (Paris: la Mission Scientifique du Maroc, 1910), tome 11, 4e année, Mai, No 5, 422–427, 422.

[77] Ibid.

[78] Lapanne Joinville, "Note sur l'esclavage au Maroc" to be circulated within members of the administration only, Centre de Hautes Etudes d'Administration Musulmane, 3 Novembre 1950, 9.

[79] Spain also controlled the land in the southwest desert known as the Tarfaya strip until 1975.

the establishment of the 1912 French Protectorate in Morocco, the public slave markets in the cities and the countryside were suppressed.[80] In 1912 the French Anti-Slavery Society conducted an inquiry into slavery in Morocco.[81] The colonial authorities replied on the impossibility of an outright abolition of slavery but held out hope for abolition as a gradual process.[82] In the same year, Louis-Hubert Lyautey, resident-general of the Moroccan French protectorate from 1912 to 1925, closed the slave market in Marrakesh.[83] Around 1919, Jérôme (1877–1953) and Jean Tharaud (1874–1952), two brothers who made long trips to Morocco, noticed that there were only three slave merchants in Fez and that the sale of slaves was conducted discreetly by slave brokers. One of these merchants was an intriguing old man by the name of Ben Kiran.[84] So intriguing was Ben Kiran that he appeared in a Moroccan eminent novel entitled *Dafanna al-Madi* (*We Buried the Past*), not only as a slave merchant but as a slave breaker and as a symbol of fear analogous to the central authority in Morocco.[85] Indeed, some European travelers described the persisting practice of concubinage in Morocco. For instance, Jérôme and Jean Tharaud wrote:

First, there is the Negress of the bed. Rather than marry, many people prefer Black concubines, who are allowed by the Qur'an. There is no dowry to pay, no wedding ceremonies involving ridiculous expenses[…]. It even happens frequently that the mother of a family who wants to retain her authority in the house, pushes her son to satisfy himself with one or more Negresses in the hope of keeping them under her thumb. The slave is always more docile, more prone to admire the master, and of a more obliging nature. The *hadith* [reads]: "There is no Negress who would refuse love when it is offered." And if the lover is deceived, he always has a source of consolation in thinking "The Prophet told us so." But what binds the man of Fez to his Negresses above all is that their skins, it would

---

[80] Michaux-Bellaire reports that there were "masters" who intentionally impregnated their slaves to make more slaves either for their own use or for sale, especially when sub-Saharan West Africa was under European colonial rule and the trans-Saharan slave trade was blocked or extremely difficult. See Ed. Michaux-Bellaire, "L'esclavage au Maroc," 425.

[81] See Albert Navarre, *Un voyage au Maroc* (Paris: Ch. Delagrave, 1913), 136–142.

[82] See Ghita Aouad, "L'esclavage tardif au Maroc sous le Protectorat," *Revue Maroc Europe* (Rabat: Editions La Porte, 1991), I, 139–142.

[83] Navarre, 1913, 142.

[84] Jérôme Tharaud and Jean Tharaud, *Fez; ou les bourgeois de l'Islam* (Paris: Plon, 1930). Reprinted in *Maroc. Les villes impériales*, compiled by Guy Dugas (Paris: Omnibus, 1996), 174–175.

[85] See 'Abd al-Karim Ghallab, *Dafanna al-Madi* (Beirut: al-Maktab at-Tijari li-'t-Tiba'a wa 'n-Nashr wa-at-Tawzi', 1966), 27–34.

seem, are warmer than those of white women. For a Moroccan all illnesses spring from coldness, and conversely all cures come about through the effect of heat. A burning black skin is a remedy for all ills.[86]

The assertion of the authors that this kind of sexual desire for black women is endorsed by the Qur'an and the Hadith is explained in Chapter 1. The Tharaud brothers were right that slaves as concubines were mostly attained at a far lower cost than wives with the added advantage that concubines did not have the same legal status as wives under Islamic law. They also reported popular fantasies about black sexuality that enforced the perception of the black female body as the other.[87] In many respects, owing to patriarchy, life for women in general was hard, not only for the concubines, but for the wives as well, who no matter how hard they tried, surely could not rid their heart entirely of its natural jealousy over sexual inequality and male philandering. Concubines navigated very difficult situations between the resentment of the wife and the demands of the "master." Many of these women were brought into the household as slaves for specific occupations, after which some were taken as wives by one of the male members of the household, and some of them even freed. It was not uncommon for men of high status to marry women who were slaves, which in turn gave these women unprecedented power. Cases from legal opinions (*nawazil*) confirm such attitudes and practices. Moroccan jurist Abu 'Isa al-Mahdi al-Wazzani (d. 1923) reported that the mufti Muhammad al-Warzazi was once asked by a man who had a wife and a concubine if it was permissible for him to favor his concubine over his wife. The mufti advised against the preferential treatment of the concubine as it was unjust to the free woman.[88] The issue raised in this case by a layperson is more important than the answer as it revealed the kind of emotional attachment expressed by the master of the house. In another case, a master of the house also seemed to treat his concubine, who bore him a child, as a co-wife. Al-Wazzani reported this case and advised that if a wife refused to share the house with "a mother of child"

---

[86] Jérôme et Jean Tharaud, *Fez*, in *Maroc. Les villes impériales*, 171–173. English translation by John Hunwick and Eve Troutt Powell, *The African Diaspora in the Mediterranean Lands of Islam* (Princeton: Markus Wiener Publishers, 2002), 129.

[87] The existence of these sexual fantasies are confirmed by local sources, see Ennaji's description of family and sexuality in the nineteenth century: Ennaji, *Serving the Master*, 31–41.

[88] Abu 'Isa al-Mahdi al-Wazzani, *an-Nawazil as-Sughra al-Musammat al-Minah as-Samiyya fi 'n-Nawazil al-Fiqhiyya*, Wizarat al-Awqaf wa 'sh-Shu'un al-Islamiyya (al-Muhammadiyya, Morocco: Mataba'at Fudala, 1992), vol. 2, 107.

(*umm al-walad*) then her husband should not force her to do so.[89] It is important to note that compilations of legal opinions avoided using the term concubine (*jariya*) for a female slave who had borne her master a child. The term used instead was *umm al-walad*.

These accounts of slavery by European travelers to Morocco give fascinating insight into the treatment and lives of female slaves. But they focused more on the benevolence of the enslavers and the benignity of the Islamic institution than taking into account the agency of the enslaved persons. On one hand, as "slaves," their agency as free persons was surely limited. Yet, on the other hand, they were given considerable legal protection under Islamic law, and in many cases, forged strong emotional bonds with their owners that allowed them to improve their lot, particularly in cases where concubinage resulted in offspring. Consider the following confidential French note written in 1950 about a 1948 court case in which the court was asked to make a determination under Islamic law of the inheritance rights of the son of a slave fathered by the deceased:

(Ruling number 7045, of the 15th of December 1948) in Islamic Court of Appeals, a young Dukkali claimed his hereditary share of the inheritance from his father. [90] His co-inheritors: a wife and other sons of the deceased contested him saying that his mother was a slave reserved for domestic tasks only [e.g., not a concubine]. The defendant having provided proof that the deceased had sent him to school, had called him his son and had been considered as a legitimate child of his by the tribe, the Muslim judge confirmed by the Islamic Court of Appeals, that his rights of inheritance should be recognized.[91]

Note that the court recognized the offspring of a free father as free in spite of the slave status of the mother; because he was considered free, he had the right to inherit.[92] In another case, where a concubine was unable to present "sufficient proof of paternity that she invoked ...her case [was] rejected [by the Islamic court]."[93]

We do not have reliable statistics about the distribution of female slaves across the social strata. Some were in rich houses but many women ended up in middle-class and even lower-class homes. And all enslaved black West Africans were assigned numerous occupations, including tasks in

---

[89] Al-Wazzani, *an-Nawazil as-Sughra*, vol. 2, 474.

[90] Dukkala region in which Azemmour and Safi were the most important coastal towns.

[91] Joinville, "Note sur l'esclavage au Maroc," 17.

[92] The document mentions many cases in which the judges ruled in favor of the defendants or plaintiffs, whose filiations to free status were questioned, and recognized them as free and had the quality to inherit. See for instance (Ruling number 4164 of December 11, 1943), ibid.

[93] Joinville, "Note sur l'esclavage au Maroc," 18.

the home, farm, mines, oasis, ports, or in the army. But most households preferred female servants for domestic service. Certainly, enslaved women would perform a wide range of domestic tasks such as cleaning, cooking, running errands, and being a nanny, and undoubtedly, some owners sexually abused their female servants even if they were not specifically taken as concubines. Many travel accounts spoke about the submissive nature of these enslaved women. But submissiveness is not at all natural. The oppression of women in North Africa is often wrongly interpreted to mean that women were obsequious or docile. One of the aspects of patriarchy is the idea that women in general, including female slaves, were supposed to submit to the authority of males because males were providers and leaders in public affairs hence they were held to be in effect superior to women. Women were considered mostly suited to domestic duties and for the bearing and care of children. Given patriarchy's essentialist gender prejudices, a system of formal slavery seems an easy transition from a patriarchal system of assumed inferior female gender essences and attributes and the social roles those attributes circumscribed for women. The use of female slaves as nannies, nursemaids, domestic servants, and even concubines was the logical extension of the preexisting notion of women in the niche of patriarchal dependency.[94] Black female slaves were tragic heroines struggling to overcome their enslavement, oppression, and sexual exploitation. Some were forced to use their sexuality and emotional resources to navigate the harsh realities of slavery and its attendant loss of personal identity and pride to rebuild new identities and enhance their agency in a manner that at times transcended servile conditions, race, and color prejudice. The striving for survival and the tragic drama of the female slaves' lives entailed emotional and sexual bonds via concubinage within a society where gender was hierarchical – patrilineal and patriarchal. If it was legally and socially established for a male to be entitled to female slave sexuality, it was, as well, legally and socially conventional for the progeny of female slaves to inherit their fathers' legal status. As has been discussed, some enslaved black females became the matriarchs of the kings' households – that is, their offspring had a legal and social status that allowed them to stand as potential and actual successors to the throne.

[94] This dependency seems to be a pattern in other parts of Africa where the status of "wife" was quasi-similar to that of "slave." See for instance Susan Herlin Broadhead, "Slave Wives, Free Sisters: Bakongo Women and Slavery c. 1700–1850" in Claire C. Robertson and Martin A. Klein, eds., *Women and Slavery in Africa* (Portsmouth: Heinemann, 1997), 160–181.

Moroccan society lacked gender equality: women's status in general was one of dependency and most interpretations of Islamic law differentiated between the social roles and status of men and women. Men, under most interpretations of Islamic law, assumed all positions of leadership and in family life were allowed to take up to four wives and to have as many concubines as they wished.[95] A woman could have sexual relations with only one man – her husband – and often the pair had never touched each other until the night of the wedding. These different gender roles, articulated in the religious ideology of enslavement and codified in legal treatises derived from Islamic law, mostly determined the life possibilities of male and female slaves. The phenomenon of concubinage could only be fulfilled by a slave because free women were legally entitled to the benefits of marriage before sexual relations could occur. Hence, the acceptance and practice of concubinage increased the demand for female slaves. Men were entitled to sexual rights over their female slaves,[96] but a female slave owner never had sexual rights over her male slave. In Islamic households, those who could afford it separated the living quarters of the males and females. All of the females of the household, including wives, domestic slaves, and concubines, resided in a part of the house called the *harem*. The only males allowed to enter the harem were adolescent children, other close family members, and eunuchs, who served specifically to guard or to provide domestic services to the residents of the harem. In the hierarchy of females, the mother of the male provider of the house had the highest status as a matriarchal figure, after which came the wife or wives. It is important to note that in practice polygyny existed only in a small percentage of households, usually among the wealthy. Often, race or color did figure into the positions, tasks, and status of servants and female slaves. For example, young light-skinned Circassian women were generally thought to be beautiful and were highly valued and ranked, but their numbers were few. Women of Ethiopian origin, known as *habashiyyat*, were also "renowned for their beauty and sexual temperament."[97] The majority of Moroccan domestic slaves in the harem were usually blacks from sub-Saharan Africa who performed domestic duties and other menial and hard tasks. Some enslaved women might not have

[95] Murray Gordon, *Slavery in the Arab world* (New York: New Amsterdam Books, 1989), 85. For more information see chapter 4 on sex and slavery in the Arab world.
[96] Notwithstanding Qur'anic injunctions to the contrary.
[97] Morderchai Abir, "The Ethiopian Slave Trade and its Relation to the Islamic World" in *Slaves and Slavery in Muslim Africa, edited by* John Ralph Willis, vol. 2 (Totowa: Frank Cass, 1985), 124.

been identified as slaves by outsiders because in some cases the female slaves shared family life – they ate with the family, were well dressed, and were educated according to their talents and to their duties. Almost all slaves quickly converted to Islam or were already Muslims, which was a grave contradiction and violation in the application of Islamic law.[98] Indeed, until 1912, the annual trans-Saharan trade continued to bring more enslaved blacks mainly from Bambara to many parts of Morocco, especially the south, for agricultural or domestic purposes. But it was not until 1923 that a circular signed by Urbain Blanc (délegué of the resident general in Morocco), was distributed among French officials declaring that the slave trade was abolished.[99] The trafficking of slaves was officially abolished, but officials were prohibited from interfering with households that had slaves.[100] How slaves were to be handled was set down in this official circular listed the following protocols:

1. In all cases where the controlling [colonial] authorities find a runaway slave, they should make sure, if he did not object, to see him immediately liberated of his servile condition, either voluntarily by his master or by the local [Islamic] authorities.
2. In the case of a male slave, the regulation will eventually be applied to his children. For women who have children, it has to be determined whether their masters consider the children theirs and in this case they will be free and legitimate or whether they were conceived by someone in the same slave condition.
3. The controlling authorities, who will continue to prohibit all public commerce of slaves, must make sure to block all legal proceedings by the local authorities, Muslim judges or notaries on this subject.[101]

These measures did not lead directly to an outright abolition of slavery. The protocols essentially reiterated, and, to their credit, enforced what was already found in Moroccan Islamic legal codes regarding slavery. The French colonial authorities were also reluctant to undertake proceedings

[98] See an-Nasiri, *al-Istiqsa'*, vol. 5, 133–134.
[99] It was the Residential Circular no. 17 S.G.P. of September 21, 1923 cited in Noël Maestracci, *Le Maroc Contemporain; Guide à l'usage de tous les Officiers et particulièrement à l'usage des Officiers des affaires indigènes et des Fonctionnaires du protectorat* (Paris: C. Lavauzelle, 1928), 164, but Joinville in "Note sur l'esclavage au Maroc," 12, gave a slightly different date: September 12, 1922.
[100] Maestracci, *Le Maroc Contemporain*, 164; Joinville, "Note sur l'esclavage au Maroc," 12.
[101] Ibid.; Ibid.

against Moroccans who owned slaves. The colonial authority thus gave tacit consent to slavery where slaves were already owned and used primarily for domestic purposes. Official action was undertaken only in cases of obvious excess and abuse, as implied by this 1950 French circular: "The Government [e.g., French colonial authority] is thus limited to take administrative measures against those aspects of slavery that shocked us the most."[102] As of 1935, the Moroccan royal establishment cooperated with the French authority to combat the horrors of clandestine sale of slaves. As a result, Ben Kiran, the slave broker in the city of Fez, was apprehended and sentenced by the Royal High Court to six months in prison.[103] Fatima Mernissi, a renowned Moroccan sociologist, in her memoir vividly recalled the oppression of two enslaved black females and the impact of the High Court. Yaya was a concubine of her grandfather living in a large farm in the area west of Fez, and Mina was a former slave living in her household. Speaking of the horrors of slavery, Mernissi wrote that Mina would say, "and when the slave traders were given prison sentences and fines, that slavery finally stopped. Only when the court steps in does violence end."[104] Mernissi was probably referring to slave merchants like the infamous Ben Kiran. In 1950, a French official's report, written by Lapanne Joinville about slavery in Morocco, stated:

Today we can no longer point to the existence of male slaves except among certain categories of the Sultan's servants and in the service of certain great lords of southern Morocco, among whom are both manual laborers and confidants. Their kind is disappearing. One can imagine that with the death of this present generation, they will be replaced with free men.[105]

Joinville also remarked that by 1950 the sources to acquire slaves were exhausted and it was impossible to prove the origin of "legal" capture. He insisted that "the quasi-majority of persons in servitude are Muslims from southern Morocco, victims of rapes and of kidnapping. These supposed slaves are nothing more than pseudo-slaves. In the state of uncertainty, one must grant the enslaved the presumption that they are of a free origin and one must return them to that state."[106]

It is, nevertheless, curious to note that the French colonial regime, which put so much emphasis on the abolition of slavery as one of the

[102] Joinville, "Note sur l'esclavage au Maroc," 11.
[103] Tahar Essafi, *La Marocaine: mœurs, condition sociale, évolution* (Marrakech: Imprimerie du Sud Marocain, 1935), 35.
[104] Mernissi, *Dreams of Trespass*, 165.
[105] Joinville, "Note sur l'esclavage au Maroc," 13.
[106] Ibid., 15.

principal justifications for its colonial enterprise, did not seek firmly to prohibit slavery except through procedural means. According to Lapanne Joinville, the French authorities were less audacious than Muslim scholars who attacked the principle of the right of ownership of human beings.[107] Indeed, Muslim scholars were instrumental in popularizing the abolition position. They started to push the position of the Protectorate. They maintained that the conditions of legal slavery were no longer present at their time.[108] Indeed, Moroccan voices against slavery preceded the Protectorate; for example, Ahmad an-Nasiri (1835–1897) was one of the most influential Moroccan historians who condemned his compatriots for the heinous acts they committed against blacks throughout the centuries. He wrote:

Even if you assume that some of them are pagans or belong to a religion other than Islam, nevertheless the majority of them today as in former times are Muslims, and judgment is made according to the majority. Again, even if you suppose that Muslims are not a majority, and that Islam and unbelief claim equal membership there, who among us can tell whether those brought here are Muslims or unbelievers? For the basic assumption in regard to the human species is freedom and lack of any cause for being enslaved. Whoever maintains the opposite is denying the basic principle.[109]

The growing force of the abolitionist movement influenced Moroccan jurists; certain among them did not hesitate to declare that slavery had disappeared.[110] Mernissi recorded, in her memoir on the Moroccan harem during the 1940s, the sentiment of the Moroccan nationalists who contributed to the disappearance of the practice of slavery among the burgeoning bourgeoisie. She wrote: "[G]randfather [Mernissi] was a nice man, but he bought slaves. It was the natural thing to do back then. Now he has changed, and like most of the notables in the big cities, he supports the nationalists' ideals, including respect for the individual, monogamy, the abolition of slavery, and so on."[111] The following report from Lapanne Joinville in 1950 captures some of the changes in attitudes and behaviors regarding slavery under the influence of the abolitionist activities:

I know of the personal case of a scholar from Rabat who, around 1925–1930, acquired a black slave having originally belonged to a governor of the Chiadma

[107] Ibid.
[108] Ibid.
[109] An-Nasiri, *al-Istiqsa'*, vol. 5, 131. English translation by Hunwick and Troutt Powell, *The African Diaspora*, 48.
[110] Joinville, 1950, 15.
[111] Mernissi. *Dreams of Trespass*, 36.

after changing hands six or seven times. Having doubts about the real condition of the slave, since he lacked the proof that testified to the condition of capture and unbelief, the single legal source of slavery, he hesitated, he said, to have sexual relations with her which might lead him to the sin of fornication. He thus freed her, and married her legally and had three children with her. He had, at the same time, another legitimate white woman with whom he also had children. In 1944, he repudiated his black woman, but because she had nowhere to go, she is still living with him as a domestic and continues to raise his children as well as those of the other wife.[112]

This text, however, implicitly reflects an established social order based on race. The man in the report exploited the labor and the sexuality of his black wife and after he repudiated her he still used her as a domestic servant rearing his children and those of his white wife. Although this black woman was free, she knew the limitations of her resources and was forced to navigate within the constraints of the male-dominated culture. But not all enslaved people had the same opportunity of social mobility as did concubines. The majority of slaves were black women used as domestics in large households throughout many Moroccan cities. According to Lapanne, Arab and Berber Moroccans, especially the people of Fez, were fond of black maids.[113] But the mentality of the urban bourgeoisie vis-à-vis legal slavery and the condition of domestic servility gradually changed from a legal status to an inherited social condition. Lapanne stated that "A certain number of slaves, above all women, rather than take advantage of the possibility to claim their freedom choose to remain within the Moroccan families where they find food and lodging."[114] Indeed, they were passed down from generation to generation in domestic service, from one family to another, without being declared as property in the inheritance will. The label that came to be used for these people in domestic service is "*khdem*,"[115] meaning house servants.[116] In rural areas, especially in southern Morocco, blacks and especially the Haratin provided the crucial labor in agricultural production. These Haratin tended Berber and Arab-controlled oases and were often forced into a caste system working as sharecroppers called *khammasin*. They paid one-fifth of what they produced to the landowners and were prohibited, according

---

[112] Joinville, "Note sur l'esclavage au Maroc," 15–16.

[113] Ibid., 9.

[114] Ibid., 13.

[115] *Khdem* is a local variation of *khadam*.

[116] Rita Aouad Bedaoul, "«Esclavage» et situation des «noirs» au Maroc dans la première moitié du XXe siècle," in Les relations transsahariennes à l'époque contemporaine, edited by Laurence Marfaing and Steffen Wippel (Paris: Karthala, 2004), 351.

to customary laws, from owning land.[117] The French occupation imposed a new capitalist mode of production in Morocco. The capitalist system altered the Moroccan social structures by transforming local human labor power into a class of wage earners. The creation of a wage-earning system influenced the migration of blacks from southern Morocco to the big cities, resulting in the eventual emergence of slums. Consequently, the number of slaves continually dwindled and the institution eventually died a natural death.

The slave trade was never abolished by a *dahir* or a royal decree from the royal authority of Morocco, but rather ended as a consequence of the French colonial occupation and the introduction of the capitalist mode of production into Morocco. The memory of slavery is still a personal issue among the descendants of enslaved people living in the rural south of Morocco, in places such as the Tata and Aqqa oases. In the words of as-Sudani, the grandson of an enslaved man who belonged to a rich family in southern Morocco:[118]

This ambivalence [in talking about slavery in Morocco] is further compounded by a deep upwelling of frustration at the beliefs and attitudes shaped by the historical legacy of slavery and injustice to black people. Yet, there is still a fear of stirring up the ashes, lest they would start a fire that might hurt me and my nation, instead of helping it to overcome the scars of the past. Yes, slavery existed, especially in the south of Morocco, for a long time, and into the twentieth century. Of course, it has faded slowly, but in the beginning of the century people were still bought and sold. The majority of African people who were enslaved were Muslims, including my own grandfather and the "guard" slaves in my village. One of my uncles still remembers the names of twenty-five slaves still owned by rich white Berbers.[119]

Mr. as-Sudani thus confirms vividly what was inflicted upon his people, upon his family and, consequently, upon him personally – a crime without punishment. And for Moroccans collectively, it constitutes a history we should not forget.

The memory of slavery is still passed on through songs performed by the Gnawa group: a spiritual order of a traditionally black Muslim people who are descendants of enslaved sub-Saharan West-Africans. The

---

[117] Mezzine, *Le Tafilalt*, 254–255. For information on these customary laws see pages 240 to 259.
[118] The family is that of Shaykh Ma' al-'Aynayn. Ma' al-'Aynayn, a famous religious scholar and anticolonial leader, was born around 1830 in Mauritania. In the early 1890s, he moved with a large number of slaves to live in the south of Morocco, where he died in 1910.
[119] This is an excerpt of my interview with as-Sudani in June 2001.

Gnawa have retained many of the rituals and beliefs of their ancestors and express them through their unique musical traditions. Songs dealing with the Gnawa's origins, integration, and cultural syncretism are still performed. Many Gnawa musician masters in Essaouira and Marrakesh point out that blacks occupy a marginal position in Moroccan society as a result of their past as an enslaved people, a subject to which the next chapter turns.

8

The Gnawa and the Memory of Slavery

The most important single element of Morocco's folk culture is its music [...]. The entire history and mythology of the people is clothed in song.[1]

Paul Bowles

It is difficult to define the initial ethnic identity of the Gnawa, but it originally developed in reference to blacks from West Africa – from Senegal to Chad and from Mali in the north to Nigeria in the south. The term *gnawa* refers to black people from West Africa as well as their religious/spiritual order and musical style. In the case of ethnicity, sources consistently agree that the Moroccan Gnawa were originally black slaves freed over time under various circumstances, as discussed in Chapter 3. Over many generations beginning with their initial forced presence in Morocco, the Gnawa created acceptance within the Moroccan social landscape while at the same time maintaining their ethnic and group solidarity. The diaspora of black West Africans in Morocco, the majority of whom were forcefully transported across the Sahara and sold in different parts of Morocco, shares some important traits with the African trans-Atlantic diaspora, but differs at the same time. Gnawa music and its spiritual order are visible mainly where black people live in large numbers, large enough to form a distinctive community like those found in Marrakesh, Essaouira, Meknes, and Fez. These cities are known to have had slave

---

A version of this chapter has been published: Chouki El Hamel, "Constructing a Diasporic Identity: Tracing the Origins of Gnawa Spiritual Group in Morocco," *Journal of African History*, 49 (2), 2008, 241–260.

[1] Paul Bowles, *Their Heads Are Green and Their Hands Are Blue* (New York: Random House, 1963), 97.

markets connected to the trans-Saharan slave trade. However, even in remote areas where blacks migrated in relatively small numbers, they founded communal centers where their culture is celebrated. This culture is officially and publicly associated with slavery, hence these centers as well as Gnawa public performances represent both a commemorative site and the memory of slavery.[2]

Of all the musical and mystic traditions found in Morocco, the roots of Gnawa music are probably the most obscure. The study of the Gnawa is instructive because of their relation to slavery and its legacy in Morocco. In this chapter I attempt to reconstruct the historical odyssey of the Gnawa in Morocco and their fascinating integration into the Moroccan social landscape, an integration that has allowed them to preserve elements of their culture and forge a new identity within the dominant Arabo-Berber culture. This chapter focuses not only on the struggle of the Gnawa in their subaltern relationship with the ruling institutions, but also brings out how the Gnawa, as a marginal group, had a profound influence on the religion, rituals, and music of the greater Arabo-Berber culture. In the latter part of this chapter I will look at some work on slavery in the antebellum American South to present relevant analogies.

The best-known genre of music in Morocco comes from the Andalusian legacy; it is regarded as the classical Andalusian music,[3] reflecting Morocco's historic relationship with Spain. Andalusian music is recognized as a Moroccan national music and enjoys wide popularity mainly among middle and upper classes and especially in cities historically connected with Muslim Spain. Another musical genre stems from the Berbers (or Imazighen), which is an older traditional music and tends to be more rural, whereas the Andalusian genre is more urban.[4] The Sephardic population has also contributed to Morocco's musical heritage, but unfortunately the folksongs from the Jewish communities in Morocco are vanishing because most of Morocco's Jewish population has relocated to Israel. Another important but often neglected genre of Moroccan music is that of the Gnawa. Although the Gnawa are now fully integrated into

---

[2] On memories of slavery see Rosalind Shaw, *Memories of the Slave Trade: Ritual and the Historical Imagination in Sierra Leone* (Chicago: University of Chicago Press, 2002).

[3] It is also known colloquially as *al-Ala* (the instrument) as opposed to *Sama'*, which is a musical genre using only human voices. For more information on Andalusian music see: Ahmed Aydoun, *Musiques du Maroc* (Casablanca: EDDIF, 2001).

[4] The Berbers usually refer to themselves linguistically and ethnically as *Imazighen*. The term *Berber* is a foreign word most likely of Roman origin.

Moroccan society and represent a symbol of confluence of cultures, they retain a cultural and a social distinctiveness.

As a religious or spiritual order, the Gnawa are traditionally a mystic order, and this marks their exclusiveness within Islam. As a style of music, the ancestral memory of a displaced and enslaved people brought to Morocco has been preserved in their songs and dances.[5] The religious and spiritual components of Gnawa practice are likewise expressed through their music. Although the Gnawa have adopted the Arabo-Berber-Islamic form of social identification, their music represents a fascinating syncretism and a mixture of resistance to enslavement, the rigors of forced migration, and the challenges of integration into their new social landscape. In the discussion that follows, I will elaborate on each of the three meanings of Gnawa in turn, with the caveat that in the case of Gnawa as a religious spiritual order, and Gnawa as a style of music associated with this order, there is a good deal of overlap between these meanings, for they cannot be regarded as entirely separable. Indeed, in many ways they inform one another. By way of conclusion, I look at how Gnawa music has attained a degree of "pop" status in the contemporary Moroccan social landscape.

The Gnawa are a diasporic culture and one finds artistic and spiritual parallels between the Gnawa order and other spiritual black groups in Africa: the Stambouli in Tunisia,[6] the Sambani in Libya, the Bilali in Algeria, the Zar cult in Sudan, and the Bori among the Hausa of Northern Nigeria and Niger.[7] Outside Africa, a parallel can be seen in the case of the Candomble in Salvador, Brazil, where the African enslaved population found their beliefs in African spirits compatible with local beliefs and, with the introduction of Catholicism, created a syncretic religious form while still under the horrors of servitude. The Vodoun or Voodoo

---

[5] On the connection of Gnawa to memory, Bilal, and Islam, see Earle Waugh, *Memory, Music, and Religion: Morocco's Mystical Chanters* (Columbia: University of South Carolina Press, 2005), 107–120.

[6] Sophie Ferchiou, "The Possession Cults of Tunisia: A Religious System Functioning as a System of Reference and a Social Field for Performing Actions," in I. M. Lewis, Ahmed Al-Sa, and Sayyid Hurreiz, eds., *Women's Medicine: The Zar-Bori Cult in Africa and Beyond* (Edinburgh: Edinburgh University Press, 1991).

[7] Among the scholars who have written excellent books discussing the impact of Islam on the cults of possession: Janice Patricia Boddy, *Wombs and Alien Spirits: Women, Men, and the Zar Cult in Northern Sudan* (Madison: University of Wisconsin Press, 1989); Adeline Marie Masquelier, *Prayer Has Spoiled Everything: Possession, Power, and Identity in an Islamic Town of Niger* (Durham: Duke University Press, 2001); and A. J. N. Tremearne, *The Ban of the Bori: Demons and Demon-Dancing in West and North Africa* (London: Cass, 1968).

religion practiced in Caribbean countries is also a mix of Roman Catholic ritual elements and traditional rituals from Dahomey.[8] The syncretism and the similarities in the artistic, spiritual, and scriptural (e.g., related to Abrahamic written traditions) representations seem to reflect a shared experience of many African diasporic groups. As in these other spiritual traditions, the belief in possession and trance is crucial to Gnawa religious life and their music has served a patterned function in this belief and practice. The Gnawa music embodies their specific historic and cultural memories celebrated and invoked in songs, dances, and musical chants, all of which are claimed and used by the Gnawa as the means to access the spiritual realm. Although present-day Gnawa musicians speak only Arabic and/or Berber, some West African religious words and phrases do survive even though their meaning is lost.

The Origins of the Gnawa

The term *gnawa* refers particularly to physical color, from which a good deal of insight into the origin of the Gnawa can be inferred. Historically, at least since the twelfth century, it means "the black people." Some scholars, such as Viviana Pâques[9] and J.-M. Lesage, argue that the term *gnawa* derives from medieval Ghana, a Sahelian kingdom north of Mali in the eighth century through the twelfth century, as much linguistically as historically.[10] But this connection seems unlikely, as J. D. Fage explains, "if only on the ground that the pronunciation of the initial letter of Ghana, which is the Arabic *ghain*, is more nearly 'rh'[11] than 'gh.'"[12] Thus, in Arabic, Ghana and the adjectives Ghani or Ghanawi are different from Gnawi, Knawi, or Jnawi.

Another possible etymology for *gnawa* may derive from the influence of sixteenth-century Moroccan historian Leo Africanus, who used

[8] For more information, see Yvonne Daniel, *Dancing Wisdom: Embodied Knowledge in Haitian Vodou, Cuban Yoruba, and Bahian Candomblé* (Urbana: University of Illinois Press, 2005); and Margarite Fernández Olmos and Lizabeth Paravisini-Gebert, *Sacred Possessions: Vodou, Santería, Obeah, and the Caribbean* (New Brunswick: Rutgers University Press, 1997).
[9] Viviana Pâques, "Le monde des Gnawa," in Jean Poirier et François Raveau, eds., *L'autre et l'ailleurs: Hommage à Roger Bastide* (Paris: Berger-Levrault, 1976), 171.
[10] Jean-Marie Lesage, "Gnawa" in *Encyclopédie Berbère* (Aix-en-Provence, France, 1999), XXI, 3165.
[11] Something like the French "r."
[12] J. D. Fage, *Ghana: A Historical Interpretation* (Madison: University of Wisconsin Press, 1959), 39–40.

the words *Jinni* or *Jenne* to refer to Guinea: "This kingdom called by
the African merchants Gheneoa, by its inhabitants Genni and by the
Portuguese and by anyone among Europeans who knows these regions as
Ghinea."[13] The term was adopted by the Portuguese and appeared perva-
sively as Guinea on European maps dating from the fourteenth century.[14]
Jenne (also spelled Djenné) is a city situated in present-day Mali, on the
Bani, a tributary of the Niger River. The seventeenth-century Timbuktu
historian, 'Abd ar-Rahman as-Sa'di, believed the foundation of Jenne to
be around A.D. 767.[15] But it is more likely that Leo Africanus conflated
Guinea and Jenne, assuming they were one and the same. Hence, linguistically speaking there is no connection between Gnawa and Jenne.[16]

Linguistically, the meaning of the term *gnawa* most likely derives from
the Berber word *gnawi*, which is connected with skin color. It means
"black man" in contrast to the light-skinned Berber. In the Sanhaja
language (or Zenaga), *gnawa* derives from a word root *gnw*, meaning
"black."[17] The "g" sound as in "goal" does not exist in Arabic, hence the
use of the equivalent sound of, usually, "j" or "k" and less commonly "q."
Therefore, Arab writers or scribes transcribed *gnawi* as *knawi* or *jnawi*
(sometimes vocalized as *kanawi* or *janawi*) interchangeably. This word
could be the origin of the name Guinea because *akal n-iguinamen* (sing.
aguinaw) in Berber means the "land of the black men," synonymous
with the Arabic term *bilad as-sudan*, which means "land of the black
people".[18] According to René Basset (1855–1924), a French specialist in
North African languages, in Algeria one calls "Guennaouyah" the languages of black peoples in general and in Jabal Nafusa (northwest of
Libya) *agnaou* means black.[19] It is interesting to note that there are other
words that derive from the same root *gnw* and that have different import,

---

[13] Leo Africanus, *Description*, tome 2, 464. The Arabic translation, vol. 2, 162.
[14] See for instance the sixteenth-century Portuguese explorer Duarte Pereira, *Esmeraldo*,
    2–3.
[15] As-Sa'di, *Tarikh as-Sudan*, 12 of the Arabic text and 23 of the translation.
[16] The two terms did not mean the same thing. Italian scholar Giovanni Lorenzo Anania
    (born in 1545 and died between 1607 and 1609) reported that Genni was the capital of
    Guinea. Dierk Lange and Silvio Berthoud, "L'intérieur de l'Afrique Occidentale d'après
    Giovanni Lorenzo Anania (XVIe siècle)," *Cahiers d'Histoire Mondiale* (Neuchâtel,
    Switzerland: Editions de la Baconnière 1972), 14 (2), 327.
[17] According to René Basset, "nègre, gennoui كنوي, pl. gennoun كنون of the root G N." See
    René Basset, *Mission au Sénégal* (Paris: E. Leroux, 1909), 147.
[18] See Maurice Delafosse, "Relations du Maroc et du Soudan à travers les âges,"
    Hespéris-Tamuda (Rabat: Éditions Techniques Nord-Africaines, 1924), vol. 4, 155–156.
[19] René Basset, "*Les noms des métaux et des couleurs en Berbère*," in Mémoires de la
    Société de linguistique de Paris (Paris: Impr. Nationale, 1895), tome 9, 87.

for instance, in the Zenaga language the word *ignwi* (pl. *guinawn*) derives from the same root *gnw* and means Sérère and Wolof (ethnic groups of Senegal).[20] Also, in the Tuareg language, *iguinawin* means "a mass of dark clouds."[21] Nevertheless, all these meanings have one thing in common: a dark complexion.

Historically, the oldest evidence that indicates the origin of the term *gnawa* comes from Arab historian az-Zuhri, who wrote in the 1140s. He noted that *janawa* (or *kanawa* in another copy) designated the land of the blacks, whose capital was Ghana. He placed the territory of Janawa, which represented the southern termini of Moroccan caravans, at the end of the land of the Sanhaja (Berber people).[22] Az-Zuhri possibly collected his information while he was in Andalusia from the Sanhaja or Masmuda people. These Berbers of the Saharan desert had an early (pre-Arab conquest) encounter with the Sahelian and sub-Saharan people of West Africa because of their shared proximity. Additional evidence comes from a twelfth-century Islamic legal scholar, 'Ali al-Jaziri (d. 1189), who wrote a legal document in the form of a model contract of manumission of an enslaved person: "A person so and so manumitted his slave so and so al-Janawi or ar-Rumi with the description such and such and this manumission is definite."[23] Yaqut al-Hamawi (1179–1229), a Muslim geographer, used the spelling *kinawa*, but may have confused the term to refer to the Berbers who occupied the region adjacent to the land of Ghana with the ethnically different black population that lived in Ghana.[24]

Hasan ibn al-Qattan, a Moroccan historian who lived around the middle of the thirteenth century, reported that in a battle of the Almohads against the Almoravids in Aghmat (a Berber town in southern Morocco east of Marrakesh) in 1130, three thousand blacks from Jnawa were killed.[25] Ibn al-Qattan's historical reference gives little detail, but those blacks killed in the battle were presumably soldiers in the service of the Almoravids.

Another piece of evidence comes from the Portuguese during their fifteenth-century Atlantic seafaring that referred to black West Africa

[20] Basset, *Mission au Sénégal*, 237.

[21] Charles de Foucauld, *Dictionnaire Touareg-Français* (Paris: Imprimerie Nationale de France, 1951), tome I, 458.

[22] Muhammad Az-Zuhri in Hopkins and Levtzion (eds.), *Corpus*, 98.

[23] 'Ali Al-Jaziri, *al-Maqsad al-Mahmud fi Takhlis al-'Uqud* (Rabat: Bibliothèque Royale, ms. 5221), 230.

[24] Yaqut al-Hamawi in Hopkins and Levtzion (eds.), *Corpus*, 173.

[25] Hasan ibn al-Qattan, *Nuzum al-Juman li-Tartib ma Salafa min Akhbar az-Zaman*, annotated by Mahmud 'Ali Makki (Beirut: Dar al-Gharb al-Islami, 1990), 158.

Black Morocco

using a descriptive term for blacks that likely derived from their encounter with the Berber people. In the words of fifteenth-century Portuguese explorer Gomes Eannes de Azurara, "Now the people of this green land are wholly black, and hence this is called Land of the Negroes, or Land of Guinea. Wherefore also the men and women thereof are called 'Guineas,' as if one were to say 'Black Men.'"[26] Clearly, "Guineas" in this passage corresponds to the Berber word *guinwi*, which has the same meaning as black. In Western Europe, Guinea did indeed come to be associated with black West Africa. Olaudah Equiano (circa 1745–1797), wrote: "That part of Africa, known by the name of Guinea, to which the trade of slaves is carried on, extends along the coast above 3400 miles, from Senegal to Angola."[27]

In the writings of a seventeenth-century Islamic legal scholar, Muhammad al-Masmudi, concerning some legal issues in a model contract of manumission of an enslaved person in Sijilmasa (an old city in the south of Morocco, presently in ruin), substantively similar to that written by 'Ali al-Jaziri (cited earlier), states, "A person so and so manumitted his slave al-Kanawi (or al-Janawi in another copy), with a specified name and specified characteristics. This manumission is licensed and is an accomplished fact."[28] Hence, according to these Islamic texts, Janawi or Kanawi (e.g., Gnawi) were used interchangeably as a generic term to designate a black from West Africa.

My analysis so far points to the conclusion that the origin of the name Gnawa derives from the writings of North Africans who used the designation Gnawa as generally referring to blacks from West Africa. *Gnawa*, as a term that came to describe a diverse group from West Africa transplanted by forced migration into Morocco, lumped together in one category: a fictional "ethnic black" group that had no differentiated ethnic or linguistic reality. Gradually, the Gnawa as a distinct ethnic group turned their marginalized status into a collective identity. Yet the oral history preserved in Gnawa songs contains names of West African peoples and places that confirm their diverse origins. For instance one particular song with a refrain using the phrase "*Lalla Yamma*" ("Oh, our Mother") to stress a feeling of melancholy, recalls the different ancestors of the Gnawa: Sudani ("Oh, our Mother"), Fulani ("Oh,

[26] De Azurara, *The Chronicle of the Discovery*, 177.
[27] Equiano, *The Interesting Narrative*, 32.
[28] Muhammad al-Masmudi, *al-Watha'iq as-Sijilmasiyya*, edited by Musatafa an-Naji (Rabat: Markaz Ihya' at-Turath al-Maghribi, 1988), 28.

our Mother"), Bambarawi ("Oh, our Mother"), and Hausawi ("Oh, our Mother").[29] We can thus name among the ancestors of the black Moroccans of today the Soninke, the Bambara, the Fulani, and the Hausa. Hence, the Gnawa as a spiritual and a musical group became a quasi-corporate community that absorbed and empowered all black participants from different ethnic backgrounds, old as well as newcomers such as in the case of the Gania family members who live in the city of Essaouira and provided me with valuable information on Gnawa oral traditions.[30]

The Gnawa's Agency and Impact

Relations between Morocco and black West Africa, two regions separated by a sea of sand, historically shared a remarkable continuity, given that a dominant aspect of that continuity was the slave trade. Historically, as a racialized minority, the Gnawa suffered much discrimination and injustice at the hands of the Arab-Berber majority within the regions that the Gnawa inhabited. Gradually, enslaved black people were freed either by manumission, by running away, or because their masters were forced to grant them freedom under different circumstances. After many generations, these freed black slaves eventually formed their own families and communities, such as those of the Gnawa mystic order.

Although the Gnawa adopted Islam, they did not totally abandon their animist or West African religious traditions; they continued to observe ritual possession.[31] They combined Islamic belief with pre-Islamic African traditions, whether local or sub-Saharan West African. Gnawa "spirit possession" practices were not fundamentally outside of standard Moroccan Islamic Sufi practices, because, first, the notion of a spirit world is accepted in Islam, namely angels and *jinns* (spiritual beings) are basic to Islamic literature as well as practice, and, second, most Sufi orders sought a form of spirit possession through study and meditation.

[29] Interview with Mokhtar Gania, Essaouira, June 20, 2005. For more information see Viviana Pâques, *La religion des esclaves: recherches sur la confrérie marocaine des Gnawa* (Bergamo : Moretti et Vitali editori, 1991), 263–271.
[30] The head of this family was Boubker Gania (1927–2000). His father was kidnapped from West Africa and sold as a slave in Morocco.
[31] For more information see the work of Bertrand Hell, a French anthropologist who specializes in spirit possession mainly in Morocco. I refer, in particular, to his article entitled: "L'expérience du corps et des émotions dans les cultes de possession" in Ysé Tardan-Masquelier, ed., *Le Corps médiateur* (Paris: Dervy, 2006), 87–106.

Black Morocco

The Gnawa also use music as a crucial part of their rituals. Music is not outside of standard Moroccan Islamic Sufi practices, although the official Islamic discourse insists on the distractive effects music has on the sacred text, nonetheless there is a kind of music in the delivery of the *azan* (the Islamic summons to prayer), the recitation of the Qur'an, and other litanies. In all Moroccan Sufi orders, music is a fundamental part of worship in order to be in motion toward God. For Gnawa, the training of the soul is done through worship, communion, incantation, and hearing.

The Gnawa do not have a holy place or a sanctuary (*zawiya*) where the master spiritual founder (*wali*) would be buried and to which they can be linked according to the model of the Sufi brotherhoods. To accommodate their needs, they usually used other Sufi orders (*turuq* plural of *tariqa*) as a model. Wherever they resided, they chose the local holy person or persons to whom they performed ritual visits (*ziyyara*).[32] There are other significant differences between Gnawa practice and Sufism. For the Gnawa, the spirit world is inhabited by ancestral spirits who, among other spiritual creatures, can be used for either good or evil purposes. Ancestors are believed to act as intermediaries between the living and the supreme God, and the Gnawa communicate with their ancestors through prayer and sacrifice. The spirit world is also invoked through special ceremonies in which drumming, clapping, the sound of the castanets, and dances were designed to enlist the aid of ancestral saints. Thus, human beings were protected from evil spirits and other predicaments such as illness or misfortune. These rites often involve spectacular trances in order to contact ancestral spirits and appeal to them for their assistance.[33]

After their initial conversion to Islam, while probably still in their country of origin, the Gnawa adopted Bilal ibn Rabah (died in Damascus circa 641), as their ancestor and patron saint.[34] Bilal was the first black person to convert to Islam and became a companion of the Prophet Muhammad. Hence, the Gnawa asserted another line of charisma beside the Sharif status. Claiming Bilal as a patrilineal figure not only emphasized the nobility of belonging to Bilal but also legitimized their identity in Islamic terms. Conscious of their difference and their blackness, they chose Bilal, a

---

[32] Abdelhafid Chlyeh, *Les Gnaoua du Maroc: Itinéraires initiatiques, transe et possession* (Casablanca: Editions Le Fennec, 1998), 17–32. Chlyeh uses the word *pilgrimage*. This is not accurate, because pilgrimage (*hajj* in Arabic) is reserved specifically for the performance of the fifth pillar of Islam: pilgrimage to Mecca.

[33] For more information about ritual practices of the Gnawa see the work of Pâques, *La religion des esclaves.*

[34] Bilal is also discussed in Chapter 3.

black man, as agnate.[35] Bilal was a special man whose special relationship with the Prophet brought him baraka (divine blessing).[36] Furthermore, it is reported in the *Sahih* of the traditionist al-Bukhari (d. 870) that the Prophet once said that he heard Bilal's footsteps in Paradise.[37] The Gnawa have constructed their Islamic identity by claiming a privileged status among Muslims – they converted to Islam even before Quraysh, the tribe to which Muhammad belonged. By emphasizing this early conversion, the Gnawa deny the stigma of slave origin. Hence, it is not surprising to find the name of Bilal in many Gnawa songs.[38] Additionally, to honor their spiritual and emotional link with Bilal and Islam, the Gnawa built a unique shrine in Essaouira dedicated to Bilal: the Zawiya Sidna Bilal, a place to celebrate their culture. Bilal is the symbol of the dialectic between diaspora and homeland. Given that Bilal's burial place is not in Morocco, but rather in Damascus (Syria), the Gnawa also venerate the local holy persons to whom they perform ritual visits. The creativity of the Gnawa is fascinating – they navigated between conformity, resistance, and syncretism within the Arabo-Islamic cultural standards.

Bilal was likely known to the Manding people of West Africa as early as the eleventh century. Muslims traders who inhabited Kumbi Saleh, the capital of Ghana, related narratives of the life of the Prophet and his companions in their sermons, highlighting the story of Bilal as a device to appeal to black people in order to establish trust. As Islam took root in the courts of West Africa, the Manding creatively adopted many elements of Islamic literature to serve their political agenda. The Keita dynasty, the history of which was well chronicled by their griots, a professional group of oral historians, used the case of a black man tortured by unbelievers and liberated by a Muslim as a source of black Islamic pride. Although ancestry from Bilal is difficult to prove, it nonetheless represents the importance of lineage for political stature among the Manding people.

---

[35] Viviana Pâques, "The Gnawa of Morocco: The Derdeba Ceremony," in Wolfgang Weissleder, ed., *The Nomadic Alternative: Modes and Models of Interaction in the African-Asian Deserts and Steppes* (The Hague: Mouton, 1978), 319–329. She describes the Gnawa as "sons of Sidna Bilal" and as masters of possession rituals. She gives an interesting analysis of the symbolic elements of the Gnawa spiritual order.

[36] On Bilal, see W. 'Arafat, "Bilal" in *The Encyclopedia of Islam*. He is also discussed in Chapter 3.

[37] Al-Bukhari, *Sahih*, 214. It is important to note that Bilal was also a transmitter of the Prophet Muhammad's reports.

[38] Such as the following lyrics:
Father Bilal man of God
The Prophet's servant, father Bilal.

The griots were responsible for preserving the history of the Mali empire. They composed the epic of Sundiata Keita (d. circa 1255), the founder of the Mali empire; they traced his family lineage back to Bilali Bounama[39] or Bilal ibn Rabah whose eldest son "left the Holy City and came to settle in Mali."[40] In the Manding oral traditions, the Keita family founded the first dynasty of the Mali empire in the thirteenth century, claiming descent from Bilal in order to legitimize its rule through an Islamic identity.[41]

Ibn Battuta (1304–1368), famed for his historical travel accounts, wrote about the social status and musical function of the Mandé bards (griots or Jeli) during his visit to Mali in 1352–1353. Griots were also storytellers, praise singers, and master musicians.[42] The use of musical instruments and verses celebrating the legendary exploits of historical figures gave the griots considerable artistic status. The story of Bilal and the use of musical instruments, rhythms, and lyrics are clearly present in the culture of the Gnawa in Morocco. Indeed, the Gnawa lyrics emphasize their link with their Manding heritage. The Africanist scholar, Thomas Hale, argues that one finds a strong referential relation between the words *gnawa* and *griot*: "The word *agenaou*, so deeply imbedded in the intertwined cultures of the North West African region, was most likely a step in the process of linguistic change that began with *ghana* and went on to *gnawa*, *agenaou*, *guineo*, and *guiriot* to produce *griot*."[43]

The great French abolitionist and human rights activist Henri Grégoire (1750–1831) compared the West African griots to the French *troubadours*, the German *minnesingers*, and the Scottish *minstrels*.[44] Grégoire's reference was from notes made by Sylvain Meinrad Xavier de Golbéry (1742–1822), a French traveler to West Africa. De Golbéry observed that griots were men and women and were poets and musicians. He reported that the female griots played as important a role in the production of

---

[39] It is a Mandé pronunciation of ben Hamama. Hamama was his mother.

[40] Niane, *Sundiata*, 2.

[41] See David C. Conrad, "Islam in the Oral Traditions of Mali: Bilali and Surakata," *The Journal of African History* 26, no. 1 (1985), 33–49.

[42] On the culture of the griots, bards or *jeliw* (sing. *jeli*) among the Manding people of West Africa, see the interesting article by David C. Conrad, "Oral tradition & perceptions of history from the Manding peoples of West Africa" in Emmanuel Akyeampong, ed. *Themes in West Africa's History* (Athens: Ohio University Press 2006), 73–96. See also Tal Tamari, "The Development of Caste Systems in West Africa," *The Journal of African History*, 32 (1991): 221–250.

[43] Thomas A. Hale, "From the Griot of Roots to the Roots of Griot: A New Look at the Origins of a Controversial African Term for Bard," *Oral Tradition*, 12/2 (1997): 258.

[44] Henri Grégoire, *On the Cultural Achievements of Negroes*, translated by Thomas Cassirer and Jean-François Brière (Amherst: University of Massachusetts Press, 1996), 78.

culture as the male griots, "[t]he griotes are the female jesters; they are very numerous, and not so amiable as the Almehs of Egypt; like them, however, they sing histories, dance, narrate amusing adventures, make astrological calculations, and they are likewise the agents of concupiscent love."[45] However, the study of female griots has not received the same attention as has the study of male griots. Thomas A. Hale, one of the few scholars who attempted to remedy this gap, noted that "[t]he paucity of scholarship on griottes in particular and women performers in general seems to be symptomatic in a larger sense of the basic gender bias that has marked much social science research by scholars trained in the West, African and non-African."[46] The Gnawa as a whole have received even less scholarly attention, until recently mainly in the fields of ethnography or musicology and as a focus of tourist attraction. The lack of female Gnawa public presence stems from gender division – the external Gnawa activities are dominated by male Gnawa and the internal ones are a female affair.

The lack of primary written sources concerning the Gnawa makes the historian's task difficult in tracing an accurate history of this fascinating people. It is only from fragmentary primary records that I was able to assemble this description of the Gnawa people; this situation was made more difficult because Arab Muslim scholars avoided writing about the rituals of animal sacrifice, spirit possession, and mystical trances. Even *The Encyclopedia of Islam*, one of the more reliable sources about the world of Islam, has no entry on the Gnawa. Islamic orders that include such practices were considered heretical and a deviation from the Sunna (the right path of the Prophet Muhammad) or at best a folkloric rite and therefore dismissed altogether from any local scholarly inquiry. Fatima Mernissi, a Moroccan sociologist, in her book on the Moroccan harem during the 1940s, reported that Moroccan nationalists looked down at these trance rituals and considered them un-Islamic.[47] 'Abd al-Karim Gallab went further, portraying

---

[45] Sylvain Meinrad Xavier de Golbéry, *Travels in Africa, Performed by Silvester Mainrad Xavier Golberry, in the Western Parts of That Vast Continent: Containing Various Important Discoveries*, translated by William Mudford (London: Jones and Bumford, 1808), 297.

[46] Thomas A. Hale, *Griots and Griottes: Masters of Words and Music* (Bloomington: Indiana University Press, 1998), 218. Hale uses the French gender-specific term *griottes*. Recently, some scholars have started to fill the gap. See for instance Raphaël Ndiaye, *La place de la femme dans les rites au Sénégal* (Dakar: Nouvelles Editions africaines, 1986); and the great scholarly work on Gnawa by Deborah Kapchan, *Traveling Spirit Masters: Moroccan Gnawa Trance and Music in the Global Marketplace* (Middletown: Wesleyan University Press, 2007).

[47] Mernissi, *Dreams of Trespass*, 159.

blacks in the perception of slaveholders in the city of Fez in the 1950s not
only as a different and inferior racial category but as the superstitious cultural other. Hence the slaveholders allowed their servants and concubines
to attend Gnawa activities, which they perceived as witchcraft.[48] English
anthropologist Nina Epton, during her fieldwork in Morocco in the 1950s,
remarked that Moroccans "prized black women as concubines and black
men as soldiers and bodyguards, but they resolutely ignore the negro world
of superstitions."[49] The historian must resort to ethnographical studies and
Gnawa oral sources to reconstruct the historical background behind the
formation and meaning of the Gnawa spiritual order.

   Another way to recover the opaque history of the Gnawa is to trace
their cultural practices and beliefs among other spiritual orders and
brotherhoods. The Gnawa have influenced Berber or Arab mystic orders
and brotherhoods, as can be seen in the case of the 'Isawiyya (sixteenth
century) and Hamdushiyya (seventeenth century). These brotherhoods
added new elements to the usual Sufi devotional rituals, such as trances
and contacts with spirits, most likely influenced by contact with the
Gnawa order. Curiously, these Zawaya and other Sufi Berber and Arabic
orders have been far more socially accepted within the regions where they
are found than that of the Gnawa. Among Muslim intellectuals, these
brotherhoods, including the Gnawa, are considered an inferior form of
Sufism – a cult influenced by pagan black traditions and embraced mostly
by lower-class people with little or no literacy and learning. The association of Gnawa with slavery and sub-Saharan traditions was a prejudice
that blinded local scholars to the merits of Gnawa contributions to and
influence on the rich cultural traditions of Morocco. Viviana Pâques, an
ethnologist who has written extensively on the Gnawa, says that dismissing the influence of the Gnawa:

is a serious mistake, because their cosmogonic system is not different from the
other brotherhoods' systems; regarding Gnawa practices, they have greatly influenced other brotherhoods, who at the end of their ceremonial songs and dances,
add, for example like the 'Isawiyya brotherhood, something from the Gnawa
such as the veils of colors characteristic of their mystical journey.[50]

English anthropologist Edward Westermarck (1862–1939), after
spending seven years conducting fieldwork in Morocco between 1898

[48] Ghallab, *Dafanna al-Madi*, 1966, 56–70.
[49] Nina Epton, *Saints and Sorcerers* (London: Cassell, 1958), 4.
[50] Viviana Pâques, " Couleurs et Génies au Maghreb," in Abdelhafid Chlyeh (ed.), *L'univers des Gnaoua* (Casablanca: Éditions La Pensée sauvage, 1999), 60. See also Pâques, *La religion des esclaves*.

and 1926, observed and speculated that "this influence [on other mystic orders] is very conspicuous [from] the rites of the Gnawa, and will probably prove to have had a considerably larger scope than is known at present."[51] With respect to the origin of Gnawa practices, he concluded:

There can be no doubt that various practices connected with the belief in the *jnūn* [spirits] have a Sudanese origin.[52] We have seen that there are intimate relations between the *jnūn* and negroes, and the Gnawa, chiefly consisting of negroes, are experts in expelling *jnūn* from persons who are troubled with them.[53]

French ethnologist René Brunel, who studied the mystic order of the 'Isawa in the 1920s, argued that ritual sacrifice used by the 'Isawa as a means to establish contact with the spirit world is a Sudanese (mainly Bambara)[54] practice borrowed from the Gnawa group.[55] Brunel observed that "the 'Isawa extensively devote themselves to the practices of spiritual possession and exorcism peculiar to the Gnawa."[56] He added, "the Gnawa are experts in exorcism and the 'Isawa master healer-exorcists have adopted many Gnawa practices and rituals, including using the blood of those possessed to hasten the departure of demons incarnated in them."[57] The Gnawa rely on their musical instruments to communicate with the spirit world, one of which, a three-stringed lute-tambour (*guenbri*), is used as the primary invocation to call on the *jinns*.[58] The 'Isawa too use musical instruments to communicate with the spirit world, but turn to an oboe-like Andalusian instrument (*ghaita*) as their primary means to call on the *jinns*. Another inference that can be made about the influence of the Gnawa on the 'Isawa derives from the 'Isawa belief in at least five black spirits and, even more suggestive, the king of their *jinns* is black and called al-Gnawi. One finds other Arab-Berber brotherhoods similar to the

---

[51] Edward Westermarck, *Ritual and Belief in Morocco* (New Hyde Park: University Books, 1968), vol. 1, 13.

[52] *Sudanese* derives from the Arabic term '*as-Sudan*' (plural of *aswad*); it means black people and it was the general name in medieval Arabic sources for the region of sub-Saharan West Africa.

[53] Westermarck, *Ritual*, 379.

[54] During his field work, René Brunel noticed that the Gnawa perform some of their songs in the Bambara language. René Brunel, *Essai sur la confrérie religieuse des Aissaouas au Maroc* (Casablanca: Ed. Afrique Orient, 1988), 181.

[55] Brunel, *Essai sur la confrérie*, 10–11.

[56] Ibid., 178.

[57] Ibid., 186.

[58] See Edward Westermarck, "The Nature of the Arab Ginn, Illustrated by the Present Beliefs of the People of Morocco," *The Journal of the Anthropological Institute of Great Britain and Ireland*, 29, no. 3/4. (1899): 252–269.

'Isawa who practice the saint-cult and the spirit-possession-cult, such as the Hamdushiyya brotherhood founded by Sidi 'Ali Ben Hamdush, who is associated with a black she-spirit (*jinniyya*), Gnawiyya Lalla 'Aisha. An American anthropologist, Vincent Crapanzano, also concluded from his fieldwork in Morocco that "[t]he Hamadsha themselves, as well as most other Moroccans of their background, recognize the Gnawa origin of many of their named-jnun."[59]

This discussion points to the indelible influence and contribution of the Gnawa to Moroccan mysticism. Gnawa trance ceremonies generally take place after sundown; for this reason they are called *lila* ("night" in Arabic). They are also called *derdeba* (ritual of possession).[60] The Gnawa believe that many misfortunes are hardly accidental, but probably caused by evil spirits. Through their musical ceremonies and trances the Gnawa claim to cure insanity, freeing its victims from these malign influences. Many people from all walks of life who suffer from acute illness, infertility, or depression seek the spiritual intercession of the Gnawa's art. Sometimes people seek their intercession to preserve their good fortune.

The trance functions to heal social illnesses and disparities and serves a dual purpose of therapy and protest. It provides a cultural text to read the history of oppression and subjugation of this particular group of black Moroccans.[61] According to Gnawa, the spirit never completely leaves the body it inhabits or possesses, hence the necessity to repeat the ceremony. This repetition becomes an act of memorization and implicitly suggests that the initial wound is indelible. Slavery itself was the initial wound and because it was never officially recognized or healed it was therefore destined to repeat itself. Although only a few Gnawa still remember slavery, such as Mokhtar Gania whose grandfather was a slave, the trance remains a ritual of remembrance and a narrative of suffering, healing, and coping. Furthermore, other forms of prejudices, humiliation, and marginalization perpetuate the wounds of slavery.

The space that Gnawa created also attracts all those who share similar wounds. Deborah Kapchan observed: "These ceremonies attract those whose wounds are bound up with oppression, whether racial or sexual."[62]

---

[59] Vincent Crapanzano, *The Hamadsha; a Study in Moroccan Ethnopsychiatry* (Berkeley: University of California Press, 1973), 141.
[60] The Gnawa of Essaouira use the term *lila* but the Gnawa of Marrakesh use the term *derdeba*.
[61] See the insightful analysis on the multidimensional meanings of the Gnawa trance of Deborah Kapchan, *Traveling Spirit*, 33–46.
[62] Ibid., 35.

Indeed, the majority of Gnawa devotees are women who have been historically sexually segregated and suffered the psychological distress of a male-dominated culture. Hence, the two crucial figures in the ceremonies are the *m'allem* (pl. *ma'llmin*), the master of the ceremony, and the *mqaddema* (pl. *mqaddemat*), the overseer of the ceremony. They are usually related by blood. Mqaddema could be a family relative such as a spouse, a sister, or a daughter of the m'allem. In the case of the Essaouira Gania family,[63] the mqaddema Jmiaa (d. 2003) was the daughter of the late m'allem Boubker Gania and the sister of Mokhtar Gania.[64]

Mqaddema supervises the ceremony and makes sure all ritual procedures flow smoothly for the benefit of the afflicted persons who seek Gnawa healing. She commands the material organization of the ceremony. Mqaddema is also a clairvoyant and a healer and is equipped with magical powers to treat persons haunted by *jinns*, and is in charge of collecting the magical objects that she deems necessary for the healing process. These objects are deposited in a tray called *tbiqa*, used to diagnose the nature of the affliction caused by *jinns*. This tray contains sea shells, cowry shells, and stones of different colors that symbolize saints and spirits. Another tray has seven boxes of different colors each of which symbolizes a particular function of the spirits in nature and in the spirit world. These boxes contain different kinds of incenses. The incenses are used for fumigation in the ritual possession in order to identify the spirit that harasses the patient.[65] Among the names called upon during the ceremonies are female spirits (*jinniyyat*) such as Lalla 'Aisha Qandisha, Lalla Mira, and Lalla Mimuna, in addition to male spirits. The trance dance floor scene is dramatic; women start the trance dance slow and gradually speed up in sync with the hypnotic rhythms of the music in their loose robes and long hair swinging in the air from side to side or over the face until they fall into a trance under the watchful eye of the mqaddema and her female helpers. And in the end, they feel relieved. Hence the trance is a therapeutic act that serves as an outlet for frustration and suffering.

The Gnawa shrine offers a social event for women, especially for those living in a sexually segregated society and affected by its discourse. They find in the shrine an outlet to their seclusion and an escape by which grievances are shared among the attendees and addressed to God and His

---

[63] Interview in Essaouira, June 20, 2002.
[64] For more information of the different roles of the mqaddema see Kapchan, *Traveling Spirit*.
[65] For more information see Chlyeh, *Les Gnaoua du Maroc*, 74–77.

saints. The shrine, whose guardian is usually the mqaddema, provides a support system through its therapeutic exercises – women perform trance dances to release the tensions of the heavy tasks of the household and the suffocation of their limited freedom (freedom of movement and sexual taboos), hence it articulates a gendered subjectivity. Kapchan noted that "the ceremonies born of the wounds of slavery go on to cure wounds originating in other forms of domination."[66] Consequently, the ceremonies attract mostly people from poor families. Occasionally, wealthy families do attend Gnawa ceremonies but their motivation is usually out of curiosity or entertainment rather than devotion. Gnawa performers are aware of this fact, which is why they distinguish between the practice of rituals for their devotees and an entertaining performance for those who appreciate Gnawa as a musical art. Fatima Mernissi noticed that Mina, an ex-slave woman who lived in her household, attended the Gnawa trance ceremony in the city of Fez once a year:

"For the rich the *hadra* [trance] is more of an amusement," explained Mina, "while for women like me, it is a rare opportunity to get away, to exist in a different way, to travel." For a businessman like Sidi Belal [the Gnawa master], of course, the rare attendance of women from high-ranking families was absolutely vital, and they came to his house, bearing expensive gifts. Their presence and generosity were appreciated by all as an expression of women's solidarity, and their support was much needed.[67]

Indeed, the material support of women attendees and devotees is crucial to the sustainability of the Gnawa. The Gnawa perform for multiple purposes: they perform their spiritual order rituals, they "work the spirits" in order to appease their devotees, they participate in religious festivities such as the celebration of the Prophet's birthday, and they use their artistic skills for entertaining the public in venues such as wedding celebrations or private parties and in the streets or the markets in order to support themselves.

Women have been active participants in the Gnawa rituals and the preservation of Gnawa heritage. Many famous Gnawa masters and musicians have received their Gnawa training from their mothers, for example, m'allem Si Mohammed, whose grandmother was a mqaddema (overseer of the ceremony).[68] Another example is the popular Gnawa musician Hassan Hakmoun, a Moroccan expatriate living in New York

---

[66] Kapchan, *Traveling Spirit*, 35.
[67] Mernissi, *Dreams of Trespass*, 159.
[68] See Kapchan, *Traveling Spirit*, 20.

since 1987. Hakmoun grew up in Marrakesh in a Gnawi environment, but he is not a master spiritual healer; he is a professional singer in the field of entertainment. He has emphasized repeatedly that he learned his art and craft from his mother, who was a mystic healer in Marrakesh.[69]

Gnawa Spiritual Music and the Diaspora

The Gnawa orchestra has many musicians: the *m'allem* (master or lead musician) plays the *guenbri* (a three-stringed bass lute-tambour) and other members of the group play *tbel* (drums) and *qarqaba* (metallic castanets). Generally they dance as well, for music and dance are spiritual partners to the Gnawa. According to Boubker Gania (1927–2000), an old Gnawa master and a native of Essaouira:

The *guenbri* is a crucial instrument in Gnawa rituals. It is through this device that the trance occurs. For this reason the Gnawa do not say "they play music" but they say "they call out to [i.e., they request the sprits to appear]." If there is no *guenbri* there will be no trance. The *guenbri* provides the rhythm for the trance.[70]

The ceremony usually takes place inside the house; shrine, or center of a Gnawa family or group and likely will last throughout the night. The first part of the ceremony (or *lila*) is called *al-'ada* (the custom), it is something of a warming-up exercise for what follows. It is also accompanied by dates, milk, candles, and incense. This task is usually reserved for women. The first séance that follows is called "Kuyu" or "Awlad Bambara"[71] which starts with the invocation of blessings upon the Prophet Muhammad and the remembrance of Gnawa origins. Afterward, it is *ftuh ar-rahba* (opening of the spirits repertoire of songs), a crucial ritual that sets the stage for the *mluk* (supernatural entities).[72] The traditional Gnawa ceremony includes seven sections; each section represents seven saints or ancestral spirits. Each section is also associated with a particular color (white, light blue, dark blue, red, green, black, and yellow) each of which

---

[69] From a discussion with Hassan Hakmoun during his visit at Duke University in 1998.

[70] The interview was conducted in the house of master Boubker Gania (also spelled and pronounced Guinia), Essaouira, on July 7, 2000 with myself, Paul Lovejoy, Yacine Daddi Addoun, and Abdul Karim al-Asiri, author of the book *'Alam at-Tuqus wa 'l-Alwan Dakhil al-Layla al-Gnawiyya* (Essaouira, Manshurat as-Safriwi, 1999) I also conducted another interview with his son, Mokhtar Gania, in Essaouira, on June 20, 2005.

[71] Bambara is the name of the ethnic group and their language in present-day Mali.

[72] *Mluk* (sing. *malk*) means the possessors; it derives from the verb *malaka*: to possess or to own.

symbolizes a particular function in nature and in the spirit world.[73] The
ceremony is characterized by well-established rituals, such as a sacrifice
of a sheep or a goat, cloths of different colors, eating dates, drinking milk
with rose water, and the burning of incense. Sacrifice is crucial in Gnawa
ceremonies; it is an act of offering a slaughtered animal to the spirits in
propitiation. As Deborah Kapchan observed, "sacrifice is central to all
propitiation ceremonies, an offering to the spirits and an initiation of a
lifelong relationship with them. It both appeases the spirit and nourishes
the community."[74] The most visible and fundamental trait of the ceremony is something of a versicle and response chant coupled with dance.
Some participants go into a trance through which a particular spirit may
express its wish for the appropriate tune and the preferred color. *Lila* will
continue until the goal is achieved, the trance over, "the spirits have been
worked," and the participants have been cleansed of their afflictions.

It is important to note that Africans in the Americas performed similar
roles as traditional healers, as Du Bois observed:

He [Priest or Medicine-man] early appeared on the plantation and found his
function as the healer of the sick, the interpreter of the Unknown, the comforter
of the sorrowing, the supernatural avenger of wrong, and the one who rudely but
picturesquely expressed the longing, disappointment, and resentment of a stolen
and oppressed people. Thus, as bard, physician, judge, and priest, within the narrow limits allowed by the slave system, rose the Negro preacher, and under him
the first Afro-American institution, the Negro church.[75]

Through similar ceremonies and practices, the Gnawa transformed
themselves, having first arrived as forced migrants then reembodying
themselves with a socially and spiritually constructed identity through
centuries of acculturation into Moroccan society.

As a spiritual order within Moroccan Islamic society, the Gnawa were
and continue to be marginalized. They believe that God is too powerful
for bilateral communication or even direct manifestation and thus can
only be reached through spiritual manifestations in our world. Hence, the
Gnawa receive little attention in Islamic scholarship,[76] presumably because
they are not a mystic order proper, as they do not seek the conventional

[73] For more information see the work of the Moroccan scholar Abdelhai Diouri,
    Lahlou: Nourriture Sacrificielle des Gnaouas du Maroc (Madrid: Agencia Española de
    Cooperación Internacional, 1990).
[74] Kapchan, *Traveling Spirit Masters*, 73.
[75] W. E. B. Du Bois, *The Souls of Black Folk* (New York: Dover, 1994), 119.
[76] A few Moroccan scholars have recently embarked on the study of the Gnawa people
    mainly in the disciplines of music, ethnotherapy, and ethnology. Abdelhafid Chlyeh, who
    holds a PhD in ethnology, is one of these contributors to the study of the Gnawa.

personal union with the divine. Instead, their contact with the spirit world acts as an intermediary through which divine communion may be accomplished. The Gnawa have found legitimacy for their cultural identity within the regions and societies they inhabit, despite their unusual, often marginalized, religious rites, ceremonies, and musical practices. The images conveyed in their songs construct a coherent representation of displacement, dispossession, deprivation, misery, and nostalgia for a land and a former life kept alive through their unique musical and ceremonial practices. The historical experience of the Gnawa sketched in this essay is very similar to those found in all forced African diasporas. Through their ceremonies, songs, and gatherings, they reconcile themselves with their fragmented past. Thus, connected with their origins, they have a sense of location, sharing a common experience through enslavement and its legacy. The Gnawa provide a fascinating story of how a people reconstruct its identity against a broken cultural continuity. Drawing on their African musical heritage, the Gnawa have also created a musical genre in Morocco that enabled them to cope with the horrors of servitude and its legacies. The Gnawa originally used their music and dance to express the feeling of being subalterns and to heal the pain of their abduction. Gnawa lyrics contain many references to the privations of exile and enslavement. Kapchan emphasizes the musical dimensions of language and trance experience in her analysis of the Gnawa narrative about trance. She identifies three main functions in the Gnawa narrative: emotive, phatic, and poetic. She explains, "this narrative repeats the ontological register of trance time in its poetic function, while asserting a politics of representation and control in the domain of referentiality."[77]

In this regard, Gnawa music is very similar to the spirituals and blues that are rooted in black American slave songs. American historian John Blassingame (d. 2000) wrote that "spirituals served as much more than opiates and escapist fantasies. [They] enabled blacks to transcend degradation and to find the emotional security to endure pain [...]. Having a distinctive culture helped the slaves to develop a strong sense of group solidarity."[78] On spirituals, also called "the Sorrow Songs,"[79] African American theologian James Cone wrote:

Through song, they built new structures for existence in an alien land. The spirituals enabled blacks to retain a measure of African identity while living in the

---

[77] Kapchan, *Traveling Spirit*, 83.
[78] John W. Blassingame, *The Slave Community* (New York: Oxford University Press, 1972), 145–147.
[79] See Du Bois, *The Souls*, 155.

midst of American slavery, providing both the substance and the rhythm to cope with human servitude.[80]

American abolitionist Frederick Douglass (1818–1895) explained that these songs also reflected the masters' unwillingness to see the humanity of the enslaved people:

[T]hey would sing, as a chorus, to words which to many would seem unmeaning jargon, but which, nevertheless, were full of meaning to themselves. I have sometimes thought that the mere hearing of those songs would do more to impress some minds with the horrible character of slavery, than the reading of whole volumes of philosophy on the subject could do [...]. Every tone was a testimony against slavery, and a prayer to God for deliverance from chains.[81]

In some Gnawa songs we find words in a form of an open plaint generally to God and His saints that express the trauma of being displaced and the sorrow of losing their homes:[82]

> They brought from the Sudan
> The nobles of this country brought us
> They brought us to serve them
> They brought us to bow to them
> They brought us Oh there is no God but God
> We believe in God's justice.[83]

In another song:

> The Sudan, oh! Sudan
> The Sudan, the land of my people
> I was enslaved, I was sold,
> I was taken away from my loved ones.[84]

René Brunel recorded similar lyrics during a Gnawa séance of possession in the city of Meknes. The group still plays the same instruments today in Essaouira or Marrakesh that they played in the 1920s when Brunel was engaged in his fieldwork – the three-stringed lute *guenbri*, castanets, and drums and singing a song entitled "Sidi Mimoun":

---

[80] James H. Cone, *Risks of Faith: The Emergence of a Black Theology of Liberation, 1968–1998* (Boston, 1999), 16.

[81] Douglass, *Narrative*, 20.

[82] Earle Waugh, a Canadian scholar of Sufi mystical traditions thinks that many Gnawa songs are meant to preserve the memory of their historic migration. Waugh, *Memory*, 110.

[83] Translation, with emphasis added, from al-Asiri, *'Alam at-Tuqus*, 33.

[84] Al-Asiri, *'Alam at-Tuqus*, 18.

> O Saint Sidi Mimoun!
> Our lord goes to the land of Sudan.
> He brought a servant Gnawiyya.
> O God! O Prophet![85]

Since their initial enslavement they devised ways to confront their lot. Richardson reported how they protested and lamented their abduction in verses during their journey in the middle passage of the Sahara in the area of Murzuq south east of Libya:

This evening the female slaves were unusually merry and excited in singing, and I had the curiosity to ask Said what they were singing about. As several spoke the language of his own country, Mandara and Bornou, he had no difficulty in answering the question. I had often asked the Moors about the merry songs and plaintive dirges of the negresses, but could never get a satisfactory answer.

Said replied at first, "Oh, they're singing of Rubbee (God)."

"What do you mean?" I rejoined impatiently.

"Oh, don't you know," he continued; "they ask God to give them the Atkah [freedom].

I. – "Is that all?"

Said. – "No; they say, 'Where are we going to? The world is large, O God! Where are we going? O God! Shall we return again to our country?'"

I. – "Is that all, what else?"

Said. – "They call to their remembrance their own country and say, 'Bornou was a pleasant country, full of all good things, but this is a bad country and we are miserable, and are ready to sink down.'"

I. – "Do they say anything more?"

Said. – "No, they repeat these words over and over again, and add, 'O God! give us our âtkah, let us go to our dear home.'"[86]

Interestingly, William W. Brown (1814–1884), who escaped from slavery in the American South in 1834, recorded a song with similar lyrics sung by the enslaved Africans as they were taken away:

> See these poor souls from Africa
> Transported to America;
> We are stolen, and sold to Georgia–
> Will you go along with me?
> We are stolen, and sold to Georgia–

---

[85] Brunel, *Essai sur la confrérie*, 181–182.

[86] James Richardson, *Travels in the Great Desert of Sahara, in the Years of 1845 and 1846* (London: R. Bentley, 1848), 377–378.

Come sound the jubilee!
See wives and husbands sold apart,
Their children's screams will break my heart; –
There is a better day a coming–
Will you go along with me?
Come sound the jubilee![87]

To find out more about slave songs, I was able briefly to interview[88] m'allem Boubker Gania before death took him away shortly after my first interview in 2000. He was himself a son of an enslaved father in Essaouira. His father (although Muslim) was kidnapped from Mali or Guinea, taken to the Sahara, and then sold as a slave in Morocco. Master Gania, who had a huge repertoire of songs, said that the Gnawa songs belonged to the whole group. They represented a collective memory of their life experience. According to Master Gania, the oldest Gnawa song is the Mbara song. Mbara is a diminutive for Mbarak (a typical name given to an enslaved male). This historical slave song goes:

Oh! God our lord,
My uncle Mbara is a miserable man
What a fate does he have?
My uncle Mbara is a poor man
Our lady eats meat
Our master eats meat
My uncle Mbara gnaws at the bone
Our lady wears elegant shoes
Our master wears beautiful shoes
My uncle Mbara wears [ragged] sandals
Oh! God is our guide
This is the predicament of the deprived
Oh poor uncle Mbara.

It is important to note that this particular song, like all other songs characterized by improvisation, sometimes includes contemporary terms such as:

My master goes to the cinema
My uncle Mbara entertains in the market.

The song is also performed with reference to women by repeating the same verse with the name aunt Mbarka (a typical name given to an

---

[87] William Wells Brown, *From Fugitive Slave to Free Man: The Autobiographies of William Wells Brown*, edited with an Introduction by William L. Andrews (Columbia: University of Missouri Press, 2003), 48.
[88] Interview with Mr. Gania, Essaouira, July 7, 2000.

enslaved female). Thus, this song is a musical plaint reflecting the pained consciousness of successive wrongs suffered by these enslaved black people. The historic and contemporary inequalities of the Gnawa's social and economic status in Morocco are clearly displayed in this song.[89] How deaf is the audience to their sounds of sorrow and misery and how blind it is to the wounds and scars of their enslavement and its legacy. A similar observation was made by William Faux, an English farmer during his visit to Charleston, South Carolina, in 1819:

I noticed to-day the galley-slaves all singing in chorus, regulated by the motion of their oars; the music was barbarously harmonious. Some were plaintive songs. The verse was their own, and abounding either in praise or satire, intended for kind and unkind masters.[90]

In 1830s, Frederick Douglass reported the lyrics of the following song to indicate in his words "the meanness of the slaveholders":

> We raise the wheat,
> Dey gib us de corn;
> We bake de bread,
> Dey gib us de crust;
> We sif de meal
> Dey gib us de huss;
> We peel de meat,
> Dey gib us de skin;
> And dat's de way
> Dey take us in.[91]

In another song:

> Massa sleeps in the feather bed,
> Nigger sleeps on the floor;
> When we'uns gits to Heaven,
> Dey'll be no slaves no mo'[92]

These examples from American and Moroccan slave songs show the parallels in African diasporic cultures. They represent an open plaint about

---

[89] This historical analysis is relevant to contemporary issues. This means that the historical lessons still hold true today. The legacy is still alive and in order to establish a free society, taboos must be questioned.

[90] William Faux, *Memorable Days in America: Being a Journal of a Tour to the United States, Principally Undertaken to Ascertain, by Positive Evidence, the Condition and Probable Prospects of British Emigrants* (New York: AMS Press 1969), 78.

[91] Frederick Douglass, *Life and Times of Frederick Douglass: His Early Life as a Slave, His Escape from Bondage, and His Complete History* (New York: Collier Books, 1962), 146.

[92] Blassingame, *The Slave Community*, 122.

suffering as a result of extreme poverty under displacement and enslavement. Emile Dermenghem witnessed the Gnawa ceremonies in North Africa
in the 1950s and observed: "This is the form that can easily be taken by the
mysticism of a displaced, oppressed and exiled minority which has accom-
modated itself to Islam in Africa as it did to Christianity in America."[93]

For the Gnawa, their historical memory of forced migration is primarily preserved in their music. The Gnawa do not appear to have any desire
to return to their ancestral homeland; their diaspora is positively constructed around the right to belong to the culture of Islam, and it is Islam
and not their consciousness of their ancestral roots and forced migration
that has allowed the Gnawa to integrate into their new homeland. Black
Moroccans perceive themselves first and foremost as Muslim Moroccans
and only secondarily as participants in a different tradition and/or belonging to a specific racial or linguistic origin, real or imagined. Similar to the
manner in which Berbers see themselves as having been absorbed into
the larger collective consciousness of Arabo-Islamic historical experience, while preserving their singular identity (ethnic and cultural), black
Moroccans have found a way to reconcile and to integrate themselves into
a Moroccan collective identity. The distinctiveness of the Gnawa within
the dominant and coercive culture fits the cultural patterns of the African
diaspora in the Americas, as Michael Gomez in his analysis of African
American culture in the colonial and antebellum South observed: "In the
presence of the host community, reinterpretation was the lone option
available to the slave. Once removed from the gaze, however, the slave
was free to Africanize the religion, thus engaging in reinterpretation and
true synthesis simultaneously."[94] Gnawa people have created a distinct
place for themselves in Moroccan society. They play a social and spiritual
role and in recent decades have become well-known public performers. As
early as the 1920s, Carleton Coon, an American anthropologist, made the
following observation on the Gnawa during a trip to Morocco:

[They] are racially full Negroes, very black and broad-nosed. They are said to
come from Rio de Oro. They wear rags and comic headdresses, belts covered with
cowrie shells, and leather sandals. In their hands they carry pairs of iron clappers.
Wandering through the streets of the towns, singly or in pairs, the Gnawa sing to
attract a crowd. Once a few people have paused to see them, the Gnawa break

[93] Emile Dermenghem, *Le culte des saints dans l'islam maghrébin* (Paris: Gallimard, 1982),
260.
[94] Michael Angelo Gomez, *Exchanging Our Country Marks: The Transformation of
African Identities in the Colonial and Antebellum South* (Chapel Hill: University of
North Carolina Press, 1998), 10.

into a fast jazzy dance, clicking out the time on their clappers, and singing a little song. They collect the few coins given to them, bow and bless the audience, and move on.[95]

The character and practice of the Gnawa changed over time. In the 1920s, Coon saw Gnawa as disorganized beggars often forced to perform in the streets for survival. Now they are more organized and have become professional singers and musicians.

Over the past fifty years in North Africa, Gnawa music, like the blues in America, has spread and attracted practitioners from other ethnic groups, in this case Berbers and Arabs. Public, nonceremonial performances outside the Gnawa mystic order are a recent development.[96] The Gnawa have turned the mystical aspect of their music into a more popular musical art. In the 1970s, when the most popular music available was of the Middle Eastern type, some Moroccan artists started to look into other Moroccan traditions. One striking example is the group Nass al-Ghiwan, who created an original Moroccan pop music inspired by Gnawa music and mystical beliefs. One member of the band, Abd er-Rahman Paco, was a Gnawa master musician from Essaouira. In subsequent years, Gnawa music has engendered a style of pop music that appeals to a wide audience of listeners. Groups such as Nass al-Ghiwan and Jil-Jilala were the most listened to bands in Morocco in the 1970s and 1980s. In the 1990s, other groups such as Nass Marrakesh emerged, blending traditional music with new songs that connect with contemporary themes and audiences. Yet, for the Gnawa, their music is still primarily spiritual and used for healing purposes. The Gnawa however express a deep concern and even a fear of being dispossessed of their culture. Hence, the emergence of the concept *tagnawit* to distinguish between what is Gnawa "authentic" and what is Gnawa "imitation."[97]

Gnawa music has inspired the development of popular Moroccan music in general and is analogically similar to the African American spirituals, gospels, and eventually the genre known as the blues, also founded by former slaves. Recently, Western musicians interested in

---

[95] Carleton S. Coon, "North Africa," in Ralph Linton (ed.), *Most of the World; the Peoples of Africa, Latin America and the East Today* (New York: Columbia University Press, 1949), 431.

[96] Paul Bowles made several recordings of Moroccan music that included Gnawa performances. One segment is entitled "Sudanese slave song in Arabic sung by a Gnawi." See Paul Bowles, Christopher Wanklyn, and Charles F. Gallagher, *Morocco, ca. 1959*. This sound recording was deposited at the Archives of Traditional Music at Indiana University, Bloomington, in 1962.

[97] See Kapchan, *Traveling Spirit Masters*, 138–144.

African traditional music have encountered the music of the Gnawa. As a result, much collaboration has ensued between Gnawa musicians and famous jazz artists such as Randy Weston.[98] The Gnawa are modernizing their style to make it more secular with more commercial appeal. With these recent developments and their appeal to tourists, the Moroccan government in 1997 established The Gnawa and World Music Festival in Essaouira.

The legacy of the Gnawa has become another rich thread woven into the cultural cloth of modern-day Morocco. As such, the Gnawa spiritual group provides a window through which we may view the history of blacks in Morocco, making it possible to discover and recover West African roots and dialogue that still live on in Morocco.

---

[98] Randy Weston and other Western artists, who admired the rhythmic richness of the Gnawa, such as Richard Horowitz, Henri Agnel, Pharoah Sanders, Adam Rudolph, Loy Ehrlich, and Banning Eyre helped raise the appreciation for Gnawa art both inside and outside Morocco.

Conclusion

I have argued that in legal discourse, the institution of slavery in Morocco seems not to have been dissimilar from premodern and early modern notions of slavery held in the Mediterranean basin in general. Here we see that, at least in relation to slavery, religion was not much of a boundary marker. But in addition to the common, if not analogically shared, legal foundations for the practice of slavery, this study demonstrates that historical racial attitudes toward slavery and its practice were exchanged throughout the Mediterranean basin and the Atlantic Ocean – one country's practice of slavery was informed by another's. Thus, it also proves that the notion of "Islamic slavery" held among some scholars in the West such as Bernard Lewis is misleading. In Western literature, Lewis is arguably the most cited author in the field of slavery and race in the Islamic world. Lewis essentialized the narrative of "Islamic slavery" for the entire Islamic world from the beginning of Islam to the European colonial period in a book that consists of less than 150 pages. He wrote: "We thus have two quite contradictory pictures before us – the first contained in [Toynbee's] *Study of History*, the second reflected in that other great imaginative construction, *The Thousand and One Nights*. The one depicts a racial egalitarian society free from prejudice or discrimination; the other reveals a familiar pattern of sexual fantasy, social and occupational discrimination, and unthinking identification of lighter with better and darker with worse."[1] Lewis relied on external sources and on myths and fantasies of the Arabian nights (possibly of Persian origin) as an historical source to portray an unchanging reality of slavery in the Islamic

[1] Lewis, *Race and Slavery*, 20.

world. He falsely suggested that the Hamitic myth was an Arab invention and maintained that Arabs had a preconceived notion that blacks were of an inferior and lesser breed, so much so that the latter were "almost entirely missing from the positions of wealth, power, and privilege."[2] This wholesale oversimplification undermines the agency and the achievements of many black individuals all over North Africa. Here Lewis is ignorant of the history of the Maghreb as he is unaware of historical figures such as renowned Moroccan Sufi figure Abu Yi'zza (d. 1177), politician Ibn Marjan (d. 1728), vizier Ahmad b. Musa (d. 1878), and grand vizier and governor of Fez 'Abd Allah (d. 1885).

Morocco shared patterns with and in fact participated in the global African diaspora. The cultural exchange of racial attitudes endemic to the African diaspora justified slavery even where such justification was inconsistent with the tenets of Islam as explicitly expressed in the Qur'an and Hadith. On one hand, slavery in Morocco was organized according to the rules of Islamic law. On the other hand, Moroccan Muslims some-times enslaved black Muslims under the false accusation of heathenism. Legal texts such as *Daftar Mamalik as-Sultan Mawlay Isma'il* (the regis-ter of the slaves belonging to Mawlay Isma'il) provide coherent critical testimony of the practice of slavery in Morocco under Mawlay Isma'il at the beginning of the eighteenth century. This legal register homogenized the various statuses and backgrounds of blacks into the single category of slaves. At this point, the egalitarian message of Islam became alien to many Muslims in Morocco. The moral principles suggested by the Qur'an and Hadith regarding the emancipation of enslaved people and the promotion of human rights and dignity conflicted with the interest of the dominant class and slave culture. Mawlay Isma'il's example is by no means the only one, as there are many precedent cases. Historical docu-ments such as *Mi'raj as-Su'ud* of Ahmad Baba from the city of Timbuktu in the beginning of the seventeenth century are examples of legal texts that illustrated how identities and otherness were constructed and vio-lated in the name of Islam. What is unique about Morocco is not so much the practice of racial prejudice and slavery, as such attitudes and practices existed all over North Africa. According to Shawn Marmon, black slaves in Mamluk Egypt (1250–1517) were marked by racial boundaries that generally privileged whites over blacks.[3] Indeed the Mamluks, who were

---

[2] Ibid., 61.
[3] Shaun Marmon, "Black Slaves in Mamluk Narratives: Representations of Transgression" *Al-Qantara* 28, 2 (2007): 435–464.

originally white military slaves, soon integrated in Egyptian society, created their own dynasty that lasted for more than 250 years, and remained as a privileged group until the colonial period. Blacks on the other hand remained generally stigmatized as a subaltern group. According to Eve Trout Powell, Egypt's Sudanese people during the colonial period were Egyptians' racial other.[4] Similarly, Arabs and Berbers in Morocco perceived the 'Abid al-Bukhari's high upward mobility as a transgression against the social order and at times reminded them of their origins, slavery, and blackness.

The exceptionality of Morocco, however, was in the methods, the racial factor, and the scale of Mawlay Isma'il's operation that resulted in gathering, humiliating, and violating the legal rights of more than 221,320 black persons, namely their natural right to freedom provided by being Muslims and long-time residents within the authority and protection of Islamic jurisprudence. Although Mawlay Isma'il's decision to forcibly conscript all black people into his army was political, he invoked racial distinctions conflated with heathenism to justify his enslavement of Moroccan blacks. His avowed intention was to convince influential Islamic scholars that the needs of the state – to create a formidable army to defend the land of Islam – provided the warrants for enslaving free black Muslims whom he believed had all formerly been slaves. As a consequence of this mass forced conscription, the perception of blacks was radically altered; it reinforced prejudices and determined the future image of blacks in Morocco. Mawlay Isma'il needed people whom he could trust in the military, soldiers who owed their allegiance solely to him and who were not split by tribal affiliation and solidarity. But his initiatives gave rise to cruel practices and racial conceptions that affected how Islam was interpreted with respect to black people.

Yet the idea of a professional loyal army was not Mawlay Isma'il's invention, as he was inspired by the Ottoman Janissary model. There is still no comprehensive published work that compares the two models, but that is perhaps because there is a relative dearth of research on Moroccan slavery. As I have shown in this study, there is sufficient historical evidence that allows us to address this issue. By contrast, there already exists a vast literature on the Ottoman empire and the Janissaries.[5] The goal of

[4] Eve Troutt Powell, *A Different Shade of Colonialism: Egypt, Great Britain, and the Mastery of the Sudan* (Berkeley: University of California Press, 2003).
[5] For more information see Halil Inalcık, *The Ottoman Empire: The Classical Age 1300–1600* (London: Phoenix Press, 2002) and Bernard Lewis, *Istanbul and the Civilization of the Ottoman Empire* (Norman: University of Oklahoma Press, 1990).

both models was the same – to create an army devoted to the sultan. The corps of the army was their home and the sultan was their father figure. They shared a symbol of devotion and obedience in the form of a spiritual pledge. For the Moroccan army it was sealed through the sayings of the Prophet as contained in *Sahih al-Bukhari*, whereas the Janissaries made their pledge through the Sufi order Bektashi. The military training of both was done at a young age, but Moroccans acquired additional skills, mainly masonry. The training of the Janissaries insisted on the conversion to Islam and the learning of Islamic sciences; however, that was not necessary for the 'Abid al-Bukhari as they were already Muslims. The black army was established mainly for defensive purposes. As Morocco's authority was fragmented prior to the creation of the black army; it was a crucial part of Sultan Isma'il's plan to resolve political instability and maintain internal security. On the other hand, the Ottoman Janissary corps was a tool of conquest from its inception, aspiring to the expansion of the Ottoman empire. Unlike the Janissaries, the black army never attempted to assassinate any heirs or 'Alawi pretenders to the throne after the death of Mawlay Isma'il and replace him with their own military leaders, as they honored the Moroccan tradition of Sharifian rule.

This book also demonstrates Morocco's centrality in the history of the trans-Saharan diaspora and slavery in the Islamic world. It also corrects the general assumption made by many scholars who considered the Haratin either former slaves or freed slaves. A popular etymology falsely suggests that the name Haratin derives from a combination of two Arabic words, *hurr* and *thani*, literally meaning "the second-class free man." This study has problematized the status of the Haratin. It is indeed a story of a great injustice against a particular group of Moroccans who happened to have a different complexion, slightly darker than those of the Arabs and Berbers. The racialization of this group confused and homogenized the history of the diversity of all blacks in Moroccan from free natives to imported slaves. Consequently, the name Haratin, originally designating those who were among the first inhabitants of southern Morocco, changed from an ethnic designation to a legal term meaning former slaves or freed slaves, and, at the time of Mawlay Isma'il, as maroons and then conscripts and servants of the government, and as a result after the gradual disintegration of the black army they all became former slaves again.

The enslaved people were both sexes, young and adults, but the tragic heroine in Moroccan slavery is female. Female slaves, mainly black, originally from West Africa, endured an unimaginable burden especially as domestic servants and concubines. French anthropologist Claude Meillassoux insisted on the crucial role of women in African agriculture and interpreted the notion of double exploitation of women in labor and childbearing. A similar duality existed in Morocco; it defined the preference of women over men for domestic labor and sexual exploitation.[6] From the nineteenth century to the beginning of the twentieth century, the nature of slavery in Morocco was largely domestic, hence the preference for female slaves over male slaves. This gender preference was the foundation upon which a larger burden rested on females. If it was legally and socially established for a male to be entitled to female slave sexuality, it was, as well, legally and socially conventional for the progeny of female slaves to inherit their fathers' legal status. It is through this legal status of *umm al-walad* that the offspring of genetically dissimilar parents were homogenized. In this instance, the interplay of color, consanguinity, and social function complicated the racial equation in Moroccan society. This is how the Moroccan definition of race accepted blacks in the Arab family as long as they possessed a "drop" of Arab blood. However, this process of assimilation camouflaged the dismissal of the sub-Saharan African affiliation of the blacks and manufactured Arab hegemony and political unity by insisting on the sacredness of the language of the Qur'an and Arabic culture. Hence, even people descended from mixed marriages may not see any ambivalence in claiming one identity, namely, their Arab lineage.

Enslaved black women who became concubines of their masters might have used sexual liaisons with their masters to secure a better position within a society where gender was hierarchical – patrilineal and patriarchal. There were cases when a concubine might even be freed and marry her master. For instance, Zaydana's bond with Mawlay Isma'il seemed to go further to the point that he freed her and made her his prime wife. Concubines often experienced an amelioration of their status as a result of becoming *ummahat al-awlad*, as there is fairly substantial evidence of this practice in terms of manumissions and inheritance of property. It must be noted that the male slave owner, given the nature of the slave relationship, gender, and the common age differences involved, initiated the sexual and emotional relationship with their concubines. It also

---

[6] Claude Meillassoux, *Maidens, Meal, and Money: Capitalism and the Domestic Community* (Cambridge, England: Cambridge University Press, 1991), 75–78; Claude Meillassoux, "Female Slavery" in *Women and Slavery in Africa*, edited by Claire Robertson and Martin Klein (Portsmouth: Heinemann, 1997), 49.

happened that masters who could not afford concubines initiated sexual relations with their maidservants. The evidence of concubines falling in love with the masters with whom they experienced sexual relationships is difficult to substantiate, as I have not come across any direct evidence such as love songs, love letters, or slave narratives. Hence, we may never get a closer or accurate picture of the concealed reality of the harem because of the lack of written literature on this taboo subject.

Indeed, oral traditions contain many tales of oppression of vulnerable women such as servants and concubines. It is only with the emergence of the novel in colonial modernity that this tradition found its voice, albeit fictionalized. The fictionalization of the reality of victimized women in Morocco was a way to circumvent the social and religious taboos that had the force of law. Moroccan novels suggest that slavery was still prevalent among the Fasi mercantile bourgeois families and landed aristocracy in the 1950s. Novels talk about men buying young servants specifically to fulfill their sexual desires. Novelist 'Abd al-Karim Ghallab (1917–2006) used the medium of the novel genre to expose and protest such social ills in modern Morocco, hence the title *Dafanna al-Madi* (*We Buried the Past*), which referred to unjust practices such as slavery and concubinage that have no place in a modern society. Ghallab and other writers of the same era such as Driss Chraibi (1926–2007),[7] Tahar Ben Jelloun,[8] and Fatima Mernissi,[9] depicted female slaves' suffering within the general pattern of women's oppression in traditional Moroccan society as inconsistent and hypocritical to morality and Islamic piety as well as to modernity. Gallab explains the dilemma of the concubine's condition:

Yasamin was not happy with her position in the house of Al-Haj Muhammed.... She was a sexual partner, yet she was not a lawful, official wife, and therefore she did not live the life of either a wife or a mother. She could not wear make-up the way wives do, and she could not attend parties in the presence of visitors.... Yasamin was not happy, not because of her social position or the rights refused to her, but because she was the mother of Mahmud. She was able to bear everything when it came to herself; the fact that she was and was not a wife at the same time, but she was not able to bear the distinctions made in relation to her son. After all he was Al-Haj Muhammed's son and even if his color was a little bit darker than that of the other sons, why should he suffer because of it?[10]

[7] Driss Chraïbi, *Le passé simple* (Paris: Denoël, 1986).
[8] Tahar Ben Jelloun, (*Moha le fou, Moha le sage* (Paris: Editions du Seuil, 1978).
[9] Mernissi. *Dreams of Trespass.*
[10] Ghallab, *Dafanna al-Madi,* 71–72. Translation of Evelyne Accad, *Veil of Shame: The Role of Women in the Contemporary Fiction of North Africa and the Arab World* (Sherbrooke, Canada: Éditions Naaman, 1978), 85.

Tahar Ben Jelloun criticized the Moroccan practice of concubinage and pondered the irony of the piety of a family patriarch in his novel *Moha le fou, Moha le sage* (*Moha the Fool, Moha the Wise*), who, during his solemn pilgrimage to Mecca, brought with him a female slave named Dada to attend to his personal and sexual needs. Ben Jelloun intensified the wound of Dada's servitude by making her mute and hence suppressing her in a world of silence and apathy.

It is important to note that childbearing validates the function of motherhood as the greatest value of women's role in society and by extension it may bring freedom and amelioration to the condition of concubines. The concubine's son or daughter may legally inherit their father's status, kinship, and wealth but they also may inherit their mother's stigma as they are called "children of servants" by their kin members as an insult at times of quarrel and jealousy to stress not only a social ranking but also a racial distinction.[11] However a mulatto category did not exist as in Latin America. In Brazil, for instance, the mulatto class blurred, to a certain extent, the racial line and was a crucial factor in the formation of white hegemony. The common crucial key is the female slave's womb that generated racial intermixing. Brazil did indeed have far greater miscegenation among the countries in the Americas. But whiteness was still held to be superior to blackness, by the people who considered themselves white, in a way that did not define miscegenation as generally corrupting the blood of the dominant white group, but rather was perceived as an opportunity to gradually "whiten" Brazil.[12] Similarly, in Morocco miscegenation was not perceived to corrupt the blood of those who considered themselves white. However, the so-called mulatto people do not exist as a single category in Morocco; instead they are imbedded in the dominant Arabo-Berber lineages as demonstrated in Chapter 2.

The practice of slavery in Morocco conformed to a certain extent to Orlando Patterson's thesis that slavery meant social death, as slavery extinguished all civil rights of the "slave," giving their owners total control over their lives. Patterson relies on the assumption that the master–slave

[11] Ghallab. *Dafanna al-Madi*, 50–52.
[12] For more information on the construction of race, color and racial attitudes in Brazil, see: Edward Telles, *Race in Another America: The Significance of Skin Color in Brazil.* Princeton[u.a.]: Princeton University Press, 2004; Larissa Viana, *O idioma da mestiçagem: as irmandades de pardos na América portuguesa.* Campinas, SP, Brasil: Editora Unicamp, 2007; Hebe Maria Mattos de Castro. *Das cores do silêncio: os significados da liberdade no sudeste escravista, Brasil século XIX.* Rio de Janeiro: Arquivo Nacional, 1995.

relationship always involves the cruel domination and oppression of a socially dead person (e.g., the enslaved person). However, this assumption, when applied to slavery in Morocco, overlooks the enslaved person's agency and important differences in how cultural factors and Islamic law shaped the institution of slavery. It is clear that slavery in Morocco was a coercive system of exploitation and fits the description of Paul Lovejoy that slavery in Africa was "fundamentally tied to labor"[13] and that "[c]ontrol of women enabled the domination of production and reproduction."[14] It is therefore only one segment of female slaves, mainly concubines who bore children for their masters, who can be usefully understood along the lines advanced by Suzanne Miers and Igor Kopytoff, whose work brings out the nuances and the uniqueness of pre-Atlantic slavery and the ways that the marginalized outsider/slave incorporated himself or herself into the dominant society of the master. Miers and Kopytoff argue that in sub-Saharan Africa, one finds that slavery's relation to the structure of social relationships can be understood as a "slavery-to-kinship continuum" in which "the kinsman, the adopted, the dependent, the client, and the 'slave' abutted on one another and could merge into one another."[15] But this argument should not suggest an apology for the exploitive ideology of slaveholders but rather a measure of social power and agency of the black Moroccans navigating the margins of the dominant community. This view is partly supported by the fact that the concubinage system did allow a similar mobility but was not typical of the entire slavery system in Morocco. Hence, the ethnically mixed Moroccan social landscape is in part a result of laws that protected the offspring of miscegenation, and has often been cited as evidence that Islamic societies in general have a benign attitude toward slaves.[16] This is partially true, especially in the case of soldiers and officers, sharecroppers, or female slaves who lived in close contact with their masters performing domestic services as maids or as wet nurses suckling the master's children. Yet, the notion of a "benign attitude" toward slavery as it was practiced in Morocco exaggerates the social status and social mobility of the enslaved woman regardless of the status of her offspring under Islamic law. The extent to which attitudes toward slavery could be seen as benign was more aptly applied to the offspring of concubinage rather than the

---

[13] Lovejoy, *Transformations in Slavery*, 5.
[14] Ibid., 20.
[15] Suzanne Miers and Igor Kopytoff, eds., *Slavery in Africa: Historical and Anthropological Perspectives* (Madison: University of Wisconsin Press, 1979), 23.
[16] This is explained in the introduction and Chapter 2.

concubines themselves. Even in the case of the *umm al-walad* status that provided integration and miscegenation, by bringing blacks into equal association with Arabs, it implicitly enforced the notion of Arabness and the power and the authority of Arab rule. Concubinage is above all a forced sexuality that ironically created a mixed society of whiteness and blackness. Nonetheless, given the reality of what women faced as both slaves and concubines, forging emotional bonds with their masters presented an opportunity to improve their status in the household and thus the conditions of their lives. But emotional navigation within the constraints of concubinage and even within the landscape of Arab and Islamic patriarchy in general, should not be taken to imply emotional liberty. Research into how women in male-dominated Arab and Islamic societies expressed their emotions has produced some insights into this aspect of women's agency. Notably, Lila Abu-Lughod, in her study about women's emotions in the Egyptian Bedouin society,[17] wrote about how nomadic Arab women in Egypt used poetry to express their deepest emotions that were repressed in the cultural and religious customs of a society dominated by men, hence a double discourse of emotions. A double discourse of emotions means that on one hand it is a response to the male code of honor that dictates women's behavior and on the other hand women express themselves freely in women's own space. By extension, enslaved females under the oppressive and exploitive system of slavery developed survival skills including an "emotional refuge"[18] to allow some relief by forging emotional bonds with their enslavers. Under Islamic law, a female slave who gives birth to a child of her "owner" acquired certain legal rights and her child was considered free as a consequence of being fathered by a free male. The children of concubinage received the same rights as legitimate free children. The *umm al-walad* also gained some legal rights, in the sense of a morganatic marriage, which included freedom upon the death of her "owner." In a patriarchal society where women are relegated to subordinate roles of dependence, concubinage did offer some liberty for female slaves.

Just as I demonstrate that the complexities of concubinage are based on partial liberty, so I also show how the black army and their families gradually separated themselves from the Makhzan and claimed

---

[17] Lila Abu-Lughod, *Veiled Sentiments: Honor and Poetry in a Bedouin Society* (Berkeley: University of California Press, 1986).

[18] A phrase William Reddy used in his book, *The Navigation of Feeling: A Framework for the History of Emotions* (Cambridge, England; New York: Cambridge University Press, 2001), 129.

their original status of freedom, as a great number of them (such as the Haratin) were indeed free before their enslavement by Mawlay Isma'il. The great dispersion of the blacks across Morocco happened during the period of Mawlay Isma'il. Since then blacks were scattered as far as Oujda in the northeastern part of the country as well as in the new cities such as Essaouira where they founded communal centers where their culture is celebrated. Their syncretic culture is manifested in the practice of Gnawa. The Gnawa is a spiritual order of a black Muslim people who are descendants of enslaved sub-Saharan West Africans. This cultural phenomenon associated with slavery was the product of the confluence of African cultures. My goal has been to reconstruct the forgotten past of the Gnawa who over many generations productively negotiated their forced presence as slaves in Morocco to create acceptance and group solidarity. I have highlighted a relation between slave songs in America and slave songs in Morocco culminating with the insight that the common experience of suffering gave rise to similar memories of slavery and aesthetic expressions.

A consistent abolitionist movement is a modernist idea but the moral rejection of slavery existed throughout Islamic history. Scholars such as Ja'far b. Muhammad as-Sadiq (d. 765), Hamdan Qarmat (fl. ca. 860–900), Fatimi ruler al-Hakim (d. 1021), Ahmad an-Nasiri (d. 1897), and Muhammad 'Abdu (d. 1905) made moral conclusions based on the Qur'an that would justify their position on the abolition of slavery. They made arguments that used specific textual statements in favor of the texts' general disposition on social justice. But these kinds of moral interpretations were ineffective to most Muslims until the nineteenth century, during the contact with Western modern ideas and consistent campaigns on abolition. Thus isolated and silenced voices against slavery appeared to fit better modern circumstances. The advanced moral stance of such scholars never made it as a mainstream movement in Morocco because the knowledge of the mainstream was controlled through the Maliki dogma and the official discourse of the ruling class and afterward by the populist Wahhabi movement. So contradictory are the interpretations of the sacred text that Tunisia made slavery illegal in 1846 even before France. By contrast, slavery in Morocco was never abolished by any decree from the royal authority. Slavery vanished rather as a consequence of the capitalist system introduced by the French colonial occupation of Morocco.

The study of race and slavery in Morocco (and by extension in the rest of Islamic Africa) has only recently attracted the interest of Moroccan scholars although there is a rich body of evidence on the practice of slavery in this region since the seventh century. The sources are scattered but abundant in many *fiqh* (Islamic jurisprudence) books, legal registers, hagiographic books, and chronicles. Indeed, a number of scholars (Western and local) have begun to restore the forgotten role of blacks in North Africa. In this project I join recent scholars in exploring documents and oral sources until now overlooked that can shed light on how enslaved people navigated within the harsh conditions of slavery and used all means available to them to claim their dignity and creatively negotiate their survival. The objective of my book fits in the mission of this new scholarship to recover the silenced histories of slavery in North Africa. It is my hope that it will contribute to our general understanding of the concept and practice of slavery in African societies influenced by Islam.

Figure. Kitab Mawlana Nasarahu Allah ila 'Ulama' Misr (Letter from Mawlay Isma'il to the Learned Men of Egypt). Reprinted with permission from Rabat: Bibliothèque Royale, ms. 12598.

لغيره مجاورة (نعوذ الكرام) واحتياجا عاماً إلى المطاعم ودبر بهم أشلاء ... إدانته وإقامته والتراوع
والنار ... صلاحي عناية من ... والله أعلم ... وأشار إليه توفيقه معاً أبو جردته ... وجيش متكامل في
خصيف ... بناتو بن زاد ماء ... الهيئة ... إسلامه وإنجاه والدعاية نصف خطبة أخبار
وقد كان بعد المغرب ... منذ الله تعالى ومريم دأوار سفلة منه الله ودخل دهمت ولذ ... لله
الدولة بإسلامه عفيته أخرى ... أربعاً وكذا ولله جاء ... ذغراخرى تغير العيش فرأيتك موجوداً
موفراً مرزقاً عافياً ... كم بقية الحزن ومعوضة قوانيه وصوابكه وهم ... وتحو
بيوتاً ... اشوا تعمرون وتشرحون ... والعزة ... متربة مموقة ... وكل دولة تستقيم الدولة لنت ... كانت
... العادة الدولة بنير ها طائل ... حين جاء الله بنا نصر المغرب ... وإذا الله أراد وإن ... منها
... يشر فضله ... حيناً عليه خير وبتة من أهله ... وجعلناه مارجة من الجيش ... أنفعت
وجيف العبد ... بعبرا المعبر ... بغلامة ... وراماية ... بسبب تلك العترة ... نفترة ... وأنت ... تحو
... لست حتى نسوسه ... أمور المملكة وسياسته ... وأصعبة ... وأوطاء الملكة ولزم
... وخولع وهرج ... كنهما أعاد الله ... على المسلمين ... ما نحرجته أقامة الله ... ونصف ... ما
... المبارك ... العفو ... بالعين ... للنزال ... تشرقه النسير ... وأذكر ... من أولها ... وبعض معالم ...
... وكذا وبنا مبدء من أنعم سألتم الله ... علم ... نوا أراد الله سبحانه عفو وضاً واختيار
... أعاناوا عاملنا ... تعوذ وصوله ... وعوت وصولة ... وكان الله كار الله له ... وتعالم ... عربي
هذا المغرب ... إنه ... الله منزو وأنا لله أراد ... أن ... جنزا ... مغينا مزيداً ... نوع ... بعض عليه ... وتحير بشر ... بأهله
... المغرب ... جعلنا ... بقور ... الله تعالى وتوبع ... إقبال ... الله تعالى ونبش منش
... الجبرية ومن يليق به ... مبرا ... قاوا نقاً ... أصل المغرب لهذا الأعمر ... علو ... الحبرية
والشبون به ... ومعود تشوء صلوا عليه ... وتكتأشير والتقلاد ... وغاية أشعوة وكنة ... طا
... المركوزة منكم ... بأصباء ... جيش لا ينتخى ... منهم القبيل ... ويستصعر ويقول
... قليل وحسبنا ... على معك وخوذ العين ... وزكنا ... عاماً عليه ... وأشق ... إلا
... ووزد ... علينا منا معر ... ووجدوه ... المسلمين تم ... والله وحير ...
... صواب المماليك ... واشتري بهم ... وإشراكهم ... وقد ... عنهم ... والتعيش بهم ... ... الشرقي
... البحريين ووجدنا صفاء المماليك ... منهم ... أبو ... كبيرا ... وخرج ... وسم
وبك ... ومعاشهم ... واصلاح ... ومركحف ... وصف ... طاناو ... وعة ... بترقبل ... ابراء ... وتحزه
... ومعز ... كأبله ... وعرموا ... واد ... كوها ... ينزغور ... وانبغور ... ومن ... أولها ... أبو
... وخجوائع ... أبزيم ... وأشكا ... وتمرة ... واسيلتهم ... مبرح ... أبواهم ... عسير ... وبشوى
... وبناز ... أي ... أوسنتز ... أي ... سنج ... أوقيم ... عصميته ... منتهكاً به ... وعرابس
... لانه ... وأودي ... وأصل ... مكنبة ... وتشتبو ... إضطرابا ... أنفلان ... وأفكاروا ... حيوو
... والخرج ... ثم ... خلافة ... مصرح ... المغرب ... أعاد الله ... حتى ... أشاخوي ... أبنور الكثير من هذا ... المماليك هذا مع إن ... ظلم مري ... الشهود ...

ونهزهم ... الیهم النجح حسرتاه ... ومغایر طوطوا ... وطا ... خلاف ... زمنهم الدیوان خرجت
دار الخلافة عمّا لنا ... وادار عنّا به ... عینه لعمر ... وقفارا ... لعل الخیر وغیر ذلک ... الخطیئة
والنصواب بدعوا الیه هذه الوجوه کلها ... تلیک هؤلاء الامراء تسمیهم زربا للاسلام
ونشأ ورثا ونعاوضنا مع العلماء ... وبعضه ... والبعضة وانقال العشوی والمدبسر والبدو المهذب
واظل الصلاح والبر ... وطا هذه انعا صل المغرب اشهد الله ... ووجوهه ... وقبائله ... مشارقة
هؤلاء الجهالیة وشرحنا لهم ... وأخبارهم ... کانوا علیه ... فبلجهم هذا الجمع ... مطهرا
وازدکاء ... امور الشیعة والعساکر الشیعة ... میهم فالمع الغربی والناس لعبی
والخطاف والشاری ... انعادرامی ... والمتربی بغیر زیه ... وبیضا ذلک علیه للبعض ... د
والخلاف عنهم ... وعرفوا ... ووقصوا علی بعضه ذلک غنا ... جلبوا لها اجلبوا الظهر بالامور
عیر دروفه ... واتلغتی ... طهویه المغربه اجاز ... سایف لها ... نواصلة
الیهم ... ان شاء الله تعالی ... عاملد ... اصحابة انجم وطالبتم القفور علیکم صدق
الخلاف ... لفشاء علیه مسکن عصوم وابدیعم ایرروا بها ... نسروا رایته وعزلوا
علیبرم ... النصوص لبعضهن وطاقا ... المشهورة ... المرصید ... لعیم ... وعده
من اظل العشوی ... وار ... کنبر وبایز واحد ومصای اطبا ... اظل المغرب ... طاوهرا انتم هبته
بد ... واقتار وشهرله ... لعر ... والتسبریز اظل انصر ... بوعبار ... بعول علیه ... العشوی لیعول
والمنفول بحیر اذا ... اوصال بابعول ... عشر ... مرضة دائمة ... الجمع علی
صلاة ... ویدراعم اجماعة ... العشاله ... وارکا وانجعلنه ... عنا ... عنکم ... اطلها
واغسادهم رماطبا ... کانا ... علی علماء انصل المغرب ... حربار ... وما ملرعلنا ... الشر
سیا ... ... کدررا ... نا ... مشارکتکم بد ... اجبارهنا ... واستطهاری عنکم من انعم
بد اوصا ... الحق للجمیع علی انجنس ... وعلی ... معروص هم بعضین ... وقوة الحق
خبرالحق ... وضوح ما جمبونا اعنکم الله ... مدع البشارة ... بعضه کم ...
وسبیله ... وبیشر البر ... ودلیله ... ومدکبته ... المعونة ... البشارة ... تعدیم قبلاوی
هؤلاء ... واطعا ... ومقصود ... نصبری ... جضورکم وخطابکم ... والسلام

انتهی کما وجد
من خط السید الشریف
الکاتب والله
المنّ

Appendix

The complete translation of Mawlay Isma'il's Letter to Scholars of the al-Azhar Mosque

From the servant of God, the contented in His grace, the obedient to His authority, the commander of the believers, the struggler in the path of the Lord of the world, ash-Sharif al-Hasani [i.e. descendant of the Prophet Muhammad], may God give him support and victory.

To most eminent scholars, honorable jurists and men of legal advice and wisdom of the Islamic land in the East, living in Egypt; may God preserve it; and especially among you the muftis and teachers of the al-Azhar mosque; may God forever preserve it in repeating His name and may He fill it with His benevolence and munificence. May God be your supreme guide, illuminating your insight and directing you always toward virtuousness. May He make the light shine through your knowledge and let it be a source of benefit for all Muslims; and may He guide us all so that we may be of those who apply justice and equity. [...]

We are writing to you from the seat of the government, may God preserve it, for the good of these territories of the Maghreb and the frontiers of war; may God guard them. We have chosen you for your knowledge of God's benefactions and for your interpretation on His successive and new favors, proof of your loyalty in the expression of His extreme goodness, and also for the qualities that we recognize in the good intentions of the scholars, their inclination to perform kind deeds and fine convictions in worldly and religious affairs. You, our distinguished scholars who are the example of a model behavior, by your knowledge problems are illuminated, doubts and obstacles are erased; by your insightful legal opinions the darkness of ignorance is enlightened. You are the judges and we are the executants. Knowledge and governorship are brothers. They hold equal worth, like the camel's knees. Scholars need governorship and governorship needs scholars. One cannot manage without the other. We wish, may God guide you toward the straight path, to know your advice, your opinion, and to consult you about a religious question of great importance in which we desire, with the blessing of God the most high, to take the path of well-guided beings and follow in the footsteps of virtuous assiduous jurists. The essential of the matter, to keep from boring you, and also because the best composition is the least in size and the greatest in significance, concerns the states of the Maghreb. These states are in reality borderline areas and fortified places neighboring the infidel enemy and therefore needing, up and down the border, the presence of combatants and defenders fighting with perseverance in the name of Islam. There is therefore no doubt that the ruler of these lands is in need of a strong army consisting of united and prudent soldiers in order to defend the security of the Muslim community. Many Islamic states have succeeded one another in the long time in the Maghreb. Each time one of the states disappeared, another came immediately to take the reigns of power. Each of these states found an existing army, ready, trained, and experienced following the practices of the central authority, knowing its laws and rules, and following its methods and conduct. It also found the state treasury well filled and supplies well stocked. Each state therefore fed off its predecessor following the erstwhile practice. When we were given the power to govern the Maghreb, thanks be to the will of God, we found it empty: the army was inexistent, supplies were rare, and the population was small; it was far from what the caliphate and what the emirate ought to be, because of the crisis that had invaded it and in which it has persisted for around eighty years to the point of forgetting political affairs and policies. The general state, may God keep the Muslims from reliving such a situation, was completely degraded, famines followed riots and insurrection to such a degree that when we arrived where God wanted to put us in order to exercise the functions blessed by His will, we were in charge of putting together the foundation of administration from the very beginning, and God alone knows what we would have endured in these tasks if it hadn't been for the divine providence that had supported us, because if you belong to God, God will be with you. Not having found upon our arrival in power an organized and available army on which we could rely and which could inspire confidence and security, we turned to God, imploring His help in the choice of convening and building up an effective army. We then realized that free men and the inhabitants of the Maghreb at this time would not be suitable for a military engagement and this for multiple reasons. Slothfulness and laziness were established in their habits, and the force of want as well as greed had become a character trait; such that none among them was able to be satisfied by the little which he had disdain for as being too little. Having noted the state of these souls, we let them tend to their livelihoods and preoccupy themselves with their interests, letting them off the hook except in their duty toward the treasury of the Muslims, may God replenish it. It was then that we shifted our interest to slaves whom we bought from their owners, this having been done after searching for them and conducting investigations on them following the law and in respect for the tradition of [the Prophet].

We have noticed that the majority of these slaves had become fugitives and that their masters no longer had power over them. There was not a single one who was not a runaway slave. They have become accustomed to running away for many generations. They are aware of this insubordination and they would not refrain from it. At the first chance, they deserted their master and rebelled against him. Each one left his master and adopted a new one; allied himself with a tribe or had recourse to a sheikh or the head of a clan in order to go against his legitimate master to whom he owed his loyalty. In this way they were dispersed in the countries and regions, especially when the drought and disorder had plagued the country and the power of the caliphate had weakened, may God forever preserve the Muslims from this experience. The years of famine had therefore annihilated a large number of these slaves.

These slaves were originally pagans from the Sudan [black West Africa] from where they had been brought by their neighbors who attacked to conquer them, they were the object of long-standing commerce, the buyers were different at each epoch in their interest by reason of their usefulness and the assurance of need. Thus, some slave buyers have more slaves than others, just like the people of the East from among the slaves they possessed, be they European slaves, Ethiopian slaves, or those from other pagan races of the southern regions. For a long time, these slaves were permitted to marry and to have children and it is not unlikely that this procreation was done in an illegitimate, sinful manner and through crime, particularly in perilous rural areas. The situation stayed this way for long periods of time. It remains, however, that these slaves were mostly rebels, as we have already pointed out, and that those who obeyed their master and remained in his service were rare. This situation was a result of the lack of authority among the masters and the absence of any power capable of commanding and reprimanding the slaves in order to bring justice to their masters. At the moment when God led us toward these slaves, it became clear to us that ease implies permission and when God approves an act; its outcome is always a success. In this way, the Prophet, each time he had to make a choice, opted for the easiest choice as long as it was not a sin; if it was, he distanced himself from it. Intention always takes precedence over action, that way each person gets only what he projects and the intention of the believer is worth much more than his actions. Besides, our master Salim b. 'Abd Allah had written to our master 'Umar b. 'Abd al-'Aziz (may God bless them): "Know this, oh 'Umar! That the support of God for His worshiper is always in accordance with his intentions." We had the intention of pushing forward with the legal investigation concerning the origins of these slaves until we established the roots and identity of each one of them. We had also looked for their masters, their various inheritors, and their filiations, in all legality, respecting the requirements of the law and its methods. The result of all these investigations, which is in the content of the questions and answers you are going to receive, with the help of God, proves that all transactions were correct and took place in respect of Muslim tradition concerning buying and selling. Because of the simplicity of this affair and the general interest that it contains, and since any person charged before God with human affairs has the duty to accomplish his task conscientiously by fixing before himself the objective of protecting the interests of those he governs and by favoring the affairs of great importance before any others, and the people owe him obedience and submission in anything he decides. According to Shaykh Abu Bakr at-Tartushi (may God have mercy on him): "when a person to whom God has given the responsibility of the affairs of Muslims makes a decision relating to religious and worldly matters, which he judges to be in their interest, it is upon them to follow his decision and to conform to it even in matters in which they are ignorant of the impact and consequences."

We have chosen these slaves to make soldiers and to make up the shield of Islam because they possess distinctive traits not found in others, such as the fact that this stock is not very costly, that it is content with little, and that it is very satisfied with whatever is offered to it. In addition, this group of slaves is better qualified for the blessed task for which it has been chosen, and especially the surveillance of the frontiers and the combat fronts and the protection of the land of Islam. They are sufficiently strong and patient to put up with the movements and voyages imposed by this function. Because of this fact, they are worthy and can accomplish their task in the best way. Our intention was also to save them from the predicament in which they were involved, a behavior in which the son followed in the footsteps of his father, in pledging their allegiance to the masters who were not theirs without the authorization of their legitimate masters, an act which a report [of the Prophet] condemns: "Whoever takes as his masters other than his real masters without the permission of his real masters, will incur the curse of God, the angels and all the people, and God does not accept any repentance or redemption from him." It was also our desire to obtain forgiveness from God Almighty by having united, trained, and disciplined them, as well as for what they have acquired in the way of good conduct and exemplary behavior in being next to the royal court and in being in the service of the government, may God preserve it and keep it in His favor.

We carefully examined the question in all its aspects by researching the interest and usefulness of the investment in owning these slaves for making a shield of Islam out of them. In this matter we got together with scholars, jurists, judges, muftis, teachers, eminent notaries, and virtuous religious men and especially noteworthy persons from among the people of the Maghreb, may God preserve them. We explained to them the life and past experience of these slaves before ordering their round up, the insubordination in which they were, and the repulsive wrongdoing which they committed, and among them lives the outlaw, the pillager, the embezzler, the bandit, the perfidious, and the usurper. We explained all this to the jurists and scholars, until they understood it and have witnessed themselves some of it. They then gave us their immediate response, without hesitation or stammering; these are written responses according to the Maliki legal school just as those we bring to you through our messenger, if God wills it.

The text you have in your hand was written by them; they cite their legal references and their jurisprudential sources. The number of these muftis and narrators was large. There is no scholar among them from the Maghreb that was not well known in other countries and scholars recognize his grasp of the sciences and proficiency in the domains of jurisprudence and in reason and revelation. It is, by the way, known that never do ten people of this community gather around error and God is for all. We wanted to bring you into this matter even though we charged the scholars of the Maghreb with it, may God preserve them, and we could have kept from consulting you on this subject. We still preferred to have your opinion, because truth can hide neither from two nor from any person who carefully examines it. What's more, by delving deeper into research, the truth can only become clearer.

Please respond to us on this matter according to what seems to you to be the way of truth and conforming to its proofs; you will have less work, since eminent scholars have already voiced legal opinions on this matter, nevertheless our goal is to honor your writing and your response.

Index

BOOKS IN THIS SERIES

Made in the USA
Las Vegas, NV
10 December 2022

61753934R00208